Also by Donald S. Passman

The Amazing Harvey
The Visionary
Mirage

All You Need to Know About the Music Business

NINTH EDITION

Donald S. Passman

Illustrations by Randy Glass

Simon & Schuster
New York   London   Toronto   Sydney   New Delhi

Simon & Schuster
1230 Avenue of the Americas
New York, NY 10020

This Simon & Schuster hardcover edition November 2015

SIMON & SCHUSTER and colophon are trademarks of Simon & Schuster, Inc.

For information about special discounts for bulk purchases,
please contact Simon & Schuster Special Sales at
1-866-506-1949 or business@simonandschuster.com.

The Simon & Schuster Speakers Bureau can bring authors to your live event.
For more information or to book an event contact the Simon & Schuster Speakers
Bureau at 1-866-248-3049 or visit our website at www.simonspeakers.com.

Manufactured in the United States of America

1 3 5 7 9 10 8 6 4 2

Library of Congress Cataloging-in-Publication Data is available.

Passman, Donald S.

ISBN 978-1-5011-0489-3
ISBN 978-1-5011-0490-9 (ebook)

Did You Know That . . .

- Most record deals don't require the record company even to make a record, much less to release it?

- You don't have to register in Washington to get a copyright?

- If we write a song together, and you write only the lyrics and I write only the music, each of us owns a piece of the music and each of us owns a piece of the lyrics? And that neither of us can use just the music, or just the lyrics, without paying the other?

- Prior to 1972, the United States had no copyright law prohibiting the unauthorized reproduction of records?

- Some film music composers can't even write music, much less create the arrangements for each instrument of an orchestra?

- A brain surgeon and a rock star have something in common?

To my precious Shana, and our growing family:
Danny, David, Rona, Josh, Lindsey,
Jordan, Dorianne, Benjamin, Talia, and Billy

Acknowledgments

PLEASE READ MY THANK-YOUS. I KNOW IT'S A BUNCH OF PEOPLE YOU'VE PROBABLY NEVER HEARD OF, BUT THINK HOW MUCH YOU'D WANT OTHER PEOPLE TO READ IT IF YOUR NAME WAS HERE.

No creative work is ever the product of one person alone (no matter how tempting it is to believe our own hype), and I want to acknowledge and thank all the following people for their inspiration and help:

Payson Wolff and Bruce Ramer, my mentors and spiritual brothers.

Bea Shaw, my mommy, who helped edit the first edition, and who paid for my first soft-drink stand.

Snuff Garrett, for believing in me early on.

Mike Gorfaine and R. Diane McKain, for their invaluable advice on film and TV music.

Gene Salomon, for his input, and for always making me look good.

Ethan Schiffres, for going over this entire edition in detail.

Rob Light, for help with the touring section.

Ed Ritvo, for the confidence to do all sorts of things.

Steve Bigger and Larry Apolzon, for help with protecting the rights in group names.

Chris Castle, for help with the classical music chapter.

Dave Dunton (in the beginning) and Jofie Ferrari-Adler, for getting this book into the hands of readers.

Alan Garner, for his extraordinary communication skills and advice on conversation, books, and salesmanship.

Kim Mitchell, my incredibly indispensable assistant.

Jules Levine and Corky, for having bulldogs.

In addition, the following people (in alphabetical order) generously gave the benefit of their expertise: David Altschul, Jill Berliner, Don Biederman, Kevin Breen, Nancy Chapman, David Cohen, Gary Cohen, Glenn Delgado, Bruce Eisenberg, Steven Fabrizio, Gary Ford, Russell Frackman, Dell Furano, Steve Gawley, Neil Gillis, Mark Goldstein, Lauren Gordon, Trudy Green, Jeff Hill, Zach Horowitz, Cathy Jacobson, Howard Kaufman, Larry Kenswil, Steve Lyon, Jay Morgenstern, Jay Murray, Michael Ostroff, Ed Pierson, Peter Reichardt, Bruce

Resnikoff, Jack Rosner, Tom Ross, Joe Salvo, Rose Schwartz, Joel Sill, Patricia Smith, Lon Sobel, Sandy Tanaka, Lance Tendler, Ray Tisdale, Tracie Verlinde, Wayne Volat, Lenny Waronker, and Ron Wilcox.

FOR THIS NINTH EDITION, special thanks to (alphabetically): Christos Badavas, Lenny Beer, Tom Cavanaugh, Patti Coleman, Matthew Cox, Richard Feldstein, Darryl Friedman, Marc Geiger, Susan Genco, Lee Goforth, Phil Graham, J. Grannis, Randy Grimmett, Susan Hilderly, Liz Kennedy Holman, David Israelite, Justin Kalifowitz, David Kokakis, Peter Lubin, Tom MacDougall, Alli Macgregor, Brian Meath, Irwin Nachimson, Chad Peterson, Diarmuid Quinn, Bruce Resnikoff, David Ring, Paul Robinson, Stu Rosen, Bobby Rosenbloum, Andrew Ross, Steve Schnur, Cary Sherman, Alison Smith, Helen Stotler, Ann Sweeney, Lisa Thomas, DA Wallach, Emily White, Ron Wilcox, and Pat Woods.

But most especially, thanks to all the garage bands out there—you're the lifeblood of our business.

Introduction to the Ninth Edition

Well, kiddies, we've certainly seen a lot of changes since we last we got together.

The good news is that streaming is growing at a wonderful pace. And that's about it for the good news.

CD sales are under 25% of the business and dropping. Downloads have fallen 15% per year for the last few years. Piracy is alive and well, hiding under cyber-rocks, and YouTube delivers more audio-only music than all the other sites put together (including the pirate sites), for which the creators are paid very little (we'll talk more about that later). All in all, the industry earnings are almost half of what they were in 2003. Also, we're going through a major upheaval in the songwriter world that could radically change the industry.

Otherwise, it's a lovely afternoon.

On the brighter front, we're seeing huge growth in vinyl (to younger people, it's a new technology; go figure) that's only held back because every vinyl plant on the planet is at full capacity. The bad news is that it's less than 2% of the business. But in the current state of affairs, we'll take what we can get.

Now if you're reading this and trying to decide whether the music business will disappear and if you'd be better off putting the price of this book into your stamp collection, there actually is a beautiful weather forecast. As we'll discuss, streaming has the potential to make the music business bigger than it's ever been in history. People who never would have gone into a record store are listening to streams, and the numbers are growing fast. So stick around (and buy the book).

As these new ways to exploit music take hold, you might wonder how artists get paid. Well, my friend, you've come to the right place. The book in your hands has the latest scoop on all these newfangled gizmos. And at no extra charge (if you act RIGHT NOW), there's an update of what's happening with traditional music business deals recording, songwriting, merchandising, touring, and so forth.

So step right up. All these secrets and more are revealed just inside the tent.

P.S. Congrats if you read this. It means you're a real Go-Getter, since most folks skip the introductions to books.

IMPORTANT

Contents

PART III
Songwriting and Music Publishing

PART IV
Group Issues

PART V
Touring

PART VI
Merchandising

PART VII
Classical Music

PART VIII
Motion Picture Music

All You Need to Know About the Music Business

NINTH EDITION

I

First Steps

OPEN UP AND SAY "AHHH"

For many years I taught a class on the music business at the University of Southern California Law School's Advanced Professional Program. The class was for lawyers, accountants, record and film company executives, managers, agents, and bartenders who want to manage groups. Anyway, at the beginning of one of these courses a friend of mine came up to me. She was an executive at a film studio and was taking the class to understand the music industry as it relates to films. She said, "I'm here to open up the top of my head and have you pour in the music business." I loved that mental picture (because there are many subjects I'd love to absorb that way), and it spurred me to develop a painless way of infusing you with the extensive materials in this book. So if you'll sit back, relax, and open up your mind, I'll pour in all you need to know about the music business (and a bit more for good measure).

HOW I GOT STARTED

I really love what I do. I've been practicing music law for over thirty years, and I represent recording artists, record companies, film companies, songwriters, producers, music publishers, film music composers, industry executives, managers, agents, business managers, and other assorted mutants that populate the biz.

I got into this gig on purpose, because I've always loved creative arts. My first showbiz experience was in grade school, performing magic tricks for assemblies. I also started playing accordion in grade school. (I used to play a mean accordion; everyone applauded when I shook the bellows on "Lady of Spain." I gave it up because it's impossible to put the moves on a girl with an accordion on your chest.) In high school,

I graduated from accordion to guitar, and in college at the University of Texas, I played lead guitar in a band called Oedipus and the Mothers. While I was with Oedipus, we recorded a demo that I tried to sell to our family friend, Snuff Garrett (more about him later). Snuff, a powerful record producer, very kindly took the time to meet with me. That meeting was a major turning point in my life. Snuff listened to the record, smiled, and said, "Don . . . go to law school."

So I took Snuff's advice and went to Harvard Law School. While I was there, I played lead guitar with a band called the Rhythm Method. However, it was quickly becoming clear that my ability to be in the music business and eat regularly lay along the business path. So when I graduated, I began doing tax planning for entertainers. Tax law, like intricate puzzles, was a lot of fun, but when I discovered there was such a thing as music law, the electricity really turned on. In fact, I took the USC class that I later taught, and it got me so excited that I left the tax practice for my current firm. Doing music law was so much fun that it wasn't even like working (I'm still not over that feeling), and I enjoyed it so much that I felt guilty getting paid (I got over that).

My first entertainment law experience was representing a gorgeous, six-foot model, referred to me by my dentist. (I promised him I would return the favor, since most of my clients had teeth.) The model was being pursued (I suspect in every way) by a manager who wanted a contract for 50% of her gross earnings for ten years. (You'll see how absurd this is when you get to Chapter 3.) Even then, I knew this wasn't right, and so I nervously called up the guy to negotiate. I still remember my voice cracking as I said his proposal was over the industry standard, since most managers took only 15% (which was true). He retorted with "Oh yeah? Who?" Well, he had me. I wasn't even sure what managers did, much less who they were. So I learned my first lesson in the art of humility.

As I began to really understand how the music business worked, I found that my love of both creative arts and business allowed me to move between the two worlds and help them relate to each other. The marriage of art and commerce has always fascinated me—they can't exist without each other—yet the concept of creative freedom, and the need to control costs in order to have a business, are eternally locked in a Vulcan death match. Which means the music business will always need lawyers.

Anyway, I now channel my creative energies into innovative business deals, and I satisfy my need to perform by teaching, lecturing, and playing guitar. Just to be sure I don't get too straight, however, I've kept up my weird assortment of hobbies: magic, ham radio, weight lifting, guitar, dog training, five-string banjo, karate, chess, poker, backgammon, and real estate investment. I also write novels, which you are all required to buy.

BRAIN SURGERY

Speaking of marrying creativity and business, I've discovered that a rock star and a brain surgeon have something in common. It's not that either one would be particularly good at the other's job (and I'm not sure which crossover would produce the more disastrous results), but rather that each one is capable of performing his craft brilliantly, and generating huge sums of money, without the need for any financial skills. In most businesses, before you can start earning big bucks, you have to be pretty well schooled in how the business works. For example, if you open up a shoe store, you have to work up a budget, negotiate a lease, bargain for the price of the shoes, and so forth—all before you smell that first foot. But in entertainment, as in surgery, you can soar to the top without any business expertise.

Making a living from a business you don't understand is risky. Yet a large number of artists, including major ones, have never learned such basics as how record royalties are computed, what a copyright is, how music publishing works, and a number of other things that directly affect their lives. They don't know this stuff because (a) their time was better spent making music; (b) they weren't interested; (c) it sounded too complicated; and/or (d) learning it was too much like being in school. But without knowing these basics, it's impossible for them to understand the intricacies of their professional lives. And as their success grows, and their lives get more complex, they become even more lost.

While it's true that some artists refuse to even listen to business talk (I've watched them go into sensory shutdown if you so much as mention the topic), others get very interested and study every detail of their business lives. The vast majority, however, are somewhere in the middle. They don't really enjoy business, but they want to participate intelligently in their career decisions. These artists are smart enough to know one simple thing: No one ever takes as good care of your business as you do.

It was for my moderately-to-seriously interested clients that I developed a way to explain the basics in simple, everyday language. With only a small investment of time, these clients understood the essential concepts, and everyone enjoyed the process (including me). It also made an enormous difference in the artist's self-confidence about his or her business life, and allowed them to make valuable contributions to the process.

Because the results of these learning sessions were so positive, several clients asked if we could explore the subjects more deeply. Thus the conception of this book. It's designed to give you a general overview of the music industry. You can read it as casually or intensely as suits your interest level, attention span, and pain tolerance. It's not written for lawyers or technicians, so it doesn't include the minutiae you'll find in a textbook for professionals. Instead, it gives you a broad overview of each segment of the industry, then goes into enough detail for you to understand the major issues you're likely to confront.

JUNGLE MAPS

When I was in high school, a policeman named Officer Sparks spoke at an assembly. Mr. Sparks hyped us on the life of a crime fighter, seeming sure we all secretly wanted to be cops. In the process, he showed us something I'll never forget.

Officer Sparks ran a film in which the camera moved down a street. It was a grainy black-and-white movie, only about thirty seconds long, filmed by a camera bobbing along a sidewalk. When it was finished, he asked if we'd seen anything unusual. No one had. Apart from a couple of people bouncing in and out of the doorways, it looked pretty much like pictures taken by a camera walking past a row of boring shops. Mr. Sparks then said that a "trained observer" who watched the film could spot six crimes being committed. He showed the film again and pointed out each of the incidents (there was a quiet exchange of drugs, a pickpocket, etc.). This time, the crimes were obvious. And I felt like a doofus for missing them.

Any time I learn a new skill, I go through a similar process. At first, things either look deceptively simple, or like a bewildering blur of chaos. But as I learn what to look for, I see a world I never knew was there.

The best way for me to become a "trained observer" is to have a guide to the basics—a framework in which to organize the bits and pieces. So that's the purpose of this book—to be a map through the jungle, and show you where the crimes are.

DETAILS

There is no way one book (even one filling several volumes) could poke into every nook and cranny of a business as complicated as the music business. So the purpose here is to give you the big picture, not all the details. (Besides, for some of those details, I charge serious money.) Also, even if I tried to lay out all the little pieces, as fast as everything moves in this biz, it would be obsolete within a few months. So the goal is to give you a broad overview (which doesn't change nearly as quickly). That way you'll have a bare tree on which to hang the leaves of your own experience. Oddly, it's easier to pick up details (from trade publications, gossip at cocktail parties, etc.) than it is to learn the structural overview, because few people have the time or patience to sit down and give it to you. In fact, giving you the overall view turned out to be a much bigger job than I thought when I started. But you're worth it.

SOME RESULTS

Since this is the ninth edition, I now have feedback from experiments using this book on actual human subjects. Of all the responses I got, I thought you'd enjoy hearing about two in particular:

First, I received an irate call from a music lawyer, who was upset because he charged thousands of dollars to give clients the advice I had put in the book.

Second, I received an equally irate call from a manager, who said that most of the artists he'd approached kept pushing my book in his face.

Way to go! Keep shoving.

And if you'll permit me a momentary lapse of modesty, my favorite compliment was from someone who said this was the first book he'd ever finished in his life.

STAPLE, SPINDLE, AND MUTILATE

When you go through this book, forget everything you learned as a kid about taking good care of books, treating them as sacred works of art, etc. Read this book with a pencil or highlighter in your hand. Circle or star passages you think you'll need, fold over pages, mark them with Post-its, paper clips, or bong water—whatever helps (unless you're reading an electronic edition, then you might want to just smudge it here and there). This is an action book—a set of directions on how to jog through the music biz without getting mugged. So treat it like a comfortable old pair of shoes that you don't mind getting dirty. It doesn't matter what they look like, as long as they get you where you're going.

CHOOSE YOUR OWN ADVENTURE

When my sons, David, Josh, and Jordan were little, their favorite books were from a series called Choose Your Own Adventure. They work like this: You start reading the book on page one and, after a few pages, the author gives you a choice. For example, if you want Pinocchio to go down the alley, you turn to page fourteen, but if you want him to go to school, you turn to page nineteen (my boys never picked school). From there, every few pages you have more choices, and there are several different endings to the book. (The boys liked the ending where everyone gets killed, but that's another story.) These books are not meant to be read straight through; if you tried, you'd find yourself crashing into different plots and stories. Instead, you're supposed to skip around, following a new path each time.

This concept gave me the idea of how to organize this book. You have a choice of reading for a broad overview or reading in depth, and the book tells you where to skip ahead if you want to do this. However, unlike the Choose Your Own Adventure books, you can read straight through with little or no damage to the central nervous system.

Here's how it's organized:

Part I deals with how to put together a team to guide your career, consisting of a personal manager, business manager, agent, and attorney.

Part II looks at record deals, including the concepts of royalties, advances, and other deal points.

Part III talks about songwriting and publishing, including copyrights and the structure of the publishing industry.

Part IV explores things you'll need to know if you're a group.

Part V deals with concerts and touring, including agreements for personal appearances, and the role of your various team members in the process.

Part VI, on merchandising, tells you how to profit from plastering your face on posters, T-shirts, and other junk.

Parts VII and VIII explore classical music and motion pictures.

They're the last sections because you need to understand the other concepts before we can tackle them.

Now, to choosing your adventure. You have four mouth-watering ways to go through this book:

1. **EXTREMELY FAST TRACK**
   If you *really* want a quick trip, then:
   (a) Read Part I, on how to pick a team of advisors;
   (b) Get people who know what they're doing;
   (c) Let them do it;
   (d) Put this book on your shelf to impress your friends; and
   (e) Say "Hi" to me backstage at one of your concerts.
2. **FAST TRACK**
   Short of this radical approach, if you want a broad-strokes overview of the business, without much detail, skip ahead each time you see the **FAST TRACK** directions.
3. **ADVANCED OVERVIEW**
   If you want a more in-depth look, but less than the full shot, then follow the **ADVANCED OVERVIEW** directions. This will give you a solid overview, plus some detail on each topic.
4. **EXPERT TRACK**
   For you high achievers who want an in-depth discussion, simply read straight through.

Feel free to mix and match any of these tracks. If a particular topic grabs your interest, keep reading and check out the details. (Amazingly, topics that grab your interest tend to be things currently happening in your life.) If another topic is a yawn, Fast Track through it.

So let's get going. Everybody starts with Part I.

PART I

Your Team of Advisors

2

How to Pick a Team

GETTING YOUR TEAM TOGETHER

Let's talk about the professionals you'll need to maximize your career and net worth. The main players are your:

1. Personal manager
2. Attorney
3. Business manager
4. Agency
5. Groupies

With respect to number 5, you're pretty much on your own. As to the others, let's take a look:

BUSINESS PHILOSOPHY

Before we talk about the specific players, let me share a bit of personal philosophy. (If "share" is too California for you, try "Let me tell you some of my personal philosophy," or the New York equivalent, "Yo, listen up, I'm talkin' to *you*.")

Take a hard look at some facts:

1. **You are a business.**
   Even though your skills are creative, you're capable of generating multimillions of dollars, so you have to think of yourself as a business.
2. **Most artists don't like business.**
   This is not to say you aren't good at it. Some artists are unbelievably astute in business. However, those folks are the minor-

ity, and whatever their love and skill for business, their love and skill for creating and performing are much bigger. So even if you've got the chops to handle your own business, it's not the best use of your time.

3. **Success hides a multitude of sins.**
   This is true in any business, from making widgets to making records. If you're successful, you can get away with sloppy operations that would bankrupt you if times were bad. For example, putting all your pals on the payroll, buying lots of non-income-producing assets (such as houses, jets, and other things that cost you money to maintain), as well as an overindulgence in various legal and illegal goodies, can easily result in a crash and burn if your income takes even a small dip, much less a nosedive. You can make more money by cutting costs than you can by earning more income (see page 417 for proof of this), so the time to operate efficiently is NOW, not later.

4. **Your career is going to have a limited run.**
   Don't take offense at this—"limited" can mean anything from a year to fifty years, but it's going to be limited. In most other careers, you can expect to have a professional life of forty years plus, but as an entertainer in the music business, this rarely happens. And the road is strewn with carcasses of aging rock stars who work for rent money on nostalgia tours. So take the concentrated earnings of a few years and spread them over a forty-year period, and you'll find that two things happen: (a) the earnings don't look quite as impressive; and (b) this money may have to last you the rest of your life.

It's certainly possible to have a long, healthy career, and to the extent you do, the need for caution diminishes radically. However, even the best entertainers have slumps, and very few have lengthy careers. So it's best to plan as if your career isn't going to last, then be pleasantly surprised if it does. Setting yourself up so that you never have to work doesn't stop you from working all you like—it just becomes an option, not an obligation.

HIRING A TEAM

The way you pick your professional team will either set up your career and finances for life, or assure you a place on the next Electric Prunes tour. So be very careful and pay attention *personally* to the process of assembling them. I know you don't like to deal with this stuff, but it's your career and your money, and you have to do it every now and then. If you pick the right people, you can set your life on automatic pilot and just check up on it periodically. If you pick the wrong people and set it on automatic pilot, you'll smash into a mountain before you know what happened.

Pre-team Strategies

Since you wouldn't open a store without something to sell, before you start assembling a team, you want to be sure your music is ready for the big time. And how do you know when it's ready? You ask your tummy. Do you believe, in your gut, that your music has matured to the point that you're ready for a professional career? If the answer is yes, then you're ready. (Tummies are reliable indicators once we learn how to listen to them and dismiss the goblins that yell, "You're a phony and nobody wants you." Even the superstars have these goblins; they've just learned to ignore them.)

The first thing is to record your music. The recording doesn't have to be expensive or elaborate—with the advent of relatively inexpensive multitrack recorders, synthesizers, and computer recording software, you can get a very professional sound in your bedroom. The important thing is to capture your energy, enthusiasm, and drive. You know what I mean.

A word about what kind of music to make. It's simple—you make the music that moves your soul. No one has ever had a serious career by imitating others, or trying to guess what the public wants. And I'll tell you a secret: What the public wants is someone whose music resonates from their heart. Doesn't matter whether you're the commercial flavor of the month, or an obscure blend of reggae and Buddhist chants. All the superstars I've known have a clear vision of who they are and what their music is.

So you've got a killer recording and you're ready to boogie. Next question is whether you want to sign to a record company or do it yourself. We'll discuss that question later (on page 70), but the first things you do are the same whether you're looking to sign to a company or go it on your own—namely, you have to build a fan base and, also build what the industry calls "a story." A story is something that comes after the line "You won't believe what's happening with this artist!" In other words, something that sets you apart from the pack.

So how do you get yourself a fan base and a story? A lot of artists start by playing whatever local gigs they can get. This is not only to attract fans, but also to tighten up their musical chops and get experience playing live. At the shows, get your fans to sign onto your email list. It's crucial to build a database (as we'll discuss in a minute), and many artists give away something (pins, stickers, etc.) to everyone who signs up. Even if you only add a few new folks at each gig, you can eventually get a following that spreads the word and grows itself virally (assuming your music doesn't suck).

Another way to build the database is by giving a free song to anyone who signs onto your email list for the first time. There's software to capture email addresses in exchange for songs at places like CASH Music (www.cashmusic.org), FanBridge (www.fanbridge.com), and Bandcamp (https://bandcamp.com). Of the three, CASH Music has the advantage of being an open source (and free), as it's based on the principle that everyone donates resources and uses the platform to help other artists. You can also expand your base by giving away songs in exchange for Tweets on Twitter, using something called "Tweet for a Track" (Tweet for a Track tools are located at the cleverly named www.tweetforatrack.com.) If you want a one-stop shop for all these schemes, sites like BandPage offer a full set of tools (www.bandpage.com).

Once you have a list, stay in touch with your fans on a regular basis. Direct them to your sites on YouTube, Facebook, Twitter, SoundCloud, Tumblr, Bandcamp, Instagram, Meerkat, Periscope, etc., and promote yourself through email and text messaging. When you contact the fans, have something interesting to say. Give away tickets. Give away songs. Give away merchandise. Release video footage of yourself. Raffle off your collection of sponges.

Don't be afraid to tell your fans what you want them to do: Come to a show. Email clubs saying they want to see you. Write about you on their Facebook pages. Tell their friends about your music. Write to bloggers about you.

And speaking of bloggers, it's important for you to write to bloggers yourself. A lot of them love to hear from artists who genuinely like their blog (insincere kissing-up doesn't work, unless you're *really* good at it).

A good database can also put your booking strategy on steroids. Facebook Insights and Google Analytics let you see where your fans are clustered, so you can strategically target those markets rather than just booking gigs in East Bumbleton and hoping the farmers show up.

A great way to build visibility is by getting your songs placed on TV

shows or in commercials. Sites like Music Dealers (www.musicdealers
.com), Pump Audio (www.pumpaudio.com), Jingle Punks (www.jingle
punks.com), Secret Road (www.secretroad.com), and Zync (www.zync
music.com) can help with that. You won't likely get much money for
the use of your recording, but you'll spread your music to a wider base.
However, if it's a big enough use, and you wrote the song, you can earn
some decent monies from airplay of the TV show or commercial (these
are called **performance royalties,** which we'll discuss on page 240).
This kind of activity can also get you noticed by a music publisher, who
may give you money for your songs. (We'll talk a lot about publishers in
Chapter 16, but essentially they handle the business of songwriters, as
opposed to the business of recording artists.)

If you get noticed by a "tastemaker" (an important blogger, journal-
ist, radio station, etc.), be sure to connect with them on Twitter and say
thanks. Apart from building goodwill with the tastemaker, it hopefully
spreads your name to their audience. Similarly, it can help expand your
base if you're able to connect with other artists on Twitter and start a
tweety conversation. Fans love to eavesdrop on artists talking shop, and
you can also get exposed to their fans.

When you're more established, give your database fans a chance to
get your music ahead of everyone else. Tell them about a secret show.
Let them have first crack at your tickets. Some bands do **lifecasting**,
where they communicate with fans a number of times each day. For
example, they might iChat on the way to a gig; blast out backstage
updates through Twitter; send pictures of themselves onstage through
Instagram; forward videos of themselves in the bathtub with rubber
duckies, etc.

Of course, with all these techniques, be sure to stay on the right side
of the line between keeping people intrigued and becoming the pomp-
ous egomaniac at the party. And just as importantly, make sure you
stay focused on your music as the first priority, with marketing as the
second. Some people recommend no more than an hour a day on social
networking/promotion, so that you don't use up all that creativity and
have none of it left for your music.

There are obviously a lot more ways to market yourself, so let your
imagination take flight and go for it. A number of websites can help
with marketing, both in terms of specific tools and general advice, but
because I don't use them myself, I can't really recommend any particular one. When I asked some friends, they suggested CASH Music,
BandPage, Bandcamp, Hyperbot, and Taxi.

Okay. So let's assume you've decided you want to sign to a record company (we'll discuss later, on page 73, whether you actually want to sign or not, but for now, let's assume you do). In this day and age, before you sign, the companies expect you to have a decent-size fan base and hopefully one or two other goodies in your story, like positive words from an important tastemaker. And even after you've done that, and even though most labels have scouts monitoring the Internet for hot new artists, unless a lot of people are going nuts over you, it's not likely anyone will call out of the blue. As with most things in life, you gotta make it happen yourself.

And now, ladies and gentlemen, a bit of a bummer: The major record companies (not so much the independents) don't listen to new artists' material unless they're submitted by someone in the business. It's usually a manager or attorney, though it could be an agent or a respected tastemaker. (I hate delivering bad news, but look at the bright side: I just saved you two months of waiting for a form email that says they won't consider your stuff because it didn't come from someone in the biz.) The reason is that record companies can get 300 to 400 submissions *per week*, and restricting who can send in material is one way to regulate the floodgates. However, it's also a Catch-22: How can you get your music heard if you're not already connected in the business, and how do you get connected in the business if you can't get heard? Don't despair; I'm going to give you the key to the door. The key consists of finding yourself a lawyer or manager to shop your music, which leads nicely into our next topic.

Who's on First?

The first person on your team is almost always a manager or a lawyer. In your baby stages, the manager is not likely to be someone in the business; it's more likely a friend or relative with a lot of enthusiasm. While this can be a major plus (as we'll discuss in more detail when we talk about managers on page 28), it may or may not get your music to the record companies. So if you have an inexperienced manager, or if you have no manager at all, an industry lawyer can really help. Record companies prefer to deal with people they know, so your music will get heard much faster, and by more important people, if it's submitted by an industry lawyer.

It's much easier to get a music lawyer than a manager. Why? Because the time required of a lawyer is minimal compared to the time a manager has to devote. The manager is expected to help you with songs, image, bookings, babysitting, etc., but the lawyer only has to spend a few hours getting people to check out your music. It's the lawyer's relationships—not their time—that count.

A word of caution about hiring a lawyer to shop your music. Most of the lawyers consider it important to maintain their credibility with the record companies, and thus will only shop artists they really believe in. Unfortunately, there are a few who will shop anything that walks in the door as long as they get paid a fee. Being shopped by one of these sleazoids is no better than sending the music yourself, and may be worse, because the record companies know these lawyers don't screen out any of the garbage, so their clients' music goes to the bottom of the pile. To prevent your music from being thrown out with the tuna cans, you should carefully check out the references of any lawyer you're thinking of using. Ask them for the names of people whose music they've shopped (both successfully and unsuccessfully, so they don't just give you the few success stories that slipped through the cracks), then call up the references and find out how it went. You can also check around other industry sources to see who's legit. (We'll talk more about checking references later on.)

You'll of course need a lawyer and manager even if you don't go the record-company route, and the criteria for hiring them (which we'll discuss in the next chapters) is exactly the same.

A business manager (the person who handles your money, investments, etc.) is usually the last on board for the opposite reason of why the lawyer is first: It's expensive (in terms of staffing and labor) for a business manager to take you on, and new artists need a lot of work just to keep financially afloat. Another reason they come on last is that very few business managers are willing to "take a flyer" with a totally unproven, unsigned artist; the business manager's potential upside is not nearly as great as a personal manager's or agent's, and yet they have to incur substantial expenses. (As you'll see in Chapter 4, business managers aren't paid as much as agents or personal managers.) But don't sweat it. Until you have some decent money coming in, you don't need a full-fledged business manager. A good accountant can take care of your tax returns and answer basic questions.

The Search

Where do you find warm bodies to begin assembling your team? Well, start with the age-old ploy of asking every human being you know for a recommendation. Talk to people involved in music, even if it's only your high school choir's piano accompanist. You can lead yourself into any unknown arena by diligently following your nose, and the music business is no exception. You'll be amazed how many things fall into your life when you open yourself up to the possibilities. The only frustrating part is that the people you really want don't have time for you in the beginning. (Be assured, as soon as you're successful, they'll fall all over you and say they "knew it all along.")

The major players are almost all in Los Angeles and New York, with a growing number in Nashville, though of course that leans heavily to country. That isn't to say there aren't qualified people in other places—there most certainly are—but the music industry is centered in these three towns, and the people who live there usually have more experience. On the other hand, major managers are increasingly popping up in other places. For example, I've dealt with managers of world-class artists who live in Vancouver, Atlanta, Austin, Philadelphia, and Boston. However, the better ones spend a lot of time on airplanes visiting Los Angeles, New York, and/or Nashville.

Here are some specific suggestions for building your list:

1. *AllAccess*
   There's a website called www.AllAccess.com that has a pretty comprehensive online directory of people in the music biz. I'm told it's updated often, and it has the major advantage of being free. You'll need to register for the site (don't be intimidated by the radio station questions—anybody can register), then click on Industry Directory.
2. *Hits Magazine*
   Hits is the *MAD* magazine of the music biz. It's full of current news and gossip, reported with a college-humor-magazine style, and is very funny reading. (www.hitsdailydouble.com)
3. *Billboard Magazine*
   Billboard is the major industry trade magazine, with lots of news, interviews, charts, and other goodies. (www.billboard.com)

By no means are these three an exhaustive list of sources; they just happened to be the ones lying nearby when I grabbed for something to give you. Frankly, I've been doing this long enough to know everybody I need to get to, and I don't use references on a routine basis. So don't take my suggestions as gospel. Check the Internet for more references.

Here's some more ideas for developing your list of potential team members:

1. Read interviews with industry figures online and in music publications, and note the names. As we just discussed, the major industry trade magazine is *Billboard*, a weekly publication that's available at newsstands and online. Here's some major *consumer* magazines (meaning magazines for fans, as opposed to trade magazines that are geared to business people), in alphabetical order:
   (a) *Music Connection*, www.musicconnection.com.
   (b) *Spin*, www.spin.com.
   (c) *Vibe*, www.vibe.com.
   (d) *Rolling Stone*, www.rollingstone.com.
2. Watch for quotes, stories, or blurbs about music industry people online, in the newspapers, on radio, and on TV.
3. Try these online places: TAXI (www.taxi.com), Music Business Registry (www.musicregistry.com), RecordXpress (www.recordxpress.net), PureVolume (www.purevolume.com), and Songwriter 101 (www.songwriter101.com).
4. Some artists list the names of their professionals, together with their jobs, on their websites, info page of Facebook, or in tour programs.
5. The liner notes of CDs (not that you buy any of those . . .) often list managers, lawyers, business managers, or agents in the Special Thanks section. Unfortunately, they may only list the people's names and not their roles (so you might end up managed by someone's yoga instructor if you're not careful). Still, when you're compiling a list of names, every little bit helps.

Using the above and anything else you can think of, write down the names and develop a "hit list." Just keep moving forward—follow any lead that seems promising.

Once you assemble a bunch of names, prioritize who you want to contact first. If you've heard any names from two or more sources, the odds are you are on to a person who is "somebody," and he or she should move up in priority. Also look for the professionals surrounding people whose music you admire and whose style is similar to yours. While this is less critical with lawyers and business managers, it's important to make sure that agencies, and especially personal managers, handle your style of music. For example, the agent who books Wayne Newton is not likely to book Lil Wayne, and I guarantee you they have different managers. On the other hand, you may be surprised to find that acts just as diverse are represented by the same agency (with very different individual agents). And the legal and business management lives of different artists are a lot alike. Rock 'n' rollers (like Green Day, the Rolling Stones, etc.) and divas (like Adele, Barbra Streisand, etc.) have similar needs in music publishing, record royalties, touring, merchandising, sponsorship, etc.

Once you've prioritized your list, start trying to contact the people on it. It's always better to come in through a recommendation, friend of the family, etc., even if it's only the person's dry cleaner. But if you can't find any contact, start cold. You can try calling people on the phone, but expect a lot of unreturned phone calls, or at best to be shuffled off to an underling. That's okay—talk to the underling. Be sure you're brief and to the point if you get someone on the phone, because these folks are always in a hurry. It's a good idea to rehearse your rap with a friend in advance.

You can try emailing folks, with a brief story about yourself and a link to your music. Be short and straightforward—good people are always busy, and you'll be lucky to get five seconds of their attention. If you can't grab 'em fast, they'll hit "delete." Repeated emails to the same person help get their attention, and may even have the subliminal effect of making your name sound familiar if anyone ever asks. It can also be annoying and get your name into their spam filter, so don't overdo it.

You could also use that old-fashioned thing you may remember, called the "U.S. Mail." Since so few people do that anymore, you might even get more attention. In this case, include CDs or a USB stick, pictures, hundred-dollar bills, and anything else to distinguish yourself. (I once had a guy send me a recording stuffed inside a rubber chicken. For real.) If you've gotten any local press, that's a good thing to add. Use a yellow highlighter so they don't have to search the page for where you are. Just like the emails, be short and sweet, or you're off to the round file.

However you approach it, expect a lot of unacknowledged letters and unanswered emails, but don't get discouraged.

If you successfully snag someone's attention but find out they can't get involved with you, ask who they would recommend. This is valuable for two reasons: First, you've got a lead from someone actually in the industry. Second, when you reach out to the recommended person, you can tell them "So-and-so" told you to contact them. If "So-and-so" is a big enough name, it should at least get your phone call or email returned. (Maybe.)

Someone, somewhere, will nibble, and you can parlay it into real interest by being persistent. All the superstars I've known have heaping helpings of drive and perseverance, and they'll continually hound people to further their careers. So hang in there and keep following up, despite the discouragements thrown in front of you. Virtually every record company in America passed on the Beatles and Elton John, so don't expect people to be any smarter about your music. And don't get discouraged—it only takes one enthusiastic person to get the ball rolling.

Screening the Sharks

So you've honed your list, run up hours of chasing people, and hopefully found two or three nibbles on your line. At this point, you should fly, drive, bus, or hitchhike to meet these people in their natural habitat. You can't tell everything from a phone call; you want to see their body language, meet their associates, see if they work out of a trailer, etc. Basically, use your instincts to feel how they vibe you, and don't be afraid to trust your gut. If you think you're meeting with a piece of slime, you probably are. But if they dazzle you, be even more cautious—charming crooks are the most dangerous!

The fact that someone works with a lot of big names is helpful, but not a final determination. There have been a lot of big names associated with disasters over the years. Here's a bit of personal history to illustrate:

When we first got married, my wife and I decided to buy a vacuum cleaner. For reasons I still don't understand, we called a door-to-door salesman. This buzz-cut, square-jawed man bounced into the house and fractured my pinkie with his handshake. Buzz used the vacuum's suction to pick up seven-pound metal balls, then used it to slurp up some blue gunk that he'd poured on our carpet. He started bragging about how he'd sold vacuum cleaners to the wives of several celebrities, and while he was rattling off a list of big names, I said, "Excuse me, but do these people know anything about vacuum cleaners?"

The point, as I'm sure you see, is that a big-name celebrity isn't necessarily a good recommendation. It may just mean the celebrity pays no attention to his or her business, or that the celebrity is an imbecile.

So how do you protect yourself? Like this:

References.   Have the potential team member give you references. And check them out carefully.

In asking for references, it's important to get people at your level of success. The fact that someone takes good care of their biggest client doesn't mean he or she will give you the same attention, or even have the time to take care of you. Odd as it seems, some people don't even pay much attention to their big-name clients, usually because they're too busy. There's an old joke (based on truth) about a major artist who couldn't get his lawyer on the phone to fire him. Also, try to get the reference from someone who's been using this professional for a while, so you don't just get a report on their honeymoon period.

Although it may seem obvious, be sure the professional's expertise is in music. There are brilliant real estate accountants who would be lost in the music business, just as the opposite is true. In fact, even people with extensive film, television, or book expertise may not understand music. So be sure you're talking to someone who does.

Use Your Other Team Members.   You should consult the other members of your team anytime you hire someone. First, you want their input and suggestions, and second, these people have to work together, so you want to be sure you're hiring someone who can get along with the team. But beware of this: Benjamin Franklin once said (and I'm too lazy to look up the exact quote, so I'll paraphrase it) that when you gather a group of people for their collective wisdom, you also gather their collective prejudices and hidden agendas. In other words, there will almost always be a political reason why your other team members want something, and this may or may not coincide with your best interests. For example, a business manager may have just referred a very important client to a personal manager. The personal manager may therefore be pushing you toward this particular business manager in order to pay back the favor, regardless of whether the business manager is right for your situation. (I don't mean to make you paranoid; most people are ethical and won't recommend someone unless they genuinely believe he or she would be the best person for the job, even if it's a payback. But a great deal of politicking goes on in the music business, just like any other business, and you should be aware of it.) So, always ask people *why* they're making a recommendation, rather than just the bottom line of who you should use. Make them give you specific, factual reasons. Facts are something you can evaluate yourself, and you should make the final decision.

Look Beyond the Sales Pitch.   Everybody looks great when they're selling. When you interview someone, all the seller's attention is focused on you, and you are absolutely the most important creature on the planet. This is almost never the case when you actually get down to business; the realities of other people's needs take their toll. It's extremely difficult to know this in your first meeting, as "giving good interview" can take people very far in their professions.

So how do you get beyond this? Once again, you have to check their references very carefully. Ask the references about their entire experience of working with this person, such as their promptness in returning phone calls, how fast he or she gets work done, what's their zodiac sign, etc. It's a good idea to make a list of questions in advance, so you don't forget anything.

Don't be lulled by promises that sound unbelievably fantastic. If they sound too good to be true, they probably aren't. Many people will promise things they can't possibly deliver, just to get the job. They figure you won't fire them when they can't deliver, because they know most artists don't like to make changes in their lives. (These are the same people who will stop returning calls if your star fades.) They also figure they have to lie just to ace out the next guy, who they assume is also lying to you. The truth is that there are no real miracle workers. The secret of success in the music business is no different from that in any other business—intelligent planning, solid work, and smart execution. Promises of "shortcuts" usually don't come through.

Who Does the Work?   Ask exactly who is going to be involved in your day-to-day work. It may not be the person you're meeting with. This isn't necessarily bad, but you should be aware of it from the start, and you should meet the people who will be involved. All professionals use staff people, some to a greater degree than others. With some firms the staff people divide and multiply like paramecia, so the people you're meeting today may be gone in six months. Other places are more stable. So ask, and also ask your references.

Fees.   Never hesitate to ask what someone is going to charge you. I know it's an uncomfortable subject, but bring it up anyway—you can be in for some seriously rude surprises if you don't. And when you do raise the topic, be particularly wary of someone who gives you a vague answer. (If you really can't stomach a fee discussion, have another team member do it for you.)

Personality.   It's a myth to think any one personality style is more effective than any other (assuming you don't hire a wuss). Screamers and table pounders, if they're smart and knowledgeable, can get a lot out of a deal, but no more than those who speak quietly, if they're smart and knowledgeable. Some people work with a foil, and some with a sabre. Both styles can be effective.

Remember, you're hiring people to guide your professional life, not to travel on the tour bus. It's nice if you strike up a friendship with your professionals, but it's not essential. (However, with your personal manager, I think you need at least a solid rapport, if not a true friendship.) I'm not suggesting you hire someone you really dislike, or someone who has the personality of a salamander, but I am saying these folks don't have to be your pals. In fact, some amount of distance is often helpful. Just as doctors can't operate on their own relatives, one of the main things a professional does is bring some objectivity to your life.

There is a wonderful story about Genghis Khan, the great warrior. In the midst of a pivotal battle for his empire, involving thousands of troops on both sides, an aide went into Khan's tent and was surprised to find Khan himself sitting there. The aide said, "How can you be in your tent? The troops need your command, and the battle is at a critical point." Khan replied, "I found myself getting angry over a turn in the battle, and I can't think straight when I'm angry. I came in here to cool off before deciding the next move."

Think about that. If even ol' Genghis had to detach from his emotions to do the best job, who are you and I to do any better? When I have legal problems, I hire a lawyer. This may sound strange to you, but I get emotional about my own problems (just as you do), and I don't trust my judgment when I'm too close to the situation. So I hire someone who isn't.

In sum, a bit of distance from your professionals is not a concern, but you should feel comfortable enough to have an easy communication with your team. If you think you'll dread talking to one of them, look for someone else.

Decide Now—Confirm Later. Make a decision reasonably quickly, but confirm it slowly. In other words, once you've hired somebody, continue to watch them carefully (to the extent you can stand to do it). The fact that someone came in with rave reviews doesn't mean they'll be right for you, so consider them "on probation" until you've seen enough to merit your trust. And don't just take another team member's word that it's working. Force yourself to follow their moves in the beginning, and you will earn the right to relax later. Remember: No one pays as good attention to your business as you do.

CHANGING A TEAM MEMBER

Here's what to do if something goes wrong on your team:

Even if they never pay much attention to business, I've never met an artist who doesn't have a built-in radar that tells them when something is wrong. So if you're feeling weird, then, "Houston, we have a problem."

It may be that things aren't being handled right. Or maybe you just don't feel comfortable talking to one of the team members. Ignoring the issue doesn't help any more than turning up the car radio to drown out a rattle in the engine. It's like a quote I once heard attributed to Dick Gregory: "I read so much about the bad effects of smoking that I got scared and gave up reading."

So deal with problems head on.

Talk About Your Problems

I know confrontation is difficult. I have never known an artist (or anyone else, for that matter, other than a few ornery jerks who've been divorced five times) who enjoys confrontation. But for your team members to do an effective job, you must have an open communication with them. If you can't bring yourself to talk directly to the person who is bugging you, talk to another team member and make sure they carry the message. *Fast.* Nothing is worse than letting small things snowball to the point that they build into a major drama. If you discuss them when they're small, they can usually stay small. Often they're just innocent misunderstandings.

If you talk frankly about your problems, and they still aren't getting solved, make a change. No one has the right to expect a lifetime contract with you. People and circumstances change over the years; those who were spectacular for you at one point in your life may no longer be interested in you (if your career has taken a nosedive, if they've lost interest in their job, etc.). Or they may no longer be capable of handling you (if they were unable to grow with you and your career is soaring, or if you have changed careers and their expertise is in the wrong area, etc.). I respect and admire loyalty, but blind loyalty does no one a favor. To me, loyalty means you don't turn your head and run off with every pretty face that walks by (and as you get more successful, pretty faces come out of the woodwork to try to seduce you, literally and figuratively). But loyalty is a two-way street, meaning you're entitled to the same commitment from your professionals. You're only obligated to stick with someone as long as they're doing a good job for you. If you're not getting the service you want, then loyalty means you discuss it with them and tell them what needs to be changed. (Again, if you don't want to do it directly, do it through another team member.) If things still aren't being done right, and you're sure your complaints were clearly communicated, make a change. But do it for the right reasons, not the wrong ones.

Lost Confidence

It pains me a bit to give you this next piece of advice, but you should have it. Once you've lost confidence in someone, it's almost impossible to continue with them. It's like falling out of love—it isn't easy to fall in again. I say this sadly, because many times we lose confidence in people for the wrong reasons. It may be that someone with a political ax has buried them unjustly; it may be that they are doing a terrific job, but they have the personality of a stop sign and treat you rudely or bore you to death; it may be they have just delivered bad news to you (firing such a person is known as "shooting the messenger," from ancient Greek times, when a messenger bringing bad news was killed); it may be they have done a terrific job on everything important in your life, but screwed up paying your bills one month, so you had no electricity and your spouse refuses ever to see their face again; or it just may be an uneasy feeling in your stomach that you don't trust them. When you find yourself in this situation, again, I urge you to talk to the person openly (directly or through another team member) and tell them how you feel. (I know this is easy for me to say, and I admit it's difficult for me to do as well. But I force myself, and most of the time I find that the problem is a simple mistake that's easily fixed. And even if it isn't, I always feel better just from processing it.) If you talk things out and the situation doesn't get any better, split.

COCKTAIL PARTY TALK

Let me say a word about cocktail party talk. In college, we used to play a kind of poker called "roll your own." In this game you get five cards, then draw additional cards (like in regular five-card draw). Finally, you arrange your cards in any order you want before flipping them over one at a time and betting on each card. After flipping the first three cards, everybody at the table looks like they have a spectacular hand. There appear to be straights, flushes, straight flushes, three of a kind, high pairs, and every other imaginable configuration to make you want to drop out and give up the pot. However, when it comes to flipping over the last couple of cards, most of the hands are mediocre.

I've always thought cocktail party talk is the same as flipping only the first three cards. Everyone sounds like a genius; everyone has just pulled off the greatest deal since the Louisiana Purchase. The truth, however, is in the last two cards, which you never see. The million-dollar deal turns out to be a hundred-thousand-dollar deal, with the other nine hundred thousand being there only if the artist achieves massive success (not that a hundred thousand isn't a decent amount of money, but it ain't a million). Nobody talks about their screw-ups, because self-aggrandizement is part of the dance of the sand crabs that is ritualized at cocktail parties.

The whole point of this is to say that you shouldn't take casual talk at face value. Especially if someone has an editorial point of view, like a manager trying to convince you to leave your current manager for the terrific things he or she can do for you. (Lawyers, of course, would never do such a thing. And if you buy that, I have some land in Florida we should discuss.) So make your own evaluations in the realistic light of day.

3

Personal Managers

ROLE

The personal manager is the single most important person in your professional life. A good personal manager can expand your career to its maximum potential, and a bad one can rocket you into oblivion. When the job is done properly, a personal manager is the general manager and chief operating officer of your enterprise. (There are, of course, some artists without managers, but they are very much the exception, and they usually have one or more other team members filling this role.)

The most important aspects of the manager's job are:

1. Helping you with major business decisions, such as deciding whether to do a record deal, and if so, which record company to sign with; whether to make a publishing deal (we'll talk about what those are on page 235); how much to ask for; etc.

2. Helping you with the creative process, such as selecting a producer (we'll talk about who producers are on page 125), deciding which songs to record, hiring band members, selecting photographers, etc.

3. Promoting your career by hyping you to everyone the manager meets, helping you coordinate a publicity campaign, etc.

4. Assembling and heading your professional team by introducing you to lawyers, business managers, and agents, and overseeing these people's work.

5. Coordinating your concert tours by working with your agent to make the best deals with promoters, routing the tour, working with your business manager to develop a budget, assembling your road crew, supervising the road and tour managers to make sure everything runs smoothly, etc.

6. Pounding your record company to maximize the advertising

and marketing campaigns for your records, making sure your records are treated as priorities, screaming at them when they do wrong, praising them when they do right, etc.

7. Generally being a buffer between you and the outside world, such as fielding inquiries for commercial endorsements, personal appearances, charitable requests (both for money and for your smiling face), taking the rap for tough decisions that you make but don't want anyone to think you did, etc.

Let's first take a look at the structure of your deal with the personal manager, and then we'll talk about picking one.

COMMISSION OVERVIEW

Managers typically get from 15% to 20% of earnings from new artists. Established artists can sometimes knock them lower, as we'll discuss in a minute.

These percentages are generally applied to your **gross** earnings, meaning your earnings before deducting any expenses. That means:

1. If you're an individual artist, the fee is pretty much what it sounds like for songwriting, publishing, records, etc. We'll discuss some of the finer points later, but basically, if the manager gets 15%, they take 15% of what you bring in. However, when it comes to touring, the 15% means much more than you might think. You'll see, when we discuss concert appearances (on page 395), that you're lucky to take home 40% to 50% of your gross income. That means a manager's 15% of gross can take a big bite out of your net. For example, if you earn $100,000 and net $40,000, your manager's 15% of gross ($15,000) is almost 40% of your $40,000 net.

2. If you're a group and you have more than five members, 15% of gross equals almost the same as, or more than, any one of you earns (assuming you're dividing equally). For example, if there are seven of you, everybody gets one-seventh; that's 14.28%, which is less than the manager's 15%. In fact, since the manager's percentage comes "off the top" before you divide up any monies, you only get one-seventh of the 85% left after the manager's 15%, which is 12.14%. And for touring monies, a manager's 15% of gross can be several times your individual share of **net**.

Because artists have found it, shall we say, "uncomfortable," to pay managers more than the artist makes, the classic "15% to 20% of gross" has softened over the last few years. Here's what's going down:

NEGOTIATING THE MANAGER'S DEAL

Despite the powerful personality of many managers (carefully designed to keep you in your place), it is possible to negotiate with your manager. However, just like any other negotiation, the result depends on bargaining power. If you're a major artist, bringing in $10 million plus per year, the managers will follow you like floppy-eared puppies, delighted to take whatever treats you care to drop for them. On the other hand, if you're a brand-new band negotiating with a powerful manager, then you're the doggy.

Here are the points to discuss:

Compensation. The first and most obvious issue is the manager's percentage. You should try to limit the percentage to 15%, although some managers argue that the risk of taking on a new band is worth 20%. They say it will be years—if ever—before they get paid for a lot of work (which is true). A compromise is to say the manager gets 15%, but it escalates to 20% when you earn a certain dollar amount (such as 15% of the first $2 million and 20% of the excess). I've also seen the opposite, where the manager gets 20% up to a certain level, and then 15% after that. The theory is that the manager gets a bigger percentage when you're young and the manager can't make as much, but his or her cut drops to the 15% norm when you're successful. This seems a bit weird at first, because it looks like the manager has no incentive to make you more successful (the more success, the lower the manager's take). But it's really not true—all managers would rather have 15% of a big number than 20% of a small one.

Sometimes managers share in the *net* of an artist's earnings (meaning your earnings *after* deducting expenses) rather than the gross. This is much better for the artist—for starters, the manager won't get paid if the artist loses money, which is not the case in gross deals. In one deal I'm aware of, the manager got 20% of the net of a four-piece band. Another deal paid the manager on the gross for records and publishing, but on the net for touring.

When a manager has a deal on the net, they will sometimes ask for limits on the expenses. For example, artists who decide to go on the road and charter jets, throw parties in every city, put inflatable pools in their hotel suites, etc., can easily eat up the net while having a great time with their pals. Managers don't usually enjoy these parties quite as much. Thus, the agreement might be that the manager is paid on net touring proceeds, but that the expenses of the tour can't exceed a negotiated percentage of the gross.

A variation on this theme is that the manager gets a percentage of gross, but the commission is capped at 50% of the net. In other words, the manager will never make more than the artist actually puts in his or her pocket. For example, if you gross $1,000, and have $800 in expenses, your net is $200. If the manager got 15% of the gross, he or she would earn $150. Under this arrangement, the maximum would be 50% of the net (50% of $200, or $100), so the manager gets $100 and the artist gets $100. Note, however, that if you're a group, you all have to share the artist's 50% of the net, which means the manager makes more than any one of you.

In a few situations, where the artist is a superstar, the manager sometimes gets 10% or less, and occasionally just a salary (no percentage). These salaries can run well into six, or sometimes even seven, figures.

Exclusions. It's sometimes possible to reduce (or even exclude) certain types of earnings. For example, if you're a major songwriter hiring a manager to help you become a recording artist, the manager might get 15% of your earnings as an artist, but only 10% (or even 7.5%, 5%, or 0%) of your songwriting monies. Or maybe the manager gets 15% of your songwriting monies from records on which you appear as an artist, and a reduced (or no) percentage on other songwriter earnings. Another example is an established motion picture actor who hires a manager to help with his or her music career. Or vice versa. In these cases, you normally exclude (or reduce the percentage for) the area where you're already established. The possibilities are as varied as your imagination.

If you exclude any of your earnings from commission, the manager won't be obligated to do any work in the excluded area (though they often do as a practical matter).

Money-Losing Tours. You can sometimes get managers to agree that, if a tour loses money, they'll take no commission on it. This is the same concept we discussed above, when we talked about capping your manager's commissions at 50% of your touring profits. If you can't get your manager down to zero on money-losing tours, then try for a reduced commission (meaning, for example, instead of 15%, they'd only get 7.5% on a losing tour), and at the very least, get them to defer their commission until you're more successful (meaning you agree they're entitled to a commission, but they have to wait and get paid later, when you have money coming in). Another variation is that the manager doesn't get paid for dates where you make a small amount, such as $1,000 per night (or a similar negotiated figure).

Deductions.   Certain monies are customarily deducted before computing the manager's percentage, even when a manager is paid on gross. Most managers don't take commissions on these, even if their contract says they can, but some try. So it's always a good idea to spell things out and avoid any misunderstandings.

Here's the list of no-no's:

1. **Recording costs.**
   If the record company pays you money, and you spend it on recording costs, you should not pay a commission on those monies. This is because the funds only pass through your hands (i.e., you don't keep them), and thus they aren't really "earnings."
2. **Monies paid to a producer of your records.**
   Producers are the people hired to put together your recording, as we'll discuss in detail on page 125, and you pay them advances and royalties. Just like recording costs, money you get that you have to fork over to a producer isn't really earnings, for the same reasons we just discussed for recording costs.
3. **Co-writers.**
   When you write songs with somebody else, the manager shouldn't get paid on the other person's share of the song's earnings, even if you collect them first.
4. **Tour support.**
   This is money paid by a record company to offset your losses from touring (see page 196). Whether managers should commission tour support is a bit controversial. Some managers argue this is money you get from the record company, just like any other money, and they helped you get it, so they should commission it. Most of the time, however, they'll agree it isn't commissionable, because it only compensates you for a loss.
5. **Costs of collection.**
   If you have to sue someone to get paid, the cost of suing them to collect the money (called **collection costs**) should be deducted

before applying the manager's percentage. For example, if a concert promoter stiffs you for $50,000, and it costs you $10,000 in legal fees and court costs to collect, the manager should only commission $40,000 (the $50,000 recovery less the $10,000 collection costs). Another way to look at this is to say the manager bears his or her proportionate share of the collection costs.

6. **Sound and lights.**

   It's common in personal appearance contracts for the artist to supply his or her own sound system and stage lighting. The promoter then "rents" the sound and lights from the artist for a specified dollar amount. Customarily, this rent money is considered an expense reimbursement (as opposed to a fee paid to the artist), so the manager isn't paid on the amount allocated to sound and lights. But you gotta ask for this one.

7. **Opening acts.**

   When you get to the superstar category, your deal for a personal appearance may also include monies you pay to an opening act. Again, since this money just passes through your hands, it shouldn't be commissionable.

8. **Related entities.**

   More and more often, managers now own record labels, and sometimes publishing companies. If you make a deal with one of those, you shouldn't pay a management commission on the earnings from that company. The managers don't always agree to this, arguing that they're wearing two hats (manager and record label) and should be paid for both. However, you argue that they can't be expected to beat up their own company the way they would beat up a major label. You also argue that they're getting paid much more through that entity than they would as a manager, so they shouldn't "double dip" and get paid twice on the same earnings: they'd get paid once as a label when you sell records, then again as a manager when you get paid for those sales. Also, if you leave them as a manager, they'll still get paid as your record company if that deal continues.

Term

Historically, the term of a management agreement (meaning the period of time that the manager will work for you) was three to five years. If you're an artist, you want to make it as short as possible; if you're a manager, you want it as long as possible.

For some time, there was a trend for managers to have terms geared to **album cycles,** as opposed to a specific number of years. An *album cycle* means a period of time from the commencement of recording an album until the end of the touring and promotional activities surrounding it. Usually that means the later of either the end of a tour or the end of promotion of all of the singles from the album.

A management term geared to album cycles is fairer to the manager—if the term is simply a period of years, it could end in the middle of promoting an album and the manager could get knocked out of commissions after he or she has done most of the work.

Lately, however, management terms have been going back the other way, to a specific number of years. For one thing, albums will arguably disappear, meaning the term goes on forever. And even if albums stick around, with a baby band, record cycles can be incredibly long. So from the artist's point of view, you would much rather have it tied to a specific time period.

Be very careful when negotiating the term of a management deal. Many artists have lived to regret being tangled up in long-term contracts with lousy managers. Yet there's a balancing act that has to work for both sides. Managers don't want to put their sweat into launching your career, only to see you waltz off at the first sign of success, and you don't want to be married to a moron who's holding you back.

The most common compromise is to say that if the artist doesn't earn a minimum amount, he or she can terminate the agreement early. For example, the deal might be for three album cycles, but if the artist doesn't earn $200,000 over the first two years, he or she can terminate the deal.

I hesitate to give you specific dollar figures for the earnings, because (1) they'll probably be out of date by the time you read this, and (2) they also depend on who you are. If you're a heavy touring band, the numbers are much higher than if you write folk songs and sing in coffeehouses. Here's an example from a beginning rock artist's contract: The deal was for two years, and the manager could renew for an additional two years if the artist earned $300,000 over the first two. The manager could then renew for another (third) two years if, during the second two years, the artist earned $500,000.

The manager, if he or she has any sophistication, will also say that the "earnings" have to include offers you turn down. The theory is that you can't refuse to work and then get out of the deal because you didn't earn enough. I usually agree to this request but require that the offers must be similar to those you have previously accepted. So an offer to appear nude at the Moscow Circus wouldn't count (unless that's your act).

Another approach is to say you must have a record deal (or a publishing deal if you're a songwriter) within a year or eighteen months after the start of the term, and if not, you can terminate. If you have a deal before you sign with the manager, then try to say you can terminate if you don't hit certain album sales figures. For example, you could terminate the deal if you haven't sold X number of albums by the end of the second album cycle. The specific sales level varies with the type of artist involved. If you're a straight-ahead, commercial artist, you want a fairly high figure. But if you're more off center and want to build slowly, the figure would be lower. Whatever the criteria, it doesn't usually kick in until the second or third album, as the managers argue that the first album is just the beginning of a building process. One manager I know agreed to a figure of 60,000 albums for an alternative, quirky band, and a figure of 200,000 albums for a straight-ahead, commercial artist. Note this includes both physical (CD) albums and digital album downloads. Managers usually want to include digital singles, on the basis that ten digital singles equal one digital album, plus some kind of streaming equivalent of an album (X number of streams equal one album sale). This gets pretty complicated, and at the end of the day, it's only about how much success they're generating, so I'm guessing the trend will go back to dollars rather than sales.

Termination for failing to clear the hurdle can be done two ways. One is a letter from the artist to the manager containing legal words that translate as "You're fired." The other is a shorter management deal that gets renewed if the artist achieves certain earnings (for example, the term of the agreement is two years, but if the artist earns at least $200,000, the manager continues for an additional two years). The only difference between these two arrangements is whether the artist has to remember to send the manager a notice.

Earnings After the Term: "The Gift That Keeps on Taking"

One of the most important points you have to negotiate is what your manager gets paid after the end of the management deal. Even though the term may end after a few years, virtually every management contract says the manager gets paid on earnings *after* the term if those earnings are generated under "contracts entered into or substantially negotiated during the term." This language means two things:

1. As to records made during the term of the management deal, the manager gets a commission from sales of these records occurring after the end of the management deal; and
2. The manager is paid on records *made after* the term of your management deal, if the records are recorded under a contract signed during the term.

All of this could mean—and I've seen it happen—that a manager is still getting paid seven, ten, or more years after he or she finished rendering services. For example, suppose six months before the end of the management deal you sign a five-album deal. Under this clause, the manager gets paid forever on sales of these five albums, most of which will be recorded after you've parted company.

I think this clause is way overreaching, and I've been pretty successful in cutting it back. Let's analyze the situation:

The major things to worry about are records and publishing. Unless you're in a television series or some other nonmusical commitment that could run for several years, records and publishing are the only areas where you're likely to have significant earnings from activities after the term under agreements made during the term. The other contracts you make during the term, such as personal appearance engagements, may be completed after the term, but this happens in a relatively short period (although it can represent millions of dollars). And if a manager is involved in setting up a tour, it's not unreasonable for him or her to be paid something for the tour. (So if you're going to dump your manager, do it before the tour gets set up.)

Sunset Clauses.   Here are some of my better strategies to cut this back. These are known as **sunset clauses,** because they end the day for commissions.

1. **Records.**
    (a) The manager gets paid only on records recorded and released during the term (and not on any others). This is the best for you.
    (b) Another solution is that the manager gets a half commission (e.g., if the manager has 15%, it's reduced to 7.5%) on records recorded during the term but released afterward. The theory is that the manager only does half the work—overseeing the recording, but not overseeing the release and promotion. (As in (a), records made after the term aren't commissionable at all.)

2. Publishing.

(a) The manager is paid only on songs recorded and exploited during the term. This is the best for you.

(b) The manager gets a half commission on songs recorded during the term and exploited after.

(c) The manager gets a half commission on songs written during the term but recorded afterward. This at least cuts off participation in songs written after the term under contracts made during the term.

3. Final cutoff.

(a) I try to have some date after which all commissions end, no matter what. Try three to five years after the term; settle for no more than seven.

(b) Even with an overall cutoff, you can sometimes reduce the commissions while you're waiting for them to die. For example, there might be a full commission for the first two years after the term, a half commission for the next three years, then over and out.

Feel free to creatively mix and match the above three approaches. For example, the manager could get a full commission on records recorded and released during the term, but only for a period of three years after the term. Or they might get a commission for a period after the term equal to the term itself (for example, if the term were three years, the period afterward would be three years; if it were four years, the period would be four years, etc.), and thereafter nothing else. The limits are only your imagination and the manager's patience.

A particularly thorny problem (and another reason you should pay so much attention to the commissions after the term) is the fact that, after the term, you'll need to hire a new manager. As you can imagine, there aren't too many managers who want to work for free, and there are even fewer artists who want to pay 15% of their gross to two managers (30%!). Thus, it's very important to limit or eliminate commissions after the term. In truth, most new managers will take a reduced (or even no) commission on earnings that another manager is commissioning. But they're only going to do this for, say, the first album or the first tour, and they'll only do it if you're pretty successful. If they can't start making money relatively soon, managing you isn't going to be worth their time. So while you can live with paying a prior manager something on after-term projects, you should limit it as much as possible.

Key Man

Another important aspect of your management deal is called a **key man** clause (hopefully soon to be called a "key person" clause). Although you have a relationship with a particular personal manager, your contract might be with their corporation or a partnership. Thus it's possible that "your person" could leave the company, and since your deal isn't with that manager personally, you can't just get up and go with them. Accordingly, you could find yourself managed by a stranger. Or someone you know but who smells like the Cuyahoga River.

To prevent this, you should insert a clause that says the person with whom you have a relationship (the *key man*) must personally act as your manager, and if not, you can terminate the deal. If the company buys this concept (some bigger ones won't), you can easily get a clause that says you can terminate if the key man dies or is disabled, and you can sometimes get the same right if he or she is no longer employed by the management company. Much trickier is the situation where they're alive and kicking, and still employed by your manager, but taken off your account. It's much harder to say the key man must be "actively involved" in managing your life, because the manager worries that, even if the key man is still working on your career, you'll try to use this clause to get out of your deal—you'd argue that the manager is doing a mediocre job (and thus is not "actively involved"), and therefore the management company is in breach of your contract. (For exactly this reason, from your point of view, the broader you can make the language, the better.)

Double Commissions

If, for tax planning or otherwise, you set up a corporation to conduct your entertainment activities, you want to be sure this doesn't trigger a **double commission.** (See page 203 for a discussion of using a corporation in record deals, and page 381 for corporations used by groups.) Observe:

Management contracts say that the manager's commission is based on your earnings at the corporate level. This is perfectly reasonable—otherwise you could easily pay the gross monies into the corporation, pay yourself only a small salary, and claim the manager only gets his or her commission on the small amount that comes out to you. For example, if your corporation gets $100,000 for your appearance at a show but only pays you $10,000, it wouldn't be fair to pay the manager only 15% of the $10,000. However, it's not reasonable for the manager to take a second bite at the money. Once he or she has commissioned it at the corporate level, there should be no further commission when it comes out to you in the form of salary. (In the previous example, this means the manager can't commission both the $100,000 and the $10,000.) Most management contracts would technically allow the manager to do this "double dip" (after all, the salary is your gross income), but in practice it isn't done (by reputable managers). Still, it's a good idea to specifically say so.

Power of Attorney

Another provision to watch for is one that says the manager has a **power of attorney** (meaning the power to act for you), such as the right to sign your name to contracts, hire and fire your other representatives, approve use of your name and likeness, cash your checks, etc. I like to wipe out most of this nonsense. You should hire and fire your own representatives, and definitely cash your own checks. The only time I let a manager sign for an artist is if (a) the deal is for personal appearance engagements, of no more than two or three nights, which will be performed within the next four to six weeks; (b) you're unavailable to sign the agreement yourself; and (c) the manager has your verbal approval of the deal. If it doesn't meet these criteria, bless the piece of paper with your autograph.

As you get busier, you may want the manager to handle routine approval of the use of your name and likeness. If so, make sure it's only for certain uses (publicity for your own career is okay, but not major things like commercial endorsements), and that they can only authorize use of a likeness that you previously approved.

The Best Deals

Now that you've studied managers' contracts, you're ready for a well-kept secret. Go close the door before I tell you.

Okay, here's the secret: Many of the top managers have absolutely no written contracts with their artists. It's all done on a handshake, and the only discussion is the percentage. Their feeling, and I respect them for it, is that the relationship is more important than any piece of paper, and if the artist isn't happy, they're free to go at any time. Also implicit in this arrangement is that the artist needs the manager as much as (or more than) the manager needs the artist.

Please don't misunderstand this point. Many legitimate and well-respected managers require written contracts, and there is nothing wrong with this. But there are also a number who "fly naked" (without a written deal), and ironically they are often the ones who keep their clients the longest.

Even with these folks, I often do an email outlining the terms. It spells out the percentages, states that the term can be ended by either party at any time, and deals with the post-term earnings (see the above discussion). It never hurts to make sure there are no misunderstandings.

PICKING THE RIGHT MANAGER

So how do you pick a manager? First, review Chapter 2, which applies to picking everyone on your team. Then take a look at these specific tips.

Let's start with the absolute best. This is the yardstick to use in measuring your candidates: The absolute best is a powerful, well-connected manager, with one or more major clients, who is wildly enthusiastic about you and willing to commit the time required for your career. If you're a superstar, you can easily find such a person. If you're not, this situation hardly ever exists. The reason is that, when a manager is powerful and successful, he or she is usually not interested in anything other than a major money-earning client. The analysis is simple—it takes as much (or more) work to establish a new artist as it does to service an established artist, and guess which one pays better (and sooner)? (Yes, every once in a while, a powerful manager gets genuinely revved up over a new band. But this is rare, and you have to be extraordinarily lucky even to get such a person's attention.)

So let's look at more down-to-earth alternatives, not in any particular order:

1. A major manager with a young associate who is genuinely enthusiastic about you.
2. A midsize manager who is wildly enthusiastic about you.
3. A major, powerful manager who is taking you on as a favor (either personal or professional) to somebody who is *very* important to him or her.
4. A young, inexperienced manager who is willing to kill for you.

There are of course endless combinations of the above, but these are the major categories.

Unless you can get the best possible situation described above, you'll have to make some kind of compromise. The compromise is between power and clout on one hand, and time and attention on the other. The reason a manager is powerful is that he or she has at least one major client who takes up most of the manager's time. This means you're going to get less of it, and thus less personal attention (although these people can often do more in a five-minute call than a newcomer can do in a week). At the other extreme, a young, bright manager with no other clients will lack clout and experience, but will spend all of his or her waking hours promoting your career. And in between lies a rainbow of choices.

I personally like young managers a lot. If they're bright and motivated, I've seen their energy overcome the lack of experience and political clout with superb results. And to help you understand why, let me give you the Passman Treatise on Managers' Careers.

Managers' careers go something like this:

1. The manager is young and enthusiastic, and attaches himself or herself to a promising young act.
2. By doing whatever it takes, the manager promotes the artist into major stardom, at which point, (a) every other manager comes out of the woodwork to try to steal the artist, and (b) the manager is offered twenty-seven other acts to manage.
3. The manager is now exhausted from having worked so hard on the first act (back when he or she had nothing else to do and could literally live with the band). So the manager wants to cash in on the fame and fortune while it lasts, and, accordingly, starts hiring associates and taking on superstars.
4. This is the point at which many managers begin to lose it because they're too successful. Some of them have such huge egos that they won't take on associates of their own caliber (for fear the associate might steal the artists). So they hire less capable people and give the artists lousy service. Others hire good people, but pay them so poorly that their employees get frustrated and go out on their own (usually stealing the artists in the process). As things unravel, the manager begins to lose artists who are no longer getting the personal attention they once did.
5. After these batterings, the manager decides it was a mistake to have tried to get so big, breaks up with his or her partners, keeps one or two key artists, and starts a record label or goes into the movie business.

Of course, a few managers have been able to pull off large,

successful management companies, but they're the exception. They also ruin my theory, so I'm ignoring them. In the last few years, a number of management companies have grown by pulling together a group of major managers. Essentially, these managers share expenses and some central services, such as marketing, but for the most part, they're operating on their own.

At any rate, every major manager was a nobody at one time. While I don't suggest that a superstar take on an inexperienced manager, I do think many new artists are well advised to hire a bright, aggressive young manager. Obviously, you shouldn't do this if you have the opportunity to go with an established manager who is (or has someone in his or her organization who is) genuinely enthused about you. But if this isn't an option, the right young manager can be a real asset.

4

Business Managers

ROLE

The business manager is the person on your team who handles all your money. He or she collects it, keeps track of it, pays your bills, invests it, makes sure you file your tax returns, etc.

Listen to me!!! Did you know that in California, a person needs no credentials whatsoever to be a business manager? Contrary to popular opinion, you don't have to be an accountant (much less a certified public accountant), and you don't even have to be licensed by the state. Technically, business managers who give certain kinds of investment advice need to be "registered investment advisors" (like stockbrokers, who are licensed by the federal government before they can sell securities to the public). However, very few are.

What this means is that you could be turning your money over to someone who has no more financial training than you do. And when you stop to think about it, that's pretty scary.

I know you wouldn't have gone into the music business if you wanted to be a financial whiz—if you were good with numbers, you'd be in some back room with an electronic spreadsheet instead of winning your way into the hearts of millions. I also know that numbers make you nervous and may even intimidate you. On the other hand, there are parts of all of our lives that we don't like, and, while we can get other people to deal with them day to day, we have to be sure we choose good people to do it. For this reason, I urge you to *personally* spend some time investigating all of the people on your team, AND BE ES-PECIALLY CAREFUL WHEN IT COMES TO BUSINESS MAN-AGERS. They can range anywhere from superb to slimebag, with all variations in between. And their bedside manner and office space may tell you very little of what they're really like—the bad ones can be like a shiny used car that's rusting underneath a new paint job.

Financial disasters can come from someone who is an out-and-out crook, or they can come from an honest person, with the best of intentions, who is just a boob. My doctor once told me a story about an orderly he had when he was in the army. One day the orderly decided to go that extra mile and do something on his own initiative. So, with the best of intentions, he sterilized all of the thermometers by *boiling* them. SO BE EXTREMELY CAREFUL WHEN YOU PICK A BUSINESS MANAGER!

Hopefully I've now got your attention, so let's take a look at how to find the right person. Oh, and did I mention you should be careful?

HOW TO PICK A BUSINESS MANAGER

References

The other professionals on your team can be a great help in choosing a business manager. But remember, they may have their own agendas. For example, a personal manager may have a lot of control over a business manager because he or she handles some of the business manager's most important clients. This is a two-edged sword—it means you may get a lot of attention from the business manager, but it also means that, if you have a fight with your personal manager, the business manager is not necessarily on your side (if the business manager loses you, it's only one account; if they upset the personal manager, it could mean their whole career). This is particularly so when the business manager also does the personal manager's work. With reputable personal managers and reputable business managers, I have rarely found this to be a practical problem, but it's a sign to be extra-careful.

Family

Barring very unusual circumstances, inviting family members into your financial life is extremely dangerous. Most of them aren't qualified to do the job, and even when they are, it's difficult for them to be totally objective about you. It's the same reason that doctors won't operate on their immediate family, because they're too involved emotionally. And not only that, (a) it's very difficult to fire your brother, and (b) if something goes wrong, Mom may stop speaking to you.

BUSINESS MANAGER CHECKLIST

When interviewing business managers, take another look at Chapter 2 for general questions, then add these specifics:

1. What kinds of financial reports are you going to get, and how often? (You should get monthly reports.) Ask to see samples of the reports. Are they clear? Can you understand them?
2. What is the business manager's investment philosophy? Will they only keep your money in conservative, short-term paper (meaning bank deposits or government notes of thirty-days to one-year duration), or in highly speculative pork belly futures? Don't settle for the gobbledygook that says, "We tailor our services to every individual's needs." Ask what they'd do for *you*. And why.
3. Is he or she a **CPA** (certified public accountant)? Accountants who are certified have passed rigorous accounting exams and at least have that part of the job down. Whether they have the other skills to be good business managers is a different question, but at least they're true professionals, who have trained extensively and are responsible for adhering to the CPA's code of ethics.
4. How much do they charge? (This is discussed in detail below.)
5. What is the business manager going to do besides paying your bills and keeping track of your income? Will they do your tax returns? (Some charge extra for tax returns or send them to outsiders who charge.) Are they going to handle your investments or hire an outsider? In either case, are they paid for investments? Do they do projections, budgets, and forecasts of your income? Do they coordinate wills and estate planning? Monitor your insurance needs? Oversee divorces?
6. Do they have a dedicated tax staff? As you get more successful, you're going to need specialized tax advice. For example, touring in the U.S. may require you to file tax returns in every state you play.
7. What security systems do they have in place to safeguard your money? How strictly do they screen their employees? What checks and balances keep a bookkeeper from turning up on a yacht in Venezuela, lighting cigars with your money?
8. Does the business manager want a written agreement? Some business managers require written agreements, although many

don't. It isn't a bad idea, because it spells out exactly what's going on. However, don't ever agree to a deal that locks you in to them for any period of time—you should be free to leave whenever you want. If there's a written agreement, be sure to have your lawyer look it over.

9. Does the business manager represent music clients? This may seem like a silly question, but some very talented business managers have no expertise in the music industry, and you don't want one of them. The music industry is very specialized, and you need someone who understands its intricacies. For example, if they don't understand music publishing, they can't do a good job of making sure you're getting paid everything you're owed by the publisher. Good business managers know when something should have come in but didn't; someone without industry expertise may not.

10. Have they handled people with your particular problems and challenges? If you're a new artist, you want to be sure they know how to watch every penny so you can survive. You also want to be sure they have time for you. If you're a superstar, you want to make sure they've handled, for example, mega tours, which require massive financial controls (as we'll discuss in Chapter 23), as well as knowledge of how much venues should be charging, what you should pay for a truck rental, how to minimize taxes, etc.

11. Do they have **E&O** (Errors & Omissions) **insurance**? E&O insurance pays you if the business manager mishandles your affairs. If so, how much insurance do they carry? Also, ask if their insurance only covers accounting, or does it also cover investing advice.

12. If you live outside the United States or plan any extensive touring or other activities there, ask if they have any international experience. I probably don't have to tell you that meshing the tax laws between several countries (much less understanding the tax laws in any one of them) is a major pain, and if you have (or think you'll have) these kinds of problems, you need someone who's been down that road.

13. Do they get **referral fees** from any place they might put your money (such as buying insurance, putting your funds in a particular bank, placing your investments through a particular stockbroker, etc.)? A *referral fee* is an amount paid to the business manager for sending your business to a particular place, as

compensation for referring you there. Ideally, they shouldn't get any such fee because it could affect the advice they give you—they might be inclined to put your dough with someone who gives them a fee, even if it's not in your best interests. However, if the existence of the fee and the amount are fully disclosed up front, and if the business manager is willing to credit it against their fees, and if you get independent advice about the particular transaction, this could be okay. Maybe. But put your radar up if you see it; it's a serious red flag.

14. The check-signing procedure should be set up carefully, and if possible you should sign all the checks. When you get really busy—especially when you're on tour—it may not be possible to do this. However, I know some extremely busy artists who manage to sign all their big checks. Most of the time, larger checks can either be signed in advance or sent to you. Short of actually signing, it's now possible for artists to see and approve checks online, through a secure system. Ask if the business manager has that capability.

15. Will the business manager object to your auditing them periodically? (An **audit** means you send in an independent person to see if the business manager has properly handled your money.) A lot of people are reluctant to audit their business managers. They think it's awkward because it looks like they don't trust them. In fact, the ethical business managers welcome it—they have nothing to hide, and they understand it gives you peace of mind to know everything is as it should be. (You can figure out which ones don't want you to audit.) Auditing a business manager is expensive ($25,000 plus), and thus not worth it unless you earn substantial monies. However, when you get to the big leagues, an audit is important to consider. If you raise the issue up front, there won't be any hassles later on. It's surprising how few people raise this issue until it's too late.

16. Be sure the business manager wants to educate you, rather than just pat you on the head and say, "Trust me, kid." Most decisions can be condensed down to a fairly simple summary, and you should make all the significant decisions yourself. Be wary of someone who just wants to tell you what to do and seems offended if you question it.

FEES

How you pay your business manager varies, depending on your circumstance. The custom is for them to work on either a percentage basis (5%), an hourly rate, a flat fee, or a combination. Some people earn tons of dough and have uncomplicated lives. If this is you, go for an hourly rate or a set fee. Others earn much less and always seem to have financial troubles. If that's more your style, go for a percentage. (Ironically, if your finances nose-dive, you may need more of your business manager's time than when you're doing well—he or she has to keep the wolves away from the door and turn pennies into nickels. This, of course, comes at a time when you can least afford to pay.)

With percentage deals, a lot of business managers want a minimum fee, because they have legitimate costs to set up their systems for you. So, unless they're willing to take a flyer in the hope that you'll someday be hugely successful, they want their downside covered. These minimums are in the range of $2,000 to $5,000 a month, but can be much more for superstars. Sometimes the minimum fee is a discounted hourly rate (for example, two-thirds of their normal rate). Under these arrangements, they get more dough if they do a lot of work, but you pay less than if they were on an hourly rate. Whatever minimum you work out, it will be against (meaning a prepayment of) the percentage.

If you do a percentage deal, many business managers will accept a maximum fee (called a **cap**). You should always ask for this, particularly when they're charging you a minimum. The cap will vary with the amount of money you earn and the amount of work you require. They're generally around $150,000 to $300,000 per year (which means, if you're paying 5%, you're earning $3 million to $6 million a year). Minimum fees for people in this range are about $30,000 to $125,000 per year.

When you make a percentage deal, it should only apply to money *received* (not *earned*) while the business manager is involved. Also, ask if it applies to investment income. With some business managers it does, while with others it doesn't.

If you don't do a percentage fee deal, most business managers charge an hourly rate. In this case, spell out what the rate is, and be sure they tell you the rate for everyone involved, not just the top people.

Sometimes, if the business manager is young and hungry, or if you have a lot of clout, he or she may be willing to take a **flat fee** for all services, regardless of the amount of work. Often it's a flat fee for normal services, plus an additional amount for touring work (which is reasonable, because touring takes an enormous amount of time and resources).

Listen again! Let me say this one more time: BE EXTREMELY CAREFUL in picking your business manager. More careful than you are with anyone else on your team. This is the person who can make sure you have a cozy old age, or leave you playing supermarket openings in your fifties.

YOUR HALF OF THE JOB

Just as important as picking the right business manager is your own attitude. I remember seeing one of Elvis Presley's bodyguards at a press conference. A reporter asked why he didn't stop Elvis from taking drugs. His answer: "How do you save a man from himself?"

That answer really hit me. I've always felt it was one of the most telling statements about an entertainer's life. If you don't care about your financial future, it's difficult for anybody else to. If someone is constantly telling you not to do something (like spend money), and you really want to do it, you'll probably get rid of them rather than listen. Remember Dick Gregory's quote (see page 25). If you're going to spend everything you make, then start spending money you don't have, you're going to end up broke. It's that simple. And it doesn't matter how much you earn. So don't do it, unless you subscribe to my partner Chuck Scott's philosophy: "The best way to build a small fortune is to take a large one and dwindle it down."

Few things last forever, and an assured stream of earnings at your highest level is not one of them. So even the best business managers can't help you if you overspend on jets, yachts, houses, cars, and controlled substances. I know: You're reading this and saying it will never apply to you. But only you can make sure it doesn't.

5

Attorneys

GREGORY

"We've got Tom O'Brien on bass, Nick Weber on drums, and Jonah Petchesky on contracts."

© *Alex Gregory/The New Yorker Collection/www.cartoonbank.com*

Now for a subject close to my own heart. It's hard for me to be totally objective about this one, but I'll try.

PICKING A LAWYER

Role

Attorneys in the music business do much more than just look over contracts and advise clients about the law. They are very involved in structuring deals and shaping artists' business lives.

Lawyers have evolved into one of the most powerful groups in the music industry, odd as that may sound to you. The reason is that the power bases in the music business aren't concentrated in any one group. (For example, in the film business the major agencies are the most powerful players. In the music biz, the agents are powerful but limited in their sphere of influence, as we'll see in the next chapter.) Personal managers are very powerful, but the nature of their job limits the number of clients they can take. Business managers can have a lot of major clients, but they deal only in limited financial areas and are therefore not power bases. Lawyers, on the other hand, are involved in all areas, and because the time required for each client is less than that of a personal manager, they can handle more clients. This means the attorneys end up seeing more deals than anyone else, and therefore have more knowledge of what's "going down" around town. Consequently, they can be influential in determining which company will get a particular deal, which means the companies want to keep them happy. They can also influence which personal manager and which business manager get a client, which means these guys also want to keep the lawyers happy. This means lawyers have power (and are happy).

Style

There are distinctly separate styles of attorneys in the music business. Some are into "hanging out" and acting as if they're one of the band members, while others stick to the business side. There are power broker/agent types, who are good negotiators but not particularly good lawyers, and excellent lawyers who lose sight of the big picture. And of course there's a whole spectrum in between.

Using the techniques in Chapter 2, first assure yourself you're talking to a good, competent lawyer. After that, the match-up of style is mostly a matter of your personal taste. For example, if you like flash, you may want a flashy lawyer (although I find more often that flashy artists like their lawyers to be staid and solid). If you're honest and straightforward in your business dealings, be sure to get an honest and straightforward lawyer (your references will tell you who is and isn't). If you aren't, there are unfortunately lawyers to match you.

Clout

It's true a lawyer with clout can get through to people that other lawyers can't (or at least they can get through faster). Indeed, one of the major things to look for in a lawyer is his or her relationships in the industry. Let me illustrate with a story about remodeling my house: Over the years, I went through a number of house remodels, always looking for the cheapest possible price (which meant dealing directly with the workmen). I finally got sick of that process, so I broke down and hired a contractor. (This contractor was so good that, after the job was finished, I was still speaking to him. That's a serious recommendation.) During this job, for the first time, I realized the value of a general contractor. In the past, whenever I called up a tile man, electrician, plumber, etc., these people couldn't have cared less about me. They came to my job when it was convenient for them (if ever). If my sink leaked for a few days, they didn't care because they had a lot of other customers. On the other hand, when the contractor called, they jumped. The reason was pretty simple: If they didn't satisfy the contractor, they didn't just lose one job, they lost their next year's work.

The same applies to lawyers. Record companies can't ignore phone calls from important lawyers, nor can they afford to treat them shabbily in any particular transaction. The reason is the same as with the contractor—they're going to be dealing with the lawyers over and over, and they don't want to make enemies of them. So a lawyer with good relationships will get your deals done quicker, and if they know what they're doing, will get you the maximum that can legitimately be had.

You should also know what clout doesn't do. There is only so much you can get from any particular deal, regardless of who is asking. If a record company doesn't like your music, they're not going to sign you because of your lawyer. If they're hot for you, you'll get a deal even if you're represented by Kim Jong-un. Put another way, the real "clout" is your musical talent. (I'm not talking about a lawyer's experience and knowledge—that is truly valuable, and will indeed get you the maximum from the negotiation. But you should have a perspective on the hyped-up importance of "clout.")

Loose Lips

Be especially wary of a lawyer who tells you about other clients' lives. Some lawyers, for example, will tell you exactly what deal they got for a specific client. Apart from the fact that this violates the attorneys' Canon of Ethics, it also means they will be telling other people about your deal. It may appear that these people trade confidential information for secrets they wouldn't otherwise have, but in fact the opposite is almost always the case—everyone knows they have a big mouth, so they're only told things that people want spread around.

FEES

Most lawyers in the music business don't charge on just an hourly basis. For the ones that do, the rates are from $250 per hour for new lawyers, up to $700 or more for biggies. Some of us charge a percentage (usually 5%, though some ask as high as 10%), while others do something known as **value billing,** often with an hourly rate or **retainer** against it. A *retainer* is a set monthly fee (like the business manager's minimum fee discussed on page 48), and it's either credited against the ultimate fee, or it's a flat fee covering all services. *Value billing* means that, when the deal is finished, the lawyer asks for a fee based on the size of the deal and his or her contribution to it. If the lawyer had very little to do with shaping the deal, but rather just did the contract, the fee should be close to an hourly rate (though I'll get heat for telling you this, because it's usually more). On the other hand, if the lawyer came up with a clever concept or strategy that made you substantial money, or the lawyer made the introduction, or created the deal from scratch, he or she will ask for a much larger fee. If your lawyer value-bills, you should ask in advance what the fee is likely to be, so there won't be any rude surprises. Sometimes you can pre-negotiate the fee, based on results. (For example, if I get you X, you'll pay me Y. If I get you two times X, I get Z.) At a minimum, get a ballpark range.

CONFLICTS OF INTEREST

A lawyer has a **conflict of interest** when his or her clients get into a situation where their interests are adverse (i.e., opposing each other). This is easy to see, for example, when two clients of the same lawyer want to sue each other. However, it's also a conflict when two clients of the same lawyer make a deal with each other.

Lawyers are ethically required to disclose their conflicts of interest to you. Your choice is either to hire another lawyer, or you may **waive** (meaning you "choose to ignore") the conflict and continue to use the same lawyer.

Because the entertainment industry is a relatively small business, those of us who practice in this field are continually bumping into ourselves when our clients make deals with each other. Most of the time these situations are harmless and can be handled simply, in one of several ways:

1. Each of the clients gets another lawyer (rare unless it's a pretty serious conflict).
2. One of the clients gets another lawyer (much more common).
3. The clients work out the agreement among themselves (or else the manager, agent, or business manager negotiates for them), and the lawyer merely draws up the paperwork, not representing anyone's interest.

When interviewing attorneys, you should ask if they have or foresee any conflicts of interest. Most ethical lawyers will bring it up before you do, but you should ask anyway. For example, your lawyer might also represent your record company, your merchandiser, your personal manager, producer, publisher, etc. It's not uncommon for a personal manager to recommend his or her own lawyer, business manager, etc., and thus it's not uncommon for lawyers to represent both the personal manager and an artist. Most of the time, this isn't a problem. However, if you get into a fight with your personal manager, the lawyer will probably have to resign (or at least resign your side if the manager was there first). And you can't expect him or her to represent you vigorously against the personal manager in making your management deal.

In short, there are no hard and fast rules about conflicts. If the lawyer is straight and ethical, you can usually live with their representing a few other people in your life. But if you have a problem with another of your lawyer's clients, you must seriously consider getting separate counsel. And if you just don't like the idea of your lawyer having these conflicts (which is a perfectly reasonable way to feel), get someone who's independent.

Conflicts, by the way, are not limited to lawyers. Business managers can have conflicts when they represent both a personal manager and an artist (for example, when there's a dispute over commissions). Managers can have conflicts when they act in some other capacity (such as becoming the producer of the artist's motion pictures and negotiating a fee for themselves that affects what the artist gets paid). Managers can also have conflicts when they have two artists vying for the same gig. Like I say, it's a small business. But we generally work things out amicably.

A disturbing thing that's happened over the years is that some lawyers are selling conflicts of interest as a benefit to their clients. For example, they might suggest that you'll get a better deal with a certain record company or publisher because they also represent them. I'll give you my subtle opinion of this pitch: It's utter nonsense. For one thing, if the lawyer is being paid by a record company or publisher, it's human nature to think twice about how hard they want to beat them up and jeopardize a profitable relationship—especially for an artist who may pay them much less. Second, it's unethical for them to use any information they gain representing a company when negotiating against that company, and you can bet the company is neither going to like it nor permit it. So be wary of any pitch along these lines.

As I said earlier, it is certainly possible for you to live with a conflict, if you're fully informed and are comfortable that the lawyer will be in your corner. But a conflict is a reason to be careful, not a plus. Accordingly, the issue must be left to the tummy test. In other words, ask yourself whether your tummy feels like it's okay, or whether you're concerned about it. If you're concerned, get another lawyer.

ATTORNEY CHECKLIST

Here are some questions to ask your potential lawyer:

1. Do you have expertise in the music business? What kind of deals have you done?
2. What do you charge?
3. Do you have a written fee agreement? In California, lawyers can't enforce their fee agreements unless they're in writing, which is obviously a major incentive to have a written contract. If your lawyer requires one, ask for a copy, so you can review it.

   It's unethical in California for lawyers to have an agreement that can't be terminated at any time. If it's a percentage arrangement, be careful about what happens to the percentage after the term. See the discussion of this under management deals, on page 35.
4. You should ask if they object to your having the fee agreement reviewed by an independent advisor, preferably a lawyer, but at least a personal manager or business manager. No legitimate lawyer will object to this, and in fact they should encourage it. If it's at all possible, you should have your lawyer's fee agreement reviewed independently—especially if it involves a percentage. If

it isn't possible to do this, make sure the lawyer explains it to you in detail, and that you understand it.

5. Ask for references of artists at your level, and check them out. Does the lawyer return phone calls? Do they get deals done in a reasonable period of time? "Reasonable" in the music business is not going to be anywhere near the speed you would like. It's not uncommon for a record deal to take two to four months to negotiate, especially if you're a new artist and can't force the company to turn around their contract drafts quickly. Two to four months is a realistic time frame, but if it goes beyond that, someone isn't doing their job. I've always been amused by a story I heard from a new client when I was a young lawyer. He had been represented by another lawyer and, as he handed me his record deal, he said, "I know this is a good deal. It took over a year to negotiate."

6. Do you have or foresee any conflicts of interest?

6

Agents

ROLE

Agents in the music business are very different from agents in the film business. While agents in the film business are the major power brokers in the industry, controlling many aspects of it, agents in the music industry are involved primarily in booking live personal appearances (concerts). Music agents are sometimes also involved in commercials, endorsements, tour sponsorship, television specials, and other areas, but they don't participate in (or get paid for) records, songwriting, or merchandising, and thus aren't players of the same magnitude as film agents. That's not to suggest that agents aren't important—they're extremely so, and very influential. But their sphere of influence is limited.

FEES

Because agents aren't involved in your recording or songwriting (with the possible exception of film music, as we'll discuss on page 59), you should never give them a piece of the income from these areas. Usually agents don't ask for this, but be careful of union forms, as noted in the next paragraph.

Agents are regulated by the unions: **AFM (American Federation of Musicians)** for musicians; **AFTRA (American Federation of Television and Radio Artists)** for vocalists and actors on live, taped, and digitally recorded media; **SAG (Screen Actors Guild)** for film; and **Actors' Equity Association** for live stage. (By the way, SAG and AFTRA merged in 2012, so they're now one big, happy family, astonishingly called "SAG-AFTRA." For the book, though, I'm still referring to the music side as AFTRA because (a) that's what everyone in the biz does, (b) SAG-AFTRA is clumsy to say, and (c) I'm too lazy to change the whole thing from the prior edition. Also, on their website, they still refer to AFTRA contracts, so they're sort of endorsing this.)

The unions put a cap on how much the agents can charge, namely 10%. (For certain personal appearances under AFM jurisdiction, it can be more than 10%. However, the agents readily agree to a 10% maximum if you ask.) The AFM and AFTRA printed forms have a place for you to initial if the agency gets commissions on your earnings from records. *Watch out for it and NEVER do this.*

The union regulation of agencies is called **franchising,** and unions only allow their members to be represented by "franchised" agents, meaning those agents who agree to the union's restrictions. One of those restrictions is that the agency can only use contracts approved by the union, which results in each union having its own pet form, spelling out that union's particular requirements. So your agency contract looks like a fat coffee-table book. Actually, it's a stack of separate contracts: three for SAG (one for films, one for filmed TV, and one for filmed commercials); one for AFM; one for AFTRA; one for Actors' Equity; and two (called "General Services" and "Packaging") to pick up everything that isn't covered by a union.

Don't tell them I told you, but some agents will discount their percentage to as low as 5% for artists generating major revenues. (This is only for concerts. They stay at 10% for films, TV, etc., unless you're a major hitter in those areas—and even then, they may not budge.) Sometimes there's a sliding scale, so that as your income goes up, the percentage goes down. The industry goes through cycles as to how easy it is to get this discount, so you have to check out the situation when it's relevant to you.

DEAL POINTS

The major things to negotiate in your agent's deal are the following:

Term

The agency will ask for three or more years, and you will want to give them only one year. Shorter is better for you, because you can split if things don't work out, or squeeze their commission down if things do. The result of this wrestling match depends on your bargaining power.

If you give more than a year, you should have the right to get out after each year if you don't earn minimum levels. (See the discussion of this under personal managers' deals on page 34; agency deals work the same way, except the numbers are lower because they don't represent all areas of your life.)

If you have enough clout, you may never sign any papers at all (although some agencies get snippy about this).

Scope

If you're involved in the film business (for example, if you're a musical artist and also an actress, screenwriter, director, etc.), and if the agency is in both the film and the music business, the trend is for agencies to insist on representing you in all areas. Thus, an agency representing you in the film business will require you to sign with them for your musical concerts, and vice versa. This may or may not be to your advantage, and it becomes more negotiable as your bargaining power increases. Some agencies have a firm policy and won't let you in the door without a full package. Others are more flexible.

Exclusions

Similar to personal managers' deals (see page 31), you can exclude certain monies from commission:

1. As we just discussed, you can exclude earnings from records and songwriting without any difficulty. However, some agencies try to commission your soundtrack album royalties if the album is derived from a film in which they got you work as an actor or actress. I try to resist this, and have been pretty successful for established artists. The agencies' main argument is that, if you have no career as an actor or actress, and the agency is instrumental in creating one, they should get paid on everything you get from being involved in the film. If you do agree to this, make sure it only kicks in if you're getting a major part in the film. It isn't fair for an agent to commission your earnings from musical performances (the fee for singing the title song, soundtrack album royalties, etc.) just because you're onscreen for ten seconds to tell the doctor she has a phone call. Your argument is that you don't need the agency to get your music into motion pictures (unless, of course, you do), so they shouldn't be

commissioning an area in which you already have a career. Their argument is that, if they move you into a new arena (acting), and the soundtrack album is merely an aid to doing it, they should get paid on everything. Results vary with bargaining power.

There are agencies that specialize in getting motion picture musical work for artists. In that case, of course, the agency will get commissions on your fee for writing music and/or singing, and your record royalties as well. They normally don't commission songwriter performance royalties, which are monies we'll discuss on page 240.

2. You should exclude things like commercials (unless you've specifically engaged the agency to get you commercials), book publishing (if you're so inclined), merchandising, and record producing. Even in excluded areas, however, the agents will want to get paid if they find you work. I like to say they can't look for employment in these areas without your consent. That way they don't come running in with a basketful of offers if you aren't in the market, or if you just don't want them involved.

3. You can also exclude costs of collection before applying the commission (as we discussed in manager's deals on page 33). In other words, if you have to sue a deadbeat to get paid, you should deduct the cost of the lawsuit from your recovery before the agent gets his or her commission.

Termination of the Agency

As we discussed above, your agency deal is a stack of union forms. Each of these union agreements has a clause saying you can terminate if the agent doesn't get you work (or an offer of work) for ninety days. Since these are separate agreements, with separate terms, you want a provision that says you can get out of all these deals if you have the right to terminate any one of them. Without this, the agency would represent you in some areas but not others, because they all have different termination criteria.

This clause is a bit hard to get if you only work in the music area. Since you've never had a film career, the agency can reasonably argue that they can't be expected to produce one in ninety days. The usual compromise is to say that, if the AFM or AFTRA agreement (the ones covering the music area) can be terminated for failing to get you work, then you can get out of everything.

Territory

If you're a new or even midlevel artist, it is difficult to give an agency less than worldwide rights. However, as you move up the ladder, you can sometimes exclude territories outside the United States. This is often beneficial, because you can hire agents in Europe or elsewhere who specialize in those markets. In fact, many U.S. agencies use a local sub-agent for foreign territories, and you can thus eliminate the middleman. And at a high enough level, you might even eliminate the foreign agent and deal directly with the concert promoters through your lawyer and personal manager (if they have the expertise).

On the other hand, the U.S. agency doesn't just sit there idly while a sub-agent does all the work. The American agency oversees the foreign agent and makes sure the shows are properly promoted, that you get paid on time, etc. It's also easier to deal with someone locally than to get up at strange hours and call around the world.

Double Commissions

Just like personal management deals, there should be no double commissions if you have a corporation (see page 38).

PICKING AN AGENT

If you have a personal manager, you'll have only occasional contact with your agent. You'll see him or her at your shows, and you may meet when you first set up your tours. The rest of the time he or she talks to your personal manager and, to a lesser degree, to your lawyer and business manager. Thus, while you should make the final decision, picking an agent should be primarily handled by your manager (since he or she deals with the agent most of the time).

If you don't have a manager, the agent will report directly to you. In this case, the criteria for picking your agent should be the same as picking a manager. So take another look at page 40.

As always, make sure you get a good vibe from whoever you're hiring.

PART II

Record Deals

7

Broad-Strokes Overview of the Record Business

INDUSTRY STRUCTURE

Before we get into the various moving parts of record deals, and discuss whether you even want one, let's first talk about how records make their way from the oven to your table. There are several designer methods to choose from:

Major Record Companies

You sign a recording contract with a major label (Columbia, Warner Bros., Interscope, etc.) and hand in your recordings. The company then gives your recordings to a **distributor,** who sells physical copies of your records to the stores and distributes your music digitally (more about distributors later). The record company next gears up its advertising, promotion, marketing, etc., and rockets you to stardom.

Here are the major divisions of a fully staffed record company (in no particular order):

A&R. These are the people with "ears" who find and nurture new talent, and who work creatively with the artists (see page 125 for a discussion of A&R people).

Sales. Salespeople get your records into the stores and onto digital sites—not an inconsequential step in having a million-seller.

Marketing.   Advertising, publicity, album-cover artwork, promotional videos, web campaigns, promotional merchandise, etc.

Promotion.   These folks live solely for the purpose of getting your records played on the radio. They spend their days "jamming" radio stations, and saying "Dude," "Baby," and "Sweetheart" a lot.

Product Management.   Product managers are in charge of whipping up all the other departments (sales, marketing, promotion, etc.) to work together on your records. This is to make sure you get propelled forward by a coordinated team, rather than torn apart by horses running in different directions.

Catalog/Synch.   There is a separate marketing department for older product (called **catalog** product), but within this department are people who try to get both old and new recordings into movies, TV shows, and commercials (called a **synch** department, which we'll discuss on page 265).

Production.   Manufacturing, cover printing, assembling, and shipping physical product (CDs) to the distributors.

Finance.   They compute and pay your royalties—bless their little hearts—and keep track of the company's income and expenses.

Business Affairs/Legal.   These executives are responsible for the company's contracts, not only with artists, but with digital service providers, foreign licensees, etc. Business affairs people negotiate the deals and, in conjunction with other executives, make the decisions as to what to give and what to hold. The legal department gives legal advice and drafts the contracts. Due to industry cutbacks, business affairs and legal are now almost always the same people.

International.   As the name implies, the international department coordinates the release of your records around the world, and oversees all the functions listed above in foreign territories.

Here's a pictorial chart, suitable for framing:

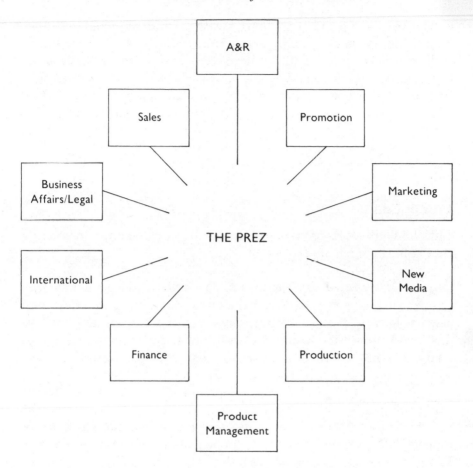

Figure 1. Divisions of a major record company.

By the way, in some companies a number of these functions are combined in a single person or department, while in other companies multiple departments handle just one of them. For example, some companies have their A&R people also act as product managers. At larger labels, there might be separate departments for advertising, publicity, and art (which are all handled by the marketing department at other companies).

The major record companies' records are all distributed by **major distributors,** which are gigantic distribution networks that coordinate digital distribution and move physical records from manufacturing plants into the stores. Ramming CDs (and this new configuration called "vinyl") into retailers is more difficult than it sounds. You need a large network to do it, like any other manufacturing business, and it's expensive to set up and maintain the warehousing, shipping, inventory controls, sales force, etc., necessary to move goods into a marketplace.

After years of consolidation, there are only three major distributors left, and they're all owned by the major labels (or, more specifically, by the labels' parent companies). They are (alphabetically): Sony (Columbia, Epic, and RCA Records); Universal (Universal/Republic, Interscope, Capitol, Island, Def Jam); and WEA (Warner Bros., Elektra, Atlantic). The labels listed after each are only the bigger labels—all of the majors distribute smaller labels as well.

Independents

Independents are record companies that aren't owned by a major, and they come in two main flavors:

Major-Distributed Independent.   This is an independent entity that has little or no staff, but rather signs artists and makes a deal with a major label to perform all functions except recording the records. The main thing these companies bring to the party is the ability to find talent and to mercilessly beat the distributing company to make sure their product gets promoted. Product released by these companies may be on the independent's own label, or it may be on the distributing company's label (in which case the public may never know the independent company exists). This type of entity is discussed in detail on page 206, in connection with independent production agreements. Here's a chart, and note that "Retailer" means both physical retail locations (which are called "brick and mortar" locations), digital stores like iTunes and Amazon, streaming sites like Spoitfy and Pandora, and anywhere else the companies can squeeze out a few bucks:

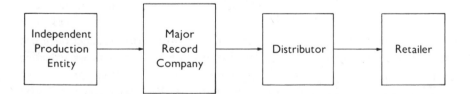

Figure 2. Major-distributed independent record company.

True Independent. A true independent is not owned by a major label, but rather is financed by its owners and/or investors. Examples of these labels are XL, Merge, Sub Pop, Epitaph, Rounder Records, and Victory. The true independents distribute their records through **independent distributors,** which are set up to deal with the specialized needs of independent companies.

Strange as it sounds, most of the big independent distributors are owned by major labels. Specifically, RED is owned by Sony; Caroline is owned by Universal; and ADA is owned by Warner.

So, you ask, how does a major distributor run an "independent" one? The answer is that they use the same infrastructure to do the shipping, paperwork, etc., but they have different sales staffs for the indie product. For example, if you're an independent label, it's a big deal to get an order for 2,000 CDs. That'd be reason to celebrate. On the other hand, a major label would yawn over an order for 20,000 units. So the whole indie distribution company is geared to this smaller scale, meaning the employees are paid commissions and bonuses based on the reality of what they can do.

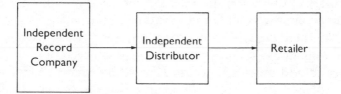

Figure 3. Independent record company distribution.

A WORD ABOUT RETAILERS

At the time of this writing, brick-and-mortar record retailers are on the endangered-species list. The pure record store is almost extinct, because there's not enough CD and vinyl business left to support them. A few independent stores are healthy, but even they have to sell DVDs, posters, and other stuff to stay afloat. And as the CD's heartbeat continues to slow down, it's hard to see how anyone (other than maybe a few specialty shops) can survive in the long run.

Today, most of the CDs in the United States are sold by Amazon and the **big-box retailers** (so named because their stores are in the shape of gigantic boxes). Specifically, Walmart, Target, and Best Buy handle the biggest chunk of the business. However, as CD sales continue to shrink, the big boxes keep cutting back the number of CDs they're willing to carry in their stores—in fact, as I write this, most of them only carry the top-selling titles. In addition, these stores are cutting back the amount of floor space they're willing to devote to CDs. That's because they want to get the most revenue from their real estate, and if selling vacuum cleaners is more profitable than selling CDs, the dirt-suckers win. All this, of course, becomes a vicious cycle: If the stores carry less product, CD sales drop even more, because there's less available to buy. Which means the big boxes cut more floor space, which means even fewer sales.

Now guess who's the biggest retailer of music in the United States? By far it's iTunes. (Did you get it?) And while its business continues to be healthy, the sale of downloads is dropping because consumers are moving to the streaming services. In fact, **streaming** (meaning music on demand to your mobile phone, computer, etc.) is the fastest growing area of the business (other than vinyl, which is faster growing but under 2% of sales).

You might ask why you need a distributor for streaming. Can't you just license it to Spotify and be done? Well, it's not as simple as it sounds. First of all, there are a number of streaming services floating around, and the companies have to work out deals with each of them. Second, they have to add **metadata** to each recording (that's the information that tells the user the name of the song, artist, album, who to pay, etc.); store digital files; set up **SKUs** for each title (**SKU** means **Shop Keeping Unit,** and it's like a bar code for each version of a master, to keep track of who gets paid). And once that's done, they have to monitor the sales and licensing of millions of uses.

So you can see that the role of the distributor is changing. And because you don't need gigantic warehouses and big staffs to sell music digitally (in fact, there are independent services who will handle it for you, as we'll discuss later), a lot of artists wonder if they need a record company at all.

Funny. That just happens to be our next topic . . .

DO YOU NEED A RECORD LABEL?

Historically, record companies held the keys to the kingdom. As we discussed, it takes a large organization to manufacture and ship records to stores (manufacturing plants, warehouses, sales forces, shipping people, financial controls, etc.). Also, in order to really sell records, you had to get your music on the radio, which took a promotion staff and a lot of money.

In those days, the record retailers were so big that they wouldn't bother with small players. That meant, if you didn't come through a major record company, it was hard to get your product on their shelves at all. Also, frankly, the big record companies paid retailers a lot of money to position their product prominently in the stores. So even if an artist managed to get their records into the retail bins, they'd likely get buried in the back. If, somehow, an independent artist's records started selling anyway, the retailers would pay the artist late (if at all), since one little player didn't matter to them. On top of all this, as we'll discuss when we get to pressing and distribution deals (on page 218), the artist would have to put up the money to manufacture the records. So if the stores didn't sell them, they'd be returned to the artist, who'd lose the manufacturing costs, plus the freight costs in both directions. Putting this all together, it took a big player to absorb these risks.

Well, Dorothy, we're not in Kansas anymore:

1. While it's still difficult to get your product into stores (now it's because the stores carry so few titles), physical retailers are becoming less significant as CD sales decline. Conversely, digital is on the rise, and anyone can get their music distributed digitally (I'll tell you how in a minute).
2. Radio is still very important for mainstream artists, but it's become a very narrow channel—in other words, it plays only a limited range of music genres, and not a lot of different titles. Because of this, alternative ways for people to discover music are becoming more important, and the Internet and mobile devices are two of the biggest keys.
3. As we discussed on page 14, a direct relationship with fans is the next generation of marketing, and young artists are proving more savvy in this area than a lot of established companies.

On top of all this, as you'll see shortly, when you make a deal with a record company, you give up control of your recordings (as well as other aspects of your life, such as the ability to do music for films, commercials, concert videos, etc.), and you also give up a chunk of your income from both record *and* non-record areas (as we'll discuss in a bit).

So, why would you want a record company? Well, if you're a niche artist (for example, a jam band or backpacker), and you're happy staying in your niche and selling to a small group of fans, you may not need or even want a record deal. It's possible (through outfits like TuneCore) to get your music to iTunes, Amazon, Spotify, Pandora, and other digital outlets, and you can make a living doing gigs, promoting yourself directly to your fans, and selling your tracks. Because your genre limits your potential audience, you'll often make more money by doing it yourself than you will if you sign to a record company. For a record deal to make sense, the company has to generate more money for you (after they take their piece) than you would get by selling less product on your own. With niche artists, that's often questionable.

If you're more mainstream, such as pop, rock, or country, this is a much tougher question. You can of course set up a killer web presence, build a fan base, and sell directly to them. Since your music has a wide appeal, if you break through, you'll make far more money by keeping the record company's share of the pie, not to mention keeping all of your non-record income. But here's the problem: The same way that it's easy for you to set all this up, it's easy for *everybody* to set this up. At the time of this writing, there are more than ten million artists on SoundCloud and Facebook, and who knows how many on YouTube. How's anyone going to find your music?

There are some "virtual" record companies who can help. These companies, started by talented people who lost record company jobs when the industry melted down, will do everything from sales to marketing, promotion, etc., but let you keep control of your destiny. However, they charge pretty heavily for these services, which most new artists can't afford. Thus, they've mostly been successful with artists who've already released a few albums (and therefore have a fan base) but are out of their record deals.

If you decide you want to release your own music (known as **DIY** in the biz, for **Do It Yourself**), you first need a fan base. As we discussed on page 14, most artists start by playing local gigs, building a following, and most importantly, collecting a database of fans. A few people I've asked say that you shouldn't try to sell your music until you have at least 2,500 fans in your database. Before that, you should just give it away. As this philosophy goes, until you reach that 2,500 magic number, you need fans, not money. I'll leave you to decide if you agree.

When you're ready to sell your music, you can easily get it into cyberspace through sites like TuneCore and CD Baby, who charge a flat fee per year, or The Orchard, which takes a percentage of sales (though they also charge a setup fee). The Orchard and CD Baby distribute both physical CDs as well as digital, while TuneCore is only digital (though they cover both downloads and streaming).

When your music is available, it doesn't help much if no one knows about it. You have to get the word out by using the same techniques and online resources we discussed on page 14 (in the section on "building your buzz"). So take a peek back at those if you're going DIY. Then come right back.

As of this writing, most mainstream artists still want to sign to a record company. Apart from guaranteeing you money (so you can avoid sleeping on park benches while creating your music), the record companies have the resources to get your music heard over the noise of all the other artists out there—they have staffs of people with experience in marketing and promotion, and they will put up the bucks needed to push your career. Also, at least as of this writing, the reality is that no new artist has been able to move massive amounts of product by using the Internet on their own. That may well change in the future, but today it still takes radio airplay and the clout and expertise of a record company to hit a major home run. For that reason, even artists who do quite well on their own often move to a label because they feel they need the company's resources to take their careers to the next level.

So, assuming you want a contract with a record company, lemme show you what those babies look like.

WHAT'S A RECORD?

Let's start with a real basic: What's a **record**?

Surprisingly, in virtually every record agreement made since the 1960s, the contractual definition of *record* includes both audio-only *and* **audiovisual** devices (meaning one with sound and visual images), such as DVDs. (This is particularly interesting when you remember that audiovisual devices weren't even invented in the 1960s! Companies anticipated their development, even though no one knew what form they would take.) The definition of records also included (and still does) any other device *now or hereafter known* that is capable of transmitting sound alone, or sound with visual images. Even more importantly, the current deals define "records" to mean *any kind of delivery of your performances for consumer use,* whether sound alone or with visuals. This is designed to pick up the Internet, including Spotify, Pandora, YouTube, and Vevo. As you'll see later, these broad definitions in record deals can make life a bit tricky if you're a recording artist and also an actor or actress in films. Stay tuned (or peek at page 145 if you can't wait).

By the way, did you know that, originally, records were made by having the musicians and singers perform for each record sold? That's because there was no mass duplication process available, and thus the recordings were made directly onto the wax that was ultimately sold (meaning every record in a store contained a unique, one-time performance). Can you imagine how sick you'd be of a song if it sold a million copies?

MASTERS

The word **master** has two meanings:

1. The original recording made in the studio is called a *master,* because it is the master (meaning controlling entity) from which all copies are made. In the old days, it was a high-quality tape, and there were a number of machines making copies from the tape which were called *slaves*—master/slave; get it?

   Master recordings are now done on computer hard drives, and the recordings are **multitrack,** meaning that each instrument and voice part is recorded on a separate track: the drums on one track, guitar on another, voice on another, etc. When the recording is finished, the master is then **edited, mixed,** and **EQ'd.** As in films, *editing* means cutting out the parts you don't like and splicing in the parts you do. *Mixing* means getting the right level for each track, so that the drums are the right volume during each particular part of the song, the voice is raised a bit on the chorus, etc. Also, the sounds may be enhanced through processes I have never completely understood. *EQ'ing* stands for **equalizing,** and means that the bass, midrange, and treble are each adjusted to the right level (so that no one of them overpowers the others). The mixed multitrack is then reduced down to a two-track stereophonic master, which is ready for the duplication process.

   So there are two masters—the original multitrack, and the finished two-track.

2. The word *master* also means a recording of one particular song. Thus, you might say an album has "ten masters" (meaning ten selections) on it. These individual recordings are also called

cuts, because of the historical fact that each selection was made by cutting grooves into vinyl.

ROYALTY COMPUTATION

Enough about art; let's talk about money.

We'll start with your royalties.

Basic Concept

My brother-in-law, Jules, was in the used car business. He was famous throughout the West Valley because he'd trade cars for anything. At one point, he traded a car for a silver tea set, a set of golf clubs, and a mule. (Honest.) He then traded the mule, along with a stained-glass window of Daffy Duck, for an English bulldog named Rosie.

About that time, my wife and I were looking for a dog. It was before we had children, and we wanted to test our parenting skills on some-

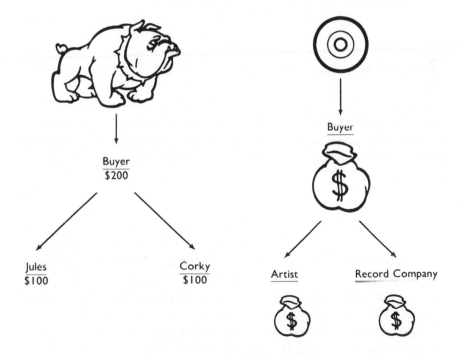

Figure 4. Bulldogs and royalties.

thing that wouldn't use drugs if we failed. In trying to decide what kind of dog we wanted, we used to take Rosie for outings on weekends. In a perverted way, we began to think of her gnarled face and drooling as cute. Anyway, Jules decided he was going to breed her, and we wanted a puppy. So I helped him find a stud dog, through a sophisticated referral system—the Yellow Pages. I called a place named Royal Family Bulldogs, which conjured up images of some country squire's dogs lounging around on velvet pillows. Well, it turned out to be a dilapidated house in Pacoima, the most impressive feature of which was its bulldog smells. But Royal Family had a brown-and-white champion stud named Winston, so Jules hired Winston, and Rosie got pregnant.

After a few weeks of this, Jules decided he wasn't interested in the headaches of small puppies. So he enlisted the help of his friend Corky. Corky's deal was that she would take care of Rosie and the puppies, then when each dog was sold, she'd get half of the sales price. So if a dog sold for two hundred dollars, Jules would get a hundred dollars, and Corky would get a hundred dollars.

What does this have to do with records? Well, your record royalty is very much like Jules's share of the bulldog proceeds. In the case of records, the artist (Jules) turns the recordings (pregnant Rosie) over to the record company (Corky), who then sells the finished product (puppies). For each record (puppy) sold, the artist gets a piece of the price, and the company keeps the rest to cover its costs and make a profit.

By the way, for the next edition I suspect I'll need to replace the picture of the CD in the above figure. I'm open to suggestions of what I should use to represent a digital download or a stream. If you have any brilliant thoughts, drop me a line at www.donpassman.com (bulldogs are taken).

Basic Royalty Computations

The division of proceeds between the artist and record company is a bit more complicated than the puppy deal. In fact, up until a few years ago, this process was more complex than NASA's formula for getting the Space Shuttle home. But then, in a surge of *Why can't we all just get along?*, most companies shifted to a much simpler system. You get off easy—I had to learn all the complicated crap. (I included a section on how it used to work at the end of the chapter because (1) a few companies—fortunately very few, and dwindling—still use it, (2) there are a lot of older deals written this way, (3) I spent hours writing that section and hate to see it go to waste, and (4) I thought you might need it some night if you have trouble sleeping.)

To follow this next part, we'll need to use a little math. Don't worry if numbers aren't your strong suit—I'll go slowly. I explained these concepts to my cousin David, who has to take off his shoes and socks to count to twenty, and he understood them.

Here's how it works:

1. The artist royalty is a percentage of the **wholesale price.** The companies also call this price the **published price to dealers** (**PPD** to its friends), or sometimes (mostly outside the U.S.) the **base price to dealers (BPD).**

   Each royalty percentage is known as a **point,** so if you have a 10% royalty, you have 10 *points.*
2. You multiply your royalty percentage times the wholesale price to find out the number of pennies you'll get. Here's an example (using easy math numbers):

Wholesale price	$10
Royalty rate	× 10%
ROYALTY	$1

That part's simple enough, but here are a few wrinkles:

Free Goods

Royalties are paid for each record **sold.** Why do I emphasize the word *sold?* Well, the companies give away **free goods,** also known as **special campaign free goods.** This started when the companies wanted to push out large numbers of a particular artist's album. To get the stores to stock more of it, they gave away 10% or more of all records shipped. Originally, these were short-term deals (a few months), but they've evolved into a near-permanent arrangement.

These *free goods* are essentially a discount of the price. The record company doesn't get paid for them, so they don't bear royalties.

As of this writing, no company is giving away free goods for digital sales. That's because there's no need to incentivize a digital retailer to stock more units—they can instantly create copies to meet any demand. The labels do, however, sometimes give away downloads for promotion. Which happens to be our next topic.

Promotion Copies

Records given away for promotion, such as radio-station copies, contest giveaways, etc., are also free goods and don't bear royalties. They are known as **promotional** or **promo** (pronounced "pro-moe") records. These don't go to retailers and the physical ones are marked "not for sale."

That's about it for the digital concepts, but there are some added goodies on the physical side. Such as the . . .

Return Privilege

To understand this next part, you need to know that physical records are sold on a **100% return privilege.** This means that, if a retailer orders one hundred records from RCA but can't sell them, it can bundle them up, ship them back to RCA, and get credit for (or a refund of) the price it paid. Such a practice is unlike most other businesses, because if you buy a load of plastic flamingos and can't sell them, you eat them.

The reason for this return policy is that records have to be pushed out quickly in large numbers, and the retailers aren't willing to take the risk of getting stuck with too many of them (especially for new artists). Thus the retailers have always said they will only stock large quantities if the manufacturer agrees to take back the stiffs. (For you sticklers, I'm aware that most companies now charge penalties for returns in excess of a set percentage of records shipped [16% to 20%, depending on the company] and they also give a discount for returning less than this percentage. For example, if a retailer buys a hundred records, and there's a 20% penalty point, it will not get a full credit [i.e., a refund of what was paid] if it returns more than twenty records. However, if it returns only ten, it gets more than a full credit [i.e., a credit for more than it paid for those ten]. The idea is to get the retailer to order more carefully, and to make it less likely that the ones ordered will come back. However, since any given artist may have 100% of his or her records returned [the 20% applies overall, to all of a company's catalog of records], I'm simplifying this to a pure 100% return privilege, like the old days.)

To see why this is important, let's go back to Rosie's puppies. Jump ahead to the time when the puppies have been born and are crawling all over Corky's living room. A customer comes in to buy one of the dogs, but she isn't sure the puppy will get along with her children. So she says, "I'll give you a check for the dog, but hold it while I take the puppy home to play with the kids. If, after a week or so, everything is going well, you can cash the check. If not, I'll bring the dog back for a refund." Corky agrees, willing to do anything to move the little nippers out. Later the same day, she tells Jules about the deal. Jules then asks for his half of the check (which of course Corky can't yet cash), and Corky suggests he have intercourse with himself. She says he can have his share when the buyer decides to keep the dog.

Reserves

The **reserves** used by record companies work exactly the same way (usually without the suggestion for self-intercourse). Because records are sold on a 100% return basis, the companies don't know, particularly with a new artist, whether the records will sell to customers, or get returned by the retailer. Because the records may come back, the companies (like Corky) keep a portion of the royalties that would otherwise be payable to the artist (Jules) until they know whether the sales to the retailer are final. This holdback is called a *reserve* against returns.

For example, if a company ships 100,000 CDs of an artist, they may only pay the artist on 65,000 of these and wait to see if the other 35,000 are returned. At some point in the future (usually within two years after the shipment), the monies are paid through to the artist. The technical term for this pay-through is called **liquidating** the reserve. Of course, if the records are returned, the reserves are never paid to the artist because the sales are canceled and the royalty is never earned.

The size of your reserves varies with how well the company thinks the album will sell, and also with how well it thinks your *next* album will do. For example, if they think your next album will sell extremely well, they'll be less concerned about holding big reserves—if they hold inadequate reserves and overpay you, they can take the money back from your next album. However, if you're a new artist and they're not sure there is even going to be another album, or if this is a "one-off" record such as a soundtrack album, or if this is the last album under your deal, you can anticipate healthy reserves and a record company attitude along the lines of "If you don't like it, stuff it." (As your bargaining power grows, you can put caps on reserves. See page 143 for more on this.)

Let's take a look at this with numbers:

Assuming you have a $1 royalty, and you sell 100,000 units, your royalties would look like this:

Units	100,000
Artist Royalty	× $1.00
	$100,000

If the reserve was 35%, the amount payable to you would be:

Artist Royalty	$100,000
Less: 35% reserve	− 35,000
AMOUNT PAYABLE TO ARTIST	**$65,000**

As you've probably figured out, none of these reserve concepts apply to digital sales. Digital copies can't be returned by the retailer, because there's no inventory in the retailer's hands—the "inventory" is only created when a sale is made. So there should be no reserves on digital sales. As a matter of practice, most companies don't take reserves on digital, but many record contracts allow them to do it. So it's a good idea to say that they can't.

YE OLDE ROYALTY CALCULATIONS

The following is how royalties were computed up until the last few years. A few companies still use these calculations, at least for physical CDs, so if you're dealing with one of them, you'll need to understand how these Byzantine provisions work. You'll also need these concepts if you've got an older recording contract (or you're the heir to one). If you don't fit into one of these categories, feel free to skip to Chapter 8 unless you're incredibly curious or you happen to enjoy pain.

Historically, the artist royalty was a percentage of the **suggested retail list price** (also called **SRLP**). The SRLP was an approximation of the price received by the *retailer,* which had nothing to do with the price received by the record company.

This royalty was based on the *suggested* retail list price, which had absolutely nothing to do with what you paid at your local record store (in my experience, no two record stores ever had the same price for the same record anyway).

From this price, the company first deducted a **packaging charge** (also called a **packaging deduction** or **container charge**). In *theory,* this was the cost of the "package," and it was deducted because the artist should get a royalty only on the record, not the package. In *reality,* it was a charge of much more than any package actually cost, and was only an artificial way to reduce the artist's royalty.

The *packaging charge* was stated as a percentage of the SRLP, and the industry norm was 25% for compact discs and other "new configurations."

The result of this (i.e., the SRLP after deducting the packaging charge) was called a **base price** or **royalty base.** This was the figure against which you applied your royalty percentage.

Here's an example of a royalty base computation using easy (not real-world) numbers:

Retail price of CD	$10.00
Less: Packaging (25% of $10.00)	– 2.50
ROYALTY BASE	**$ 7.50**

Thus, in this example, if an artist had a 10% royalty, he or she got 75¢ (10% of $7.50).

Phony Free goods

If you liked the free goods on page 77, you'll positively *love* the phony free goods that record companies used when computing royalties based on SRLP. These are in addition to the special program and promotional free goods we already discussed.

Before I tell you how this works, you need to know about my soft-drink stand.

When I was ten years old, I had a soft-drink stand in front of our house. I don't mean a card table with lemonade; I mean a serious soft-drink stand made out of genuine pine (by my stepfather), with Dr Pepper and Coca-Cola signs that, if I'd kept them, would be worth more than my first car. Anyway, I stumbled on the brilliant idea of delivering soft drinks to the workmen at a construction site about a block away, using my little wagon. Instead of selling the drinks for a nickel, like everyone else, I would sell them for a dime (delivery labor, you know).

But for every two drinks they bought, they would get two free. (Although I felt I was putting one over on the workmen, I have a feeling they really knew I was selling the drinks for a nickel each and using mirrors.)

My idea for a soft-drink scam was taken to dizzying heights by the early record company accounting magicians. First, they figured out that selling one hundred records at 85¢ each was the same as selling eighty-five records for $1 each and giving the customer fifteen "free" records for every eighty-five they bought (the retailer gets one hundred records either way, and the company gets $85 either way). Then they realized that, because fifteen of these records were "free," they

Figure 5. The author invents free goods.

didn't have to pay the artist for the free records—I mean, how could you have the gall to ask for royalties on a record for which the company wasn't being paid? So by raising the price and giving away records for "free," the companies saved royalties on fifteen records out of every one hundred while making the same money. (Remember, the artist's royalty was based on retail, so the artist didn't get any benefit from an inflated wholesale price.) Nifty, eh?

It took the workmen who bought my soft drinks about thirty seconds to figure out that the price of my drinks was 5¢ each. But it took recording artists more than twenty years to figure out that these "free" records were hardly free, because the economics to the company were exactly the same as if all the records had been sold at a lesser price. Got it?

In the last years of this old system, only a few companies actually gave away 15% of the records they shipped. Where it was done, those "free" records were known as **phony free goods** because, like my soft drinks, they were nothing more than a cute way of discounting the purchase price. (Technically, they were called **standard free goods,** or **normal distributor free goods.**) And in fact the companies that used this practice charged a higher wholesale price than those who didn't, and the difference (not surprisingly) was the percentage of "free goods." (By the way, even though it sounds like you would, you didn't get more royalties from the companies without free goods, as we'll see in a minute.)

Let's go back to our example:

Retail price of CD	$10.00
Less: Packaging (25% of $10.00)	– 2.50
ROYALTY BASE	**$7.50**

Using a 10% (75¢) royalty, and assuming sales of 100,000 CDs, the artist's earnings would be $75,000. However, since the company "gave away" 15% (or 15,000 of the units in this example) for "free," these 15,000 units didn't bear any royalties. Thus, the artist was only paid on 85,000 units, and instead of getting $75,000, the artist only got $63,750 (75¢ × 85,000 units), which is 85% of $75,000.

As noted before, most of the companies did away with the fiction of these phony free goods. But did you get more royalties? No; instead of free goods, they only paid on 85% of the sales. So the result was exactly the same as it was with free goods. It looked like this:

Units shipped	100,000
Royalty-bearing percentage	× 85%
Royalty-bearing units	85,000
Times: Royalty	× 75¢
AMOUNT PAYABLE	**$63,750**

Compact Disc Royalties

Now that you've got the gist of how royalties were computed, I can tell you that these computations were only for audiocassettes. Bizarrely, until the companies went to the simpler royalty system in 2006, all the contracts were written on the basis of cassette royalties. This of course raises the question "What kind of weirdo wrote contracts for a technology that was sleeping with the fishes?" Well, the answer is based on history.

In the beginning, CDs were much more expensive to manufacture than cassettes, so the companies paid a lower royalty for compact discs than they did for cassettes. However, even after cassettes died, the companies kept on writing their contracts for cassette royalties. That was so they could do the following for compact discs:

1. Your royalty rate for compact discs was a reduced percentage of the cassette rate. For example, your CD rate might have been 75% to 85% of the cassette rate (depending on the company and your bargaining power). So if you had a 10% royalty, you'd have gotten 7.5% to 8.5% on CDs. Sometimes you could get an escalation (say to 90%) for later albums, or maybe based on sales.

2. The computation of suggested retail list price for compact discs varied from company to company. A few companies used the actual SRLP, but most used an artificial price that, shockingly, was less than the actual SRLP. This computation was called an **uplift** of the wholesale price, meaning they multiplied the wholesale price by a percentage (130% for all the majors) to create what was known as a **constructed retail price.** For example, if wholesale was $10, the uplifted price would be $13 (130% of $10). Your royalty rate was then applied to this constructed price.

3. The packaging deduction for compact discs was 25%, as opposed to 20% for cassettes, and 10% for vinyl. (Okay—you got me. I used a 25% packaging in my examples, so it wasn't strictly a cassette calculation.)

4. At least one company charged an extra 5% of normal distributor free goods for CDs (i.e., they charged a total of 20% for CDs, when they only charged 15% for cassettes).

"90% of Net Sales"

In the early days, records were made of shellac, and were therefore breakable. So the record companies developed a practice of paying the artist on only 90% of the shipment, keeping the remaining 10% to cover their breakage.

Records haven't been made of shellac for the last sixty years, but the practice of paying on 90% of net sales persisted until the late 1990s. There was no logical reason for this—it was a total rip-off that arbitrarily reduced your royalty by 10%. Thus, where a company paid on 90%, you were being paid on 90% (for "breakage") of 85% (for free goods), resulting in payment on only 76.5% of shipments!

Aren't you sorry you missed all this fun?

One last tidbit: If you have one of these old deals, many companies apply these crazy calculations to digital downloads. In other words, they base the price on retail, but take a packaging and free goods reduction before applying your royalty rate, even though there is no package and there are no free goods. Which, by the way, their contract most likely allows them to do.

And now, we return to our regularly scheduled programming.

8

Advances and Recoupment

ADVANCES: THE BASIC CONCEPT

Back to Jules and his bulldogs. Our friends at Royal Family charged him a $300 stud fee for the services of Winston. Let's suppose Jules didn't have the $300 (or at least didn't want to invest it in this particular endeavor). So Corky (who's agreed to raise the puppies in exchange for 50% of the sales price) comes up with an idea: She says she'll pay Jules the $300, or pay it directly to Royal Family, and then take her money back from Jules's share of money from the puppies. For example, if the puppies sell for $200 each (so that Corky gets $100 and Jules gets $100 for each dog), Corky would keep Jules's $100 share of the first three puppies ($300) to get back the stud fee.

This is exactly how a record company **advance** works. The company pays a sum of money to the artist (the $300 stud fee) and then keeps the artist's royalties (the proceeds from selling the puppies) until it gets its money back. So if a company gives an artist $10,000 to sign a record deal, it keeps the first $10,000 of artist's royalties that would otherwise be payable. The process of keeping the money to recover an advance is called **recoupment,** and we say an advance is **recoupable** from royalties. The amount of **unrecouped** monies is called your **deficit** or **red position** (from the accounting use of red ink to signify a business loss), since this is the amount that has to be recovered before you get paid. So if you got a $100,000 advance and earned $75,000 in royalties, you have *recouped* $75,000 of the advance, and your *deficit* is $25,000 (you are $25,000 *in the red*, or $25,000 *unrecouped*). Once you recoup, you are said to be **in the black.**

Here's another way to look at it:

When I grew up in Texas, it was a big deal to drive just outside the city and look at the huge water tanks with the names of towns painted on the side. (It takes very little to make me happy.) In fact, Farmer's

Branch, a city outside Dallas, had a water tower that was a major local site. (Not as famous as its post office, however, because the sign there said FARMER'S BRANCH BRANCH. Honest.)

Anyway, picture a water tower with a big ol' connecting pipe that runs deep into the ground. The connecting pipe feeds into a dry well that needs a thousand gallons of water to fill it up to ground level. If there were no other access to the water, you'd have to wait until the water filled the well up to ground level (that is, until a thousand gallons had been poured in) before you could get any water. If there were only five hundred gallons, you couldn't reach it (see Illustration A in Figure 6), but when another five hundred gallons was added, you could (see Illustration B).

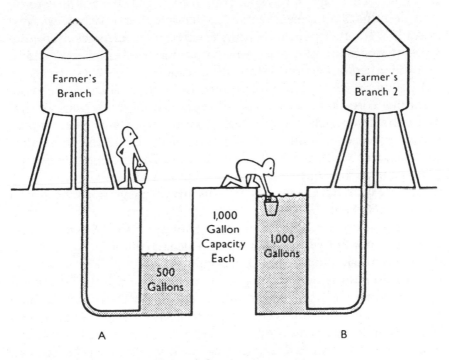

Figure 6. Separate accounts.

Recoupment works exactly the same way. The water represents your sales, and the ditch is your deficit account. If you got a $1,000 advance from the record company, your account is $1,000 unrecouped. Until you earn $1,000 of royalties (i.e., until you have enough water to fill the well), you don't get anything. In the same way that the hole has to fill with a thousand gallons of water before you can get a drink, the record company keeps the first $1,000 of royalties before you get any money.

Other Goodies

Monies paid directly to the artist are not the only recoupable monies. Recording costs are also recoupable from royalties, and so are some portion of video production costs, independent promotion costs (see page 192 for what that means), monies paid on behalf of the artist (for example, to buy equipment or to support a personal appearance tour), and anything else that isn't nailed down.

Recoupable recording costs include everything you can think of, which is often a page-long list in your record deal. It's not just studio time; it includes equipment rental, travel, arranging, instrument transportation, etc. It also includes **union scale** (*scale* means the minimum amount a union requires everyone to pay its members) that's paid to you and others to perform at recording sessions.

In addition to a specific list of recoupable stuff (like cash to you, recording costs, and video costs), almost every contract has a general provision that says all amounts "paid to you or on your behalf, or otherwise paid in connection with this agreement" are recoupable unless the contract specifically provides otherwise. You can feel the history jumping from the pages on this one—Charlie Artist asked his company to advance the cost of a trip to see his mom, and then argued the money was nonrecoupable because the contract didn't say it was recoupable. This of course is wrong, but the broad language that the companies now use is overkill—sort of like using a sledgehammer to squash a fly (which is effective, but messes up the kitchen). In fact, there are a number of costs paid on your behalf or in connection with the agreement that are never recouped under industry custom. These include such things as manufacturing costs, advertising, marketing, shipping, etc. In practice, the companies don't abuse this language, but I like to carve out the items I just ticked off, together with my own broad language, saying they can't recoup amounts that are "customarily nonrecoupable in the industry."

Risk of Loss

What happens if you don't sell enough records to get back the full amount of the advance? With very rare exceptions, such as your failure to deliver product or otherwise seriously breaching your contract, advances are **nonreturnable,** which means it's totally the record company's risk. So if you don't sell any records, it will never get back its advances. (This nonreturnable aspect is also significant because it means advances are taxable income when you get them, as opposed to when they're recouped.)

CROSS-COLLATERALIZATION

An important concept tied to recoupment is that of **cross-collateralization.** Remember the illustration on page 87, with the two towers side-by-side, and two 1,000-gallon wells? The water tank for one of the wells contains exactly 1,000 gallons, which means the well is full and the water usable. The other tank has only 500 gallons, so you can't reach the water. Suppose we dug a hole in the ground connecting these two wells. In that case, the same 1,500 gallons (500 from Well A and 1,000 from Well B) would be distributed equally between the wells (750 gallons in each), and you couldn't reach the water in either of them (see Figure 7 below).

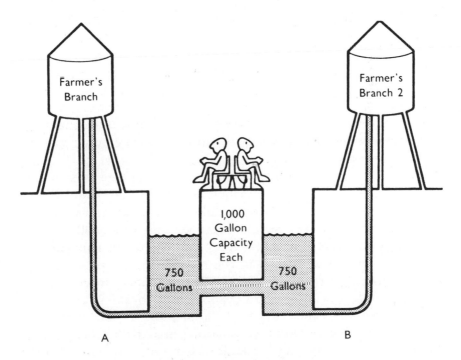

Figure 7. Cross-collateralization.

Cross-collateralization works exactly the same way as the connected wells, and it's built into every deal. Let's assume you get a $100,000 advance for album number 1, plus another $100,000 for album number 2. Now suppose album number 1 earns royalties of $10,000, and album number 2 earns royalties of $120,000. If the two albums were *not* cross-collateralized (the two wells were not connected), you would get nothing for album number 1 (it only earned back $10,000 of the $100,000 advance, so it's $90,000 unrecouped), but you would be paid $20,000 for album number 2 (the $20,000 earned in excess of the $100,000 needed to recoup the $100,000 advance). However, this only happens in Fairyland. In the real world, the two albums are *always* cross-collateralized (i.e., the wells are always connected), which means the entire $200,000 deficit ($100,000 for each album) gets recouped from the entire $130,000 earnings ($10,000 from album number 1 plus $120,000 from album number 2). Accordingly, your account is $70,000 unrecouped ($200,000 less $130,000), and this deficit carries forward against the next album(s).

Cross-Collateralization of Deals

Cross-collateralization can also apply to different *agreements*. These can be simultaneous agreements (for example, an artist signing a recording and publishing agreement with the same company), or they can be sequential (such as an artist who, at the end of one record agreement, signs a new deal with the same company). In either case, the concept is that advances under either agreement can be recouped from royalties under both. This is *never* good for the artist. NEVER.

Most companies include language in their form contract that automatically cross-collateralizes the deal with all other deals. Major record companies don't really try to cross-collateralize a record deal with a publishing deal, but small labels may (see pages 315–17). However, everyone tries to cross-collateralize *sequentially,* meaning that advances under your current recording deal are cross-collateralized with royalties under past and future record deals. The language that does this is buried innocently in the recoupment language and can easily be missed by the untrained eye. It says that advances and costs can be recouped from royalties payable, and royalties can be used to recoup advances and costs paid, "under this *or any other agreement.*" (Your eye is now trained—so don't miss it!) I've been reasonably successful in knocking this language out of artists' first deals by arguing that the issue should be discussed later, if and when there is a second contract. My argument is that there is no other deal to cross-collateralize with, and until there is, the language is meaningless. That reduces the point down to who is more likely to forget about it—the artist or the company—at the time of the new deal. (Don't worry: The company won't forget.)

9

Real-Life Numbers

OVERVIEW

Let's start to plug some real industry figures into these concepts.

What's Your Clout?

To discuss the range of real numbers, we have to know how strong your bargaining power is. Broadly, I'll divide it into three categories:

New Artist.   This is someone who has never before had a record deal, or someone who has been signed but never sold more than 100,000 or so albums per release, and with a minor social media presence. It can also mean an artist who was once successful but lost his or her following and is having difficulty finding a record deal (or, as one of my clients lovingly put it, someone who has "crashed and burned").

Midlevel Artist or New Artist with a Bidding War.   Either (1) an artist whose last album sold in the 200,000 to 400,000 range; or (2) a new artist with a lot of "buzz," such as millions of streams on YouTube, a lot of twitter followers/Facebook Likes, substantial touring base, etc. When a number of companies are chasing an unsigned artist, it's not uncommon for the deal to look like a midlevel deal, and occasionally even higher.

Superstar.   Sales from 750,000 into the stratosphere, massive social media, millions of streams on Spotify, etc.

These categories are only rough approximations, and the sales figures are dropping as the industry shifts to streaming. Also, there are a lot of variables. For example, you might be a midlevel artist but have six record companies chasing you and bidding each other up, which means you'll get a superstar deal. On the other hand, you may be a successful artist who is perceived as "out of step" with "what's happening," so you only get a lukewarm reception. Also, other factors may come into play, such as an artist with lousy album sales but massive single-song download sales and streams. But we gotta start somewhere, and this range is close enough for rock 'n' roll.

For your point of reference, a **gold album** is one that sells 500,000 units in the U.S. (qualifying sales include CDs, vinyl, and permanent album downloads, but don't include streaming); a **platinum album** is one that sells one million U.S. units; a **multi-platinum** is 2,000,000 plus. **Singles** are gold, platinum, and multi-platinum at the same sales levels, but in addition to physical singles and permanent downloads, the calculation also includes on-demand streams (100 streams equals one sale, and they count both audio-only streams and audio-video streams). The sales figures are certified by the **RIAA** (**Recording Industry Association of America**, an industry group comprised of record companies), which awards gold or platinum status.

We also have an industry joke that bombs are "certified lead."

Since we're on the topic of grading a record's performance, you may have heard the term **bullets.** Each of the major trade magazines (see page 19 for who they are) has charts that rank records numerically based on sales, downloads, airplay, and/or streams. A *bullet* is a dot or a star next to a record's number on the chart, and it means the record is moving up strongly. The lack of one means it's weakening or on its way down. So "Number 1 with a Bullet" is the best you can do. And of course there's an industry joke for turkeys: "Number 99 with an Anchor."

ROYALTIES

Range of Royalties

Using the above categories, the following is the current industry norm for royalties on U.S. album sales:

1. **New Artist:**
   13% to 16% of PPD (see page 77 for what PPD is).
2. **Midlevel:**
   15% to 18% of PPD.

3. **Superstar:**
   18% to 20% or more of PPD (royalties over 20% are rare). At this level, with an enormous amount of clout, you can sometimes make an off-center deal like a joint venture (see page 214), or even a distribution deal where the artist owns the masters (see page 211).

How much do these royalties mean in dollars and cents? At the time of this writing, most top-line CDs sell for a wholesale price of $8.50 to $10.00 or sometimes more (the higher end is for superstars or albums with bonus material, such as extra tracks). The wholesale price of digital downloads is 70% of the retail price (so if it's $9.99 retail, the wholesale price is just under $7.00; if it's $10.99 retail, wholesale is about $7.69). So to figure the number of pennies, multiply your royalty rate times those figures. For example, if you have a 15% royalty, and the average wholesale price of your album is $9.00:

PPD (wholesale price)	$9.00
Royalty rate	× 15%
ROYALTY (ROUNDED TO PENNY)	**$ 1.35**

Remember (as we discussed on page 77) that this can be reduced by 10% or more for special campaign free goods.

Streaming royalties are based on your royalty percentage times the company's receipts attributable to your streams. So if your streams earn the company $100, and you have a 15% royalty, you get $15. We'll get into how much the company gets from the streaming company later, but for now, just know that you get this percentage of what they earn. With a (very) few companies and a lot of clout, you can sometimes get a slightly higher percentage for streams than you get for downloads, but this is not easy to pull off. However, if you don't ask, you don't get.

Physical singles are typically at a lower royalty rate, on the theory that record companies make very little profit on singles (which is true). The singles rate is normally three-quarters of the album rate, but it tops out in the 10% to 12% range, occasionally up to 14% for superstars. New artists can, with some bargaining power, get to the 10% range no matter what their overall rate, and it may be possible to get escalations in your singles royalties based on sales of singles (in the United States only).

Having said that, almost no one releases CD singles anymore, but recently a few artists have released 7-inch vinyl singles. Talk about a "Blast from the Past."

Of course, digital downloads are kind of like singles, but it's a completely different market and there's no cost difference to the company, so your royalty shouldn't be reduced. Thus, be sure that your contract doesn't pay you the lower "single" royalty on downloads; you should get your full album rate. Most companies don't try to do this, but be sure your deal is clear. (We'll get into more detail about downloads on page 145.)

Escalations

It's common to escalate royalties based on sales. Typical escalations are .5% (sometimes you can get 1%) at some level between 250,000 and 500,000 album sales, and another .5% at 250,000 to 500,000 albums beyond that point. For example, if your royalty is 12%, it might escalate to 12.5% for sales over 300,000, and to 13% for sales over 600,000. The lower your royalty rate, the sooner you can expect the escalations to kick in, and in fact you may even be able to get a third bump. These escalated rates usually top out around the 16% range for new artists, 18% for midlevel, and 20% to 21% for superstars. Sometimes, you can get the company to agree that your royalty for the next album starts at the highest rate achieved by the former one. For example, suppose your royalty is 14%, and you have a 1% escalation (to 15%) at 500,000, and another 1% (to 16%) at 1,000,000. If the first album sells 1,000,000, then the second album would start at 16%, and the 1% escalations would be on top of that (to 17% and 18%). The companies put a cap on these escalations, to make sure you don't go past the 19% or 20% range.

These escalations only apply to sales occurring after the level is reached, and are called **prospective** escalations. For example, if you have 16% on the first 300,000 units, escalating to 16.5% thereafter, you don't get 16.5% on the first 300,000. If you have enough bargaining power, you can sometimes get the escalations on prior sales (called a **retroactive** escalation). This is extremely rare, and if you can get it at all, it's usually for stratospheric sales. For example, at sales of 2 million units, you might get an increase on the first 500,000.

In a standard contract, escalations apply only to full-priced retail sales, through normal retail (record store and digital retailer) channels. Typically, escalations are limited to sales in the United States, but as your bargaining power goes up, so does your ability to get escalations in other major territories (such as Canada and certain European markets) based on sales in those markets.

As single track downloads are much bigger than album downloads (in 2014, single track downloads were over 20% of the total recorded music sales in dollars, and album downloads were only 16%), the companies grumpily had to agree to count something called a **TEA** (pronounced one letter at a time, not like a drink in the English countryside). It stands for **Track Equivalent Album** and means that, if you sell a certain number of single tracks, it will count as the sale of one album for purposes of your royalty escalations. You should always try for this, especially as album sales drop, but it may not be in the form contract you get. So be sure to ask for it.

Most contracts say that the number of tracks on your album is a TEA. In other words, if you have twelve songs on your album, twelve downloads equals one album sale for purposes of escalating your royalty. Sometimes you can knock this down to ten, because the price of ten single tracks equals the price of a digital album, but that's surprisingly hard to get. If you do agree that it's the number of tracks on your album, be sure to say it's the number of tracks on the "standard version" of your album. It's becoming common to do special versions of albums with **bonus tracks** for a particular retailer (for example, an exclusive piece of product for Target with two tracks that aren't available anywhere else). These special versions shouldn't be the standard for your TEA.

The current hot issue is to argue for a **streaming equivalent album,** which is not even common enough to merit industry initials like TEA. The theory is that, as we move to streaming, downloads will continue dropping. But the streams are making money, so they should count in some fashion. If you can get this at all, and it's incredibly difficult to do, it's either based on a number of streams (such as 200 streams on a paid subscription service), or on a number of dollars to equal an album. At the time of this writing, it is just this side of impossible to get it in the U.S., unless you have the bargaining power of an Ayatollah, though it's a little easier in the U.K. But if we all keep asking, maybe we can wear them down.

"All-in"

The above royalties are known by the technical term **all-in,** which means the artist is responsible, out of his or her royalty, for paying the record producer and mixer. (Producers' and mixers' roles, and how they're paid, are discussed in Chapter 11. However, I suggest you wait 'til we get there before tackling the subject unless you're already familiar with royalty calculations.)

The practice of paying artists an *all-in* rate began in the early 1970s and is now the industry norm (excluding a few oddball situations, mostly in country music). Accordingly, the all-in rate is not what the artist puts in his or her pocket; that amount is the all-in rate *minus* the amount paid to the producers and mixers, which is called the **net rate.**

Producers are paid a U.S. royalty in the range of 3% to 4% of PPD. Some producers, who become "superstars" in their own right by producing hugely successful records, can get 5% or (very rarely) 6%. Mixers usually get a flat fee and not a royalty, but the big ones can get .5% to 1%. So your true royalty rate is the amount of your royalty less the producer and mixer.

ADVANCES

In the 1950s, artists would go to the studio, sing their little hearts out, and have almost no other involvement in the creative process. In those days, companies paid the artist a set amount of money as an advance (for example, $10,000 for an album). The record company paid all the recording costs (which are recoupable from royalties, just like an advance), and everybody went their separate ways. It took maybe two weeks to do an album; three if you were a perfectionist. (A fast-track album today takes six weeks, and more typical is three or four months. And more established artists, who are busy touring, promoting, or generally being persnickety, can take a year or more to finish an album.)

Funds

Today, most recording agreements are structured as **funds.** A fund is a set amount of money, which includes both recording costs and any amounts that may be payable to the artist as an advance (the term *recording costs* also includes the producer's advance, which we'll discuss later). Whatever the artist doesn't spend on recording costs goes into his or her pocket. For example, if the recording fund for an album is $200,000, and the recording costs are $150,000, the artist pockets $50,000 as an "advance." On the other hand, if the recording costs are $200,000, the artist pockets nothing.

Here's a rough range of all-in recording funds:

1. **New Artist Signing to Independent Company:**
   Zero to $100,000, occasionally even more. If that sounds like a big range, it is—the amount of the fund is proportionate to the number of people chasing you. It's also based on whether you want to take a big check and a smaller royalty, or a small check (or nothing) and a big royalty, or even a share of the company's profits from your records. Most new artist/independent company funds are in the range of $25,000 to $75,000.

2. **New Artist Signing to Major:**
   If you're a rock band, expect a fund in the range of $100,000 to $200,000, occasionally running up to $500,000 if you're really hot. If you're urban/hip-hop, or a pop artist, the deals (at least for the first album) are often advances plus recording costs. (We'll discuss the range of those advances in the next section.)

3. **Midlevel:**
   $300,000 to $750,000, with a few particularly hot artists kicking up higher.

4. **Superstar:**
   $1,000,000 and up. A really big artist's fund can run into multimillions of dollars. At this level, funds are computed on the basis of past track record and future expectations, as well as the bidding in the marketplace.

Advances

Fund deals are the norm in the record biz, except for urban/hip-hop artists, and for pop artists (balladeers, crooners, adolescent boy bands, and the like). (Bizarre to think those two worlds have similar deals, but hey, it's showbiz.) For the urban/pop deals, it's common for artists to have pure advances plus a mutually approved recording budget. How come? Well, as you'll see when we discuss producer deals (on page 125), urban/hip-hop producers get truckloads of money, and the albums get very expensive. This means contractual funds (if they're within the orbit of the earth) won't be enough to record an album, much less leave any money for the artist. So, at least for the first album, some companies give the artist an advance plus mutually agreed recording costs. These advances are in the range of $50,000 to $200,000. After the first album, urban/hip-hop deals are usually funds.

Pop artists are in the same range of advances, though their deals are often advances plus costs throughout the entire contract. Their deals are structured like this because (as a general rule, to which there are major exceptions) they are less involved in production, and therefore have less control over the costs.

Budget Woes

If you have a fund of $200,000, what keeps you from recording a super-cheapo album for $25,000 and pocketing $175,000? In all of these deals, unless you have a lot of bargaining power, the record company has to approve your recording cost budget for precisely this reason. Well, partly for this reason. Actually, they're more worried about the other end—that you'll have an unrealistically low budget and not be able to finish your album for less than the fund. This is particularly common with new artists, because their contractual recording funds are lower. For example, albums can easily cost $150,000 or more, and that could be the entire fund. Moreover, if you're using producers of any note, that can radically jack up the price. As we'll see when we get to Chapter 11, top producers can get advances of $25,000 or more per *master* (in addition to the recording costs for that master), and I'm sure you can see how quickly this turns into a giant sucking sound.

So what happens when you've spent your full recording fund and have three-quarters of an album? Most of the time the record companies pay to finish the record, under the age-old business strategy of "What the hell are we going to do with three-quarters of an album?" However, a recent trend is for companies to test the market before they fork over more money, to see if it's going to be worthwhile. They might release one song, or submit a song to a test group, to see what kind of reaction it gets. Or they might release an **EP** (standing for "extended play"), which is five to seven tracks. If they like the way things go, you'll get the rest of the money. If not, it's back to Poughkeepsie.

If the company agrees to cough up the extra dough, they will grumble, stomp the floor, deduct the excess money from your next album's recording fund, from your publishing royalties (I'll explain what those are later), and from anything else they can think of. Almost all recording contracts require you to write a check for the excess, but in practice this can't happen with a new artist (who doesn't have the money), and it rarely happens with a superstar (whose feathers they don't want to ruffle by asking).

Formulas

If you know enough to ask for it, most record companies will agree to something called a **formula** for advances. This is a mechanism designed to automatically increase (or decrease) your deal if you're successful (or a flop). It works like this:

Your advance for the second album is equal to a percentage (usually 60% to 70%) of all royalties *earned* (as opposed to paid) by the first album under the agreement. The advance for album number three is a percentage of album number two's earnings, and so forth. Thus, for example, if the first album earns $1,000,000 in royalties and you have a 60% *formula*, the advance for album number two is $600,000.

Historically, the formula percentage was based only on earnings in the United States, or sometimes the United States and Canada, and only on sales of albums through normal retail channels (see page 141 for what that means). As these sales dry up, those of us who represent artists are pushing to broaden what goes into the formula. Digital downloads have been included for a while, though the companies started out saying that only digital albums counted; nowadays, you can usually get single song downloads as well. We're still fighting about adding streaming income to the formula, and so far this has been really difficult (read "virtually impossible") to get. As things move more to streaming, I expect this will loosen up, so help us keep the pressure on. Tell the companies I said so.

Formulas only use earnings that happen within a certain period of time (usually twelve to eighteen months after release), so that sales trickling in over a two- or three-year period won't increase the advance for an artist who is slow in delivery. The last thing a company wants to do is reward late delivery.

If you can't get a formula, variations include delaying a formula until the third or a later album; averaging the earnings of the previous two albums (as opposed to using the earnings only of the previous one); and a limitation (or elimination) of reserves for purposes of determining the formula (reserves are discussed on page 79, and reserve limitations are on page 143).

But what happens, you say, if the first album is a dismal failure, and earns only $20,000? How can anyone make an album for $12,000 to $14,000 (60% to 70% of the $20,000)? Well, you can't, so this is handled by establishing a **floor** in the formula. A floor means that no matter how lousy the earnings of the previous album, your fund will not be less than an agreed amount (the *floor*). Not surprisingly, as soon as record companies hear the word *floor,* they think of a concept called a **ceiling,** which means that no matter how wildly successful the prior album, the fund won't exceed an agreed dollar figure. (The prospect of owing you $4,000,000 for an album makes them nervous.)

Some companies want to reduce your fund if you're unrecouped, by deducting the unrecouped balance from your formula advance. They argue that this saves them from disaster if you have a big album after a series of losers. For example, suppose the formula for your next album has a floor of $200,000, and a ceiling of $600,000, and your last album earned enough to hit the maximum $600,000. However, all your albums before that last one were turkeys, so you're $450,000 un-recouped. Under this provision, the company deducts $450,000 from the $600,000 formula advance and pays you $150,000 (even though your floor was $200,000).

One slight problem with this clause: If you were $800,000 un-recouped in the above example, subtracting that amount would eat up your entire $600,000 fund, and you'd get zippo. The same thing would happen if you were $300,000 unrecouped and only qualified for the floor advance of $200,000 (from which they'd subtract the $300,000). Since it's pretty hard to make a record for zero, you have to tell the company you need something called a **subfloor** (meaning a floor below the floor). For example, your contract might say you get the formula advance, less any unrecouped amount, but not less than a subfloor of $125,000. (We'll discuss a similar concept in songwriter deals on page 275.)

Historically, both the floors and ceilings escalated for later albums, varying with the bargaining power of the parties. Recently, some companies are trying to keep the floors at the same level (with maybe slight increases) and only escalate the ceilings, to protect the company's downside. Here's a recent new artist deal:

Album No.	Floor	Ceiling
1	$175,000	(no formula)
2	$175,000	$400,000
3	$200,000	$450,000
4	$200,000	$550,000
5	$250,000	$700,000
6	$300,000	$800,000

Don't get excited about the big numbers for the last albums. The company isn't really committed to them, as you'll see on page 108.

When the deal is for an advance (*not* a recording fund), the formula percentage is of course much less, usually in the 15% to 20% range. The floors and ceilings for option years would go up in roughly the same percentages as the funds. For example, a formula for the third album might be 15% of the prior album's earnings, not less than $125,000, nor more than $250,000.

360 RIGHTS

Welcome to the land of **360 deals.** You may not like the climate.

The name comes from the 360 degrees in a circle, because record companies now want to share in the total pie of an artist's income (or maybe it's because they want to corral you). Under these deals, the companies get a piece of an artist's earnings from touring, songwriting, merchandising, fan clubs, sponsorship money, motion picture acting, garage sales, and so forth. (Okay, I made up the garage sales part to see if you're paying attention. Don't tell the record companies, or they'll include them in their next contract.)

However you want to sugarcoat it, these deals started because the record industry was in such financial distress that the companies couldn't survive on their record business alone. So they grabbed pieces of other income. Their argument (the sugarcoating) goes like this: "In this new world, we are no longer just a record company, confined to a narrow lane. We are now an artist brand-building company. Of all the players in your life, we are the only ones who spend substantial money to make you a household name. Then, thanks to our rocket launch, you make tons of money by touring, songwriting, selling your face to teenagers on T-shirts, etc. This isn't right. We should share in all the businesses we help build for you. Besides, we'll have a much bigger incentive to spend money on you if we know we have an upside beyond records. Oh, and one other thing. We won't sign you if you don't agree."

It's true that record companies are the only ones spending substantial money to break an artist's career, so their argument has some merit. On the other hand, many people see this simply as a land grab, arguing that the company brings no value to the party beyond their record business expertise.

Whatever you think of these arguments, 360 deals are here to stay because record companies really aren't making much money. Thus, from the majors down to the independents, virtually all the companies are insisting on some kind of 360 rights. So if you want to sign a record deal, you gotta live with it.

With enough bargaining power, you may be able to trim back the 360 pie. Sometimes (actually, it's becoming "rarely") you can get a "180 deal," meaning the company only gets records and a share of one other income stream (songwriting, touring, or merchandising [selling merchandise with your name or likeness on it]) or just records plus two of the three streams (called a "270"). Sometimes, for real superstars or extremely hot bands who are free of their indie deal, it's just a record deal. But it's getting harder and harder.

Record Company Share

How do 360 deals work? Well, they vary quite a bit from company to company. Because of antitrust laws, record companies can't talk to each other about these deals, and they haven't yet fallen into an "industry custom." So we have a patchwork of practices. Most companies get from 10% to 35% of the artist's net income from non-record sources, with the majority of deals falling in the 15% to 30% range. I know that's a big range, but it varies a lot with bargaining power, and from company to company. It can also vary by category (e.g., 20% for publishing, but 30% on merchandising).

The definition of "net income" (against which the company's percentage applies) is the source of some debate in making these deals. Artists want to deduct as much as possible before paying the record company, and, shockingly, the record companies want to limit these deductions. Except for tours (which we'll discuss in a second) the language is usually something like "gross receipts less customary, third-party, arm's-length expenses." They say "third party" to keep you from cutting your brother in for a chunk, which he gives back to you in a brown paper bag. They say "arm's-length" to make sure the expenses aren't any higher than you would pay in the open marketplace.

In computing net income, most companies put a limitation on the total commissions you can pay your representatives (manager, agent, lawyer, and business manager). This is usually around 30% to 35% of your gross earnings, though at least one company tries to cap commissions at 35% of *net* (meaning 35% of your gross income after deducting all expenses other than commissions). If the cap is based on your gross earnings, 35% is probably okay, figuring 15% for a manager, 10% for an agent, and 10% to cover both the attorney and business manager. (Note: Even if your lawyer and business manager are not on a percent-

age, the limitation still applies. It doesn't matter how you actually cal-
culate their fees; if they total less than 10%, you're fine.) If you're paying
your manager 20%, and you can't keep the others down, you should ask
the record company to increase their cap to reflect reality. Results will
vary with bargaining power. (You can of course pay commissions that
exceed the cap, but you don't get to deduct the excess in computing
what you owe the record company. So it's a double hit.)

If the commission cap is 35% of your *net* earnings, that's much more
of a fight, because there's a good chance you'll go over it. This is less
of a worry for non-touring income, because the expenses aren't as significant. For example, the money you get from a publishing company
is after they've already taken their expenses, so your "gross income" is
already a kind of "net." Thus, you can probably craft some variation of
this that's livable. When it comes to touring income, however . . .

The "net income" discussion gets particularly thorny when you talk
about tours. The companies have two worries:

1. As you'll see when we discuss touring (in Chapter 23), artists are
   lucky to take home a fraction of their gross income, and when
   you're a new artist, you'll likely lose money. So the record company is worried that their share of net will mean little or nothing. (Of course, you're not doing so well, either.)
2. At the other end, when you start to make some real dough on
   the road, the companies are worried that you'll charge lots of
   questionable goodies against your tour income, for the purpose
   of reducing the amount you have to pay them.

To keep you from playing games, a number of companies insist on a
percentage of your *gross* income from touring, before you deduct any
expenses or commissions at all (the same way an agent is paid). The
gross percentage is of course smaller (from 7.5% to 15%, occasionally
less if you have some clout), and sometimes it's a minimum: for example, the company gets 30% of net, but not less than 10% of gross.
However, just like our discussion of management commissions that are
paid on tour gross income (on page 29), this could mean the record
company gets paid when you lose money.

The companies are usually willing to accommodate new artists by
saying that, if you earn less than a certain amount ($5,000 per night
is common), they don't participate at all. But when you go over that,
even if you're profitable, paying the company on gross could mean they
make more from your tours than you do.

Another concept is to pay the company on "adjusted gross" tour income, which means you're allowed to deduct certain expenses, but not others. For example, they might allow you to deduct your agent, true road expenses (like sound and lights), and maybe accounting fees, but not things such as legal fees, management commissions, and the like. The specifics vary with bargaining power.

One other thing to try. Some companies will exclude a dollar amount earned in each contract period (across all areas) before they start sharing. For example, they might not get a percentage of the first $100,000 in a contract period, just a 360 percentage of amounts over that.

Active and Passive Interests

The record company's 360 share is usually what's called a **passive interest,** meaning the company has no control over the rights involved. In other words, you make whatever kind of deal you want, then write them a check for their share. For example, you're free to make any kind of songwriting deal, with any publisher you choose, without the record company's input. When you get paid, you send over the record company's piece.

Some companies, however, actually take some of the rights involved, as opposed to just getting a piece of someone else's deal. This kind of deal is called an **active interest.** For example, they might insist that you (as a songwriter) sign with a publishing company they own (or, more commonly, it's a publishing company that's owned by the same company that owns the record company—the company at the top is known as the **parent company,** because both the record company and publishing company are its "children"). If the record company or its parent company also owns a merchandising company (a company in the business of selling artist-branded T-shirts, posters, etc.), they may insist that you give your merchandising rights to that company. And even if you don't sign a merchandising deal with them, they may want the exclusive merchandising rights to the album cover and a couple of other designs for each contract period.

Another approach is to not give them merchandising rights, but to give them a right of **first negotiation** (meaning you talk to them before you make a publishing or merchandising deal with others) and a **matching right** (meaning you can look for another deal but have to let them match it, so they have the option to take you on). We'll discuss first negotiation and matching rights in more detail on page 179, in connection with demo deals, and the concepts here are exactly the same. When you make an active deal, the contract will look just like any other publishing and merchandising deal (we'll discuss these deals in Chapters 18, 24, and 25), and you should negotiate the same protections we'll discuss later. The difference, however, is that you may only get a small (if any) advance for these rights, as some companies consider it part of your dues to make a record deal.

Some companies also want the right to operate your fan club or VIP ticketing (see page 411 for what that is).

When giving up active rights, you should try not to give the record company a passive interest in your earnings under the active deal. For example, if your company has a 25% passive right to your non-record income, and you sign to their affiliated publishing company, you want to keep all the songwriting money, rather than give 25% of it to the record company. Your argument is that they're already making money from the active rights, so they shouldn't get paid twice. Some companies are okay with this, while others still insist on a passive percentage. They argue that the active rights are not held by them (your deal is usually with a separate company that actually does the publishing, merchandising, etc., even if it's owned by the same corporate giant), and that you'd be paying them a 360 percentage if you did a publishing deal with a third party. All true, except of course that the active rights money flows into some big guy's pocket at the top.

If you can't completely knock out the record company's share of active earnings, then at worst you should give them a reduced percentage of your earnings from their affiliated company. For example, if they get 25% on your merchandising deals with a third party, they'd only get 10% (or 15%) of your earnings from a merchandising deal with their affiliated company.

> If you're on the *Fast Track* and
> haven't decided to leave the
> music business after the last section,
> go to Chapter 11 on page 125.
> Everyone else, forward ho . . .

IF YOU DON'T UNDERSTAND THE WORDS IN THE BOX, IT MEANS YOU SKIPPED PAGES 6–7. IT ALSO MEANS YOU NEVER READ THE DIRECTIONS WHEN YOU BUY A NEW ELECTRONIC DEVICE.

10

Other Major Deal Points

The other major things you'll want to know about your record deal are "How much?" and "How long?" The "how much" part of this doesn't mean royalties and advances, which we already discussed, but rather the number of albums you have to record. The "how long" sounds pretty straightforward but has taken a strange twist over the years.

AMOUNT OF PRODUCT

Pay or Play

Did you know that most record deals don't require the company to make a record? This is not only true for new artists, but also for mid-level and superstars. Almost all contracts contain a provision that says the company, instead of recording the album, can merely pay the artist a sum of money equal to (in the first draft of their agreement) minimum union scale for an album or (after negotiating) either the difference between the recording fund and the cost of the last album, or a prenegotiated, set fee. This is called a **pay-or-play** provision, meaning, as the name implies, that the record company has the option either to allow you to "play your music" or to "pay you off."

Apart from beating them up for the most *pay-or-play* money you can get, be sure that, once they pay you off, the deal is over. This shouldn't be hard to get, but it isn't in a lot of form agreements, and without it the company could hold on to you without making records. (On the other hand, since they don't want your records, they probably don't want you around either. But it's cheap insurance to add language making sure.)

Options

Record deals are traditionally structured with the company having the smallest obligation that it can negotiate, while keeping the option to get as much product as possible. For example, a company may commit to record one album of an artist, then have the option to require an additional four or five albums, each one at the company's election. Albums to which the company is committed are called **firm** albums. The others are called **optional** or **option albums.**

Options in New Artist Deals

With new artists, companies like to commit to only one album, or sometimes only two or three masters. However, the major companies insist on the right to get a total of five to six albums over the course of the deal (the indies will often agree to a maximum of three or four, sometimes even less). This is an improvement over the past—companies used to insist on options for eight to ten albums.

The company wants the right to optional albums one at a time. With a lot of clout, you can sometimes make them take two at a time (called **two firm** in industry lingo), but this has become harder and harder to do. And if you get it at all, it will most likely be later in the deal. For example, they can pick up albums two and three individually, but if they go on with the deal, they have to take four and five as a package. Can't hurt to ask for this, but expect disappointment.

If the company does commit to two albums, it may ask for the right to bail out if the first album tanks. For example, if the first album sells less than 150,000 units in the United States, the company is no longer committed to the second album. Stated another way, the second album is really optional, but the company is required to exercise its option if the first album sells more than 150,000 units. You'll want to count a number of single tracks (ten or twelve) as the equivalent of an album sale for this formula, in the same way they count toward escalating royalties (see page 96).

As we'll discuss in a bit, I'm talking here about the number of newly recorded *studio* albums you'll have to deliver. This does not include live albums (see page 119), Greatest Hits albums (see page 116), specialty albums (Christmas, Easter, Halloween), side projects, duets, or the like.

Farm Teams

In baseball, when you're not quite ready to play in the majors, they send you to a minor-league team called a farm team. The major teams all have affiliated farm teams (so named, I think, because they use them to grow their players from seeds into turnips, or whatever). In the minors, the scouts watch you in real-game situations, and as soon as you're good enough, they move you up to the majors.

Over the years, record companies have developed a similar system. Their farm teams are called **demo deals.** Under this arrangement, the record company spends some money (maybe $10,000 or so) for you to go into a studio and record **demos.** *Demo* is short for "demonstration recording," which is less than a full-fledged master but gives the company some idea of what you'll sound like on a professional record. They listen to the demo and decide whether they want to sign you to a full-blown record contract. If they do, you'll then negotiate a deal (we'll discuss exactly how this works, and how to protect yourself, on page 178).

The next step up, and more common than demo deals these days, is something called a **development deal.** This is essentially the same as a demo deal, except the company is spending more money—around $50,000 or so. In fact, under development deals, they'll sometimes record a couple of finished masters. When the recording is done, the company takes a listen and decides whether they want to go forward with you. Unlike a demo deal, the recording contract is prenegotiated, so you roll right into it.

Options in Midrange and Superstar Deals

With a midrange artist, or an artist who's the subject of a bidding war, the company may commit to two albums *firm*, and get additional options for one or two albums each (as noted above, they sometimes want the right to bail out if the first album tanks). It's rare that a company doesn't have the right to at least four albums from this type of artist, and five is the norm. At the superstar level, deals of only three albums are possible, though four is more common. Two or three of those albums are typically firm.

A few huge artists (and at the other end, a hot new artist signing to an indie label) have made deals for one album only, but this is rare.

Options Aren't Good for You

I remember a friend of mine from the high school choir who came in one day, jubilant, because she had signed a "ten-album deal" with Capitol Records. In reality, it turned out to be a deal for only one single, and she had merely given Capitol the option to require up to ten albums. While my friend has faded into obscurity after recording that one single, her attitude was not unusual. Many artists still think of record company options as being good for them (the numbers are so high at the end!), but in fact, options are only good for the record company. If you're a flop, you'll never see the money; if you're a success, it will probably be less than you're worth. So train yourself to think of options only as a chance for the record company to get out of your deal. They are never good for you.

Making the Best of Options

Despite my high-minded speech, the reality is that you have to live with options at all but superstar levels—this industry custom is too well entrenched to buck. However, since you're giving the company a chance to drop you after each album or two (in other words, to protect their tushies if there's no success), I think you're entitled to more goodies if they keep you. This can be done in two different ways:

Royalties.   For optional albums, you should get increased royalties. Typically, the increase is around 0.5% to 1%, both in your basic rate and in any escalated rates. For example, I did a midlevel deal that looked like this:

Album No.	Royalty on Sales of 0–500,000 Albums	Royalty on Sales of 500,001– 1,000,000 Albums	Royalty on Sales of 1,000,001– 1,500,000 Albums	Royalty on Sales of 1,500,001– 2,000,000 Albums	Royalty on Sales of 2,000,000+ Albums
1	16%	16.5%	17%	17.5%	18%
2	16%	16.5%	17%	17.5%	18%
3	17%	17.5%	18%	18.5%	19%
4	17%	17.5%	18%	18.5%	19%
5	18%	18%	18%	18.5%	19%
6	18%	18%	18.5%	19%	19%

Under this deal, if any particular album achieved an escalation, the next album would start at that escalated level. For example, if album one sold 2,000,000 units, album two would start at 18%, then would escalate ½ point at 500,000 units, etc. However, there was a cap of 19% on the overall royalties, no matter what the sales were.

Funds. You should also get increased recording funds for optional albums. Page 108 cites an example of a new-artist deal, and here are the numbers from a midlevel deal:

Album No.	Floor	Ceiling
1	$300,000	(no formula)
2	$300,000	$600,000
3	$350,000	$700,000
4	$350,000	$750,000
5	$400,000	$800,000
6	$400,000	$1,000,000

Don't the numbers look delicious in the later option periods? What a great deal! What a genius negotiator! DON'T BE FOOLED! OPTIONS ARE *NEVER* GOOD FOR YOU!! They only mean you'll get dropped if you're not worth the price, or you'll get too little if you're a smash. So repeat after me: "OPTIONS ARE *NEVER* GOOD FOR ME!!!" Now write it on the blackboard twenty-five times.

HOW LONG?

Term

How long the record company keeps you under an exclusive agreement is called the **term** of your deal. Record deals used to be for a term of one year, with options to renew for additional periods of one year each. These segments of the term are also called **terms,** or sometimes **periods,** such as the initial term (first year), first option period, etc. In the olden days, an artist was usually obligated to deliver two albums during each year. That worked terrifically back when records were banged out like pancakes, since most of the time artists just showed up, sang, then went to the beach. As we discussed, in those days it was not unusual to make an album in two weeks (three if the artist was a prima donna).

Every contract is a history lesson, and the contractual language dealing with the length of deals has had a particularly colorful past. Behind each clause is a story that ends with "I'm going to write something that makes sure, if this ever happens again, I won't get shafted." And unraveling these bits of history can be fun, so let's take a look.

Late Delivery of Albums

As artists took more creative control, albums took longer to make. Indeed, the more successful the artist, the longer (with rare exception) the recording process. Today, periods of years between albums are not unusual for superstars (or for flakes at any level). Many reasons for this are legitimate—if an album is successful, you need to be out touring and promoting it, which means you can't be in the studio. In fact, the more successful it is, the longer you'll be out touring and promoting, and the record company won't even want you to start the next album.

However, many of these delays don't have such a noble purpose. I'm convinced (but can't prove) that one of the reasons for delay is that artists, particularly following a major success, are a bit frightened to put out their next record. When it's actually released, they have to find out whether it does as well as the prior one; until then, it's only speculation and their fabulous track record stays intact. So, they continue to fine-tune, tweak, poke, re-record, rethink, etc., which delays the day of reckoning. And second albums are particularly troublesome. It's interesting to realize that someone's first album can actually be ten years or more in the making. That's because they were accumulating songs for a long time before they ever got a record deal, and thus had a huge catalog to choose from in making the first album. However, when the artist gets to the second album, all the cherries have been picked, so it's a matter of writing new material or going into the second tier of old stuff. And this process now has to take place within a year or two, as opposed to the unlimited time that preceded the first album. So there's much more pressure.

Record companies historically solved this slow-delivery problem by having the right to extend the term of the agreement if an album wasn't delivered on time. In other words, if your album was six months late, the current one-year term of your deal was extended by six months. This worked terrifically until Olivia Newton-John filed a suit against MCA Records seeking termination of her agreement. (The case cite is 90 Cal.App 3d. 18 [1979], for you technical freaks who like to read court cases.) In this case, she argued that her deal should be limited to the actual number of years stated in the contract, without regard to any extensions. In other words, since her contract was for a two-year term with three one-year options (a total of five years), she argued that MCA could not enforce the deal beyond five years from the start date, even though she had not given them all the product due. To everyone's surprise, the court (sort of) agreed. It reduced the duration of MCA's injunction (meaning the order saying she couldn't record for anyone else) to the five years, rather than allowing any extensions. However, I say "sort of" because the five years weren't over at the time of the case, and so the court technically didn't deal with the issue in full. Nonetheless, the case's language was strong enough to make all the companies nervous, and it forever changed the way record contracts are drawn.

Nowadays, the terms of record deals are not stated in specific time periods like one or two years. Instead, the contracts say each period ends twelve months after release of the last album required for that period, but it can be no less than a specified minimum (e.g., eighteen months) from the time it starts. For example, if you're required to record one album, the period might start upon signing your deal and end twelve months after release of that album, but no sooner than eighteen months after signing.

This language nicely solves the Olivia Newton-John problem, but the companies had to add additional provisions to deal with this little snippet of history: In 1970, Dean Martin signed an agreement with Warner Bros. Records. The agreement was unusual for those days (although it is the norm today) because the term continued until delivery of all the albums. About six years later, after everyone had forgotten about him, Dino came in and announced he was about to start recording a new album (for which he expected the substantial amount of money specified in the contract). This sent Warner into a tizzy, since Mr. Martin's star was not of the same brightness as when he signed the agreement, and they began scrambling to find a way out. So Dino sued them. Ultimately the case was settled, but it taught the companies a lesson—that contracts shouldn't be geared only to delivery of albums, or else they can go on forever. Accordingly, you'll now find provisions that say if the artist has not delivered an album within a certain period of time after delivery of the previous album (usually twelve to eighteen months, depending on bargaining power), the company can get out of the deal.

At the other end of the spectrum comes a history lesson from Frank Zappa. Also picking on our friends at Warner Bros. Records (so that they could have the distinction of being clobbered with both ends of the same stick), Mr. Zappa showed up one day with four albums under his arm. He said he was delivering all the remaining product required under his deal, and thus was free to sign elsewhere. As you can imagine, this didn't go over much better than Mr. Martin did.

The Zappa lesson is now handled by stating that you can't start recording an LP until you've delivered the prior album, and that the new album can't be delivered sooner than six months after delivery of the prior album. Record companies have a legitimate point in saying they don't have to take more than one album at a time, on the basis that (a) they can't reasonably market more than one album at a time; and (b) if they put an album on the shelf for later release, it may not be in touch with the trends in the music business (which, in case you haven't noticed, change hourly) at the time of release.

My prediction is that, in the not too distant future, we will move to deals based on a number of masters, rather than albums. That's because albums may well disappear (or at least become a rarity) as CDs whimper into oblivion, so we'll see artists putting out tracks in onesies and twosies. Ironically, in the 1950s, deals for singles (two tracks) were common. Back then, the companies could make a profit on singles, and they only did an album after the single was a success. So we may be returning to those days.

If this happens, a rather fun issue will be figuring out how long the old deals, which are based on albums, will last when albums are no longer around. In other words, if your deal ends 12 months after release of an album, and no one is releasing albums, does your deal go on forever? That should keep us lawyers busy for a while.

DELIVERY REQUIREMENTS

Apart from the number of recordings, contracts also talk about the kind of recordings you can deliver. **Delivery** is a magic word, because it means more than dumping the stuff on their doorstep. It means (a) you have to deliver a bunch of other junk along with the album (artwork, licenses for the songs, deals with producers, etc.) and (b) the company has to accept the recordings as complying with your deal. Your contract will specify what standards the company can use in deciding whether to accept the recordings, and the definition of these standards depends on your bargaining power. The extremes are:

Commercially Satisfactory

If your contract says you must deliver **commercially satisfactory** recordings, it means the record company only has to take recordings it believes will sell; in other words, recordings it finds "satisfactory for commercial exploitation" (translation: recordings it likes). If your contract has this language and they don't like your record, then (a) at best, they send you back to the studio (at your expense); or (b) at worst, they take the position that you haven't delivered an album as required by the deal, which means you're late, in breach of your contract, and they can terminate the deal.

Technically Satisfactory

At the other end of the spectrum is **technically satisfactory.** If you only have to deliver technically satisfactory recordings, then as long as a recording is technically well made, the company has to take it.

Technically satisfactory delivery standards are very rare today because of abuses that I'm sure you can imagine (for example, one of my record company clients got an album that was supposed to be a secret group of superstars but turned out to be a previously released flop from an unknown group).

Newer artists can expect to live with commercially satisfactory. Midrange/bidding war artists may get a technically satisfactory standard, but it will be subject to the company's approving the songs and the producer, plus the same limits described in the next two sentences. Superstars can expect an even more favorable version of technically satisfactory: The company may not have any approvals, but it will have language saying the recordings must be of a "style" (and perhaps even a "quality") similar to your previous recordings. They will also exclude any "specialty" or "novelty" recordings, so you can't give them a children's record, Christmas record, the Johnny Mathis songbook (unless, of course, you are Johnny Mathis), polka records, Gregorian chants, etc.

Other Delivery Criteria

The other requirements for your recordings (regardless of your level) are that they must be:

1. Studio recordings (as opposed to "live" concert recordings—see page 119 for a discussion of "live" albums).

2. Recorded during the term (to keep you from pulling out those old garage recordings).

3. Songs not previously recorded by you (I'm sure you can figure out the history lesson behind this one).

4. Recordings that feature only your performance (to keep you from bringing in the kids and your aunt Sally as guest soloists).

5. Not wholly instrumental selections (unless you're only an instrumentalist).

6. Material that doesn't cause the company any legal hassles, such as infringing somebody's copyright, defaming someone, or using obscene language (to the extent that's still possible).

7. Songs of a minimum playing time (usually two minutes).

In addition, you also have to deliver all the legal rights they need to exploit your recordings, such as producer agreements (we'll talk about those in Chapter 11), licenses to use the songs (Chapter 16), and sample clearances (we'll talk about samples on page 320).

CONTROLLED COMPOSITIONS

One of the most important provisions of your record deal is the **controlled composition clause,** which limits how much you get paid as a songwriter. However, to understand it you need a pretty extensive knowledge of publishing, which we're going to discuss later. So let's put it off until you have the background. (If you really can't wait, flip ahead to page 252, but you'll get pretty confused if you don't have a decent grasp on publishing.)

If you're on the *Advanced Overview Track,* go to Chapter 11 on page 125.
Experts, straight on . . .

GREATEST HITS

A **Greatest Hits** album (also called a **Best of**) is a compilation of songs from your prior albums, perhaps with one or two new songs. (I've always been amused by the term *Greatest Hits,* since the album is sometimes neither.) Traditionally, releasing a Greatest Hits album was a record company's way of blowing taps over an artist's career that had passed away. However, in the 1970s, Elton John released a Greatest Hits album at the height of his career and sold eight gazillion copies. Suddenly everyone rethought their position, and today a Greatest Hits album can appear at any point in an artist's life cycle.

The life cycle of the Greatest Hits album itself, however, is heading toward the endangered species list (somewhere between the hawksbill turtle and the black-footed ferret). As digital sales and streaming have soared, Greatest Hits albums have nose-dived, and the reason is pretty simple: Everyone is essentially making their own greatest hits by creating playlists on Spotify or YouTube, or buying (or stealing) their favorite tracks and sticking them on their iPhone. So as I write this, Greatest Hits albums are on life support, accented with a few death twitches. However, companies still want the rights to Greatest Hits albums.

If you don't say anything, the company will put out as many as it likes, whenever it likes, and pay you no advance. While some things about Greatest Hits albums aren't negotiable—for example, no company will count a Greatest Hits album against your delivery requirements—you can fix other issues if you know what to ask for. These are:

Limits

From the midrange level and up, and sometimes at the new artist level (depending on the company and your bargaining power), you can often limit the number of Greatest Hits albums a company can compile from your material. (Incidentally, don't ever assume there's a practical limit if you don't have one contractually—I've heard of one company that managed to put out seven different albums of an artist who only recorded two albums' worth of masters in their entire career!) The usual limit is that the company can release no more than one (or two) Greatest Hits album during the term, plus one (or two) after the term.

Greatest Hits Advances

If you have a fair amount of bargaining power, you may be able to get an advance for your Greatest Hits albums, but since the digital revolution killed off most of the Greatest Hits business as we just discussed, the companies are reluctant to pay much in the way of advances. Whether you can get one at all will depend on your bargaining power and will usually require you to deliver new recordings (see the next section). Whatever advance you get, it is typically reduced by the amount of your deficit if you're unrecouped (see page 86 if you don't remember what a "deficit" is). You want the date of determining the deficit to be as late as possible, so you can get in the maximum sales to reduce it. The date of release of the Greatest Hits album is the best.

If you have enough clout to get a Greatest Hits advance, the range is around $25,000 to $50,000 less the unrecouped deficit. So if you got $50,000 and are unrecouped by $10,000, you would get $40,000 ($50,000 less the $10,000 deficit). Independent labels will pay nothing, or perhaps $5,000 less the deficit.

Midlevel and up deals often have a "floor" on the Greatest Hits advance, regardless of the deficit. For example, I did one midlevel artist's agreement that had a Greatest Hits advance of $100,000 minus the unrecouped deficit, but in no event less than $50,000. Here's how this would work under different circumstances:

1. If the artist is recouped, the advance would be $100,000.
2. If the artist is unrecouped $25,000, then $100,000 minus the $25,000 deficit equals a $75,000 advance for the Greatest Hits album.
3. If the artist's deficit is $75,000, then $100,000 minus the $75,000 deficit equals $25,000. But the floor is $50,000, so the artist would get a $50,000 advance.
4. Can you figure the advance if the artist is $30,000 unrecouped? How about $200,000 unrecouped? (Answers on page 124.)

New Songs for Greatest Hits

Companies usually require two or three new songs for Greatest Hits packages released during the term (not after, since you'll be signed to someone else). Back when Greatest Hits packages meant something, a hit single pumped up the sales of the Greatest Hits album because it was the only place to get the song. This is of course no longer true, since you can get the new song by itself.

If you agree to do the new tracks, at a minimum the record company should agree to pay the recording costs of these new masters even if you're unrecouped (but don't assume the form agreement will say so). You should also try to get a higher advance for a Greatest Hits album that has new tracks.

LIVE ALBUMS

A **live album** is recorded during a live concert (with lots of screaming and applause), rather than in a studio. Their popularity goes through periodic ups and downs (sort of like musical movies). They were historically something a company did to keep the artist happy, because they didn't really make any money. Then, in 1976, Peter Frampton broke all the rules with an album called *Frampton Comes Alive!*, which was not only a live album, but also a *double* live album (double albums are a traditional handicap at retail because they're more expensive). This album sold in multimillion numbers that blew out all the traditional wisdom. After the predictable glut of live albums following Mr. Frampton's, the popularity again faded. Currently, live albums sell at a level I'd call "okay," but are no great shakes.

Unless you have a lot of muscle, record companies won't let you deliver a live album (or even one live cut on a studio album) without their consent. On rare occasions, superstars can get the right to deliver one live album during the term of their deal. But it will usually be for a reduced advance, both because of live records' dicey sales history and the fact that most of the songs will have been previously released.

GUARANTEED RELEASE

As we discussed on page 107, very few record contracts even build in an obligation to *record* your records, much less a commitment to release them.

With even a little bargaining power (and with some companies, as a matter of practice), you can get a **guaranteed release,** which is also called a **release commitment.** Bizarrely, this clause will never obligate the company to release your records. It will, however, let you get out of the deal if they don't.

With more bargaining power, you can sometimes get the right to buy back the unreleased album. After all, if the company doesn't think enough of it to put it out, why not let you take it elsewhere and get their money back?

Guaranteed release clauses basically turn you into a notice factory. If, within a certain period after delivery (usually 90 to 120 days) the company hasn't put out your album, you have earned the right to give it a written notice saying, "You haven't put out my album." After receiving this shocking news, the company has another period (usually 60 days) within which to actually put out the album (if they feel like it). If they don't, you now have the privilege of sending a second notice, usually within 30 days after the 60 days (and if you're late, you lose your rights). This notice says the company has still failed to put out your album; that you really meant it when you said you wanted them to; and that you are now terminating the deal. At this point you can say good-bye. (But note that the company still doesn't have to put out the record.)

By the way, the period after delivery in which the company must release is usually extended if any of it falls between October 15 and January 15. This is because no one other than the most super of superstars releases product after October 15. Beginning in early December, the radio stations start thinking about Hawaii, Aspen, or St. Bart's (or, in the current state of the biz, Fresno or Atlantic City), and they "freeze" their playlists (meaning they add no new records until after January 15). In response, the record industry closes up around the middle of December. If an artist is not well-known, their record doesn't have time to make its climb before the December shutdown, so everyone has to wait until next year. Thus, the record companies want to extend their release commitment period to make way for this phenomenon. And their vacations.

Guaranteed release clauses only let you out of your record deal if the company doesn't release your record in the United States. As your bargaining power increases, as well as your international fame, you may be able to negotiate a similar release provision for foreign territories. Certainly you should try to get a guaranteed release in the "major" territories (see page 142 for what they are) and anyplace else where you sell big numbers.

Normally you can't get out of the entire deal for failure to release outside the United States—you can only terminate for the particular territory where they blew it, and only for the specific album not released (so you can get another distributor to release that album in the territory). However, without massive clout, you won't actually get back the territory. Instead, you'll get the right to find another company to license the unreleased album from your record company. Your company will credit 50% of what it gets from this license to your account, and keep the other 50% for themselves. If you keep pushing, the company may agree that if it fails to release two consecutive albums in a particular territory, you can have back that territory for the rest of the deal. While this is not likely to be meaningful (if you're that much of a stiff in the territory, odds are no one else will want you), it's better than a sharp stick in the eye.

As the CD's heartbeat slows, an interesting issue is starting to poke out its head. Namely, can the record company satisfy its "guaranteed release" requirement by just sticking your songs in an online store, or on a streaming service? That's certainly not the spirit of these clauses, as they historically required the company's financial commitment to press CDs, ship them to stores, and do some level of marketing (though there was rarely a contractual marketing commitment). However, since most company forms don't define the term "release," dropping the songs online could technically do it.

Recently, we who represent artists have tried to get a commitment to release both physically (CDs) and digitally, and for a while most of the companies played ball. But now that CDs are a shrinking, ever-smaller piece of the business, it's really hard to get this clause.

The real goal is to have them market your music with some amount of energy, but so far there's no norm for what that means. Therefore, technically, the companies can just slap your recordings online and be done. Hopefully this will evolve into something that better protects the artist, but it's a work in progress.

INDEPENDENTS DAY

Over the last few years, deals with independent record companies have become more prevalent. That's because, over the last number of years, independent labels have become more prevalent. How come? Well, for one reason, with all the industry cost-cutting, there are far fewer jobs at the majors. So a lot of talented executives have joined or started their own companies. Also, the majors are signing fewer artists, so the indies have a lot more opportunities. And most importantly: The majors don't always understand the kind of cool music that indies love.

I think the spread of indies is incredibly healthy for the biz. It's like the record industry in the 1960s, when independent labels like A&M, Chrysalis, and Island changed the face of music. Great music has always come from doing things out of the mainstream. Keep at it!

As the independents grow stronger, their deals look more and more like major label deals. However, there are some differences you should understand, so let's take a look. We'll start with "true independents" (see page 69 for what that means), then mosey on over to production companies that have little or no staff (and rely on a major label to do the heavy lifting).

True Independents

1. As we already noted, you get less of an advance from an independent. Because a deal with them is like shopping in the bargain basement, you should make up for it by giving them the lowest number of albums possible. A few years ago, it wasn't hard to limit independent deals to one or two albums. Lately, as the independents' muscles grew, so did their desire for more albums. So now they try to get as many as five. See if you can keep it down to three or four. As a general rule, the less money they're guaranteeing, the fewer albums they should get. So with a smaller deal, you can often limit them to two or three.

2. If you're willing to take a very small, or zero, advance, some labels will give you 50% of their profits instead of a royalty. We'll discuss how profits are computed later (on page 215). For now, take my word that a profit share means a lot more money if you're a big success (though maybe less at mid level).

3. Most indie labels don't have overseas operations, and therefore you want to make sure that your records get released in those territories. If they're not released, you should get back the rights to those territories (see the discussion of this on page 120). Sometimes, you can even limit their rights to the U.S. only, and make your own foreign deals.

4. Every once in a while, the company wants to approve your manager or agent, to be sure it's someone they can work with. While you should agree with the company that a crummy manager will screw up your career, the manager's job is to beat up your record company, so I don't like the idea that they can nix someone who's doing a good job. Tell them they're free to express an opinion, but you should control your own team.

5. Most independent companies, just like majors, will want 360 rights (see page 102 for what those are). They may also want to own some or all of your publishing (your earnings as a songwriter, as opposed to your earnings as a performer on records). Since we haven't discussed publishing, I want to defer the ins and outs of this until we do. The way to protect yourself is on page 314 if you want to look ahead, but I suggest you do it only if you understand publishing pretty well.

Production Companies

When you're recording for a production company that is not a true independent, you have concerns in addition to those we just discussed. First off, you have to ask whether this company can get anyone to distribute your album. Remember, these companies aren't distributors, and thus they have no way to get your records into the stores unless they contract with someone else to do it. So here's how to cover yourself:

1. First of all, put a clause in your contract that says (a) the production company must enter into an agreement to distribute your records (ideally, you want to say the deal is for distribution both physically and digitally, though as we discussed on page 121, it's getting harder to require a physical release), and (b) the release has to happen within a certain period of time. Ideally the release should happen within six months after execution of the contract or completion of your album, but I've gone as long as nine to twelve months. If the time period is measured from completion of your album, be sure you have some outside date—otherwise, if the company never records you, the date will never arrive. For example, you might require a company to make an agreement within six months after completion of your album, but in no event later than twelve months after execution of your deal.

2. If you have a bit more muscle, you should say that the company must enter into an agreement with a *major* distributor. If you don't, you may find your records slapped on iTunes and Spotify through TuneCore (which you could have done yourself), or shipped out in Uncle Herbert's U-Haul, with no marketing or promotion behind them. If they don't use a major distributor, you want to approve who it is. Assuming the independent agrees, it will say you must be "reasonable" in your approval, so you can't use this clause to get out of the deal when some prettier face dangles more money in front of you. (You wouldn't do that, would you?) And by the way, when I represent the independent, I insist that the artist preapprove all the likely distributors (which I then list).

3. Watch out for this one: Suppose your deal with the independent is for two albums firm, but the distributor drops the company (and you) after one album. How do you make sure the com-

pany doesn't hold you for the second album even though they have no way to put it out?

Part of your protection is a guaranteed release—if they don't put your album out, you can terminate the deal (see page 119). However, as you'll remember from page 107, companies don't even have to make a record to hang on to your contract. And if they don't record any product, the guaranteed release never comes into play. Knowing this, various sleazeballs in our business have sunk their teeth into an artist and not let go if they smelled that somebody might pay them for the privilege.

The way to cover yourself is to say that the independent has six to twelve months after a distribution deal lapses within which to get a new deal, or else you're out.

Answers to questions on page 118:

If you're $30,000 unrecouped, the advance would be $70,000 ($100,000 minus the $30,000 deficit).

If you're $200,000 unrecouped, the advance would be $50,000 ($100,000 minus the $200,000 deficit is less than zero, but the floor is $50,000 no matter what).

11

Producer and Mixer Deals

WHAT'S A PRODUCER?

A record producer combines the roles of director and producer in the motion picture field. He or she is responsible for bringing the creative product into tangible form (a recording), which means (a) being responsible for maximizing the creative process (finding and selecting songs, deciding on arrangements, getting the right vocal sound, etc.), and (b) administering the whole project, such as booking studios, hiring musicians, staying within a budget, filing union reports, etc. (The mechanical aspects of administration—actually calling the musicians, doing the paperwork, etc.—are often handled by a **production coordinator,** whose life purpose is these chores.)

History

As we discussed earlier, artists in the 1950s were mostly people who just showed up to sing, then left to "do lunch." My friend Snuff Garrett, one of the most important producers of the fifties and sixties, considered it burdensome if it took him more than five days to record an album (and the artist wasn't even there for the whole time). Using this technique, Snuff produced records for Cher, Sonny and Cher, Gary Lewis and the Playboys, Bobby Vee, Del Shannon, and a host of other successes, including such strange choices as Telly Savalas and Walter Brennan.

Snuff started out (as did all the early producers) as an **A&R** man (the letters stand for "Artists and Repertoire"). A&R men (in those days there were no A&R "persons") were executives of record companies whose job was to find, sign, and guide talent, match songs to singers, and run recording sessions (in other words, doing almost exactly what producers do today). A&R executives still exist, and indeed are among the most important industry people. They are responsible for find-ing and signing talent, as well as finding songs, matching producers and artists, and generally overseeing projects. But today most of them don't actually produce the recordings (although many of the better ones come quite close to producing).

Anyway, Snuff began working for Liberty Records, which was then run by its founder and chief executive, Simon Waronker (the father of former Warner Records and DreamWorks Records president Lenny Waronker); its president, Alvin Bennett; and its chief recording engi-neer, Theodore Keep. (Do the first names of these gentlemen sound familiar? Do they remind you of a recording artist on Liberty? See page 138 for the answer if you can't guess.) Snuff (who is one of the smart-est businesspeople I ever met, but hides behind this country cornpone) figured out early on that he was making millions of dollars for Liberty while drawing a generous but small salary in comparison to what he was generating. So he summoned up all his courage and asked Alvin for a royalty of 1¢ per record. This was considered outrageous, if not treasonous—the radical idea that a guy instrumental in creating prod-uct could get a royalty—and Snuff was almost fired in the process. But due to his value to Liberty, he held out and won the point. And in so doing, he started a trend that is the reason today's producers get royal-ties on records.

ROYALTIES

We talked before about the range of royalties for producers, on page 93. However, there are some major distinctions between artists' and pro-ducers' royalties, and some fine points that will bite you in the butt if you don't know about them. For whatever historical reasons, produc-ers' royalties are computed more favorably than artists' royalties.

"Record One" Royalties

The big difference between artist and producer royalties is that pro-ducers, at some point, are paid for all records sold, meaning recording costs are not charged against their royalties. (As you know, recording costs are always charged against artists' royalties.) These are called record one royalties, because they're paid from the first record ("record one") that the company sells. Producers, of course, have to recoup the advances they put in their pocket, but if you think of those advances as a prepayment of royalties, it's the same as getting a royalty on all records. (Actually, some superstar producers are paid from record one and don't even have to recoup all of their advances, as we'll discuss in a minute).

Most producers' royalties are paid **retroactive to record one** after recoupment of recording costs at the **net rate.** What this means in English is that (a) recording costs are recouped at the artist's *net rate* (the all-in artist rate after deducting the producer's royalty—i.e., the artist's rate "net" of the producer's royalty); (b) until recording costs are recouped, the producer gets *no royalties* at all (just like an artist); but (c) once recording costs are recouped, the producer gets paid on *all* sales made, including those used to recoup recording costs. In other words, once recording costs are recouped, the producer is paid from the first record sold (*record one*), and this payment is *retroactive* because the company "goes back" and pays on sales previously made that didn't bear royalties at the time of sale.

This is easier to see with numbers. Suppose an artist's "all-in" royalty (artist and producer combined) is 60¢ a record, and the producer's royalty is 10¢ a record. That makes the "net" royalty 50¢ (60¢ all-in rate less the 10¢ producer royalty). Assume the producer gets a $10,000 advance, and that the recording costs (including the producer's advance) are $120,000. (These numbers bear no relationship to reality but make for easy math.) Here's what happens at sales of 200,000 units:

Producer's Recording Cost Recoupment Computation		Producer's Royalty Account	
Units Sold	200,000	Units Sold	200,000
"Net" Royalty	× 50¢	Producer Royalty	× 0
	$100,000		0
Less: Recording Costs	− $120,000	Less: Advance	− $10,000
DEFICIT	− **$20,000**	DEFICIT	− **$10,000**

Since recording costs are unrecouped, the producer doesn't get any royalties, because 50¢ × 200,000 equals only $100,000, which is short of the $120,000 needed to recoup the recording costs. That's why it's zero in the above example. However, once the artist sells a total of 240,000 units, the costs are recouped (50¢ × 240,000 = $120,000), and the producer is paid on all the units sold (i.e., retroactively to record one). At this point, the producer gets $24,000, which is 10¢ × 240,000 (less of course the $10,000 advance):

Producer's Recording Cost Recoupment Computation		Producer's Royalty Account	
Units Sold	240,000	Units Sold	240,000
"Net" Royalty	× 50¢	Producer Royalty	× 10¢
	$120,000		$24,000
Less: Recording Costs	– 120,000	Less: Advance	– 10,000
DEFICIT	$0	NET PAYABLE	$14,000

For you sharp-eyed purists, I'm aware that the $10,000 producer's advance would not be included in recording costs to determine the artist's royalty once it's recouped from the producer's royalty—if it were, the company would be getting it twice. But for simplicity, I've ignored this in the examples, because it's an issue in the artist's deal and doesn't bear on the producer's royalty computation.

Producers are sometimes paid **prospectively** after recoupment at the **all-in rate**, (sometimes called the **combined rate**), which means that, once the recording costs are recouped at the *all-in* rate (i.e., the *combined* artist and producer rate—**60¢** in our example), you get paid on sales *after* that point (but not retroactive to record one). This means you'll get paid sooner, but it's only a better deal if record sales die (a) after the point where recording costs recoup at the combined rate, but (b) before recoupment at the net rate. Otherwise, under the normal "retroactive-at-the-net-rate" deal, you're way ahead when you get to recoupment at the net rate—at that point, you're not only paid on the sales between the level of combined recoupment and net recoupment, but also on all the records sold *before* recoupment. This is easier to understand with numbers, so . . .

Here's an example, using our same assumptions, for a producer paid *prospectively* after recoupment at the combined rate:

Producer's Recording Cost Recoupment Computation		Producer's Royalty Account	
Units Sold	240,000	Units Sold (in excess of recoupment)*	40,000
Combined Royalty	× 60¢	Producer Royalty	× 10¢
	$144,000		$4,000
Less: Recording Costs	– 120,000	Less: Advance	– 10,000
RECOUPED	$24,000	NET PAYABLE	$0

*It takes 200,000 units at the combined 60¢ rate to recoup $120,000 of recording costs. So on sales of 240,000, only 40,000 bear royalties.

Contrast this (only $4,000 earned against the advance, meaning you get zero) with getting $14,000 on top of the advance in the prior example, for the same number of units. (Note that if there were no advance, you'd get only $4,000 instead of $24,000.)

In this example, the prospective deal would only be better than a retroactive-at-net deal if the record sells 239,999 copies and drops dead. In that case, you'd get paid on 39,999 copies under this formula, as opposed to zero under a net rate deal (239,999 times the 50¢ net rate is 50¢ short of the $120,000 needed to recoup recording costs). However, once you sell one more copy, you're way behind, as you just saw. And if, as in our example, your advance is more than the royalties on the number of sales between the combined rate and net rate recoupment points (the 39,999 in our example), you're always worse off under a combined deal. This is because you won't be paid on those 39,999 units even if you never get to a net recoupment—you already got those royalties in the advance.

ADVANCES

Producers, like artists, also get advances. These advances are recoupable from the producer's royalties, regardless of how the producer's royalties are calculated.

Producer advances fall into two categories. In one corner, weighing in as the heavyweights, you've got the urban/hip-hop producers, plus a few superstar pop producers. These folks are often considered as important as (or in some cases more important than) the artist. In the other corner, we've got rock producers and everybody else.

For rock/everybody else, the range of advances is:

1. **New Producers:**
   Anywhere from zero to $7,500 per master. If the producer is doing the entire album, advances are anywhere from zero to about $30,000 per album.
2. **Midlevel:**
   $10,000 to $15,000 per master, and about $30,000 to $50,000 for the entire album.
3. **Superstar:**
   Up to $25,000 per track, and about $150,000 to $200,000 for the whole album.

For urban/pop:

1. **New Producers:**
   Anywhere from zero to $10,000 per master.
2. **Midlevel:**
   $40,000 to $50,000 per master.
3. **Superstar:**
   $75,000 to $100,000 and up, per master.

Note these amounts are *advances* to the producer, meaning they don't include recording costs. Also, some extremely superstar producers have begun insisting that their advances are not recoupable at all, or are only 50% recoupable, so they can get their royalties much earlier.

A number of producers like to do "fund" deals. That means the producer gets a chunk of cash that includes both recording costs and the producer's advance (just like the artist funds we discussed on page 97). This is especially so with producers who own their own studios.

The important issue with funds is to allocate how much is treated as recording costs, and how much is considered the producer's advance. The higher the recording costs, the worse for the artist—remember, from page 126, only the advance is charged against producer royalties, since the royalties are payable from record one after recoupment of the recording costs. So this allocation should be spelled out in the contract.

The reality of the recording costs has little to do with this discussion (as noted above, many of these producers own their own studios, so the actual costs are minimal). The negotiation is really about how much gets charged to the producer's royalties.

OTHER ROYALTY COMPUTATIONS

Except for the record one aspect we discussed on page 126, producers' royalties are usually calculated exactly the same way as the artists' (although audiovisual royalties are different, as noted in the next section). This means they get the same "free goods" reductions and (as we'll discuss in Chapter 12) the same proportionate reduction for foreign, budget, mid-price, etc. For example, if an artist gets 75% of his or her U.S. rate in England, the producer will get 75% of his or her U.S. producer rate in England.

In situations where the artist gets a percentage of the company's net receipts (such as a license to use a recording in a motion picture, where the artist gets 50% of the fee paid by the motion picture company), the producer gets a pro rata share of the artist's earnings, based on the ratio that the producer's royalty bears to the all-in rate. For example, if the artist's all-in rate is 12% and the producer gets 3%, the producer would get three-twelfths (one-fourth) of the artist's receipts. So if the record company gets $20,000 to use a master in a film, and pays $10,000 to the artist, the producer would get $2,500 (three-twelfths of the $10,000), and the artist would get $7,500 (the remaining nine-twelfths). (By the way, I've simplified this example by omitting any special markets fee, which we'll discuss on page 144.)

Audiovisual Royalties

For audiovisual exploitations (DVDs, streaming videos, etc.), producers generally get half of their otherwise applicable rate. The theory is that the master is only half of the product (the video portion is the other half). Accordingly, when a video is licensed, if the producer had 3% and the all-in royalties were 12%, instead of getting 25% (three-twelfths) of the artist's monies, the producer would only get 12.5%. If the artist gets a royalty, for example on a DVD sale, the producer's 3% royalty would be reduced to 1.5%.

WHO HIRES THE PRODUCER?

At one time, record companies routinely hired the producers. That was in the days when one producer did an entire album (a concept that has almost vanished, since most albums today—other than rock—have multiple producers). As it became common to have four, five, or more producers per album, the companies realized their in-house lawyers were spending so much time negotiating producer deals that it was clogging up their system. So they hit on the brilliant idea that the artist should hire the producer, which has not only shifted the paperwork burden to the artist, but has also shifted the financial burden to you. Let's analyze the issues separately.

Who Actually Hires (Contracts With) The Producer?

Since the artist has a direct contractual relationship with the producer, the producer is answerable to the artist, and the artist has full control of deciding the terms of the producer's deal. That's the good news. And now for the commercial: The artist bears the legal fees for negotiating the producer's deal.

Who Pays The Producer?

Remember, in an all-in deal, you are responsible for the producer's royalties, regardless of who actually contracts with him or her. This is a much more serious issue than it may look at first glance. For reasons we'll discuss in a minute, the producer may be entitled to royalties before you're recouped under your deal with the record company. This means you could owe money to the producer at a time when the record company doesn't owe you anything. This means you could have to write a check to the producer from your own pocket. This majorly sucks.

A MAJOR POINT—PAY ATTENTION

In case you've been dozing, now's the time to wake up. I'm going to talk about something that can mean a lot of money out of your pocket if you don't do it right. This is true whether you're an artist or a producer, even though it concerns the same point.

Let's look at a producer who's paid from record one, without regard to recoupment of recording costs (it doesn't happen often, but it makes the example easier to understand). Using our earlier assumptions ($120,000 recording costs, 60¢ "all-in" royalty, 10¢ producer royalty, and $10,000 producer advance), suppose you only sold 150,000 albums:

Units Sold	150,000
Producer Royalty	× 10¢
	$15,000
Less: Advance	− 10,000
NET PAYABLE	**$5,000**

So the producer is owed $5,000. However, 150,000 units times the artist's 60¢ rate is only $90,000, meaning the $120,000 recording costs have not been recouped. Now, remember that the artist is responsible for paying the producer's royalties in an all-in deal (see page 96)? If you put these two points together, you'll see that the artist is obligated to pay $5,000 to the producer, but the artist is getting no money because he or she is unrecouped. A major bummer.

And the situation can get much worse. Continuing with these same assumptions, let's assume the artist got a $100,000 advance on top of the $120,000 in recording costs. That means the artist won't get any money until *both* the $120,000 in recording costs *and* the $100,000 advance are recouped. Meanwhile, the producer (who didn't share in the $100,000 advance) is owed royalties. For example, if the artist sells 300,000 albums, check out this Parade of Horribles:

Artist's Account		Producer's Account	
Units Sold	300,000	Units Sold	300,000
Royalty	× 60¢	Royalty	× 10¢
	$180,000		$30,000
Less: Recording Costs	– $120,000	Less: Advance	– $10,000
Less: Artist Advance	– $100,000	NET PAYABLE	**$20,000**
DEFICIT	**– $40,000**		

As you can see, you're $40,000 unrecouped (which means you have no money coming in), but you owe $20,000 to the producer. If that $20,000 number doesn't impress you, try adding a zero to make it $200,000. Do I have your attention?

This is one of the times when success can kill you, because the more records you sell, the deeper in the hole you go! (In a sense, I'm misleading you. First of all, at some level of success the artist will recoup and earn enough royalties to pay off the producer. Secondly, part of the reason the artist isn't getting royalties is an advance, which is in his or her pocket. Thus, if you think of advances as prepaid royalties, the artist has really received these royalties and is required to pay a part of them to the producer. However, unless you're very different from the artists I know, you won't be setting money aside for your producer. Also, much of this problem is caused by the fact that recording costs have not been recouped, which is not money sitting in your bank account. You can't put those monies aside to cover the producer even if you want to.)

Think that's the worst of it? Nah, we're just getting warmed up. Here's how the above example can get truly miserable:

Suppose the deal we just discussed was the artist's first album, which ultimately sold only 50,000 units. This means the album didn't recoup its recording costs, and the producer didn't recoup his or her advance.

So far, the artist doesn't owe the producer anything, and everything is fine (from the point of view of our example, that is—the artist's career is of course in the toilet). When it comes time to do a second album, the artist ditches this turkey and hires a new producer. Let's assume the second album also costs $120,000, and let's assume the artist's recording fund is $200,000 for both the first and second albums, so that the artist pockets $80,000 (the difference between the fund and the $120,000 recording costs) on each album. Also, assume the second album sells 500,000 units, so that it recoups its recording costs and the producer of album number 2 is entitled to retroactive royalties. This means he or she is owed $50,000 (10¢ × 500,000 units), less the $10,000 advance, or $40,000.

Now let's look at how the accounts stack up. First, the artist's account with the record company:

Artist's Account with Record Company

	Royalty Earnings	Charges Against Royalties	Due Artist (or Deficit)
Album 1	+ $30,000 (60¢ × 50,000 units)	− $200,000 ($120,000 recording costs and $80,000 advance)	− $170,000
Album 2	+ $300,000 (60¢ × 500,000 units)	− $200,000 ($120,000 recording costs and $80,000 advance)	+$100,000
TOTAL	+ $330,000 ROYALTIES	− $400,000 CHARGES	− $70,000 DEFICIT

Now here's the computation of album number 2's producer royalties (album number 1's producer is not owed any royalties):

Album Number 2 Producer's Account with Artist

	Royalty Earnings	Charges Against Royalties	Due Producer
Album 2	+ $50,000 (10¢ × 500,000 units)	− $10,000 (advance)	+ $40,000 PAYABLE

As you can see from the above, the producer of album number 2 is owed $40,000, but the artist is unrecouped by $70,000. If you add a few more unsuccessful albums prior to the big hit, or add a few zeros after these dollar amounts, the artist is nearing 10 on the Richter scale. And the producer ain't gonna be much happier when he or she doesn't get paid—instead of having a nice solid record company to send out the producer's royalty checks, he or she now has to chase the artist, Fred Flake, who may be vacationing in Bora Bora for the next five years. If either of these people is you, take two Valium and call me in the morning.

So what happens in real life? Any producer who has the slightest idea what they're doing will insist on the record company paying his or her royalties. Any artist who has the slightest idea what they're doing will insist on the record company paying the producer's royalties. Any record company that knows what it's doing (and they all do) will avoid this obligation like the plague.

It's simple enough to get the record company to pay the producer after the artist is recouped. That's because there are royalties from which it can deduct the producer's royalties. This is also relatively meaningless, because the artist has the money to pay the producer at that point. (It is, however, still better than not having the record company on the hook at all.) The problem comes when the artist doesn't have the cash to pay the producer.

If you have a reasonable amount of bargaining power (or if the producer does and requires this in the producer's agreement), you can get the record company to pay the producer and treat the payments as additional advances under your deal. In our example, this means the company would pay the producer $40,000 and you would then be $110,000 in the red (the original $70,000 plus the $40,000 paid to the producer). This makes you further unrecouped, but it's vastly superior to taking the money from your own pocket (few things aren't). If the company does agree, it will insist on approving the producer's deal, so that the amount it has to pay while you're unrecouped can't get out of hand. Interestingly, they'll want to keep the producer's royalty low, and the producer's advance high. Can you figure out why they want a higher producer advance? (See the answer at the end of the chapter if you can't guess.)

As your bargaining power declines, the sources from which the record company can get back pre-recoupment producer royalties increase geometrically. Not only will the company take them back from your royalties; it will also want to take them from:

1. **This album's budget,** meaning they'll hold back part of your advance money until either (a) the producer earns it; or (b) you flop so badly that it becomes obvious the producer will never get it. For example, out of a $250,000 recording fund, they might hold back $50,000 in anticipation of paying producer's royalties before the artist is recouped. If in fact the producer gets $50,000 in royalties, the artist never sees this money. If, after a period of time, it becomes clear that the producer will never be entitled to the royalties, the artist gets it (more specifically, the artist gets the portion of it not earned by the producer).
2. **Your mechanical royalties** (we'll discuss what these babies are on page 229).
3. **The next album's budget** (assuming there is a next album).
4. Some record companies attempted to take **first-born children,** but this practice died out in the late sixties.

If you don't have much bargaining power, you're going to end up giving the company anything it wants in exchange for an agreement to pay these royalties. Whatever it is, it beats the hell out of writing a check or selling your prized squeegee collection, so I suggest you take it. But fight valiantly, don't let them know I said so, and burn this page after you read it.

SoundExchange Monies

If you're a producer, you want a share of SoundExchange monies, which means nothing to you because I haven't told you about it yet. As we'll see later (on page 145), the artist is entitled to monies when masters are broadcast digitally (like on Sirius XM, Pandora, and so forth), and those monies are collected by an outfit called SoundExchange (more about them on page 347). SoundExchange gets money from the broadcasters, then pays it to the artist, record company, and unions. We'll talk about specifics down the road, but the thing to understand now is that producers aren't entitled to SoundExchange monies unless the artist tells SoundExchange to pay them.

So it's important that your deal with the artist requires them to send SoundExchange something we call a **letter of direction** (known to its close friends as an **L.O.D.**), telling them to slide the dough your way.

Your share of SoundExchange monies is the same percentage of the artist's money that you get for motion picture licenses: a fraction equal to your producer royalty over the artist's all-in royalty. So if you have a 3% royalty and the artist as 12%, you'd get ³⁄₁₂, or 25% of the artist's SoundExchange monies.

Delivery Standard

Just like artist deals, producers have a delivery standard, which is almost always "technically and commercially satisfactory"). See page 115 for what all that means.

MIXERS

Closely akin to producers are **mixers,** whose work we briefly discussed on page 74. Basically, these folks take the multitracks and throw them into a blender to produce a mystical potion of sublime music.

Great mixers can make a huge difference in the success of a record, and thus they are paid handsomely. Top rock mixers can get $7,500 to $12,500 per track, while the lower-level folk get more like $3,000. Often this is a one-time payment, meaning there are no royalties, but the mixers with clout can get a royalty as well. If there are royalties, they're usually .5% to 1%, paid exactly like a producer (retroactive to record one after recoupment of recording costs at the net rate).

The per-track money we just discussed (e.g., the $3,000 for mixing) is often a **fee,** meaning it's not recoupable from royalties. However, for the higher-paid folk, 50% of their up-front money is usually recoupable.

When we enter the hip-hop world, however, we walk through the looking glass. The top hip-hop mixers get $30,000 to $50,000 per remix, and sometimes more. When they also get royalties (and a lot of them do), it can be more than 1% (as high as 2%). As with rockers, because they're so highly paid, half their fee is usually an advance (the other half is nonrecoupable). However, at these levels, it's hard to earn enough royalties to ever recoup. A lot of remixing is done only for specific genres (like a dance remix of a pop song), which means the sales are limited.

If you're on the *Fast Track*, go to Part III (Chapter 15) on page 225.
Everyone else, read on . . .

Answer to question on page 126:

The Chipmunks.

Answer to question on page 135:

Record companies want you to pay a higher producer advance so that the producer isn't owed royalties until as late as possible, after which you've hopefully recouped more of your deficit.

12

Advanced Royalty Computations

DISTRIBUTION METHODS

Before we can get deeper into royalties, you need to know a little more about distribution.

Physical records (CDs) are distributed by four major methods: wholesale distribution entities, one-stops, rack jobbers, and licensees. Digital records are of course sold electronically, primarily via downloads and streaming. As of this writing, digital revenue is almost 75% of the business in the United States (a little less in the rest of the world) and growing. The growth is fueled by two things: (1) digital is expanding; and (2) CDs are lumbering toward the dinosaur boneyard. Still, you need to understand physical distribution for the time being, as it's still a chunk of the business, and some of the concepts carry over to the digital world.

Here's a brief look at the ways that physical records make their way from the elves in the factory to your hands:

Wholesale Distribution Entities

Record wholesalers are by far the major means of distributing records. They're just like wholesale distributors in any other business—they buy from the manufacturing company (Warner Bros., Sony, Universal, etc.) and sell to retail stores. (These are the major and independent distributors we discussed on pages 67–69.)

Rack Jobbers

Rack jobbers are people who lease floor space from department stores and put in "racks" of records. Although it looks like Wal-Mart and Target are selling your records, in fact they only turn the space over to someone who decides what product to carry, delivers it to the racks, pays rent to the store, and keeps the profits. (Would you really expect the shoe buyer at Wal-Mart to decide how many Iggy Azalea records to buy?)

One-Stops

One-stops buy from the major distributors and then sell to "Mom and Pop" record stores, who buy quantities too small for the majors to bother with. The one-stop buys in bulk (like a big retailer, so the majors will sell to them), and then sells onesies and twosies to the stores at a markup (which makes the price higher to Mom and Pop than to the chain stores). This is of course dwindling, as Mom and Pop can no longer make much money from records, so they've given the floor space over to sponge mops

Licensees

Records are also distributed by **licensees.** A *licensee* is someone who signs a "license agreement" with a record company, which allows them to *actually manufacture* and distribute records, as opposed to merely buying and distributing goods manufactured by the record company. An example would be a U.S. company that licenses a foreign company the right to manufacture and distribute records in their territory.

And Everybody Else . . .

In addition to these four major methods, there are a variety of other weird ways to get records to the public. None of these is particularly meaningful, but we'll touch on them because companies include royalty computations for most of them in their deals. They are things like direct mail by the record company (which almost never happens), distribution through armed forces post exchanges, and sales to educational institutions and libraries.

So how does all this affect your royalties? To paraphrase George Orwell in *Animal Farm*, some record sales are more equal than others. Royalties for the exact same record can be quite different, depending on how and where it's distributed. For example, a record that sells in a U.S. record store at full price will bear a higher royalty than the same record when it's sold outside the United States, or through an army post exchange. It's especially fun to watch how new technologies (such as digital delivery) go through predictable patterns of royalty shifts as they work their way from obscurity to the major way we deliver music. (See page 145 for an in-depth discussion of these patterns.)

Okay. Now you're ready to get into advanced royalty discussions. Let's boogie.

ROYALTIES FOR UNITED STATES SALES

We'll start first with United States sales, because, if you're signing to a U.S. company, all other sales are based on (i.e., a reduced percentage of) the rate for the United States.

The royalties we discussed in Chapters 7 and 9 are for records that meet *all* of the following criteria:

1. A CD or a digital download that is sold in the United States; *and*
2. The sale is:
   (a) At full price (meaning, today, a $9.00 to $10.00 wholesale price [PPD] for CDs, and approximately $7.00–$9.00 for digital albums);
   (b) Through normal retail channels;
   (c) By the company's normal distribution channels (meaning the customary wholesale distributor)

Sales that comply with 1 and 2 are known as **United States normal retail sales,** or sales through **USNRC,** meaning **U.S. normal retail channels.** The royalty rate for these sales is usually defined in record deals as something like the **U.S. basic rate.** For simplicity, let's assume that your U.S. basic rate is 10% of PPD; that makes the percentage reductions easy to follow.

FOREIGN ROYALTIES

The royalty reduction for sales outside the United States varies widely from company to company, and artist to artist. As a broad rule, companies usually give a higher rate in the "major" territories and in territories where they have an ownership interest in the foreign distributor (today the majors all have worldwide operations). Conversely, they give a lesser royalty in "minor" territories and in territories where they are only licensing their product to a wholly independent third party.

Here's the most common pattern:

Canada

Canada has evolved into 85% of the United States rate with most companies, although some still treat it like any other "major" foreign territory (see the next paragraph). Using our example of a 10% U.S. basic rate, an 85% rate means you'd get 8.5% for normal retail sales in Canada. With clout you can sometimes get 90%.

Major Territories

There are a number of markets in which American product sells particularly well, and these are known as the "major" territories. They of course vary from artist to artist, but in general they are (in no particular order): United Kingdom, Australia, Italy, Japan, Holland, Germany, and France. (By the way, France is one of the strangest record markets on this planet. Records that are total dogs in all other territories can be gigantic smashes in France, and vice versa. France is also the only country in Europe to have a television system totally incompatible with the rest of Europe, as well as with the United States. Go figure.)

The remaining European Union countries (Western Europe) and Scandinavia can be treated as "majors" if you have some clout.

The royalty for major territories again varies for the reasons set forth above (ownership versus licensing, artist clout), but it's generally 70% to 75% of the U.S. basic rate, or 7% to 7.5% of PPD in our example. With clout, you can get this up to 80%, and sometimes a bit higher for the U.K. (like 85%).

R.O.W.

R.O.W. stands for **rest of world** and means the grab bag of countries left over, which I'll leave to you and Google Maps to name. The royalty for these generally runs around 50% to 66.66% of the U.S. basic rate, or 5% to 6.66% of PPD under our assumption. If you have bargaining power, you can sometimes edge this up a bit, to 70% or so.

Having stated the general rules, let me say that if you're an artist with a huge following in any particular territory, you can usually negotiate a better royalty for that country. Superstars can get better royalties than others, but the top for an artist signed to a U.S. company is usually around 16% to 17% for the major territories, and 13% to 14% elsewhere, unless you have extraordinary bargaining power.

RESERVE LIMITATIONS

When you're a midlevel to major artist, you can sometimes get a limit on album reserves, and if you do, it will be around 35% to 50% of the records shipped. (Reserves are discussed on page 79.) This has gotten harder as CD sales dry up and the risk of overshipping gets worse. Of course, by the same token, dwindling CD sales mean that reserves are less of a money issue.

These days, the companies just want to say "reasonable reserves," and that language is better than nothing at all. It at least gives you the right to argue with them if you think they're taking too much.

You should make sure that your agreement says they can't take reserves on digital exploitations (though most companies won't do this, even if their agreement says otherwise). Digital sales are what the industry calls **one-way,** meaning that they can't be returned (other than the occasional corrupted file, and usually that's just a replacement). Therefore there's no reason to hold a reserve.

At midlevel and up, you can also force the company to liquidate (pay out) the reserves over a set period of time, usually two years. Try to make the liquidation **ratable,** meaning they have to pay an equal amount each time. For example, if the company has to liquidate your reserves over two years, that means four six-month accounting periods. If they must liquidate *ratably,* they have to pay you one-fourth of the reserves in each of the four periods. If you don't say this, they could pay you a small percentage in the first three periods and hold the bulk of your money until the end.

As a newer artist, you won't likely get any cap on reserves, so you'll have to live with the "reasonable" language we just discussed. By the way, the amount of reserves a record company holds will be larger if you're a new artist. When you're new, they hold back more money because there's no history to judge whether your sales will stick or bounce back like little rubber balls.

On the other hand . . .

SOUNDSCAN

A company called SoundScan measures how many records are sold at retail. They sign up stores, who report their cash register sales to SoundScan, and they also track online sales. SoundScan's data is used for *Billboard*'s charts and is also sold to record companies and other users.

SoundScan isn't 100% accurate for physical sales—they get exact information from a substantial portion of the retail market, then statistically extrapolate the rest. For mainstream records, I understand it's a very good snapshot of the marketplace. However, I'm told that records which sell primarily in independent stores and other outlets that aren't measured by SoundScan may be reported low. Still, it's the most accurate measure we have for physical goods.

Sometimes record companies will agree that reserves can't exceed their shipments less the SoundScan numbers, or less SoundScan plus 10%. In other words, if they shipped 100,000 albums, and SoundScan showed 80,000 sold, the reserve couldn't exceed 20,000 to 22,000 (the 100,000 shipped, less the 80,000 that SoundScan said were sold, plus a 10% cushion). This is definitely worth asking for.

In theory, SoundScan is totally accurate for digital downloads. When the record companies license digital rights to a reseller, they require them to report their sales to SoundScan—more sales helps the chart position of the record, and it also helps bolster the company's overall market share.

MASTER LICENSES

Historically, when masters were licensed by a record company for motion pictures, television shows, and commercials, the company credited the artist's account with 50% of the company's net receipts, which meant the amount paid by the user, less costs of duplication, shipping, etc. Over recent years, a fee for handling master licenses has crept into these deals. Nowadays, as we discussed earlier, all of the major record companies have what's called a **special markets** or **catalog** division, whose job is to take existing recordings and come up with ways to squeeze money out of them. For example, they promote the use of their masters in motion pictures, pitch them for commercials, put together compilation records (which we'll discuss in a minute), etc. To cover the cost of these special marketing divisions, some of the companies try to get a fee of 15% to 25% of master license receipts, which comes off the top before splitting with the artist. For example, if they get $100 for a license, and have a 20% fee, they take off $20 for special marketing, then credit the artist with 50% of the remaining $80 ($40). (In essence, all they're doing is changing the artist's split by using mirrors. In this example, the artist's 50% equaled $40 out of $100. They could have just as easily eliminated the 20% fee and said the artist gets 40%, which equals the same $40. However, that doesn't sound as good as 50%, so the charade persists.)

With enough bargaining power, you can squeeze down or eliminate the company's overhead fee.

ELECTRONIC TRANSMISSIONS, INCLUDING DIGITAL DOWNLOADS, DIGITAL STREAMING, AND THINGS THAT GO BUMP IN THE NIGHT

To record companies, every delivery of music that isn't physical is an **electronic transmission.** As you'd expect, this means download and streaming, but it includes much, much more. Typical contract language goes something like this: "Any transmission or delivery to a consumer, whether sound alone or with other data, by any means now known or hereafter discovered, whether on demand or not, and whether or not a charge is made for the transmission or delivery."

So . . . did you notice this also picks up radio, TV, and motion pictures? More about that later.

Before we hit the specifics, let me give you:

The Passman Theory of Technology Cycles

There are predictable patterns that take place every time a new technology hits the record industry. It goes something like this:

1. The record companies scramble to see what their contracts say about these devices or delivery systems. Since they didn't exist when the deal was made, the contract doesn't deal with them at all, or if it does, it usually pays a royalty that is too high now that the fantasy is a reality.
2. Because the technology is so new, no one (including the record companies) really understands its economics. Also, when it's first introduced, the thing is usually expensive, because it's a

small market. For example, when digital started, the companies had to take all their analog music and turn it into digital, as well as add metadata (see page 155 for what that is), and set up systems to keep track of the millions of digital uses, to make sure they got paid. All this while the music earned zippo.

3. The result is a grace period during which royalties on these newbies are not particularly favorable to the artist. This is to give the technology a chance to get off the ground, and to help the record company justify the financial risk.

4. Invariably, this grace period goes on far beyond its economic life, during which time the companies make disproportionate profits, and the artist gets a smaller share than he or she gets on the dominant technology.

5. As artist deals expire or are renegotiated, the rate goes up.

6. Finally, an industry pattern develops and royalty rates stabilize.

Electronic Transmission Royalties

Right now, we're well past the "what the hell is happening?" phase, and artist royalty rates for electronic transmissions are pretty much established. Before we discuss them, here's an overview of what's currently going down (no guarantee this won't be out of date fifteen minutes after I finish the book):

1. **Digital downloads.** A *digital download*, which is also called a **DPD** (standing for *digital phonorecord delivery*), is a transmission to the consumer (via Internet, satellite, cell phone, mental telepathy, etc.) that allows the buyer to download music for later use. In essence, it's the sale of a record electronically—instead of purchasing a physical copy, you buy the digital file. Examples are the iTunes download store and ringtones.

    There are two kinds of downloads:

    (a) **Permanent downloads.** As the name implies, it's yours forever, and you can copy it, burn it, stomp it, or do anything else your little heart desires. Well, actually not "anything." When you sign up with a digital retailer, the fine print you never bother to read before you click "Accept" contains something called an **End-User License Agreement** (the fraternity boys know her as **EULA**). In that hot little piece of literature, buried among exciting words and phrases, it says that the downloads are only for your personal, non-commercial use.

(b) Tethered downloads. *Tether*, which is a fancy word for *leash*, means the service provider doesn't give you complete control over the download. These are also known as **conditional downloads.** For example, Spotify allows you to load songs onto your phone so you can listen offline, but if you stop paying your subscription, they send little gnomes over the Internet to eat up the music. Another example would be a song you can download to your phone but can't copy onto another device. Or one you can listen to but not hear anything (these are the cheapest).

2. **Non-interactive webcasting. Webcasting** means streaming stuff over the Internet, and **non-interactive** means you can only hear what the programmer decides to play (just like over-the-air radio stations). Pandora is by far the biggest non-interactive streamer (though they had a little squabble over whether they were really non-interactive, as we'll discuss later). Another example is iHeartRadio, and there are tons of local radio **simulcasts** (meaning a broadcast at the same time both over the air and on the Internet. For example, the local FM station in Cow Springs, Arizona, streams its signal over the net at the same time it goes out on the air). On a smaller scale, there are individual webcasters who put together music they think is cool and send it out to the world.

Most of these webcasts are advertiser supported, but they can be paid subscription as well.

3. **On-demand streaming.** In contrast to non-interactive webcasting, on-demand streaming is an **interactive** service. This means you can listen to any songs in the service's database, any time you like, and you can pause, skip, rewind, and create playlists. However, you're not allowed to copy; just listen.

Examples of interactive services are Spotify, Apple Music, Rhapsody, SoundCloud, and Rdio. Essentially, these services are virtual jukeboxes. On a broader level, they are a form of **cloud server,** which means a remote server that stores any kind of data, then allows users to access it from wherever they are (like Dropbox, Google Drive, and Microsoft's SkyDrive). So, in essence, interactive services are cloud servers devoted to music.

As of this writing, Spotify and Rdio are the only major companies that offer on-demand streams for free (if you don't mind listening to annoying ads). (Pandora offers a free service as well, but it's not interactive.) However, as we'll discuss in a minute, there is pressure on them to move to a subscription-only basis, meaning the user has to pay a monthly fee to get their service. (Services that are subscription-only sometimes offer a free introductory period to try it out, but it's for a limited time. Spotify and Rdio are now unlimited.)

In the future, I think it's clear that on-demand streaming will become the biggest part of the business. At the time of this writing, streaming is about 16% of the recorded music income (up from a little over 14% the year before), and Billboard now uses streams as a measure of their chart success. As of this writing, there are over 25 million paying subscribers (I'm sure there will be more by the time you read this), and the advertiser-supported users are a multiple of several times that number. In contrast, digital download sales have dropped around 15% per year for several years, and CD sales are falling off a cliff. After all, if you can get unlimited music for a monthly fee, you don't need to buy as much.

The industry today is about half what it was a few years ago, but as streaming spreads more and more, I think the industry can be bigger than it's ever been. Let me explain.

Spotify makes an interesting argument along these lines: In the heyday of the music biz, the average consumer spent $40 per year on CDs. If subscribers pay $10 per month, that's $120 per year—three times what people spent on CDs.

I would also add that on-demand subscribers include people who would have never gone to a record store (when those existed). For the most part, people stop buying mainstream pop music when they get past their early 20s, but if they subscribe to a streaming service, we can keep them in our eco-system for a long, long time. (I know there's an argument that this generation has been trained to get music for free, and that's true, but these same folks will have no problem paying for cable TV or a mobile phone service, so I think it's just a matter of mindshift).

However, there is a problem with Spotify's argument that they're getting a lot more money per user. As we discussed, Spotify offers a free ad-supported service, then hopes you'll pay a subscription fee to lose the ads. This ad-supported service is called **freemium** in the biz, because in the beginning Spotify only allowed its free service on your PC, meaning you had to pay for their premium service (without ads) to get Spotify on your mobile device. That worked for a while, but music consumers moved so heavily over to mobile that they felt they had to allow the full service on mobile to bring in customers, so its service is a *free premium*, or *freemium*.

At the time of this writing, Spotify freemium users outnumber paid subscribers about three to one. The reason that's a problem is because freemium brings in *way* less money than paid subscribers. Over-the-air radio has about 14 to 16 minutes per hour of advertising, while Spotify has much less. That means: (a) Spotify ads don't generate a lot of money (the rates are cheaper and there's not much time sold); and (b) there is not enough advertising to annoy people into paying a subscription fee.

Accordingly, the $120 per year from subscribers is majorly diluted by the freebie users. Which means the earnings per stream come out to a much smaller number than they would on a pure subscription service (like Apple Music). For example (and I'm making up numbers), assume Spotify had only 1 paid subscriber and 3 freemium users. If it got $2 from each paid subscriber and fifty cents per subscriber for the ads played to freemium users, it would get $3.50 for the 4 users ($2 for the paid guy, and three times $.50 for the other 3). That's an average of 87.5 cents per user ($3.50 divided by 4), which is obviously far less than the $2 per paid subscriber).

So, now you understand why the music biz is pressuring Spotify toward paid subscription.

Newer services, like Apple Music, are offering only a paid subscription (no freemium, other than a three-month introductory period). Spotify argues that they need their free service to get people into the habit of listening, and then they can convert them to paying subscribers. But since the ratio is (today) three to one for free vs. pay, the companies have been impatient with the slow rate of conversion.

As I write this, the fight is still raging, so it remains to be seen how things shake out.

An even bigger problem is that some services (like YouTube and Vevo) offer *video* streaming on demand for free. In other words, you can call up your favorite artist's music videos and watch to your little heart's content, make playlists, and even turn off the video to essentially get free music. A few video subscription services are starting up, and some audio subscription services are talking about adding on-demand videos, but the massive majority of video streaming is free.

Now, why is this a problem for the industry?

Well, can you guess who delivers more audio content than any other website? In fact, more than all the other sites put together, including the pirate sites? It's . . .

YouTube.

As we just discussed, the free, ad-supported service dilutes Spotify's revenue, and this problem is on steroids when it comes to YouTube, who doesn't have any paid service other than Google Play, which doesn't earn much. When you put that together with the fact that YouTube delivers more music than anyone else, it means they pay *very*, very little. It also means the paying services have to compete with "free."

Despite all this, paid on-demand streaming is growing nicely. You can do the math and see that if there are 25 million paid subscribers at $10 per month, that's $250,000,000 per month, or $3 billion per year. That's of course nowhere near the $13-billion-dollar industry we used to be, but this rapid growth shows the potential to grow the music business larger than it's ever been in history.

Now, how that money trickles down to the artist is also part of the current battle, which we'll talk about later.

So stay tuned for the exciting season finale.

4. **Ringtones** and **ringbacks.** *Ringtones* are short clips of songs that play when your cell phone rings. *Ringbacks* happen when you call someone and instead of hearing an annoying ringing signal, you hear an annoying song. Ringtones are something you download and own, while ringbacks are held on the server of the phone service provider, so you're only "renting" them.

Ringtones started out as **polyphonic,** which means the song was played by a synthesizer, but nowadays almost all of them are the actual master recording by the artist (called a **mastertone** or a **truetone**). If it's polyphonic, you have nothing to do with it as an artist—the only one who gets paid is the songwriter (we'll discuss how much the songwriter gets on page 254). If it's a master recording, the record company gets paid, and then pays you.

Ringtones were at one time a surprisingly strong business

(doing sales in the billions per year), but they took a major nose-dive when it became easy to make your own for free. Currently they're not a big source of income.

5. **Lockers.** A *locker* is a place where you can store your music on someone else's server, then stream it to yourself whenever you want (to your mobile phone, home computer, etc.). Lockers are also a type of cloud service (which we discussed on page 147). At the time of this writing, Apple, Amazon, and Google offer locker services.

    There are two different locker models: **upload lockers** require you to upload your own music, then allow you to access it from wherever you want, and in essence are just a music-optimized cloud service like Dropbox. **Full lockers** don't require you to upload your music. Instead, they send little elves over the Internet to your computer, who match the songs on your device against the ones already sitting on their cloud, then allow you to stream their copy whenever you want (this process is called **scan and match**). The advantages are that you don't have to spend hours uploading your collection, and also that you get access to a high-quality recording on their system, even if yours is a low-quality one. The only exceptions are things they find but can't match to something already on their system (like a live recording you made at a concert, or your significant other's sexy voicemail), which they then upload.

    At the time of this writing, the full lockers are charging for their service (though Google gives it to you free when you use their Google Play service), while the upload lockers are free.

6. **Bundled services.** A *bundled service* is a combination of products (a "bundle" of products) that you get for a single price. For example, if you buy a CD, you get a code that allows you to download the album for free. Or you get a streaming service if you subscribe to Amazon Prime.

7. **Satellite radio.** For a monthly fee, you get music via satellite radio or as an audio channel on your television. Sirius XM is by far the largest one. The channels are non-interactive, meaning you have to listen to whatever they decide to play. And unlike Pandora, you can't skip songs or customize the content (other than by changing channels, which has been a form of interactivity since a second radio broadcaster started in the 1920s).

8. **Apps.** *Apps*, in case you've been living in a cave, mean little programs you install on your smartphone or tablet. Most of them

don't use music at all, but some are very music-based, such as allowing you to identify songs (like Shazam or SoundHound), edit a preloaded song, learn to play an instrument, or play a game that uses the song as an integral part (like Tap Tap).

9. **Podcasting.** This is a download of a program, such as an interview with an artist, or a radio show like *This American Life*, maybe with some songs interspersed. Usually it's free to the user, as the websites sell advertising around it. At the time of this writing, there's no industry standard for podcasts, and as streams take off, they're not as big an issue as they once were.

The record companies don't want full songs in podcasts, because they could displace a paid download of the song, so if they allow their music to be podcast, they limit each song to thirty seconds or so (which is viewed as promotional), or maybe longer for developing artists. Sometimes they insist on a voice-over during the song.

Now, having given you a detailed play-by-play, it's time to tell you that music industry gurus lump all of the above technologies into two buckets:

1. **Permanent downloads** (meaning the kind you buy on iTunes and own forever, which includes ringtones); and
2. **Streaming.** In industry parlance, streaming includes everything that isn't a permanent download, such as on-demand streaming, tethered downloads (which they think of as another way to deliver a stream on demand), interactive and non-interactive streaming services, satellite radio, lockers, apps, bundled services (just a fancy way to deliver streaming), ringbacks (remember, those aren't downloaded), and armadillos (just kidding about the last one; sometimes my Texas roots leak through).

So what do you get paid for all these electronic transmissions? After a lot of stumbling around, the industry settled into a routine between the companies and the artists. Under all the record deals made in the last few years, and in the renegotiations of older deals, you get a percentage (usually your royalty rate) applied to the amount received by your record company. So if you have a 15% royalty, and they get $100, you get $15. If you look back at my theory of technology cycles (on page 145), I am certain that the artist's percentage of electronic transmissions will move up as time goes on. However, this is where we are now.

What exactly do artists get a piece of? Essentially, the companies that deliver digital products to the public (called **DSPs,** meaning **Digital Service Providers**) pay about 70% of their income for music rights. This includes *both* the master rights and the rights to the songs (we'll discuss what songwriters get later), which means the record companies don't get the full 70% (they get 70% less what the songwriters get, though in some cases they collect the full 70% and then pay the songwriters).

Here's more specifics:

1. For iTunes-type **permanent downloads,** the record companies get what they call a "wholesale price" equal to 70% of the retail price. So, for example, they get about 91¢ for a 1.29¢ download.

   In the case of downloads, the U.S. record companies get the money for both themselves and the songwriters, then turn around and pay the songwriter. (Technically, they pay the publishers, who are the folks that collect for the songwriters, but we haven't talked about them yet, so for now I'll just call them "songwriters.") This is the same way it works for physical CDs, and it means you get paid on the full amount that the record company gets (the 91¢ in the above example), in the same way that your CD royalty is based on the full wholesale price. So if you have a 10% royalty and the record company gets 91¢, you'll get 9.1¢. (Outside the U.S., DSPs pay the songwriters directly, so the record companies get only their share of the money).

   Why do the record companies call it a "wholesale price"? Well, under record deals made before digital rights existed, artists got 50% of all income from licensing masters. So when downloads came along, the record companies did everything they could to treat downloads as "sales" of records, and not "licenses." That way they could pay the artist's royalty percentage (generally 10% to 20%) of these monies, as opposed to the 50% licensing percentage.

   You may have seen news stories about artists filing lawsuits against record companies, claiming that downloads aren't really "sales" but are in fact "licenses." These cases are based on the licensing language we just discussed, and the artists argue they are entitled to 50% of the earnings. The companies feel otherwise.

   The highest-profile of these cases was brought by Eminem (for you technical freaks, the case was actually brought by the production company to whom Eminem was signed, and the cite is *FBT Productions, LLC v. Aftermath Records* 621 F. 3d 958 (2010)). The record company won this case in the trial court (the court said downloads were a sale, not a license), but lost on appeal (turns out they were a license after all). The record company then asked the U.S. Supreme Court for their thoughts. When the Supreme Court refused to hear the appeal, the case was over and the record company grumbled off to write a check.

In addition to Eminem, there were some **class actions** (meaning an action on behalf of everyone in the same situation), plus a few cases brought by individual artists making the same claim. At the time of this writing, most of these have settled.

Interestingly, this argument doesn't affect as many artists as you might think. First, it very much depends on the specific language in each contract—in the Eminem case, the record company claims the language was a mistake, because they were using a short-form agreement, and not a long-form contract that would have spelled this out. Second, most of the bigger artists have renegotiated their deals in the last five to ten years, and when that happened, the record companies stuck in clauses that specified what they got for digital exploitations, regardless of whether it was a sale, a license, or a horned toad. Third, even if the artist didn't renegotiate, the successful artists have **audited** their record companies (meaning they sent over an accountant to look at the company's books and see if the artist was paid properly). When the artists settled these audits (in other words, they gave up their claims and got a chunk of money), most companies fixed the digital royalty rate from the end of the audit period into the future. And even if they didn't do that, they settled all the claims for the past, so there isn't a lot of back money sitting out there. You may be wondering why the record company thinks it should get such a big chunk of download money. In other words, if an artist has a 15% royalty, why should the record company keep 85% of the digital wholesale price? They could justify a big chunk of the CD monies, because they had to pay for manufacturing, shipping, returns, etc., but none of those exist for digital sales. Isn't the profit on digital much bigger?

The companies argue that they are making roughly the same percentage profit margin on digital sales as they did on physical product. They still pay unions (see page 199) and songwriters, and in fact the songwriter monies are often higher on digital sales (for reasons we'll discuss on page 251, but don't skip ahead because you need more information before you can really understand it). As we discussed on page 70 the companies also argue that they have expenses for digitizing product, adding **metadata** (the information that tells the user the name of the song, artist, album, who to pay, etc.), storing digital files, setting up **SKUs** for each title (SKU means **Stock Keeping Unit,** and it's like a bar code for each version of a master, to keep track of who gets paid), as well as monitoring the sales and licensing of millions of micro-transactions. In addition, they need to allocate some portion of the cost of their staff that does marketing, sales, etc.

As we discussed in my theory of technology cycles (page 145), it's really hard to tell, even at this stage of digital rights, whether this is fair. It's possible that it is. However, if history is an example, I expect digital royalty rates will climb as the technology grows.

2. For **ringtones,** the companies get about 50% of the retail price charged to the customer, sometimes with a minimum amount per sale (the minimum puts a floor on what the record company gets, no matter how low the ringtone folks drop the price). So if a ringtone is $2.00, they get $1.00, and if you have a 10% royalty, you'll get 10¢.

Just like downloads, the U.S. companies pay the songwriters, but you're paid on the full amount they get. Outside the U.S., the ringtone companies pay the publishers and record companies separately, but the total comes out to about the same 50%.

3. **On-demand audio streaming deals** pay the record companies about 60% of the advertising revenue and/or subscription fees, pro-rated for each master based on the number of plays. (The record companies don't pay the songwriters for this or any of the other uses we're going to discuss [except certain videos], which means your royalty is applied to a lower amount for these uses. In these cases, the digital service provider (DSP) pays the songwriters, and we'll talk about how much on page 274)).

At this writing, the DSPs are putting pressure on the labels to reduce the 60%, arguing that they need the money for marketing. Also, the songwriters are pressing for more money, which also puts pressure on that figure. So it may be heading south.

For subscription services, most of these deals have a **per-subscriber minimum,** also called a **per sub** minimum, meaning the company gets a certain amount for each of the DSP's subscribers, regardless of what the DSP actually collects. For example, the deal might say that payment for the service's use of master recordings can't be less than 60% of $10 per subscriber. This is to discourage the DSPs from dropping their prices too low; the companies are worried the DSPs might do this just to build up subscribers. Or to drive traffic to another product, similar to a big retailer who discounts CDs just to bring in people who buy toaster ovens.

This per-subscriber minimum is pro-rated amongst all the masters, based on the number of plays. Here's how it works, using the above example: The DSP is obligated to pay a total of $6 per subscriber (60% of $10) for all the masters that it uses. If your company's masters were 30% of the DSP's total streams in a month, they'd get 30% of the $6, or $1.80 for each subscriber. This $1.80 is then prorated over all your company's masters, based on each master's number of plays.

For example, assume your masters were streamed 200,000 times in a month, and all of your company's masters were streamed 1,000,000 times. That means your streams were 20% of the company's streams (200,000/1,000,000), and therefore 36¢ per subscriber (20% of $1.80) would be attributed to your masters. You would then get your royalty rate based on that, so if you had a 10% royalty, you'd get 3.6¢ per subscriber. (Of course, if 60% of subscriber fees are worth more than $6, you'd get more money, which would be allocated the same way).

A hot issue around subscription services today is **breakage.** Particularly for newer services, the record companies ask for advances against their streaming income (because new companies have this nasty habit of going broke and stiffing record companies). The record labels sometimes also get stock in the DSP as part of their license, or they might buy the stock as an investment.

Here's how breakage works. Assume your record company gave a two-year license to a DSP and got a $1-million advance (I'm making up numbers for the example—they actually get much more than that). At the end of the two years, the company may have only earned $600,000, so $400,000 of the $1 million is unrecouped. This $400,000 is called *breakage*, and the company gets to keep it because the advance was non-returnable. The question is, do the artists share in it? The companies argue that it's not payment for use of your masters, so you haven't earned a piece of it. We who represent artists argue that there wouldn't be an advance if there weren't any artists in the catalog, so they should divvy it up with all the artists.

It's worth asking for a piece of breakage in your deal, and some companies are willing to do it (in fact, some do it even if it's not in your deal), but others fight back hard. Some (but not all) companies will also share the money they make from taking stock in the DSP if they got it as part of a license. None of the companies want to share proceeds from stock they purchased, on the theory that it's an investment they made with their own funds, and they took all the risk that it would flop. We argue that they couldn't have made the investment without the masters in their catalog, but so far without success.

4. For **non-interactive webcasting** and **satellite radio**, the copyright law requires record companies to license their masters at a rate set by the government (we'll talk more about this on page 347). The money is collected by an outfit called **SoundExchange** (more about them on page 347).

    Under a very cool system, SoundExchange pays a portion of the money to the record company, and a portion directly to the artist. So you don't get any share of what the company gets, but the monies you get directly are outside your record deal. That means the company can't use them to recoup your advances. Very good news.

    Exactly what gets paid is pretty complicated, and I want you to stay awake for the moment, so I stuck them further back in the book (on page 348 if you can't wait). In general, Sirius XM pays a percentage of their advertising revenue and subscription fees, non-interactive webcasters pay a fee for each time they play your master, and Pandora is a mix.

5. For **upload lockers** (where you upload your music to their server), you may be surprised to hear that they pay nothing to the record companies (or to any other rights-holders). They argue that (a) uploading to their server is exactly the same as if you made a copy on your home computer—no one but you can access it; (b) personal, homemade copies are exempt from the U.S. copyright law (as we'll discuss on page 294); and therefore (c) the upload lockers don't need the copyright owner's permission. In fact, that's all probably true, at least in the United States. However, it's not necessarily true in other territories, where they don't have a personal-copy exemption in their copyright laws,

and at the time of this writing, the upload lockers have only launched in the United States.

The **full lockers** (who scan and match your music to theirs) have to pay all the rights-holders, because they need the right to copy songs onto their server and the right to stream them back to you. These models share revenue with the record company at somewhat under the 60% rate because they pay more to songwriters than the other services, which we'll discuss on page 278.

6. **Bundled services** are all over the map, and unfortunately can't be generalized. It depends on what music is offered, whether you automatically get the music as part of the purchase or whether you pay additional money for it (called an **add-on**), what the other product is, how much the service is getting for the bundle, and what the executives had for breakfast. Some deals are a flat fee, some a percentage of revenue, and some a bundle of $100 bills in a leather satchel (just kidding about the last one, in case you're taking notes).

7. **Video streaming** deals are around 70%, including both the record company and the songwriters. (We'll discuss what songwriters get on page 278.) For record company–produced videos, the streaming services pay 70% to the record companies, who (in the U.S. and sometimes Canada) pay both the artist and the songwriter. Outside those territories, the service pays the songwriter money to a collection society, which means the record company gets a smaller percentage (generally 70% minus what they pay for the songwriter).

All other videos that use music (such as a little old lady dancing to a Nas track) are called **user-generated content** (known in the trade as **UGC**). For those, the record company is paid only for use of the master, and the songwriter is paid separately by the service. If the UGC is a video of someone sitting at a piano and playing a song, then the record company gets nothing because it's not a use of their recording. Only the songwriters get paid, and we'll talk about what they get later (on page 278).

8. **Apps.** Here we're talking about apps that use music either primarily (like Garage Band, karaoke apps, instructional music apps, etc.) or secondarily (like Flipagram, Sayic, or a video game with music in the background). I'm not talking about apps that just let you access streaming music, such as Spotify, Apple Music, or iHeartRadio, as those were covered above.

The payment for music in apps has taken more shape than it had in my last edition, but it's still a work in progress.If the app isn't primarily a music product (for example, a game where you chase turkeys around the barnyard while listening to Flo Rida), the deal is usually a flat fee in the range of $500 to $10,000 per song, depending on usage and the stature of the song. The licenses are always short—generally one year to eighteen months—so if the app succeeds, the publishers can go back and price accordingly.

If an app is monetized, meaning it generates money after the initial download (for example ad sales, subscription fees, in-app purchases, emoticons, virtual currency, etc.) there may be a revenue share on top of the fee, running anywhere from 15% to 35%, depending on usage and the song. In computing these percentages, the app developer first deducts a 30% fee that is charged by the platform (e.g., the iTunes store). So the label only gets its share of the 70% that the app developer gets. For example, if an app sells for a dollar, iTunes takes 30 cents for selling the app, and the app developer gets 70 cents. If your company's share of the money is 20%, it gets that portion of the 70 cents, meaning 14 cents.

If there are downloads through the app, there may also be a minimum number of pennies per download.

In these deals, there's almost always an advance against the royalty. The amount is totally dependent on the specific situation, importance of the song, and the nature of the use. It can run from a hundred dollars per song into the thousands.

Even if the app has no revenue after the initial download, the record companies sometimes charge a yearly fee (a flat fee or a minimum per user) for as long as your music is in the app. The app developers are willing to pay this, even though they're coming out of pocket to pay it, because they're more interested in building users (which makes their business more valuable) than making a profit in the short-term.

You might be surprised to hear that song-identifiers like Shazam and SoundHound don't pay for music at all. That's because they don't actually have any music in their apps. All they do is digitally **fingerprint** the music (meaning they break it down into little digital chunks), then match those identifiers against what they're "hearing."

As I said at the outset, this area is still developing, so none of the above is set in stone. The ground is still shifting, and the house may crack a few times before it settles.

9. **Podcasts** are pretty much done on a flat fee basis, sometimes with a percentage of the ad revenues. The fees are small, and there aren't really any standards.

COUPLING AND COMPILATIONS

The practice of putting your performances on records with performances of other artists is known as **coupling,** and albums with a bunch of different artists are called **compilations.** They include television-advertised compilation albums (*Texas Punk Bands of the Sixties,* etc.); soundtrack albums from motion pictures with diverse music (*O Brother, Where Art Thou?*; *Pulp Fiction*; etc.); and any other marketing device the record companies can dream up.

The digital business (where you can buy or stream all the individual tracks you like) has slaughtered these kinds of projects. If compilations exist at all, they sell a fraction of what they could rack up in their glory days. The only exceptions are the NOW series, which seems to be doing reasonably well, and soundtracks have picked up a little from their deepest slump.

Royalties

The royalty on coupled product sold by your record company is pretty much what you'd think—if there are ten cuts on the album and you did one of them, you get one-tenth of your normal royalty; if you did two cuts out of ten, you get 20%, etc. This process is called **pro-ration,** and you are said to have a **pro-rata** royalty (meaning your royalty is in proportion to the number of cuts on the album). (Every once in a while *pro-ration* is based on the playing time of your cut versus the total playing time of the record, but this is rare. It's almost always based solely on the number of cuts.)

The royalty on coupled product that's licensed to someone else by your record company is usually 50% of the company's licensing receipts, sometimes less the overhead fee we discussed for other licensing (on page 203). Remember, in an all-in royalty deal, your half includes the producer's royalty (the producer's share of this is discussed on page 124).

Control

You should always try to control coupling, both for (1) the artistic reason that you don't want to be on a record with someone you hate; and (2) the financial reason that you don't want to be the major cut selling an album of dorks when you only get a small part of the royalty. With moderate bargaining power, you can control this during the term of your deal, but the companies carve out things like playlists on streaming services, kiosks, jukeboxes, in-transit uses (like inflight programs), and similar stuff. With more bargaining power, you can control it after the term if you're recouped. With massive clout, you can control it forever.

If you can get control, it's normally just for the United States, unless you have incredible bargaining power. These compilation albums are still a source of revenue in foreign territories, and the foreign licensees tend to do whatever they feel like, regardless of what your contract says.

Even as a new artist, you should at least be able to get a limit on the number of couplings. A common provision is to say the company can't couple more than two of your selections per year, and can't put you on more than two albums per year. Note the difference between these two concepts: If the company's only limit is two selections per year, they could put one of your hits on 37 different compilation albums.

JOINT RECORDINGS

A close cousin to coupling is a **joint recording** (keep the puns to yourself). A *joint recording* is where more than one royalty artist gets together on the same song, such as a duet. Unlike compilations, this is alive and well.

These are also called **guest artist** deals, because one of the artists is "guesting" on the other artist's record.

Royalty

The most common arrangement for joint recordings is to split the royalty among the artists in proportion to their numbers. So if it's a duet, each gets half; if it's a trio, each gets a third; etc. While this is usually pretty straightforward, there are a couple of twists:

1. If you do a duet with a five-piece group, be sure that the group only counts as one entity. Otherwise, the company might say

there are six royalty artists instead of two (you and the group), and you'll only get one-sixth of the royalty instead of one-half.

2. Whose royalty gets divided, yours or theirs? If you're the star, be sure your price is a share of *your* royalty, because it's likely to be higher than the other guy. If you're new and singing with a star, try for a piece of theirs.

   Whatever is divided, it's after deducting third-party expenses, like producers and mixers.

A lot of times, joint recordings are done on a "trade-out" basis (called a **swap** in the biz). In other words, if Sally records a duet on Fred's album, Fred agrees to record a duet on Sally's album some time down the road, and neither one pays anything to the other.

If the guest artist is also a writer, the artist who is signed to the label will ask the guest artist to go along with their controlled composition clause. That means nothing to you because we haven't talked about it yet, but it's a major point, so stick around; we'll get to that baby on page 252.

Control

It's easy to get control over joint recordings. Just ask and the record company will readily agree. The reason they're so cooperative is pretty simple—no one goes into the studio with someone he or she doesn't like.

"GREATEST HITS" ALBUMS

The royalties on Greatest Hits albums (see page 116 for what a Greatest Hits album is) are pro-rata royalties (see page 160), based on the album they come from. For example, if your first two albums were 12%, and the others 13%, and if half the Greatest Hits album was from the first two albums (12%) and half from the others (13%), your royalty on the Greatest Hits album would be 12.5% (50% times 12%, plus 50% times 13%). But these calculations are trickier than they seem.

For example, suppose that some of the earlier albums had royalty escalations because of sales success (see page 95). Which royalty do you use? The initial release royalty? The escalated royalty? And do you also get an escalation based on sales of the Greatest Hits album itself?

The answer is usually one of three:

1. You get the lowest royalty for the album from which each selection is taken (i.e., the royalty before any escalations based on sales of that album), and then a negotiated escalation based on sales of the Greatest Hits album. Under this formula, the starting royalty is pro-rated based on non-escalated rates.
2. You get the highest royalty rate achieved by the album from which the selection is taken (i.e., the escalated rate based on sales of that album) with no further escalations for sales of the Greatest Hits album. These rates are then pro-rated the same way we did it in the first example.
3. You get the lowest possible rate and no escalations for anything. This is what you get if you don't ask.

Let's look at examples of the first two:

1. Suppose a Greatest Hits album contains ten selections, consisting of three selections from the initial term, when your rate (before escalations) was 10%; two selections from the first option period, when your (non-escalated) rate was 11%; and five selections from the second option period, when your (non-escalated) rate was 12%.

    Under the first approach (no escalations count), the result would be the following:

Masters	Album Royalty
3 Masters recorded during initial term: These masters are $\frac{3}{10}$ of the album (30%), because 3 of the 10 selections on the album are at this rate. Thus, the royalty for these cuts is 30% of 10% (the initial period royalty):	3.0%
2 Masters recorded during first option term: 2 of 10 (20%), at 11%:	2.2%
5 Masters recorded during second option term: 5 of 10 (50%), at 12%	6.0%
TOTAL ROYALTY ON ALBUM	**11.2%**

This 11.2% royalty might then escalate based on sales of the Greatest Hits album. For example, you might get an additional

1% (to 12.2%) at 1 million units, and another 1% (to 13.2%) at 2 million.

2. Now let's look at the second method (where escalated royalties are pro-rated). We'll use the same figures as the first example, but assume the royalties on early albums escalated because of sales, to 12% for the album made in the first option period, and to 14% for the album made in the second option period. (Assume there are no escalations for the initial term album.)

Here's how the royalties look now:

Masters	Royalty
Initial Term: 3 of 10 (30%) at 10%:	3.0%
First Option Term: 2 of 10 (20%) at 12%:	2.4%
Second Option Term: 5 of 10 (50%) at 14%:	7.0%
TOTAL ROYALTY ON ALBUM	**12.4%**

As noted above, under this method there are no escalations for sales of the Greatest Hits album.

MULTIPLE ALBUMS

The **multiple album** has gone through an enormous change since vinyl fell off the cliff. Originally, it meant an album that couldn't fit on one vinyl disc, since vinyl discs were limited to a maximum of fifty-some-odd minutes of playing time. Then it meant more than one cassette. When CDs appeared, they could hold substantially more music than a vinyl disc or single cassette, so it took a lot of material to require two CDs. Thus *multiple albums* (in the classic sense of a two-CD package) have been rare. (Box sets of three or four CDs are a special category, which we'll discuss in the next section.)

Two-CD packages don't sell as well as single-CD packages, if for no other reason than the fact that they're more expensive (at the time of this writing, a double CD package has a PPD of $12 or $14, as opposed to roughly $10 for a single CD). Because of this, and serious mechanical royalty issues (we'll get to that on page 229), every form contract says you can't deliver a multiple-CD album without the company's consent.

If the company does consent, your royalty will likely be reduced. The reduction works like this: Your royalty is adjusted downward in the ratio that the selling price of the double album is less than two times the price of a single-album price. That's not as confusing as it sounds if we use numbers: For easy math, assume the PPD of a single-album CD is $10. That means you'd only get a full royalty for a double album if its PPD were doubled to $20 (i.e., if the company were getting the full price of two single albums). If the price of the double album is $15, that is only three-fourths (or 75%) of $20, so you'd get 75% of your normal royalty, applied against the $15 price. If your normal royalty is 10%, you'd get 7.5% (three-fourths of the 10%) for a $15 double-album set. Thus, even though the price is higher, you get a reduced royalty because the costs are more for the two CDs.

If an album has more than fourteen selections, even if it's on a single CD, some form contracts consider it a multiple album. Your royalty shouldn't be reduced for a single-CD album just because it has a lot of tracks, but many contracts would do that. Moreover, because the price of the single CD isn't increased (or if it is, maybe just a small amount), the PPD is nowhere near double that of a single album, so your royalty could be cut in half. Watch out for this.

Interestingly, most record contracts don't distinguish between multiple-CD albums and multiple digital albums. So, technically, your royalty could be reduced on a digital album if it falls within the definition of "multiple," even though they have no additional manufacturing costs. However, they do have to pay additional royalties to the songwriters, as we'll discuss later.

Regardless of how you define it, and no matter how your royalty gets computed, all record companies treat a multiple album as only one album for purposes of your delivery commitment. Accordingly, if you thought you'd knock out your obligation to deliver two albums with a multiple album, they got there ahead of you. Sorry.

BOX SETS

Box sets are a collection of three, four, or sometimes more CDs or vinyl sold in a single package, usually with an expensive booklet, and for a very high price. Usually these are retrospectives of an artist's career, and may contain unreleased cuts, alternative versions of well-known songs, demo recordings, compromising photos, etc. They can also be a retrospective of a company (for example, Capitol or Motown) or a genre (the Blues, the Definitive Polka), etc.

The royalties on box sets are always negotiated at the time, and are very specific to the particular package. They'll depend on the selling price, the number of selections (which affects the songwriters' royalties—we'll discuss those later), the size of the artist's original royalty rate, and your leverage. Unfortunately, there are no real guidelines, since each deal is made separately, except that there's almost always a reduced songwriter royalty, and usually a reduced artist royalty as well.

TELEVISION ADVERTISING

A number of years ago, record companies figured out (only in Europe at the time) that they could sell a lot of records by doing short bursts of television advertising. In fact, this worked so well that it quickly exported itself to America and other territories. However, television advertising is very expensive, and the companies said they couldn't afford it unless the artist gave them some kind of a break.

What kind of break?

Companies want to reduce your royalty on the advertised album to 50% for as long as they can get away with. They love to get two years, and I love to give them much less. Here are some things to ask for:

1. Get approval of the campaign before they can deduct anything. On several occasions, I've seen the company ask the artist for more money than the artist could make from the excess sales that the company expected to generate from the TV campaign.
2. Try to restrict the reduction to the sales occurring in the semiannual accounting period during which the campaign is launched and the following period (maybe a third period after that, if you have to). The idea is to keep the reduction period close to the campaign, so the reduction is only for those sales generated by the TV ads.
3. The total amount taken from your royalty shouldn't exceed half the cost of the campaign.
4. Make certain they can only reduce the royalties in those territories where the campaign is running—you'd be surprised what their little forms say about taking reductions everywhere.

As the music biz shrank, so did the TV advertising. Other than for the biggest selling acts, there isn't enough profit in the additional sales to pay for the TV ads. So today it's virtually nonexistent in the U.S., but it's still a factor in foreign territories for major artists. However, these provisions are in every deal, so you should get the best you can in case the biz rebounds and TV ads come back. More importantly, you want to be protected when you're the biggest-selling act on the label!

DVDS AND OTHER HOME VIDEO DEVICES

DVDs that are *purely audio* (a practice that is pretty much dead) are treated just like CDs.

If a DVD has a substantial video component (e.g., the entire album plus promotional videos), some companies pro-rate the royalties (see page 160 for discussion of pro-ration) between audio and video, meaning they pay your audio royalty on a portion, and your video royalty on a portion. The same thing happens if a package has both an audio and a video disc (like a studio album plus a video of a concert, or a portion of a concert). For example, if there's thirty minutes of music, and thirty minutes of video, you would get half of your audio royalty rate (thirty minutes over sixty minutes), plus half (thirty minutes over sixty minutes) of your video rate. Sometimes this is in the contract, and sometimes they just argue that's what the contract means.

So what's the video rate that they use for this? It's what they pay for a purely audiovisual DVD, like an audiovisual concert recording, and those royalties are:

Manufactured Units

If home video units are manufactured and distributed by your record company, you get a royalty that falls in the range of 10% to 20% of PPD for U.S. normal retail top-price sales. Most companies vary their royalty in this range depending on the wholesale price—for a higher price, you get a higher royalty. Foreign royalties tend to be the same proportionate reduction of your U.S. royalty as you get for CDs (e.g., 85% for Canada, 75% for major territories, etc.). All royalties are reduced for very low-priced videos, called **budget line** (usually to a one-half royalty), and they don't pay you on free goods. (Budget-line records are discussed on page 170, and the same idea applies to home video devices.)

Recently, there is a trend with some companies to pay the same royalty on video that's paid for audio.

Licensed Sales

While the major companies don't do this for their mainstream sales, smaller record companies may license someone else to manufacture and distribute home video. In this case, that company pays a royalty to the record company, and the company pays you 50% of its net receipts. "Net receipts" are what's left after the company deducts the following:

1. A **distribution fee** for the record company, which is a percentage of gross and therefore taken first. This is a key lesson in computing percentage fees: If you get a percentage of something, always take it first, so that it's against the biggest possible dollar amount. The distribution fee is supposed to cover the company's overhead for handling the licensing, and it ranges anywhere from 10% to 25%, depending on your bargaining power. It can sometimes be eliminated (if you're the ruler of a moderate-size nation).
2. **Distribution expenses,** meaning the costs of duplicating, shipping, etc., necessary to distribute the product.
3. **Third-party payments** to unions and guilds, though many companies now try to charge these against the artist's 50%.

The company's gross receipts, less the above expenses, equal their net receipts, and you get 50% of that.

Digital Sales and Streams

We've indirectly discussed what you get from digital video uses, but let's now make it direct: You get your royalty applied to what the company gets. For downloads, they get about 70% of the retail price, and for streaming, they get about 60% of the streaming service's revenue attributable to your video.

All-in Video Royalties

When you have an all-in record deal (see page 96), then you're responsible for these little goodies out of your share of video monies:

1. Just like audio records, your royalty includes all third-party payments, meaning the *audio* producer of the master recordings used in the video, the unions, and anyone else entitled to a royalty.

2. Unlike audio records, the company also deducts all copyright royalties payable for songs used in the videos (see page 262 for what these are), except for cases where a third party (like YouTube) pays the songwriters. With enough clout, you can sometimes make the record company pay these royalties out of their share.

Recoupment of Video Costs

All the costs of making videos go into a pot, to be charged against your video royalties. Half of these costs are also charged to your audio record royalties, under the theory that "we're a big record company, and you're not, so we can do this." When you make your deal, be sure you don't end up getting charged twice for the same cost—in other words, once the costs have been taken from your audio record royalties, the same amount can't be taken from your video royalties, and vice versa. Many record company forms would technically allow this, although I'm not certain it's intended, and I've never seen them do it.

So now we have a pot with chargeable costs in it. The company next takes your video royalties and throws them into this pot. When these monies equal the costs charged, the excess royalties are credited to your audio royalty account (in the same way that audio record royalties are credited after recouping recording costs). Of course, if your audio account is unrecouped, you won't see any of the dough, because the monies are gobbled up by the black hole of your deficit.

You can sometimes get the company to pay an advance for a home video release—after all, you're giving them something beyond what's in the deal. And sometimes you can even get them not to cross-collateralize the home video with your record deal, so that you at least have a shot at seeing royalties.

As single song videos have started to make more money (we'll discuss this on page 190), there is a trend with some companies to pay the same royalty on video that's paid on audio records, and to throw all the audio and video costs and royalties into the same big, happy pot. When the pot gets to recoupment, they start paying you on both.

MID-PRICE RECORDS

After a record has had its initial run in current release, it is known as a **catalog item,** meaning it's listed in the company's catalog of available titles but isn't being currently promoted. Some catalog items are issued at **mid-price,** meaning a reduced price that's designed to encourage consumers to buy older titles. The contractual definition of a mid-price record (with slight variations from company to company) is one "with a PPD between 65% and 80% of the price for newly released top-line records." Some companies go as high as 85% for mid-price. A lower percentage is better for you, because your royalty goes down when you get there, as you're about to see:

Royalty

The royalty for mid-price is usually from 66.66% to 75% of the U.S. basic rate (6.66% to 7.5% if you have a 10% royalty). Note this is a double whammy—not only is the royalty rate lower, but the PPD on which it's based is also lower. The record companies justify this because their wholesale price is less, and accordingly so is their profit margin. Their thinking is that the lower price will generate extra sales that more than make up for the lost revenue.

As you gain clout, you can negotiate a period of time after initial release before a record can be sold at mid-price (usually twelve months, moving up to eighteen with clout), or sometimes even a flat prohibition without your consent. This provision used to be easier to get than it is today, because (a) in recent years it's become routine to issue catalog items at mid-price and (b) the companies have "developing artist" price programs that we'll discuss in a minute.

If you do get restrictions, it will only be for the United States. This is because, in some foreign territories, mid-price is customary for the first release. Presumably, your interests and the record company's are the same, since they want to maximize their profits in that territory. Thus they won't put something out at mid-price unless they believe the reduced price will promote enough extra sales to justify the lower profit margin.

Presumably . . .

BUDGET RECORDS

The next step down from mid-price is **budget,** which means the company doesn't think it can sell the stuff unless it knocks the price way down. The contractual definition of budget records is one with a price of less than 65% of the top-line price, but sometimes there is no mid-price definition and the contract says everything under 80% of the top-line price is a budget record.

Royalty

The royalty on budget records is usually 50% of the top-line royalty rate, or 5% in our 10% example. With some clout, you can hold back budget records for a period after initial release. Because your being on a budget line is a statement about what the company thinks of your career, you can usually get a longer holdback than you can for mid-price. For example, in the United States, the company might agree to wait twelve to eighteen months after initial release (which you can push to two years with clout). Again, foreign markets have their own peculiarities, and there will be little you can do unless you're a major artist in a particular territory.

As your muscle increases, you may be able to get a flat prohibition against budget, at least during the term of your agreement. And, if you can't get the right to consent to budgets after the term, a compromise is to say they can't do it as long as your account is recouped. The idea is that, if they've lost money on your project, they can do whatever they want to get even, but otherwise they must keep you off the budget line.

Over the last few years, this has been harder to get, as companies are insisting on flexibility in pricing. One reason is:

NEW AND DEVELOPING ARTIST PRICES

There's a practice of releasing new artists at what's known as "new and developing artist prices." The theory is that people will fork over a few bucks to try something new but will balk at a steeper price. So a number of debut albums are released at mid-price (so far, this is mostly a CD practice, though a few companies have done it for digital albums). Because this works pretty well in pushing new artists, the companies have gotten tougher about controlling pricing, and it's harder to get limits in your deal.

Some companies take this to the extreme and put out radically discounted CDs (for example, a $6 PPD) to get a buzz going on the artist, pump up initial sales, etc. If your company wants to do that, they'll ask you to give up your royalties on the cheapies—they make very little money at these prices, and it's really just another form of marketing. You should ask for a limited run (say 100,000 units or so), but many companies won't agree to limits. They say they don't make much money on these, so they'll only put out enough to launch your career, and after that, it's in both your interests to raise the price. Variations on the theme include trying to limit the reduced pricing to physical only, and trying to limit it to your first album only.

RECORD CLUBS

Record clubs are mail-order "clubs" that you join by agreeing to buy a certain number of records, and they're pretty much dead. I'm only including this section because, for some inexplicable reason, every record deal has a provision for it. If it was me reading this book, I'd skip to the next topic, but, hey, you're in charge.

Royalties for record club sales are the *lesser* of (a) half of your top-line royalty rate, or (b) 50% of your company's net licensing receipts from the record club (these sales are licensed to the record clubs, who manufacture and distribute the records, and pay license fees to your company). Usually, by asking, you can get a straight 50% of the company's net licensing receipts. However, since the company doesn't get such a high rate from the club, this is what you'd get anyway (half the company's net is usually less than half your royalty rate).

Record club free goods are interesting creatures. Guess how many records they can give away for every hundred they sell? Remember (from page 78) that the norm for retail sales is 5% to 10% for free goods. With clubs, it's a bit more. What's your guess for each hundred sold? If you said 100, you're right—the company's contract with the club only limits them to giving away *100%*, meaning one free for every one sold! In other words, out of every 200 shipped, 100 can be free!

So you should ask for a limit in your contract of one free record for every sale, right? Wrong. The one-to-one limit is for the company's *entire catalog*, which means they might give away more of your records and less of someone else's, as long as the *total* doesn't exceed one to one. At superstar levels you can get your own one-to-one limit (the companies have the right to do it for a few artists, but they don't like to tell you this). Even with your own limit, however, they only "settle up" the difference between one to one and whatever they did to you every couple of years.

Unfortunately, without a lot of clout, you'll have to live with this nonsense. As your leverage grows, you can sometimes control the company's right to put your records in clubs, or at least delay the club release (the idea is that, if you hold back record clubs until, say, six months from release in stores, club sales won't compete with retail sales during the hottest period).

CUTOUTS, DELETES, SCRAPS, AND OTHER FOOD FOR BOTTOM FEEDERS

Every company publishes a catalog of records that it currently offers for sale. **Cutouts** and **deletes** are records that have been taken out of the company's catalog, and this isn't done until a title is pronounced dead, rotted, and buried. When a company finds that an album isn't selling at mid-price or budget, either because nobody cares about it or because the company overmanufactured and/or had gigantic returns, it deletes the title and looks for a way to bail out for whatever it can get. These leftovers are sometimes sold as **scrap**, to be broken up for their component parts. If not, they're sold as **schlock**, which means they're put in the bins for 99¢, $1.50, etc. Artists get no royalties whatsoever for these, as the company says (correctly) that they're sold at cost or below, just to get rid of them.

With negotiating power, you can say that the company can't schlock your records until they're deleted from the catalog, and in no event sooner than twelve or eighteen months after initial release, or with some clout, twenty-four to thirty-six months after release. (Note you can do this for schlock, not scrap. You can't restrict their ability to sell records as scrap because the public never knows about it; schlock, however, tells the world that your records are fit for lining parakeet cages.) You can also get the right to buy these records at the best price offered to the record company, but I've never felt this is of any practical value. You're not likely to be able to sell them at a better price than the company, and what are you going to do with 100,000 dogs?

PREMIUMS

Send in a Wheaties box top and get the latest T-Pain single. Records sold this way are called **premiums**, which means they're sold in conjunction with a product or service, typically at a very low price (or for free). The royalty is correspondingly low—usually at half rate—and is based on the price at which the record company sells the record to the advertiser (also very low). (There may in fact be no other price, because these records are often given away or sold to the public at less than cost.)

Historically, even with very little bargaining power, you could prohibit premiums without your consent. That was because they really constitute a commercial use of your name, likeness, and voice (by tying you into the product of the people offering them). As we move into a world where advertising supports "free" music to consumers, the companies are getting tougher about this. However, you have a legitimate right to be at the table when they're discussing these things. For example, if you're a major artist, and you have a deal with Coke, you would be in breach of that deal if the record company featured your music in a Pepsi campaign. So push hard for consent to anything that ties you to a product. And even at the beginning levels, you should be able to get restrictions against things like alcohol, tobacco, political causes, firearms, X-rated products, and anything else that rings your particular chimes.

Premiums aren't a big deal these days. There's the occasional oddball, like getting a download code when you buy a carton of Coke, or putting a CD in a cruise-ship cabin, or companies that buy downloads to give out as employee incentives. But for the most part, they're waiting for their appointment with Dr. Kevorkian.

VIDEO GAMES

Master licenses for video games are done on a flat-fee basis. So far (except as noted below), no one has gotten a royalty. Nor are they likely to get one, because video games sell a lot of units, and the video companies don't believe that any particular song means additional sales.

The fee for video game licenses can be anywhere from nothing (if the record company just wants to hammer the song into the heads of teenage gamers for three hundred hours) to $50,000 or so. Most licenses are in the $8,000 or $10,000 range for lesser-known songs and artists, and around $30,000 to $50,000 for big hits.

Interestingly, video game license fees are one of the few things in the music business to have gone *up* in the last few years. Historically, the gaming companies only licensed music for a short period (five to seven years), and only for specific video game formats. Then two things happened: (1) many of the games kept selling beyond the period that the manufacturer anticipated; and (2) the games expanded beyond their little boxes to online, mobile phones, etc., which were not covered by the licenses. So the game manufacturers had to go back and get additional rights, for which the record companies happily charged gobs of money. As a result of all this, video game licenses nowadays cover "all media now or hereafter known," and they last for "perpetuity." To compensate for these additional rights, the rates went up, but they're still just one-time payments, without any royalties.

The only exception to flat fee video game licenses is for music-based games, such as Guitar Hero and SingStar. These licenses allow the manufacturers to sell games with music embedded in them, and also to sell downloads (of songs or packs of songs) that can be added to the game. Because music is essential to these products, the gaming companies are willing to pay a royalty for every game sold. The specifics of these licenses are confidential, so I'm not free to repeat them, but the deals are structured to pay advances against either (a) a penny-rate royalty for each game unit sold and each download), or (b) a percentage royalty, which is set aside for all the music rights, then pro-rated amongst all the music involved in the sale or download).

DART, DIGITAL PERFORMANCE, AND WEBCASTING MONIES

Recording artists are entitled to monies payable under the Audio Home Recording Act of 1992, also known as the DART Bill (standing, I think, for "Digital Audio Recording Technologies," or possibly "Dallas Area Rapid Transit"). Also, in 1995, Congress added a right to be paid for the digital performance of masters, and in 1998, the right to be paid for streaming. Most of this sounds like gibberish because I haven't given you any background to understand what it means. The reason is that I want to wait until we've discussed copyright, publishing, and a few other concepts. So use a little of the patience that driven musical artists are so famous for, and hang on 'til we get there.

For a preview, as we discussed in the streaming section, the important thing to know is that with each of these, the artist is *paid directly* for these rights, meaning the monies don't go into the record company's tight little fist and therefore can't be used to recoup your deficit. This is a wonderful thing.

Since you are paid directly, your record deal will say that you're not entitled to share in the company's monies. In other words, if whoever collects streaming monies pays you and the company separately, you won't share in each other's dough. What you want to add is that, if anyone ever pays all the monies to the record company, you get 50% of those. And also try to say that the company can't use these monies to recoup your deficit. Your argument is that they didn't expect to have them for recoupment in the first place.

PUBLIC PERFORMANCE OF MASTERS

In many countries outside the United States, the *artist and record company* are paid a royalty every time a recording is played on the radio, but it was not the case in the U.S. until 1995. (This is different from public performance royalties that are paid to a *songwriter and publisher* of the *musical composition* when a recording is played on the radio, and which have always been paid in the United States, as we'll discuss on page 240.)

In 1995, the U.S finally created a performance right for masters, but it is limited to *digital* uses of the masters. So unlike other countries, there's no performance money for use of the masters in over-the-air radio broadcasting (also called **terrestrial radio**), even if it's a digital signal. We'll discuss this in more detail on page 346.

In foreign territories, however, the master performance monies can be really significant. That sounds like good news, except that U.S. artists aren't usually entitled to collect them. The reason is pretty simple: since the U.S. doesn't pay foreign artists when their masters are performed in the U.S., foreign countries don't pay U.S. artists when their masters are performed over there. In part, this comes from a sense of fairness, and to keep a balance of monies going in and out of the territory, but it's also a way to make more money available to the local foreign artists (U.S. artists aren't taking any part of a pool that gets allocated to the performance of masters).

In recent years, it's been possible for Americans to get paid by some countries, but only if you jump through some hoops. Those hoops vary from place to place, and something called the Rome Convention (which is an international treaty dealing with intellectual property) is a key player in this process. If your country signed the Rome Convention, you get performance monies from all the other countries that signed, and they get paid by you. Most of the countries that signed it are in Europe and Scandinavia, though Japan and Australia also came to the party. Guess which country didn't sign it? Right . . . the U.S. of A.

Still, you can get some foreign monies. Portugal, Romania, Hungary, Russia, and Spain pay everybody. Germany pays if the record is released in a Rome Convention country within 30 days of its initial release in a non–Rome Convention territory. The other countries generally will pay if you record (or partially record) your masters in a Rome Convention country, or if you're signed to a label based in one.

By the way, Canada is a party to the Rome Convention and they have great recording studios . . .

ACCOUNTINGS

When do you get your royalties? Twice a year, within sixty to ninety days after the close of each calendar six-month period (except for some companies that use weird, noncalendar six-month periods).

Objections

Your contract will say that each accounting becomes "final" (meaning you can no longer argue it's wrong) one or two years after the statement is sent to you. If the companies didn't say this, you'd have until four years after the statement (in California) or six years after (in New York) within which to sue them. That is, of course, precisely why they say it.

You can increase the objection period to two years, and often three years, with minimal clout. Superstars can sometimes get four years. Always do it, because it's uneconomical to audit unless you can do a number of years at once. What's auditing? Funny you should ask . . .

Audit Rights

Closely following the accounting clause is an **audit** clause, which says you can *audit* (meaning send in an accountant to verify) the record company's books. This is a way of ensuring that you're getting a fair reporting, and if you have any success, you should do it. Audits are expensive ($25,000 to $50,000 or more), so you'd better be recouped before you start. (There's not much joy in proving that, instead of being $1,000,000 unrecouped, you're only $900,000 unrecouped.) Most reputable auditors will give you an indication of whether an audit is worthwhile before you engage them. They do this by looking at your accounting statements and contracts and knowing what the various record companies do.

Nowadays almost every record contract has a built-in right to audit, although in the past you had to ask for it. The audit clause will also say you can't audit more than once in any twelve-month period; that you can't examine any particular accounting statement more than once; and that you have to audit before the period to object has expired (see the above section).

13

Advanced Record Deal Points

ADVANCED DEMO DEAL NEGOTIATION

If you're making a demo deal (see page 109 for what that is), read this section. They're rare these days, so you can always come back here if one shows up.

If you're going right into a full deal, you can skip to Exclusivity on page 183, or read this for the thrills and chills.

OK, so this section deals with *demo* deals, as opposed to *development* deals. In **development deals,** where the company is spending a lot more money, they prenegotiate the terms of your full-blown record deal. In other words, you hammer out the advances, royalties, number of albums, etc., before they shell out any bucks. Then, if they like what they hear, those terms automatically become your record deal. The terms you'll get are the same as all the other record deals we've been discussing; they're just optional on the record company's part. Development deals are becoming less common, as they're being replaced by deals for a single, with the company having the option to get more product.

Under **demo deals,** the companies are only spending a little money (maybe $10,000 or so) to record demos. Since you're on the *el cheapo* plan, they don't take the time (or spend the money) to negotiate an entire agreement. (Demo deals are also rare these days, though they do come up occasionally. Unless you're facing one, feel free to skip ahead).

Demo deals work like this:

First Refusal

Suppose you make a demo deal and record a spectacular demo. Can you thank the company very much for their help, and then go shop the demo to other companies, thereby running the price of your deal through the roof? Not very likely. The company that paid for the demo attaches the following strings:

1. In exchange for the company's giving you demo money, you have to give it a period of time after it gets the demos (about thirty to sixty days) before it has to decide whether or not it wants you. You're sitting in limbo while the company thinks about it—you can't go to another company during this period—so the shorter the time period, the better for you.

2. If the company decides it wants you, you're required to negotiate with them and try to make a deal (called a **first negotiation** right). If you make a deal, everything's great. If you don't make a deal, however, the company gets a **first refusal** (also called a **last refusal** or **matching right**). This means that, if you get an offer from another company, you can't just accept it. Instead, you have to go back to the original company and give it a chance to match your offer.

Here's an example of a first refusal:

After making a demo, you first negotiate with the record company making the demo (let's call them the Demo Company). You insist on $200,000 for your first album, but the Demo Company only offers $125,000. You say you're insulted and, in a beautifully choreographed fit of righteous indignation, you walk away to shop your deal around town. Finally, another company offers you $150,000. In steps the Demo Company, saying, "Not so fast, Charlie." Under the first refusal, you have to go back and offer the deal to the Demo Company at $150,000. If the Demo Company wants it at that price, you have to sign with that outfit; if not, you're free to go elsewhere. (However, you can't sign for less than the other company's offer—in this case $150,000—without giving the Demo Company a chance to match that deal. I'm sure you can figure out why the Demo Company insists on this.)

Here's some goodies to negotiate in your first refusal:

1. You only have to come back to the Demo Company if the other offer is less than the last offer that the Demo Company made to you. So in our example, since the Demo Company only offered you $125,000, you wouldn't have to come back if somebody offered you $150,000 (it's more than the Demo Company's last $125,000 offer). This is pretty hard (read "next to impossible") to get. Remember, when you're making a demo deal, you

haven't got a lot of bargaining power (if you did, you'd be making an album deal).

2. You only have to come back if the offer you get is less than the last offer you made to the Demo Company. Note this wouldn't change anything under our above example. Since the new company offered you $150,000, and you last offered the Demo Company $200,000, you'd still have to come back (the $150,000 is less than the $200,000 you offered the Demo Company). This provision is a bit more possible to get, but the Demo Company may still insist on your coming back with any offer, higher or lower.

3. However you end up under point 1 or 2, you should limit the time within which the Demo Company can accept or reject your offer. From your point of view, the shorter the better. Ideally, I like to get five business days, but more realistic is ten or fifteen business days. ("Business days" are Monday through Friday, excluding holidays. So ten business days is two weeks if there are no holidays.) Companies may want as long as forty-five to sixty days (regular "calendar days," not business days), which is an outrageous amount of time to hold you in never-never land. You could sit around all this time only to discover that (a) they decided not to take you; and (b) your other deal has gone away. Try never to go beyond thirty days—after all, the Demo Company heard your demos a long time ago.

Cost Reimbursement

If the Demo Company doesn't want you after you do the demos, or if it passes on your deal when you come back under a first refusal, you're free to go elsewhere. Yippee. When you sign with another company, however, the Demo Company will want back its demo money. Not so Yippee.

Since you're not likely to be in a position to write them a check, the Demo Company will want it from your new record deal. Most record companies who are "second in line" (meaning the ones that follow the Demo Company) are willing to reimburse the cost of demos. (After all, sometimes they're the Demo Company, and they want their money back, too.) This cost, of course, will be recoupable from your royalties, and thus it's ultimately your money. However, it beats smashing your piggy bank.

Here are a couple of things you can do to protect yourself:

1. Provide that the Demo Company should *only* get its money back *if* you make a new record deal. *Period*.
2. There should be a time limit. Otherwise, five years later you might get a deal based on totally different music and owe money to the Demo Company. Try a year or so.

Non–Record Company Demos

Record companies aren't the only folks who may be willing to fund your demos. I've seen deals where demos are funded by recording studios, producers, engineers, rich people who want to be in rock 'n' roll, poor people who want to be in rock 'n' roll, rich people who became poor people trying to get into rock 'n' roll, etc. Indeed, one of the more bizarre stories I came across was a guy who funded an entire album, but would never tell any of us where the money came from. He lived in a walled estate and always paid in cash (I have my guess about his occupation; how about you?). Ultimately, after the album was finished, this guy disappeared, and we haven't heard from him in years. It would really round out the story to tell you this was a hugely successful album, but they never got a record deal. (Sorry.)

Since non–record company sources can't actually make and distribute records, their contracts don't look anything like the demo deals offered by majors or independents. Also, because these aren't mainstream deals, there's basically no rules, and I've seen them run all over the map. Here's some of the more common arrangements:

1. If and when you get a record deal, you reimburse them for the cost of the demos, and the demo funder (let's call them the Funder) gets a 1% or 2% royalty on your records. This royalty is known as an **override**, because it rides on top of your deal. However, the record company will take this override out of your royalties, under the age-old theory of "It's your problem, not mine." Sometimes Funders also get a proportionate share of advances paid to the artist, in the ratio that their override royalty bears to the all-in rate. For example, if the artist has an all-in rate of 10% and the Funder gets a 2% override out of the 10%, they would get 20% (two-tenths) of the advances.
2. You want to limit the participation to as few records as possible. The minimum is where the Funder gets an override only on the specific demo recordings that are finished into masters on your record. Your argument is that the other demos didn't

interest the record company. I've also seen deals where there is a smaller override if a song in the demo is re-recorded, as opposed to the demo being turned into a master. For example, the Funder might get a 2% royalty if you fix up and use their actual recordings, versus a 1% royalty if the same song is re-recorded.

3. At the other extreme, the Funder may ask for an override on every record under your deal, which I think is overreaching. If you agree to this, you'll be married to this yutzo forever, in exchange for their relatively small investment in your career. Ideally the override should only apply to the first album, but perhaps you can throw in a couple more if it's necessary to make the deal. Another compromise is not to limit the number of albums on which the Funder gets an override, but to say they only get the override until they get back twice (or three times) their investment. So if the Funder puts up $10,000, they only get an override until they receive $20,000 (or $30,000).

4. If the Funder only gets a royalty based on the use of specific recordings or songs, then be sure to specify that their royalty is **pro-rata** (see page 160 for a discussion of *pro-rata*).

5. The Funder's royalty should only be payable after recoupment of the amounts charged to you in connection with the records on which they have a royalty, such as tour support, videos, etc. (Note this is recoupment at your rate plus the Funder's royalty, not all from the Funder's royalties.) It's not fair, however, to charge the Funder for recording costs of records on which they don't get an override, nor should they be charged for advances they don't share in.

6. If you make one of these deals, you should thoroughly understand the discussion on page 127 concerning payment of producer's royalties when you have no royalties from which to pay them. The exact same thing can happen here on the override— you could owe the Funder money before you are recouped. Ideally, when you make your record deal, try to get the company to pay the override obligation even though it's taken out of your royalties (in the same manner as discussed on page 124 for producers).

7. Recently, Funders have figured out they can ask for 360 rights (see page 102 for what those are). Since you'll have to give those to the record company, try to hold them back from the Funder, or at least only pay them until the Funder gets back their money. If all that fails, at least keep it small, and try to limit what income streams they share in.

EXCLUSIVITY

I'm sure you won't be shocked to learn that every record contract includes a provision stating the deal is **exclusive.** In other words, during the term of the agreement, you can't make records for anybody else. However, just like a TV commercial for prescription drugs, here's a list of side effects:

Re-recording Restrictions

All contracts say you can't re-record any song you recorded during the term of a deal for a certain period of time *after* the term. This is known as a **re-recording restriction.** When you think about it, it's perfectly logical—without it, you could go out the day after your deal is over and duplicate your albums for somebody else. The usual period is five years from the date of recording, but with a minimum of three to five years after the end of the term. The minimum keeps you from re-recording an album delivered in the first year of a six-year deal immediately after the term, even though it is more than five years since recording it. The five years from recording is pretty much carved in stone; you can almost always get the period after the term down to two years.

Historically, re-recording restrictions applied only to "records," which meant there was no restriction on re-recording for motion pictures, commercials, etc., which fell outside the definition of records (see page 73 for the definition). However, as artists started re-recording songs for movies and commercials, instead of using the original master (for which the record company could have charged a fee), the companies did two things:

1. As we discussed on page 73, the companies expanded the definition of "record" to include everything imaginable, so you can't re-record for any purpose during the restrictive period.
2. Most companies now say you can *never* re-record your songs to sound just like the masters you've given them, whether it's for records, commercials, or any other purpose. So nowadays, even after your re-recording restriction expires, you can only record a wholly different arrangement of the songs.

By the way, the world's record for re-recording restrictions belongs to Decca Records, who structured a deal under which Bing Crosby had a *perpetual* re-recording restriction for the song "White Christmas."

Motion Picture and Television Issues

Exclusivity clauses apply to all "records" made during the term, and, as we just discussed, companies now define "record" so broadly that the term includes motion pictures, television appearances, webcasts, DVDs, and Ninja Blenders (maybe not the last one). Thus, the companies can stop you from recording for motion pictures and television without their consent (for which they'll want a nice piece of what you make), even where there's no phonograph record involved. And even if there's no music involved, like the case when you're the actor in a film, or making an appearance on a TV talk show without singing. Nice, huh?

You can usually negotiate some slack in these, if you know enough to ask.

If there's no music involved, most companies will easily agree that you can be an actor and let you keep all the money (though they may want their 360 share of the money). When you start performing music, things get trickier. With respect to films, the most common compromise is to allow you to perform one or two songs in a film with a laundry list of restrictions, such as keeping the size of your name the same as other artists, requiring a credit to the company, etc. (This is not true for television or webcasts, as we'll discuss in a minute, on page 186). With more leverage, you can do more songs as long as you don't give the film company any record rights. However, in either case, the record company will be looking for money. They usually want 100% of what you're paid to perform in the film. They then keep half (for releasing you from your exclusivity) and credit the other half to your account (meaning it's paid to you if you're recouped, or it's used to recoup your deficit if you're not). If you've got some clout, you may be able to knock down their percentage (say to 25%), or even keep the entire fee yourself.

But what about record rights, you ask? You've seen lots of artists with recordings on soundtrack albums, often on different labels. How does that happen? Short answer: with difficulty.

Record companies don't want you freely dropping recordings on others, for the legitimate reasons that (a) they want to be exclusively identified with you; (b) they don't want someone else releasing a record at a time that would conflict with one of your own singles or albums (incidentally, neither should you, as you normally make a lot less on a soundtrack album); and (c) if they bend on these mighty principles, they want to get paid.

So how do people get on soundtrack albums? Well, it's handled one of two ways in your record deal:

Forget It.   At some record companies, this is an absolute "religious issue" ("sacred cow," "irrefutable principle," etc.—you get the idea), meaning you have no right to let anyone else put out a soundtrack album with your recording on it. In these cases, the artist throws himself or herself on the mercy of the record company each time a film company asks them to perform a song in a movie. The record company either agrees to let the artist perform (with restrictions—see below), or it refuses and the issue is closed (unless your manager can yell loud enough to reopen it). The other choice is to force the film company to give the soundtrack album to your record company, because then there is no conflict. If you're important enough, you can do this, even if you're only on one track.

Contractual Exclusions.   If you have clout, you can negotiate an automatic contractual soundtrack exclusion in your record deal with some companies (or even with the sticklers if you're King Kong). These typically have some or all of the following laundry list (which will also apply if you have no exclusion but the company consents):

1. You can't perform on more than one (or two at most) selections for inclusion in the album.
2. You can't do recordings for more than one soundtrack release during any one-year (or two-year) period of the term. Sometimes it's an overall limit, such as a maximum of three cuts over the term.
3. You must not be late in delivery of your product at the time.
4. All the royalties and advances must be paid to your record company. (Note that here we're talking now about advances against your royalties, as opposed to a fee that you may get for using your recording in the film, which we already discussed.) Just like the film fee, after the company gets your royalties and advances, it will want to keep 50% for releasing you from the exclusivity and credit the other 50% to your royalty account.

   If the soundtrack album is being released by your own company, you should be able to get 100% of the monies credited to your account, either to reduce your deficit, or to be paid out if you're recouped. If you really have a lot of bargaining power, you can get 50% or more of the royalties paid to you even if you're unrecouped. Your argument is that the film recording is in addition to the product they're entitled to get under your deal, and thus should be treated separately.

5. You must try to get the right to use the recording on one of your albums. The film company, if it gives these rights, will ask for a holdback period before you can do so. (This is discussed on page 423.)

Websites

Back when websites were strange and unknown creatures, the companies began registering the website names of all their artists without bothering to ask. And without regard to the fact that most of their record deals, which were made before websites existed, didn't give them the right to do this.

After the predictable shouting, gouging, and karate chops, most deals now provide that, during the term, the company will have the exclusive right to set up the artist's website and control social media (Twitter, Facebook, etc.). Their argument is that they want to present a coordinated marketing campaign across all platforms and, oh by the way, we're the big record company and you're not. Nowadays, you can often exclude social media, based on the argument that your fans believe it's you. Whatever is posted reflects on your overall image and therefore has to be authentic.

Some companies, if you ask, will allow the artist to set up an "unofficial" website during the term. After the term, the rights go back to the artist, although companies keep the right to have an artist section on their company website. Logistically, it requires you to give them written notice before they fork over the site.

Companies want to recoup the costs of creating and maintaining the artist's website and social media. It's hard to make this go away, but sometimes you can limit the amount they can charge, to, say, $25,000 over the life of the deal.

Streaming, TV, and Radio Broadcasts

There are three flavors of streaming:

1. Non-interactive streaming (see page 273);
2. On-demand streaming of audio and/or videos on the Internet

> (Spotify, Apple Music, Rhapsody, YouTube, Vevo, etc.; see page 274); and

3. Broadcast of your concerts on the Internet.

Numbers 1 and 2 are relatively straightforward. The company has these rights (it's a use of your masters, which they control), and you get your royalty. Number 3, however, gets immediately into your pocketbook, as people will offer money to put your concert on the Internet. And this problem also comes up if you play in a festival that insists on streaming everyone's performance.

As we discussed earlier, record companies have now made their exclusivity provisions so broad that they cover all transmissions, whether over television, satellite, Internet, or a tin can and string. This is because the contracts define "records" to include *any delivery* of music to consumers, whether it's a CD or a package of electrons. Thus, a stream, television, or radio broadcast of your music is a "record" (since it delivers music to consumers).

Because your company has the exclusive right to distribute your "records" during the term of your deal, if you want to do any kind of broadcast, you have to go to them (meaning get their permission and, if they're obliging, pay them a chunk).

If it's purely promotional (like appearing on *Saturday Night Live, Jimmy Kimmel,* etc), they want to be in the loop but won't get in the way—in fact, they usually help set these up. Their major concern is the afterlife of your performance, such as on-demand streaming or DVDs. They negotiate directly with the TV producers to work this out, and the customary deals allow the TV show to use your performance as part of the show, but not separate from it. They may also limit the amount of time they can make your performance available online. Because the labels and shows deal with each other all the time, this usually gets worked out with a minimum of fuss.

For concert simulcasts on the Internet, however, they'll be all over you. Superstars may be able to prenegotiate some exceptions, but record companies have become increasingly touchy in recent years. They view it as competitive with their own streaming of your music. This can eventually get worked out, but the record company will want something for it, which is negotiated case by case.

There's an interesting issue about these simulcasts that comes up after the end of your record deal. Because of the re-recording restriction we discussed on page 183, you can't re-record a song you delivered to them for a number of years after the term. And since a simulcast is a recording, they could stop you from webcasting a concert with those songs after the deal is over. As we just discussed for streaming during the term, the labels see these streams as competitive to what they're doing, so don't expect milk and cookies. If you have enough clout, you can sometimes make this go away in your deal, but otherwise you have to deal with it at the time.

Sideman Performances

Isn't it nice how all the superstars seem to be playing instruments and singing background on everybody else's records? These nonfeatured appearances are known as **sideman** performances, and there is hopefully a trend toward calling them **sideperson** performances. Now that you're educated, don't you wonder how this is possible? Doesn't it violate the exclusivity provisions of the superstar's agreement when she sings background for her pals on another label?

The answer is yes, it does violate their exclusivity. However, there's a strong custom in the industry (and you can usually have the provision inserted in your contract just by asking) that sideman performances are permitted, on the following kinds of conditions:

1. The performance must be truly a background performance, without any solos, duets, or "stepping out."
2. Your exclusive company must get a "courtesy credit" in the form of "[Artist] appears courtesy of _____ Records." (Before I started in the music biz, I always thought they did that just to be nice.)
3. You can't violate your re-recording restriction (see page 183), even as a background performer.
4. If you're a group, no more than two of you can perform together on any particular session. This is because your record company doesn't want your distinctive sound showing up on another label.
5. Some companies require you to get the other artist's label to give up a sideman clearance in exchange for letting you go (sort of like a future draft pick).

This is usually handled by an exchange of correspondence between the record companies in each specific instance, and it's usually just a "rubber stamp" process (unless one company is having a fight with the other about something unrelated to the sideman). After all, if one of the companies makes an issue of it, they won't have such an easy go when the other company's artist shows up as a sideman on their label. The process is something like porcupines dancing carefully with each other.

Guest Artists

If it's a true duet, or featured performance on another label, and therefore more than a sideman, the deal between you and the other artist is what we discussed in the section on joint recordings (page 161). However, the two record companies also have to make a deal with each other to let this happen, because each of them has their artist signed up exclusively. You won't be directly involved in this deal, but if they get into a fight, no one can use the track. So you should understand the principles in case you or your manager need to jump in.

The deals vary from situation to situation, depending on the bargaining power of the artists and whether the labels are getting along with each other at the time. However, this happens quite a bit, so the labels try to accommodate each other because they'll be on the other side at some point. Basically it's handled with some kind of override royalty, or if the artists are really big, there may be a profit share. Or, there may be a right to use the other artist on your records, with neither company getting money from the other.

VIDEOS

Promotional videos are the ones you see on YouTube, Vevo, and the like. The video production is paid for by the record company to promote the sales of your records, and all the provisions concerning them are in your record deal.

History

Did you know that music videos (which only became popular in the United States when MTV started in 1981) have been around since the 1960s in Europe? They were invented because it was cheaper for artists to make videos than to tour Europe. But videos have an even longer history than that. There are some great treasures that came from something called a "Scopitone" (pronounced "scope-ih-tone"). This was a Jukebox that played videos on 16mm film, and it enjoyed a brief life in the late 1950s and early 1960s. Today the Scopitone videos are collectors' items, and they include a number of color videos from such artists as Sonny and Cher, Neil Sedaka, Dion, Nat King Cole, Bobby Darin, etc. And if you really want to delve into the past, there are black-and-white videos that were shown in cinemas in the 1940s and 1950s, with such artists as Fats Waller, Louis Jordan, Lena Horne, Bing Crosby, Spike Jones, and many others. But back to today.

Commercial Market

Historically, monies came from sales of DVDs that use music videos either as (1) a **compilation** (meaning a program "compiled" from a number of individual video clips, of the same or different artists); or (2) occasionally music videos plus a "making of," an album documentary with behind the scenes footage. (For the royalties on these, see page 160.) But the market for DVDs is very small.

After a long dry spell, there's starting to be some money for single-song videos. The download market (meaning sales through digital retailers like iTunes) generates a little, but the ad-based streaming video market (meaning Vevo and YouTube, which are free to consumers with annoying advertising around each video) are starting to churn out some meaningful money from the ads surrounding the videos.

We talked about the company's money for this on page 169, and you get your royalty applied to those monies.

The video issues in your contract are:

Is the Company Going to Make a Video of Your Song?

This is the first question, because if the answer is no, there's not much else to talk about. Until you have quite a bit of bargaining power, the record company, totally by itself, decides whether or not to make a video. As your bargaining power increases, you can require the company to do one or two videos per album. But even in this case, almost every company will say they only have to make videos for as long as they're doing it for artists of a stature similar to yours. Their concern (with justification) is that videos may not be a useful means of promoting records.

Control

Control means two things: (1) the content of the videos; and (2) the manner in which they're exploited. Unless you have an enormous amount of bargaining power, you generally can't control the commercial exploitation of your videos. This is because the company wants every opportunity to get its money back, and it doesn't want you stopping them over some silly concept like artistry. You may get the company to agree it won't commercially exploit a video if you repay the cost of it, but this isn't of any practical value unless you're an extremely rich prima donna. More realistically, you may be able to limit the exploitation a bit. For example, you can (with some clout) prevent the company's putting your videos in a DVD that also contains videos of other artists.

Creative control over the content of videos is very limited. Companies don't want to spend $50,000 for a video, then have you say the "vibes" don't hit you right and you don't approve. That would mean they're stuck with a turkey they can't unload. If they give you any approval rights, it'll usually be a bare-bones approval of the story, director, and maybe producer. If you have serious bargaining power, you may be able to get approval of all elements, including the final edit. Some superstars even take over control of making the video.

Recoupment

Typically, the record company charges 50% of the cost of videos against your audio royalty, and 100% against your video royalties. One of the things you want to make sure is that they don't double-dip—in other words, if they charge 50% against record royalties, they can't take the same 50% against video royalties, and vice versa.

Most companies have a "bright line" beyond which they'll charge 100% against your audio royalties, even if the costs are within an approved budget. For example, a contract might say that if an approved video budget exceeds $50,000, they'll charge 100% of the excess against audio royalties (as well as of course against video royalties).

As we discussed earlier with DVDs, there's now a trend to treat audio and video the same. In other words, the companies want to pay the same royalty rate for both, and throw all the audio and video costs into one bucket.

Budget

Budgets for shooting a video are typically designated or approved by the company. As your stature grows, you may be able to put in a minimum budget amount. The cost of videos has dropped radically over the years, and most are in the $15,000 to $50,000 range. A real superstar video can cost up to $400,000 or more, but videos over $250,000 are rare.

Once a video budget has been approved, record companies get very touchy about your running over the limit. Sometimes they flatly refuse to pay, and the artist (only superstars can afford this "luxury") actually writes a check. Other times they grudgingly, grumblingly, bitchingly pay the excess, but they charge it against anything they can grab—future advances, songwriting monies, etc. And, of course, 100% of the excess is recouped from your audio and video royalties.

For some artists, sponsors will pay money to have their product included in a video (called **product placement**). It's up to your own personal Cheese-O-Meter to decide if you're willing to hold a soft drink while you're hang-gliding. If you are, the placement dollars can offset a lot (and sometimes all) of the video costs.

INDEPENDENT PROMOTION

There is an important phenomenon known as **independent promotion.** Promotion people (as noted on page 66) get records played on the radio, and they have relationships with station programmers to help ensure this. Some of these promotion people are independent of the record companies; they work for themselves and are hired by the companies on a project-by-project basis. They are cleverly called **independents,** to distinguish them from record company employees who do promotion.

The independents are paid handsomely for their services by a record company (in most cases) or by the artist (in others). And by handsomely, I mean the costs for multiformat promotion (meaning Top 40, Alternative, Hot AC [Adult Contemporary], AAA [Adult Album Alternative], Rhythm, or Urban) can run $75,000 to $400,000 *per single*. As high as those numbers sound, they've come way down over the years. It started with Eliot Spitzer, when he was attorney general of New York state (and before his hot nights with various ladies), who launched a probe into the record companies' promotion practices. In response, the companies cut back on independent promotion, and consequently the promotion prices came down.

The trend these days is to promote a record in one radio format, get some traction, then spend bigger money to take it to other formats. Top 40 is the Holy Grail of radio, meaning your record has a chance to be massive if they play it. For that reason, Top 40 is also the most expensive to promote, so the companies like to see a record doing well in the smaller formats before they spend the big bucks taking it to Top 40. Also, the better your record has done in other formats, the more likely Top 40 will pay attention.

Whatever the company spends will be 50% to 100% recoupable from your royalties. It's worth putting up a fight to keep the company from recouping more than 50% of independent promotion costs. If they're charging 100% to you, they don't have the same incentive to reduce spending as they do when 50% comes out of their own pocket.

Another form of promotion is what's known as **radio-promoted concerts.** Those of you in the bigger cities have seen local radio stations promote gigantic concerts with all kinds of big name acts. You probably didn't know that these acts are paid much less than their normal fees (or maybe no fee, just a reimbursement of their costs) to show up. They do it to generate goodwill with the radio station (which makes a large profit on these concerts), in exchange for the hope that these stations will play the artist's music. So, in essence, the artists are paying for promotion of their own recordings by cutting their fees.

MERCHANDISING RIGHTS

Over the years, some record companies have tried to take artists' **merchandising rights,** also known as **merch rights.** These are the rights to put your name on T-shirts, posters, etc., and we'll discuss them in detail in Chapters 24 and 25. (Note: I'm not talking about the rights to put out promotional posters, T-shirts, etc., which are distributed free to promote records, and for which all record companies have the rights. This section is about record companies who want the right to sell merchandise at concerts, in stores, etc.)

Now that we're in a 360 world (see the discussion on page 102), many record companies are trying to get merch rights. Some companies actually manufacture and distribute your merchandise, in which case they pay you the royalties we'll discuss in Chapters 24 and 25 (these are the *active rights* we previously covered). Other companies (usually independents) take these rights even if they don't have any manufacturing facilities. In other words, they're taking active rights, but they don't have the ability to exploit them. Instead, they turn around and license the rights out to a merchandiser, then pay you 50% of their receipts from that merchandiser. So not only do they get a bigger piece of the money, they also *control* your merchandising rights, meaning they can decide which merchandise company gets them (as opposed to you making that decision). On top of that, since the record company collects the money, they can cross-collateralize your merchandise earnings with your record deal (see page 89 for what that means). If you collect the money and pay them, they can't do this.

So if your company insists on merchandise rights, try one of these:

1. The company gets no merchandising rights, but gets a **first negotiation** right. This means you have to talk to them first before you talk to anyone else, and if you can't make a deal, you can then go elsewhere.

2. If the company won't agree to just a first negotiation, the next step is to give them a **matching right,** which means you can go out and shop around all you like, but you must come back and give them a chance to make the deal on the same terms as your best offer. They will also want a first negotiation as well as the matching right, meaning you first have to try to make a deal with them, and if you can't, then you can go shopping. However, if you get an offer for your merchandising, you have to come back and let them match it before you can give the rights to anyone else.

   We discussed the details of a first negotiation and matching right in connection with demo deals, on page 179, and the same principles apply here.

   This situation isn't ideal: The requirement to come back makes your shopping more difficult. Bidders aren't so interested in negotiating a whole deal if someone else can waltz in and take it away. But it's better than giving away the rights.

3. Some record companies not only want a matching right, but also a discount. For example, they may want to pay only 80% of what someone else offers. So if you had an offer for $10,000, they would be able to take the deal for $8,000. In case you didn't figure it out, this is not good for you. If you must give a matching right, it should be at 100%.

   In the real world, when the record company has a matching right, you usually go to them first and, if they're interested, just make a deal. If they're not interested, sometimes they'll let you go and forget about the matching right. But under the contractual language, they don't have to.

4. If all else fails, and you have to give up merchandising rights, make the best possible royalty deal (see Chapters 24 and 25),

and don't let them cross-collateralize merchandise earnings with your record deal. You can usually knock out the cross-collateralization just by asking.

Many companies, even if they don't get your overall merchandising deal, will take the right to merchandise one image (usually your album cover). Other companies want more images but will limit their rights to sales over their website. If you agree to any of these, try to get 50% of the profits, or at least a decent royalty (see Chapters 24 and 25 for the royalty range). This should be separate from your record royalty account, so they can't use merchandise monies to recoup your advances. Also, make sure they can't sell this stuff at your concerts, only in retail stores or on their website. And it's worth trying to limit them to online only, so you can be the only one offering your merchandise in physical retail stores.

Some companies also try to grab **digital merchandise.** *Digital merchandise* is, not surprisingly, the digital use of your image. Examples are **wallpaper** (which means the background on a mobile device or computer desktop) and **voice tones** (a recording of your *speaking* voice that plays through a cell phone, saying things like, "Yo, my main man ain't here"). Another example is a website with avatars, where users can buy virtual T-shirts for the character, or hang a virtual poster in their virtual crib. Weird, but people actually pay for that.

If you don't specifically give your company virtual merchandise, you will control those rights. But that's not the case with voice tones. Under the terms of most record deals, you can't give your voice tones to anyone but your record company—they have your exclusive recording services, and the exclusivity covers nonmusical performances as well as musical. However, you've got some leverage because the companies can't force you to record voice tones (though that's changing in newer contracts).

Wallpaper falls in between. You might be able to license wallpaper on your own, because it's your name and likeness, and it's not for records. However, you could run afoul of the broad exclusivity clauses that the companies are now using. You need to look at your specific language.

Try not to give up digital merchandising. If you have to do it to make your record deal, try to make a separate deal for the money, not crossed with your royalty accounts, and try for 50% of the profits. And be sure to build in creative controls for yourself.

TOUR SUPPORT

And now for a bit of my personal finances. Remember my soft-drink stand (on page 81)? Well, here's that summer's take: 250 drinks, at 5¢ each, equals $12.50. Not bad for sweating in the sun for seven days a week over ten weeks, eh? But here's the real coup: I convinced my mother to pay for the drinks, so it was *all profit*. (I hope you're impressed.) If she hadn't, the drinks would have cost me $6.25, and the lumber for the stand was $18. So the expenses were $24.25, and I took in $12.50, resulting in a loss of $11.75. If it hadn't been for Ma, I'd have had to file for bankruptcy.

This is not unlike the situation of a new band going on tour. As we'll see later (on page 404), it's virtually impossible for a new artist to go on the road and do anything besides lose money. Even assuming everyone in the band only has a "share of profits," and therefore you don't have to pay salaries to the musicians, the costs of rehearsal, equipment, travel, hotels, agents, managers, etc., are more than any band can earn in their baby stages. Indeed, even by the time you're midlevel, you'll be doing well to break even on the road.

Why would you ever tour under these circumstances? (As the joke goes, if you buy widgets for $1 and sell them for 50¢, how do you make a profit? Answer: Volume.) The reason, of course, is to become better known, build an audience, sell more records, play bigger concerts, and generally further your career. As we discussed (on page 14), the future of the music biz is to find ways other than radio to reach fans, and touring is still one of the best. On top of that, being on the road builds your performing skills. There are a lot of artists who explode on their first album but have a lousy live show because they haven't spent time getting their act down. Many of those careers die shortly afterward.

So touring is a good thing. However, if you go out and lose money, who's going to pay for the loss? The answer is one of two possibilities: (1) a rich relative; or (2) a record company. Guess which one happens more often.

Monies that record companies give you to make up tour losses are called **tour support.** Tour support used to be much easier to come by than it is nowadays. Record companies are more and more skeptical about whether an artist really sells more records by going on the road. Also, it depends on the type of artist you are. If you're a heavy metal band, being on the road sells records better than anything else. You may never get on Top 40 radio (Top 40 is today called **CHR,** standing for "contemporary hit radio"), but there will be a direct relationship between your appearing in a town and the sales of your records in that town. If you're more the ballad type, it's much harder to convince the company you should go out. If you fall in between, the amount of your tour support will depend on how well your manager does the Tijuana Two-Step.

Tour support is defined as the actual amount of your loss (you'll be required to give accountings to the company), but of course it has a maximum limit, usually in the range of $50,000 to $100,000 per tour for a major record company, and more like $10,000 to $15,000 for an independent. In this era of 360 deals, the companies say they'll be more generous with tour support if you're more generous with their share of touring income. Contractual guarantees of tour support are usually limited to the first album.

Record companies have gotten pretty sophisticated about tour support. For example, some companies won't let you charge a management commission in computing losses, on the theory that the manager shouldn't get paid when everyone else is breaking even. Also, if you use any of the money to buy equipment, the company sometimes tries to own the stuff.

Tour support used to be nonrecoupable. For a while, the record companies bought the argument that it was "promotion" of their records, and wrote it off just like any other advertising and promotion expense. But those days have gone the way of eight-track cassettes. Today, tour support is always 100% recoupable (if you need it, your bargaining power ain't so great).

Many record companies are reluctant to commit to tour support in the contract but are pretty good about doing it at the time of the tour. If you can get it up front, it's a great thing to have; if you can't, go in and pound the table when you need it.

If you're on the *Advanced Overview Track,* go to Chapter 14 on page 203.
Experts, read on . . .

TERRITORY

For U.S. artists in the new-to-midrange category (unless there's a massive bidding war), the **territory** of your recording agreement (i.e., the countries where the company can exclusively sell your records) is almost always "the world." In fact, the territory is usually defined as "the universe," because some backroom lawyer worried that someone might argue satellites weren't covered by a contract that only said "the world."

This "universe" wording was the cause of one of my most bizarre negotiations, as well as my initiation by fire to the music business. I had only been practicing entertainment law a few months when a label I represented signed a jazz artist named Sun Ra. This guy said he was a reincarnated Egyptian, and he recorded records in the pyramids (for real). Anyway, his lawyer called me up to say that it was unacceptable to grant the universe, and that our territory must be limited to the Earth Zone. At first I thought he was kidding, so I said I would give him everything beyond our solar system, and maybe Neptune and Pluto, but that the Moon and neighboring planets were mine. I also asked if we had to pay him in Earth money. The lawyer, very seriously, said this was not negotiable and would blow the deal. So I added "satellites" to the territory of "the world" and caved in on the rest. (That lawyer owes me one.)

More routine negotiation of the territory comes at the superstar level, or when the artist is not based in the United States. In this case, the artist may divide North America (United States and Canada, but sometimes including Mexico) from the rest of the world, thus making two separate recording agreements.

The advantages of this are

1. The two territories aren't cross-collateralized (meaning amounts you don't recoup in North America can't be offset against your foreign royalties, and vice versa); and
2. You can always get a higher royalty outside North America because you're eliminating the U.S. company's share of it.

The disadvantages are

1. The advances may be lower (because there is no cross-collateralization); and
2. It's a pain for the artist to deal with two record companies. Dealing with two companies means shipping two sets of masters and artwork, "schmoozing" (hanging out) with two sets of executives, and most importantly, coordinating marketing efforts (which means getting up very early in the morning, or staying up very late at night, to call around the world). Also, the contracts for split-territory deals are much more complex than

worldwide deals, as you have to work out how the two companies will share the costs of artwork, videos, etc.

In recent years, more and more major companies have refused to sign you for anything except the entire world. So territorial deals are getting harder to come by. It's a bit easier if you start with an overseas deal, then come back to the U.S. and tell them you don't have those other territories. However, if you're going to a major label overseas, more and more of them are holding firm for the world.

UNION PER-RECORD CHARGES

It's important that you not be charged with any union payments based on the *sales* of records, as these are customarily borne by the record company. (This is different from union scale—see page 88 for what that is—paid to you for recording sessions, which has nothing to do with sales and is due even if the recordings are never released. Session scale payments are always recoupable as a recording cost, as we discussed on page 88.)

The most significant per-record union charges are what the companies pay to the American Federation of Musicians (AFM), which has two funds—the **Special Payment Fund (SPF)** and the **Music Performance Trust Fund (MPTF).** Through some complex computations that are beyond your and my pain tolerance, these payments total about 4.2¢ per physical album (excluding the first 25,000 units) for worldwide sales during the first five years after release of the album. For sales during years six through ten after release, only the SPF gets paid, which is about 3¢ per album. In addition, these rates escalate after the first 300,000 units, and again after 1 million units. (There's no payment for physical singles).

The AFM also gets a piece of digital sales. Currently, it's .55% (meaning a little over half of 1%) of the wholesale price for each permanent download, excluding the first 10,000 units. The AFM Pension Fund gets 0.55% for non-permanent downloads and 0.5% for streams. A combined union fund (meaning it's for both AFM & AFTRA), which is called by the brilliantly exciting name of "Intellectual Property Rights Distribution Fund," collects and distributes the digital revenue to non-featured musicians and vocalists for streaming and some international revenue sources.

This can be some decent dough. For example, the 2014 SPF distribution was just over $6 million, paid to about 15,500 of its members. The biggest portion went to studio musicians (people who get a fee for recording, but don't get a royalty), and the balance went to royalty artists. (If you're a studio musician, you get a bigger piece for working more hours, so be sure the producer or the contractor booking the session fills out the AFM B-4 [session] Report Form properly, so you get credit for your hours.)

If this stuff turns you on, you can get more info on the AFM at www.sound-recording.org.

For AFTRA (remember, AFTRA are the singers; AFM are the musicians), the record companies are required to make a contingent scale payment. AFTRA's contingent scale is also based on record sales, but it's much less money. It's only payable if there are nonroyalty background singers on a master, and if the master sells more than 157,500 physical units. (Why 157,500? I have absolutely no idea.) AFTRA contingent scale also has a ceiling, meaning it stops after the union gets a certain amount. The ceiling is a little over ten times scale for a one-hour session record, and since one-hour scale is currently $222.50, that means the maximum AFTRA contingent scale is about $2,225.00 per singer, per side. Through various voodoo computations, you'll hit that ceiling around 3 million units.

AFTRA has also figured out that music is selling digitally, so they now get a digital contingent scale payment for nonroyalty background vocalists. Currently, record companies pay .07% (⁷⁄₁₀ths of 1%) of their receipts on permanent downloads. Non-permanent downloads get .5% of receipts. Music videos are paid at .55% of receipts for the first ten years after release, then .3% of receipts for the next five years. Additionally, both unions recently negotiated percentages for the use of recordings in consumer products (e.g., toys and greeting cards) and new media, such as podcasts and webisodes.

So, as you can see, these babies add up to a chunk of change that should not be charged to your royalty account as a recoupable cost. Make sure your deal says they can't.

Another union oddity is that, each time a record company signs a new artist, they're required to pay AFTRA's Health & Retirement Funds (H&R) a Special Minimum Roster Payment for every vocalist in the group. That's the good news. The bad news is that you have to pay AFTRA a one-time new member fee to become an AFTRA member (which the company may pay and charge back against your account). The current new-member fees range from $1,150 if you live in Tennessee, to $3,101 if you live in New York or California. Additionally, if you want health insurance, AFTRA H&R will bill you about $420 per quarter for single coverage, and more if you want to cover a spouse or family (which is way cheaper than you could get anywhere else). The record companies are required to pay AFTRA H&R a fistful of money to subsidize your insurance as long as you're on the active roster of the label.

ALBUM COVER ARTWORK

At almost any level you can usually get some involvement in your album cover artwork, but you have to ask for it.

"Involvement" at lower levels means they tell you what they're doing, then go ahead and do it whether you like it or not. This process is called **consultation,** which means they talk to you but don't have to get your approval. *Consultation* is actually more valuable than I'm making it sound, because you can at least make your feelings known before the horse leaves the starting gate, and many companies will actually listen to you.

The next step up is **approval,** which means you can approve artwork that the company prepares. When you have approval rights, the company has to please you or you can stop them from using it.

Top of the line is the right to create your own artwork, subject to the company's approval. You can get this as your bargaining power grows. If you're a superstar, the company's only approval rights may be as to legalities, obscenity, and other major grossness—otherwise it's your show.

When you get the right to create artwork, the trick is to make sure you have an adequate budget, or else your creative juices will be severely hampered. So build in a set figure and escalate it over time (for inflation). I hesitate to give you specific figures because they may be out of date by the time you read this, but as of now a normal (no particular frills) artwork budget is in the range of $10,000 to $20,000, which is the most you'll likely get contractually. However, companies will usually spend a reasonable amount even if it's not in your deal (but may charge the excess against your royalties if the contract permits).

As we move more into the digital age, artwork becomes less important. If it's used at all, it's a tiny little square on someone's mobile phone screen. Accordingly, fights over album artwork are dying down. Never worry, though. There's plenty of room to fight about what the company will spend to create images and artwork for your advertising and marketing campaign, such as the cost of photographers. Major artists can sometimes get a minimum budget for photography in addition to the artwork budget, but it varies so widely that I can't really give you a range. Just know that superstar photographers are really expensive.

CREATIVE, MARKETING, AND OTHER CONTROLS

There are a number of controls you should ask for, some of which you may actually get. These are:

1. Consent to coupling (see page 160 for what this is and the details on controlling it).
2. Consent to the use of your masters in commercials.
3. Consent to licensing your masters for films, television, video games and other audiovisual works.
4. Approval of your photographs, biographical materials, and other artwork used in advertising and promotion.

If you do get approvals, they may be limited to the term of your deal, and to the United States. As your power grows, so do your territorial approvals, as well as the ability to keep your consent rights after the term.

If you can't get any approvals, at least try to get consultation rights (see the previous section for what those are).

14

Loan-out, Independent Production, Label, and Distribution Deals

LOAN-OUT DEALS

Loan-Out Corporations

As you get more successful, you will undoubtedly want a **loan-out corporation.** Everybody on the block has one. It's called a *loan-out* because the corporation (not you) enters into the deals, and "loans" your services to others for recording, concerts, etc. This is the entity you see people naming with cute little phrases (two of my favorites are "Disappearing, Inc.," and "I Want It All"). As the tax laws have changed over the years, particularly in the pension area, it's questionable whether it makes sense to have a loan-out company.

Even if you don't need a loan-out for tax planning, however, a company can shield you from liability if you get sued. For example, if the loan-out company's only assets are your record royalties, and someone sues you over a record-related claim, they can only grab your record money. They couldn't go after, for example, your personal bank accounts, your songwriting income, your stamp collection, etc. (Note I'm talking about your being sued by someone other than the record company. Record companies figured this out a long time ago, so under your record deal, they take the right to grab anything they can find, as we'll discuss in a minute.)

Bottom line: The decision as to whether to have a loan-out has to be made in light of your specific situation. Consult your lawyer, accountant, or life coach.

By the way, I'm using the term "corporation" for simplicity. It is often an **LLC** [a **Limited Liability Company**, which is something that looks and smells like a corporation, but is treated for tax purposes like a partnership], a general partnership, a limited partnership, a partnership of corporations, a cluster of worms, etc.

Anyway, for record deals, it works like this: You sign an exclusive recording contract with your own corporation, on a form that looks like a record company deal. Then the record company signs a recording agreement with your corporation, which agrees to supply your services to the record company. It looks like this:

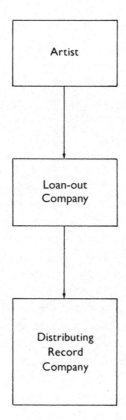

Figure 8. Loan-out deal structure.

Inducement (Side) Letters

As you can see in the above chart, you have no direct deal with the record company. So what's to keep you from walking out on your own corporation (after all, you could fire yourself), then thumbing your nose at the record company? You personally have no deal with the company—only your bankrupt corporation has a contract, and its secretary/treasurer is now in Lithuania with the masters.

Well, you know the companies won't let that happen, so they have you sign something known as an **inducement letter** or **side letter.** This is simply a piece of paper that says, if your corporation doesn't deliver your recordings to them, you will deliver them directly to the record company. So the real picture looks like Figure 9.

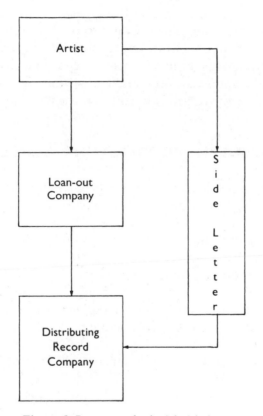

Figure 9. Loan-out deal with side letter.

The side letter is an integral part of these deals. It's like an emergency detour. If the highway is flooded, the company sends a Jeep down a back road to haul your ass back in.

Structure of Loan-out Deals

Loan-out contracts are very similar to contracts directly between the record company and artist (known as **direct agreements**), except that:

1. The parties, of course, are the record company and the corporation, instead of the company and you;
2. The corporation agrees to supply your services and recordings;
3. There are additional legal clauses, which are basically assurances that the corporation has the right to your exclusive services, that it has the right to deliver your recordings, etc.; and
4. You have to sign an inducement letter saying that the loan-out is really a phony, and if you try anything cute, you'll perform directly for the record company as if the loan-out didn't exist.

INDEPENDENT PRODUCTION AGREEMENTS

An independent production agreement is what a major-distributed independent label (we discussed those companies on page 68) signs with the major. These deals are just like loan-outs, except that the artist doesn't own the corporation in the middle (let's call the corporation the "production entity," because it "produces" the recordings). Typically, the production entity is owned by a producer or other record mogul whose "magic ears" have found you. The company then signs to a major (let's call it the "distributor") to deliver the artist's recordings. As we'll see in a minute, the inducement letter under these deals is even more critical.

There are two basic flavors of production deals:

1. A **single-artist deal** is where the production entity makes an agreement with the record company for one specific artist. Note, by the way, that the production entity may have signed more than one artist; we're talking only about the deal between the production entity and the record company.
2. A **multi-artist deal,** also called a **label deal,** is where the production entity supplies recordings of various artists, many of whom (or perhaps all of whom) have not yet been signed by the production entity. As you can imagine, this type of deal is much more complicated than a single-artist deal. So let's start with the simpler one.

Single-Artist Deals

A single-artist deal is basically the same as a loan-out deal, but because the production entity isn't owned by the artist, there are a couple of differences:

1. The deal between the artist and the production entity is now a real, arm's-length transaction, as opposed to one the artist makes with himself or herself. This means there is a true negotiation—i.e., a deal made by parties who are at "arm's length" from each other instead of hugging—and the artist asks for most of the things he or she would get from a record company, such as a guaranteed release, creative approvals, etc. (When you sign to a production entity, you should also get some things that you don't need from a record company, which we'll discuss in a minute.)

2. There is a real possibility that the artist can get into a fight with the production entity. This means it's more likely that the record company will exercise its rights under the inducement letter, and thus the terms of the inducement letter are even more critical.

Why Do It?   So why should an artist make a deal like this? Wouldn't it be better to have direct contact with your record company? Well, the answer is "maybe." A production deal has its pluses and minuses compared to a direct deal, and whether it's better for you depends on your specific situation.

Here are the negatives:

1. The production entity takes some of the royalty. Traditionally its deal with the record company provides a higher royalty than direct artist deals (by 1% to 2%) for precisely this purpose. But you still normally get a lower royalty than you would under a direct deal, and this is especially so when you're successful. The reason is that, with success, the production entity's deal with the record company "tops out" and leaves no room for them to keep anything without getting it from you.

2. It may be harder for you to coordinate marketing, promotion, etc., if you and your manager have no direct contact with the record company.

3. There may be problems auditing the record company directly

(see page 177 for what auditing is). In its contract, the production entity has the right to audit the record company. But the record company doesn't want two different people (you and the production entity) doing the same audit, and since it has no direct contract with you, it doesn't have to let you in at all.

4. The production entity might go south with your money.

On the positive side:

1. The production entity may be owned by someone who really brings something to the party. For example, there are production companies owned by major producers who will only work with a new artist if the artist signs to his or her entity. Other production companies are owned by important managers, promotion people, or industry people with good track records (translation: They have a lot of clout).

2. You may be able to get the same calculation of royalties that the production entity gets (meaning the same reduction for foreign sales, free-good limits, reserve limits, etc.). If you're a new artist and they're an established company, this can be more favorable than you could get on your own.

3. And I saved the best for last: Nobody else may want to sign you.

On balance, this is not your ideal choice (barring very unusual circumstances, like a great producer), but it can be a very desirable alternative to flipping Big Macs.

Artist Deal Points.   If you're making a deal with a production entity, in addition to all the other items we talked about for record deals (guaranteed release, advances, approvals, etc.), you should get the following:

1. You want the same computation of royalties that's in the production entity's deal with the record company (for packaging, free goods, foreign, budget, etc.). Indeed, you may want to ask for a percentage of the production company's receipts. It's not uncommon to do a deal where the artist gets 75% of the production entity's royalties (with the artist paying the producer from his or her share), or maybe 50% or 60% (with the production entity paying the producer from its share). This percentage should also apply to advances in excess of recording costs.

2. Try to get direct accountings from the record company. This may or may not be possible, depending on the production entity's own deal. Your worry is similar to the situation we discussed on page 132, where we talked about a producer being owed money by an artist when no royalties were payable. In this case, the roles are reversed: You're the one due money, and the production entity may not have any royalties coming in. This can easily happen to your production entity—especially if it signs several artists (as you'll see in excruciating detail on page 212).

3. And, of course, don't forget the points we discussed on page 123: You should have the right to get out of your deal if the production company doesn't get a distribution deal within a certain period of time, or if that deal goes wonky and they can't replace it.

Production Deal Points. Now, let's jump over the table and get the production entity's point of view. (Come on—it will make you a better-rounded person.) Here are two major areas of concern:

1. Remember how the artist wants the same computation of royalties as you? (See paragraph 1 of the previous section.) In representing production entities, I've rarely found it worthwhile to recompute the royalties. First of all, it's difficult, complex, time-consuming, and usually given to a low-level bookkeeper who doesn't quite understand what to do. So half the time they end up paying more than you would if you just used the same computation. Second, even when done correctly, the advantage you pick up is often minimal. Third, if the artist finds it out (which will happen if there's a great deal of success), you look like a pig, which is not usually good for artist relations.

2. Make sure you don't give the artist any rights you don't have in the first place. I remember a situation where one production company gave the artist approval of coupling, approval of album cover artwork, guaranteed release, etc., when they didn't have those things from the record company. If you fall into this trap, at best it will be embarrassing, and at worst the artist can walk away from your deal when you don't deliver. (Note that the artist isn't going very far—if he or she succeeds in walking away from you, they'll still have to record for the record company under their inducement letter. However, this doesn't do you any good because the record company won't pay you any royalties

if you lose the artist because of your screw-up. This position is known in show biz as "sucking rocks.")

Multi-Artist (Label) Deals

A **multi-artist deal,** as the name implies, is one where the production entity has a deal with a record company to sign and deliver a number of artists. It is sometimes called a **label deal,** as nowadays the production entity usually has its own label on the product. Sometimes, however, the producing entity has no identification on the records, and the public doesn't even know they exist.

Differences from Single-Artist Deals.   A multi-artist deal between the distributor and the production entity looks a lot like a single-artist loan-out deal, but:

1. In addition to paying a recording fund for each album, there is often some form of overhead payment to the production entity. This is usually an advance (although it can at times be nonrecoupable, at least in part) and it's used to pay the entity's rent, payroll, phone, light bills, etc. For bigger deals, it will be a number large enough to cover marketing, promotion, etc.
2. The term of the deal is usually two or three years firm, with the distributor having options for additional one-, two-, or three-year periods.
3. The number of artists the production entity can sign, and whether the distributor can approve these artists, is a matter of major negotiation. A new production entity will maybe get the right to sign one, two, or three artists over the term, but a more established company may get to sign one or two artists per year. More and more, the distributors want to approve the artists before signing, but if you have a lot of bargaining power, you may be able to negotiate (a) no approval (very difficult today); or (b) for each one or two approved artists, you have the right to sign an artist that isn't approved (which is called a **put** because you can "put it to" the company and they have to take it).
4. The minimum and maximum number of albums the production entity can deliver is also prenegotiated, both in terms of the overall number per year, and the number per artist. Normally, the distributor doesn't want you delivering more than one album per artist per year without its consent.

5. Speaking of albums, how about this great idea (see if you can find the history lesson): You are a production entity in the last year of your deal with a distributor, and you suddenly have the opportunity to sign a hot new band. Six months before the end of your term, you deliver an album of this band and say, "Please make these guys into superstars so that, six months later when my deal ends, I can (a) beat you to death in a renegotiation; or (b) better yet, take them to another company, leaving you with a gigantic deficit from my prior flops. That way I can take the royalties from this band and buy that little pig farm I've always wanted." Sound too good to be true? Of course; the deal will require you to deliver a minimum number of albums for each artist—usually three or four—even if the term is over. (Note this will put you in the position of having your deal expire for some artists and continue for others.)

6. The recording funds for the artists are spelled out up front. If you're a new entity, you'll probably have to live with something like $75,000 to $150,000 per album. You may be able to negotiate a preapproved formula for artists with previous track records (for example, a fund of $300,000 to $350,000 for an artist who has sold the equivalent of 200,000 albums or more). To exceed these figures, you need the company's consent on each specific deal. This means, if you have the chance to sign a major artist, you must sit down with the distributor and work out a special arrangement. (Sometimes the production entity and the distributor both are bidding for the same artist. You can imagine, since the distributor approves how much the production entity can spend, which one is likely to come out the winner. In this case, unless there's a personal relationship or some other good reason why the artist would rather sign to you, you can pretty well kiss them off.)

7. It's sometimes possible, although difficult, to get ownership of the master recordings under a label deal. Even in this situation, however, you normally wouldn't own the recordings during the term. So even if you win this point, the distributor usually owns the masters and assigns them back to you at some point after the end of the term (usually seven to ten years after the term). The distributor may insist on your being recouped before they'll assign; if this is the case, you should get the right to pay back the unrecouped deficit for an immediate reassignment.

Cross-collateralization.   Remember our story about a producer being entitled to royalties when the artist is unrecouped, and how the artist went further in the hole with every success? (See page 132.) Well, when you get to a multi-artist deal, this scenario gets to be a high-speed drilling rig. It is entirely possible (even easy) to have two or three real losers, together with one smash, but not get any royalties because the record company is using the winner's royalties to recoup the losers' deficit. Here's an example:

Suppose a production entity has signed three artists. Assume the following (*the numbers bear no relationship to reality;* they're just for easy math):

Multiple-Artist Deal

All-in Royalty to Production Entity:	60¢
Royalty to Artist A:	50¢
Royalty to Artist B:	50¢
Royalty to Artist C:	50¢
Recording Costs:	$60,000/album
Advance for Production Entity's Operations	$100,000

Sales:	Artist A:	Album 1: 60,000 units
		Album 2: 40,000 units
	Artist B:	Album 1: 20,000 units
		Album 2: 40,000 units
	Artist C:	Album 1: 60,000 units
		Album 2: 500,000 units

Under these assumptions, let's look at everyone's accounts:

Artist A's Account with Production Entity

	Charges (Recording Costs)	Earnings	Balance
Album 1	– $60,000	+ $30,000 (50¢ × 60,000 units)	– $30,000
Album 2	– $60,000	+ $20,000 (50¢ × 40,000 units)	– $40,000
TOTAL	**– $120,000**	**+ $50,000**	**– $70,000**

Summary: Artist A is *in the red (unrecouped) in the amount of $70,000* (the $120,000 deficit less the $50,000 earnings), and is thus owed nothing.

Artist B's Account with Production Entity

	Charges (Recording Costs)	Earnings	Balance
Album 1	– $60,000	+ $10,000 (50¢ × 20,000 units)	– $50,000
Album 2	– $60,000	+ $20,000 (50¢ × 40,000 units)	– $40,000
TOTAL	**– $120,000**	**+ $30,000**	**– $90,000**

Summary: Artist B is *in the red (unrecouped) in the amount of $90,000* (the $120,000 deficit less the $30,000 earnings), and is thus owed nothing.

Artist C's Account with Production Entity

	Charges (Recording Costs)	Earnings	Balance
Album 1	– $60,000	+ $ 30,000 (50¢ × 60,000 units)	– $ 30,000
Album 2	– $60,000	+ $250,000 (50¢ × 500,000 units)	+ $190,000
TOTAL	**– $120,000**	**+ $280,000**	**+ $160,000**

Summary: Artist C is *in the black (and owed) $160,000* (the $280,000 earnings less the $120,000 deficit).

Production Entity's Account with Record Company

	Charges	Earnings	Balance
Overhead	– $100,000		– $100,000
Artist A	– $120,000	+ $ 60,000 (60¢ × 100,000 units)	– $ 60,000
Artist B	– $120,000	+ $ 36,000 (60¢ × 60,000 units)	– $ 84,000
Artist C	– $120,000	+ $336,000 (60¢ × 560,000 units)	+ $216,000
TOTAL	**– $460,000**	**+ $432,000**	**– $ 28,000**

Summary: The production entity is *in the red (unrecouped) $28,000* (the $460,000 deficit less the $432,000 earnings), and is thus owed nothing.

Grand Summary

Artist A: Unrecouped and not entitled to royalties.
Artist B: Unrecouped and not entitled to royalties.
Artist C: Owed $160,000.
Production entity: Owes Artist C $160,000, but is in the red $28,000 and thus not entitled to royalties.

Owing $160,000 and having no royalties due you is certainly the fuzzy side of the lollipop.

So how do you get out of the box? Well, if you have enough clout, you make the distributor pay the artists' royalties without regard to cross-collateralization. Thus, if you and Artists A and B are deeply unrecouped, but Artist C is recouped, they'd have to pay Artist C's royalties. In other words, they can't cross-collateralize any artist's royalties with either your or any other artist's deficits.

If you don't have enough bargaining power for this, then at minimum you should require the distributor to pay the recouped artist's royalties and to treat these payments as additional advances against your share of royalties. In the above example, that would mean the record company would advance the $160,000 owed to Artist C, and the production entity would then be $188,000 in the red (the $28,000 original deficit plus the $160,000 paid to Artist C). You wouldn't make any money under these circumstances (until you have an awfully big success and eventually recoup), but at least you won't be breaking your kids' piggybanks to pay the artists.

JOINT VENTURES

A **joint venture** is the same as a multi-artist or label deal, except the production entity doesn't get a royalty. Instead, the production entity and the distributing record company are in effect "partners." This means they take all of the income that comes in (the gross wholesale price of records, all proceeds from downloads, streams, licensing, etc.) and put it into a pot. Then they take all the expenses of operations out of the pot, and whatever is left over gets split between the two entities. Historically, the split was 50/50, but over recent years this has become increasingly difficult to get. Record companies are shying away from joint ventures altogether, and when they do them, they're trying to pay less—40%, 30%, sometimes even lower.

By the way, these agreements aren't usually "joint ventures" or "partnerships" in the legal sense. A true partnership or joint venture means one partner can commit both of them to legal obligations. For example, if one partner signs a bank loan for $200,000, both partners can be sued if it isn't paid back. Neither you nor the record company wants this, so the agreements sometimes specifically state they aren't legally partnerships or joint ventures. Thus the name "joint venture" is not technically correct; it just describes a deal where the profits are shared as if a joint venture existed.

Computation of Profits

The economics of a joint venture look like this:

Income Side. Gross receipts for records and downloads are the price received by the record company, which is easy to compute if the distributor is independent. However, as we discussed on page 67, all the major distributors are owned by the major record companies. This means you need a different definition of *gross receipts* when the joint-venture distributor is a major. Why? Well, if the same person owns both the distributor and the record company, they can set any price they want between the two of them. To use an absurd example, the distributor might charge $10 for a record and only pay $2 back to the record company, simply to hose you.

The way it's handled is by treating each record and download's full PPD price as the gross, then taking a negotiated distribution fee off that before it goes into the pot. We'll discuss the range of those fees in the next section.

Income from licenses is also treated as gross receipts, with the same distribution fee coming off the top.

Foreign income from unrelated companies is treated as license income, and the venture usually gets the same royalty paid by foreign distributors to the U.S. company for its entire catalog. In other words, if they get a 25% of PPD royalty in Guam, that would go into the pot as gross receipts and therefore be used for determining profits.

When the foreign distributor is owned by the same company that owns your record company, they establish an **intra-company rate,** meaning the rate at which the U.S. company is paid by the foreign distributor. Usually it's somewhere in the mid-20% range. This rate is in place even when there is no joint venture, as it's used by the U.S. company to compute its profits and losses in reporting earnings to the parent company (and in determining executive bonuses based on performance, so you hope the executives are greedy enough to keep this number high). Lately, some companies have taken to paying the venture a foreign royalty that is less than the intra-company rate, so there's less money to split with you. They do this because they get to keep more money that way. There's no logic to this practice; it's just a muscle-move by the company. So you should always try to get the full rate into the pot. Results will vary with your bargaining power.

Note the result of this foreign licensing practice is that a joint venture only shares profits for U.S. sales. On foreign sales, it's simply a sharing of the royalty paid to the U.S. company.

Expenses. From this gross, the joint venture deducts its expenses and other charges. They consist of the following:

1. The first thing deducted is a **distribution fee** for the record company. (We already discussed this concept in the context of home videos, on page 168. And remember the rule we discussed there: If you're getting a percentage, take it out first.) The distribution fee is a charge to cover the cost of the record company's overseeing the distribution of records, meaning the accounting, invoicing, manufacturing, etc., of the venture. This will run somewhere in the 15% to 20% range, sometimes even higher, and it includes the distribution fee charged to the company by its distributor (it may be even higher if it includes an overhead/services fee, which we'll discuss in the next section). It's possible to reduce this fee as volume increases, usually on a yearly basis. For example, the fee could be 20% of the first $5 million each year, 19% of the next $5 million, and 18% thereafter. At the beginning of the following year, the fee would start again at 20%.

   The above is what you'll be charged in computing your profits under a joint-venture deal. It may have no relationship to what the record company is actually charged by its distributor. And what, you ask, are the labels actually charged by the distributor? Well . . .

   Before I tell you what distribution fee they get charged, let's look at the big picture. Major record labels are judged by their profits and losses, separate from the profits and losses of the company that owns them. For example, the executives at Warner Bros. Records get bonuses (or get fired) based on the financial performance of Warner Bros. Records, and the executives at Atlantic Records (which is owned by the same people who own Warner Bros. Records) get rewarded on the basis of Atlantic's performance.

   Let's use Atlantic as an example. To figure out Atlantic's profits, you have to know its costs. If Atlantic were a stand-alone company, it would have to make a deal with someone to distribute its records, and that distributor's charges would be an expense for Atlantic. Because Atlantic is owned by Warner Music Group (WMG), it's forced to make a deal with WEA Distribution (also owned by WMG). However, just because they have the same owner, Atlantic doesn't get a free ride. It has to pay a fee to WEA Distribution for putting Atlantic's records into stores and through online distributors.

In one sense, this distribution fee is a fiction, because the money moves from one WMG pocket to another. But it's not a fiction to the executives of Atlantic. The bigger it is, the more it reduces Atlantic's profits (and the executives' bonuses).

Typically, the distribution fees charged by a major distributor to an affiliated major label are in the 12% to 14% range. In your joint venture, if you've got a lot of clout, you may be able to get the same distribution fee that the label is charged. In other words, if Atlantic pays 12% to WMG (I have no idea if that's correct), you'd only be charged 12% in computing the profits. However, that's only if you've got a *lot* of bargaining power. In the beginning, you'll pay quite a bit more, as noted above.

2. In addition to the distribution fee, the record company may also charge an **overhead fee,** sometimes called a **services fee.** This is for services supplied by the label in addition to distribution, such as marketing and promotion. The more they supply, the higher this charge will be. It can range anywhere from zero to (more commonly) 4% to 7%. Often this is combined with the distribution fee discussed in point 1, so that there's one percentage that includes both distribution and services/overhead (e.g., 25%).

3. Next come all the costs of operation. In addition to the costs you would normally expect (recording costs, advances, etc.), there are a number of things that aren't charged under royalty deals. These include:
   (a) Manufacturing
   (b) Shipping
   (c) Advertising and marketing
   (d) Mechanical royalties (we'll discuss these later, on page 229)
   (e) Per-record union payments (for a definition, see page 199)

4. Lastly, the record company takes back payments it has made to the production entity, such as reimbursements for promotional and operating expenses of the company. It's a matter of negotiation whether these are charged "off the top" of the venture (so that each party bears 50%), or whether they're charged solely against the producing entity's share of the profits.

The amount left after the above calculation is the profit, and the agreed split goes to each party.

Royalty Versus Joint Venture

So how about the key question: Are you better off with a joint venture or with a royalty arrangement? To answer this requires a crystal ball. If you're extremely successful, you're better off with a joint venture. With modest success, you're better off under a royalty arrangement. (If you're a turkey, it doesn't really matter.) Here's why:

As we discussed, you're charged for more costs in a joint venture than you are under a royalty deal, and thus with only modest success, you're behind. However, many of these costs are not "per unit," meaning they're only paid at the beginning, as opposed to "per-unit" costs that are incurred for each record ("unit") made. (Examples of per-unit charges are costs of manufacture and freight for physical goods, mechanical royalties [the monies paid to songwriters for the songs in the record], union per-record charges, etc., which are only paid when a physical unit is manufactured and shipped, or when a digital unit is sold. Costs that are not per-unit are such things as artwork, videos, promotion, marketing, and advertising, which are unrelated to specific units.) Thus, with a great deal of success, the non-per-unit costs are eaten up by the first dollars that come in, and thereafter the profit per unit is far greater than any royalty arrangement.

PRESSING AND DISTRIBUTION (P&D) DEALS

If you are truly a record company in your own right, then this is the deal for you. It gives you the most autonomy and control of your life, as well as the highest profit margin. This is the deal that true independent labels make.

A **pressing and distribution agreement** (or **P&D** deal) is exactly that—the company agrees to manufacture records for you (although in some situations this isn't even so; the product is manufactured elsewhere), and then to distribute them solely as a wholesaler. This means you sell the records to the distributing entity for a wholesale price less a negotiated distribution fee (which covers the distributing company's overhead, operations, and profit). The distribution fee for physical product ranges in the 20% to 25% range (less if you're a big label), with the bulk of the deals around 24% to 25%. For example, if a CD wholesales for $10, under a deal with a 25% distribution fee, the independent company gets $7.50 per unit ($10 less 25%). Out of this, the independent pays manufacturing, mechanicals, artist royalties, promotion, overhead, salaries, and everything else.

Unless you're a really large label, or have massive bargaining power, the distribution company will only handle your physical records if they also get the exclusive right to distribute your digital records. Even though their distribution costs are less for digital, they will insist on the same distribution fee for both physical and digital product, and unless you have a lot of clout, this is hard to change. Their argument is that the physical business is dwindling, that they can't make money if they don't have digital, and there are significant costs in managing the hundreds of users, and millions of plays, in the digital world.

If you're putting out physical records, a distribution deal is not for the weak-hearted:

1. In these deals, the entire risk of manufacturing falls entirely on the independent company. Remember how physical records are sold on a returnable basis (see page 78)? This means that, if you guess wrong, the returns come back home to roost. So not only are you losing your potential profit on the sale, you're also coming out of pocket and losing the cost of manufacturing and shipping records you can't sell (although they make passable doorstops). Many deals also require you to pay a distribution fee even if the record is returned, adding injury to insult.

2. The distributing company typically offers no services whatsoever in terms of marketing, promotion, accounting, etc. You really are on your own. (You can sometimes make a deal to get these services from the distributing company for an increased distribution fee. For example, they might help with marketing, sales, or promotion, and charge an extra 3% to 5% on top of the distribution fee.)

3. You may well be treated as a second-class citizen. This is because the distributing company will favor its own product over yours; they make a bigger profit on their own stuff, and they have a bigger investment in it.

These types of deals can be made at the highest level (for example, Hollywood Records [Disney's label] is distributed by Universal under such an arrangement), down to small indie labels who make these deals with independent distributors.

A relatively new animal is the **label services deal,** which is essentially a distribution deal aimed at artists (rather than independent labels, though I'm sure they would handle the right label as well). For a known artist, the distributing label (at the time of this writing, Kobalt and BMG Rights are major players in this game) will front the money for you to not just manufacture product, but for marketing and promotion as well. They will then do a kind of profit split, but instead of taking costs off the top like a joint venture (see page 214), they instead take the costs from your share of money. That means you end up in the same place you would have been under a normal distribution deal if you'd written the check yourself (except for the fact that you didn't have to write any checks, which is no small "except"). The specifics are very negotiable, so I can't give you hard and fast rules, but for the right kind of artist, these can be favorable deals.

UPSTREAM DEALS

An **upstream deal** is a cross between an independent distribution deal and a production deal. It works like this:

An independent label goes to an independent distributor that's owned by a major label. It makes a standard distribution deal but also gives the major label a right to *upstream* the artist, meaning the deal miraculously transforms from a distribution deal into a production deal with the major label. (Technically, the upstream deal is made with the major label in the first place. The major label then "supplies" the independent distribution to the indie label. In other words, the pure distribution part of the deal is in a contract with the major label, not a separate contract with the independent distributor.)

When an artist is upstreamed, the distributing label moves the records from the indie distributor to its major distributor. It stops paying over the gross sales monies less a distribution fee, and instead pays the indie a royalty, or, if the independent has enough clout, a percentage of profits. Whether it's a royalty or profit share, the independent gets less money than it would under a distribution deal. That's because the distributing label is now taking a much bigger risk. As part of the upstream, it takes over the cost of marketing, promotion, videos, etc. (all of which were the responsibility of the indie label under the distribution deal). Also, the distributor takes the risk of records being returned, which was the indie's problem under the distribution deal.

The idea behind upstreaming is that, when an artist's sales get to a certain point, it takes the clout (and money) of a major to move those sales to the mega level. The major labels aren't willing to put out big marketing bucks if they're only getting a distribution fee, so the deal transforms.

The upstream is usually at the discretion of the major label. Sometimes it's automatic, meaning it kicks in when an artist achieves a certain sales level, but this is rare. Upstreaming is never at the independent label's discretion.

The advantage of doing an upstream deal is basically time. If there were no upstream deal in place, and an artist explodes, the indie would have to run around and make a deal with a major, which takes time and (when you change distributors) disrupts the flow of records to the stores. If an upstream deal is already there, they can immediately shift the project to the bigger system, without loss of momentum.

The disadvantage is that the terms of the upstream deal are preset, so the indie doesn't have the clout of an exploding record to make a better deal when they decide to upstream.

To date, a few upstream deals have worked well, but a large number of artists have disappeared after being upstreamed. We'll see if these deals are still around for the next edition.

PART III

Songwriting and Music Publishing

15

Copyright Basics

Before you can understand what songwriting and music publishing are all about, you have to understand how copyrights work.

When you deal with something intangible like a copyright (which you can't see, feel, or smell), it's a challenge to nail it down. Copyrights are a tremendous amount of fun—they're squiggly little critters that, every time you think you have a handle on them, take an unexpected turn and nip you in the butt. And many of the concepts have been around since record players had cranks on the side, which makes for some interesting challenges in today's world.

But don't worry. I'll guide you through the maze.

BASIC COPYRIGHT CONCEPTS

When you own a copyright, it's like playing Monopoly and owning all the properties on the board. But unlike Monopoly, you're not limited to the rents printed on the little cards. (Well, actually, there are some preset rents, but for the most part you can charge whatever the traffic will bear.)

Definition of Copyright

The legal definition of a copyright is "a limited duration monopoly." Its purpose (as stated in the U.S. Constitution, no less) is to promote the progress of "useful arts" by giving creators exclusive rights to their works for a while. As you can imagine, if you created something and everybody had the right to use it without paying you, not very many people would go through the trouble of creating anything (including you and me).

What's Copyrightable?

To be copyrightable, the work has to be original (not copied from something else) and of sufficient creativity to constitute a work, which is a pretty low threshold.

There's no specific test to know what's copyrightable; it's decided on a case-by-case basis. For example, the five notes played by the spaceship in *Close Encounters of the Third Kind* are copyrightable because of their originality, even though they're just five notes.

How to Get a Copyright

Under U.S. copyright law, as soon as you make a **tangible copy** of something, you have a copyright. *Tangible* simply means something you can touch. If the work is a musical composition, for example, it can be written down (if you write music, which many creative people don't these days), or just sung into a recorder. Once this tangible copy exists, you have all the copyright you need.

Many people think you have to register in Washington to get a copyright. Not true. There are some important rights you get from registering, but securing a copyright isn't one of them. (More on this later.)

So it's that simple. If you sing a song in your head, no matter how completely it's composed, you have no copyright. Once you write it down or record it, you have one. If you'd like to take a few minutes right now and copyright something, I'll wait.

WHAT ARE ALL THESE RIGHTS YOU GET?

When you have a copyright, you get the following rights at no extra charge. These rights are **exclusive,** which means that *no one* can do these things without your permission. (For you technical freaks, the rights are listed in Section 106 of the Copyright Act.)

You get the *exclusive* right to:

1. **Reproduce the work.**
   For example, if you write a song, no one can record it, publish it as sheet music, put it in a movie, or otherwise copy it without your permission.
2. **Distribute copies of the work.**
   Apart from the right to reproduce your song, there is a separate right of *distribution* that you also control. Notice the difference

between making a copy of the work (like recording a song or manufacturing records of it), which is one use of a copyright (it's a reproduction, as we discussed in point 1), and the *distribution* of this copy (selling records to the public), which is another, separate right. For example, if a record company hires a plant to manufacture its CDs, the plant gets the right to reproduce the songs, but not the right to distribute copies of them.

3. **Perform the work publicly.**

   With a song, this means playing it in concert venues, on the radio, on television, through a streaming service, in bars, amusement parks, supermarkets, elevators (you know your career is either soaring or history when you hear your song in an elevator), or anywhere else music is heard publicly. It doesn't matter whether the performance is by live musicians or a DJ playing records; you get to control this right. (If you're wondering how you could ever police this or get paid, stay tuned.)

4. **Make a derivative work.**

   A **derivative work** is a creation based on another work. In the music industry, an example is a parody lyric set to a well-known song (what Weird Al Yankovic does). The original melody is a copyrighted original work, and once you add parody lyrics, it constitutes a new, separate work. This new work is called a *derivative work* because it's "derived" from the original. A more common example is a song with a sample in it.

   This concept is even easier to see in the motion picture area. Any film made from a novel is a derivative work (the novel is the original work). The Broadway musical *Rent* is a derivative work based on the opera *La Bohème*. Anyway, you get the idea. (By the way, the original doesn't have to be copyrighted. If it isn't, the only parts of the derivative work that are protected are the newly created ones.)

5. **Display the work publicly.**

   Generally, this is the right to put paintings, statues, etc., on public display, and in the music area, it applies to websites that display lyrics.

EXCEPTIONS TO THE COPYRIGHT MONOPOLY

As I said earlier, the copyright law gives you an absolute monopoly, which means it's your bat and ball, and you don't have to let anyone use it. If you want to write poems and throw them into the ocean, so that no human being can ever make use of them, that's your prerogative. You may be cold and poor in your old age, but you will have entertained a lot of fish.

However . . .

Compulsory Licenses

There are five major exceptions to this monopoly rule, and they're known as **compulsory licenses.** A compulsory license means that you *must* issue a license to someone who wants to use your work, whether you like it or not. The five compulsory licenses are:

1. **Cable television rebroadcast.**
   This was originally designed for areas that had poor television reception. Cable companies set up a big antenna to receive weak signals and send them along to the homes in the area. The cable television compulsory license requires the broadcasting stations to allow the cable company to retransmit their signals in exchange for payment of set fees. Without this license, the rebroadcast would be an unauthorized distribution of copyrighted programming. (By the way, the pay channels [HBO, Showtime] and satellite channels [CNN, MTV, etc.] are original programmers, not retransmitters of over-the-air stations. That means they're not subject to compulsory licenses, so they can charge whatever they can gouge out of the cable operators.)
2. **Public Broadcasting System.**
   The PBS lobbyists did a terrific job of requiring copyright owners to license works to them at cheap rates.
3. **Jukeboxes.**
   It may surprise you to know that, until the 1976 Copyright Act, jukeboxes paid nothing for the right to use music. They were considered "toys" in the 1909 Copyright Act (really). Now they pay set license fees, the details of which have never been relevant to me, so I don't know them.
4. **Digital performance of records.**
   This baby was added in 1995, then modified in 1998, and it requires the owners of recordings to allow performances of masters on digital radio, which also includes non-interactive streaming (radio shows on the Internet). We talked a little about this on page 176, and we'll hit it harder on page 347.

5. **Phonorecords and digital downloads of non-dramatic musical compositions.**

   This is a biggie in today's music business, so we'll discuss it in detail. It's called a **compulsory mechanical license.**

COMPULSORY MECHANICAL LICENSES

To understand what the hell I'm talking about, you first need to know about mechanical royalties.

Mechanical Royalties

The term **mechanical royalties** (or **mechanicals** to its friends) developed in the 1909 Copyright Act and referred to payments for devices "serving to mechanically reproduce sound." Even though devices haven't reproduced sound "mechanically" since the 1940s, the name has stuck and the monies paid to copyright owners for the manufacture and distribution of records are still called *mechanical royalties.* The rights to reproduce songs in records are known as **mechanical rights.**

The concept of a *compulsory* license for these mechanical rights grew out of a concern in Congress that the music industry was going to develop into a gigantic monopoly (we may still make it). This desire to keep copyright owners from controlling the world resulted in the compulsory license for records, which accomplishes its mission nicely. Let's take a closer look:

Compulsory Mechanical Licenses

The compulsory copyright license for records is in Section 115 of the Copyright Act. It says that, once a song has been recorded and released to the public, the copyright owner *must* license it: (a) to anyone else that wants to use it in a **phonorecord** (which is a defined term in the Copyright Act); and (b) for a specific payment established by the law (more on this later). However, the owner is only required to issue a compulsory license *if*:

1. The song is a non-dramatic musical work; *and*
2. It has been previously recorded; *and*
3. The previous recording has been distributed publicly in phonorecords; *and*

4. The new recording doesn't change the basic melody or fundamental character of the song; *and*
5. The new recording is only used in phonorecords.

All of these conditions have to exist before you get a compulsory license. If you miss one, you have to beg the publisher for a license, and she can say, "Buzz off."

Let's look at each condition separately.

Non-dramatic Musical Work. Before you can get a compulsory license, the song must be a non-dramatic musical composition. It's not clear what a "dramatic" musical composition is, but it's probably a song used in an opera or musical—i.e., a song that helps tell a story. No one knows whether or not the term includes a "story song," which tells a story in the lyrics. My guess is that it doesn't, but it's just a guess.

Previously Recorded. You can't get a compulsory license for the very first recording of a song. The law allows the owner to control who gets it the first time, which is known as a **first use.** Even if the song was previously recorded, you can only get a compulsory license if that first recording was authorized by the copyright owner. The fact that someone sneaks off and records the song doesn't trigger the compulsory license.

Public Distribution. The first recording must have been distributed to the public. This closes a loophole from the prior law. So even if the copyright owner allowed a recording to be made, if it was never released, you can't get a compulsory license for another recording.

Phonorecord Use. A compulsory license is available only for **phonorecords,** which are defined in the copyright law to mean *audio-only* recordings. This definition was the publishers' finest lobbying accomplishment in the 1976 Copyright Act, because it excluded home video devices from the definition of phonorecords. This means there's no compulsory license for audiovisual works, and, among other things, the result has been that motion picture companies have to negotiate with every copyright owner (publisher) for home video usage of each song. It also means the song owners are free to charge whatever rate they choose. (More on how this is done on page 236.)

In 1995, the Copyright Act was revised to make clear that compulsory mechanical licenses apply to a **DPD,** which means **digital**

phonorecord delivery (such as the download of a song from iTunes). Specifically, DPD is defined (in Section 115(d)) as the "delivery of a phonorecord by digital transmission of a sound recording which results in a specifically identifiable reproduction." Those congressional folk can really turn a phrase, huh?

No Major Changes.   When you get a compulsory license, you're allowed to arrange the song "to conform it to the style or manner of interpretation of the performance." (This is in section 115(a)(2) of the copyright law, for you detail-oriented folk.) However, you can't change the basic melody or fundamental character of the work. So, for example, you couldn't write new lyrics, or add another melody.

An interesting debate over this section came up with **ringtones** (the songs that play when someone calls your cell phone). For reasons we'll discuss in a few paragraphs, the owners of songs (publishers) were always paid much more for ringtones than they were paid for the same song on phonorecords. The record companies, wanting to pay a cheaper rate, argued that a ringtone use was subject to a compulsory mechanical license. The copyright owners said "No thanks," arguing that a ringtone is a thirty-second edit of the full song, and that was too much of a "change" to fall under the compulsory license. (Remember, if it isn't subject to a compulsory license, the publishers are free to charge whatever they can get.) After a lot of screaming, it's now settled that ringtones are subject to the compulsory license, but there's a separate ringtone compulsory rate that is more than the normal phonorecord rate (as we'll discuss in a second).

If all the above conditions exist, then anyone who wants to use a song in phonorecords can do it by filing certain notices with the copyright office and paying a set fee per record. This fee is called the **statutory rate** (because it's a rate set by the Copyright Statute), and it has had a rather bizarre history. The rate was 2¢ from 1909 to 1976 (inflation didn't exist in those years, but record company lobbyists did). The 1976 Copyright Act raised it to 2.75¢, with provisions for further adjustments by a Copyright Royalty Board (more about them in a minute). It is currently the larger of (a) 9.1¢, or (b) 1.75¢ per minute of playing time or a fraction thereof. Thus, if a song runs five minutes or less, the rate is 9.1¢. However, if it's over five minutes (even by a second or two), but not over six minutes, the rate is 10.5¢ (1.75¢ × 6 = 10.5¢). If a song is over six minutes but not more than seven minutes, the rate is 12.25¢ (1.75¢ × 7 = 12.25¢). You get the idea.

As noted previously, ringtones have a separate rate, which we'll discuss in a second.

To its credit, Congress did a thorough job of research in working out the compulsory licensing legislation. There are specific accounting provisions (monthly), limits on the amount of reserves that can be withheld (see page 79 for a definition of reserves), and requirements that the reserves must be liquidated (paid out) at specific times. Also, in perhaps its most sophisticated move, the royalty is payable on all records "made and distributed" (as opposed to "made and sold"), which means the compulsory royalties are payable on "free goods" (see page 77 for a discussion of free goods).

The current 9.1¢ rate continues until December 31, 2017, at which point it will be reviewed by the **Copyright Royalty Board.** The Copyright Royalty Board (**CRB** to its pals) is made up of three administrative judges who probably have no sense of humor. They take in lots of evidence (shockingly, record companies say why the rate is too high, and copyright owners say why it's too low), then the judges sit around and think about the rates for all the compulsory licenses (meaning not just mechanicals, but also streaming, subscription services, etc.), and finally issue rulings from on high. Historically, mechanical rates escalated yearly, but since 2006, they've stayed at the same level (no doubt in a nod to the wretched state of the music business).

The current ringtone rate is 24¢, which is obviously much higher than the phonorecord rate. Why? Well, originally, ringtones were played on phones with simple synthesizer tones. Since they didn't use the actual master recording, the only rights holder who got paid was the song owner (the publisher). Thanks to some aggressive publishers, the industry norm settled in at 10% of the ringtone's retail price (ringtones were about $2 to $3, so the publishers got 20¢ to 30¢). When mastertones became the norm, meaning phones played the actual masters, the phone companies now had to pay both the publisher and the record company. The phone companies refused to pay two different parties, or to pay more money, so they made a deal with the record companies and required them to take care of the publishers out of their share. This gave the record companies an incentive to squeeze down the publisher's money, so they could keep more for themselves. Their argument, which we just discussed, was that ringtones were subject to a compulsory mechanical license, so the publishers should get 9.1¢ (as opposed to 10% of the price, which was 20¢ to 30¢). The publishers were not pleased.

This fight was settled at a CRB hearing when the publishers agreed that ringtones could be subject to a compulsory mechanical license, but only if they got a higher rate. They pushed for 10% of the ring-tone price. The CRB refused to adopt a percentage royalty and instead looked at then-current industry data, decided that 24¢ was the average, and went with that. (Ironically, as the price of ringtones fell, the publishers are getting more than 10% of the price.)

Back to Real Life

Having told you how compulsory licenses work, I will now tell you that the compulsory license is almost never used. Record companies hate to use it because the monthly accounting provisions are too burdensome. The copyright owners (publishers) would rather give a direct license because they can keep track of it easier. (Would you want a Washington bureaucrat to handle your licensing?) However, the compulsory license is still very significant because the "statutory rate" is the benchmark for setting mechanical rates in the industry. The reason is that, once a musical composition is recorded and released, the "statutory rate" is the maximum mechanical royalty anyone is willing to pay for it (if a publisher refuses to license it at that rate, the record company just gets a compulsory license). Of course, the record companies love to pay less than statutory, which we'll discuss on page 253.

First Use

Implicit in the above (which I'll now make explicit) is the fact that the compulsory license does not apply to a **first use** (the first recording of a song). In other words, until a song has been recorded under authorization of the copyright owner (until a *first use* has been made), and that first recording has been distributed to the public, the publisher can charge anything it wants. Customarily, the publisher doesn't charge more than the statutory rate, but there's no reason why it can't, other than industry custom (and the fact that no one will pay any more than that).

Foreign Mechanicals

By contrast, it's interesting to note that, other than the United States and Canada, most countries of the world use an entirely different copyright royalty system. Mechanicals over there are a percentage of wholesale price, which covers all songs on the record. This means the rate has nothing to do with the length of the composition or even the number of songs. The same amount of mechanicals is paid for an album containing eight compositions as is paid for one with twelve. Also, as we'll discuss later (on page 286), foreign mechanicals are usually paid to a government-affiliated agency.

For example, mechanicals in the United Kingdom are currently 8.5% of PPD (see page 77 for what PPD is), though there are some complexities. If you're curious, or a glutton for pain, take a look at their website, www.prsformusic.com. Finding the details is a little like navigating a Call of Duty battle, but at the time of this writing you go to the home page, click on Writers/Publishers, click on **MCPS** (standing for **Mechanical-Copyright Protection Society**), then look under "MCPS Royalty Sources, and knock yourself out.

The rate in the rest of Europe is set by an organization called **BIEM (Bureau International des Sociétés Gérant les Droits d'Enregistrement et de Reproduction Mécanique;** is that a mouthful, or what?). BIEM (pronounced "beam") is a group of agencies in each territory that collect mechanical royalties for their affiliates. Currently, the BIEM rate is 8.712% of PPD.

16

Publishing Companies and Major Income Sources

PUBLISHING OVERVIEW

Now that you're a maven on copyrights, understanding publishing is pretty simple. It works like this:

What Does a Publisher Do?

As a songwriter, you may be interested in business, but your talents are best spent in creating. However, someone needs to take care of business, and that's where the publishing industry came from.

A publisher makes the following speech to a songwriter:

"Sit down, kid. Nice shirt. You got great taste."

The publisher leans forward, rattling the gold chains on his neck. "You're a smart guy, so you'll get this right away. Your strength is writing songs, and mine is taking care of business. So let's make the following deal: You assign the copyright in your song to me, and I'll get people to use your songs. Then I give 'em licenses, make sure they pay up, and we split the dough. Simple, huh? Now sign this perfectly standard agreement. Wanna cigar?"

Administration

Okay, so I'm being a smart aleck. But these principles are the basis of the publishing business.

The rights the publisher just described—finding users, issuing licenses, collecting money, and paying the writer—are known as **administration rights.** When a publisher makes a publishing deal with a songwriter, it takes on the obligation to do all these things, and thus "administers" the compositions. In exchange, the writer signs over the copyright to the publisher (though, as we'll discuss later, it's less common for writers to give up 100% of their copyrights, or to give them up forever). The flow of rights looks like this:

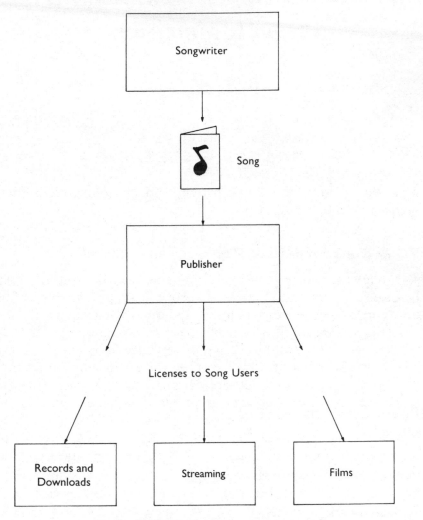

Figure 10. Publishing industry structure.

Traditionally, the publisher splits all income 50/50 with the writer (with the exception of performance monies and sometimes sheet music, which we'll discuss later). The publisher's 50% is for its overhead (office, staff, etc.) and profit. The share of money kept by the publisher from each dollar is known by a sophisticated industry term: the **publisher's share.** The balance is just as imaginatively called the **writer's share** (see Figure 11).

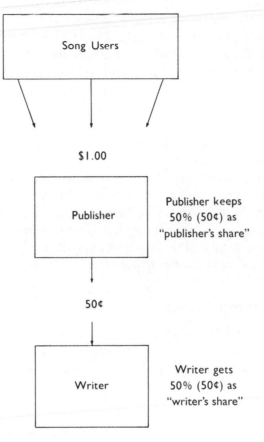

Figure 11. "Publisher's share" and "writer's share."

Publishers, from the Beginning of the Universe Until Now . . .

Following the turn of the twentieth century, and well into the 1940s, publishers were the most powerful people in the music industry. (Ever heard of Tin Pan Alley? That's where the publishers' offices were located.) In the early days, most singers didn't write songs, so they (and their record companies) were at the mercy of the publishers, who controlled the major songwriters. Remember, no one can use a song for the first time without the publisher's permission (see page 233), so the publishers decided which artist was blessed with the right to record a major new work. Because of the publishers' power, it was difficult, if not impossible, for songwriters to exploit their works without a major publisher behind them.

Publishers today are still major players, but their role has changed radically. Some are "creative" publishers, in the sense that they put their writers together with other writers, help them fine-tune their skills, match writers with artists, etc. They also use their clout to help writers find a record deal. Other publishers are basically just banking operations—they compute how much they expect to earn from a given deal, then pay a portion of it to get the rights. From these guys, you can't expect much more than a bet against your future income.

However you look at it, the reality is that publishers don't have as many major writers under contract today. This is because a lot of major songwriters keep their own publishing (i.e., they are their own publisher, retaining ownership of their copyrights and hiring someone to do the clerical function of administration). See, once a writer is well-known, he or she can get to artists as easily as a publisher can, and maybe easier (artists often call important writers directly, looking for material). Also, more and more artists are writing their own songs, so there's no need for a publisher to get songs to them.

Mechanics of Publishing

A publishing company has a lot fewer moving parts than a record company. (We discussed record company anatomy on page 65.) You only need the following (and some of these functions can be performed by the same person):

1. An administrator to take care of registering copyrights in the songs, issuing licenses, collecting money, paying writers and co-publishers, etc.
2. A "song plugger" who runs around and convinces people to use their songs.
3. A creative staff person, who finds writers, works with them to improve their songs, pairs them up creatively with co-writers, etc. If the publishing company has no writers under contract to deliver newly written songs (in other words, it just administers existing songs), you don't even need this person.

Thus, unlike the record business, it only takes a small capital investment to call yourself a publisher. You don't need a large staff (until you get to be huge), and there's no need for the expensive distribution network, warehouses, inventory, etc., necessary for records (since you're dealing with intangibles). Indeed, there's an industry term, **vest-pocket publisher,** which refers to one person, with administrative help, acting as a publisher. However, this is changing as the digital world gets more complex. It takes a sophisticated system to keep track of the millions of tiny transactions that generate money these days, so it's not quite as simple as it used to be. But publishers are still much smaller than record companies.

Types of Publishers

For this reason, there are a lot of players in the publishing biz, and it isn't nearly so dominated by the majors as is the record business. There are, to be sure, megaton publishing companies who have world-wide operations and generate hundreds of millions of dollars per year, but there are busloads of others running the gamut from a one-person show to the giants. Here's a broad-strokes view of the different types:

The 900-Pound Gorillas.   These are the major companies, such as Sony/ATV/EMI, Warner/Chappell, and Universal (all of whom are affiliated with record companies). There are also slightly lighter-weight (500-pound gorillas), such as Kobalt and BMG Rights.

Major Affiliates.   There are a number of independent publishing companies, with full staffs of professionals, whose "administration" is handled by a major. The publisher's affiliation with a major may be for the world, or it may be for only certain territories. For instance, a publisher might be affiliated with a major for the United States and have separate subpublishing deals (with other publishers) for the rest of the world.

Stand-Alones.   *Stand-alone* is my term (borrowed from the cable TV business) and not an industry one. I'm using it to mean a company that's not affiliated with a major, and instead does its own administration. In other words, it collects its own money, does its own accountings, etc. It may, however, license territories outside the United States to a major.

Writer-Publishers.   Many writers keep their own publishing. Examples are well-established writers, who don't need a publisher because people are constantly begging them for songs (such as Diane Warren), and writer/artists who record their own works. In fact, if you're a writer/artist whose material doesn't lend itself to being recorded by others (such as rap, jazz, or heavy metal), then you should only part with your publishing if you need (or want) some guaranteed money. Otherwise, you can hire people relatively cheaply to do the administration (see page 328). (If your publishing really generates a lot of money, you can even hire someone on an hourly or flat-fee basis.)

Just because the publishing game has a low entry price doesn't mean it's an easy gig. So you have to check out your publisher thoroughly. The difference between a good publisher and an unqualified one can mean a lot to your pocketbook. For example, a good publisher knows how much to charge for various licenses and where to look for hidden monies (see, for example, page 292, discussing how foreign monies get lost when they're not properly claimed, and in the digital world, it really takes know-how to squeeze out the dough). The bad ones can lose money just by sitting there and not doing what they're supposed to. An inexperienced publisher affiliated with a major publisher is a quantum improvement over an unqualified publisher trying to go it alone. However, the major will not have the same incentive to take care of the independent's songs as it will to take care of its own. Also, a major may administer hundreds of thousands of copyrights, so you can get shoved to the back of the shelf. On the other hand, a good independent publisher affiliated with a major can often do better for you than if you signed to the major directly. If the indie publisher has enough clout to become a "squeaky wheel" on your behalf (and remember, the squeaking is on behalf of themselves as well), it can prevent you from getting lost in the shuffle.

SOURCES OF INCOME

Now let's take a look at what monies a publisher collects. I'm starting with publishing income, not songwriters' royalties, because the writer gets a percentage of the publisher's monies.

The majority of revenues today come from performance monies, with mechanicals and sync (we'll talk about what that means later) coming in second and third. So let's examine these first.

By the way, this is a major change since the last edition of this book, where mechanicals were the most important monies, or at least equal to performances. Just in the last few years, there's been a tectonic shift toward performance money because record sales and downloads are dropping (which means mechanicals are going down), while TV (especially cable) and digital service providers multiply like bunny rabbits. Thank you, Mr. Marconi.

PUBLIC PERFORMANCE ROYALTIES

Remember, when we discussed copyrights, that one of your exclusive rights is the right to perform your composition in public (see page 227). These rights are known as **performing rights,** or **public performance rights.**

Every time someone uses your song, they need your permission to play the song on the radio, stream it to your mobile device, perform it on television, in nightclubs, in amusement parks, at live concerts, etc. So does that mean every radio station, nightclub, etc., in the country (of which there are thousands) has to get a separate license for every song they play (of which there are also thousands)? And that every publisher has to issue thousands of licenses to each individual user? The paperwork alone would send them off to buy that trout farm in Idaho. Well, rest easy. This is taken care of by something called **blanket licenses,** which are issued by **performing rights societies.**

So what the hell am I talking about? Here's how it works:

Performing Rights Societies

In the United States, the major performing rights societies (also called **PRO**s, meaning **performing rights organizations**) are **ASCAP** (standing for American Society of Composers, Authors and Publishers), **BMI** (Broadcast Music, Incorporated), and **SESAC** (which originally stood for Society of European Stage Authors and Composers but now stands for "SESAC"). Of the three, ASCAP and BMI are by far the largest, as SESAC only has about 10% of the U.S. performing rights. There is also a much newer company started by Irving Azoff called **Global Music Rights** that is making moves in this space by signing up major writers (and since it seems to be a rule that every PRO have nickname initials, they're known as **GMR**).

ASCAP and BMI are non-profit, meaning they collect money, pay their expenses, and distribute everything else to the writers and publishers. SESAC and GMR are for-profit, meaning they keep a chunk of the money in excess of expenses, but they say they are able to pay higher rates than ASCAP/BMI for reasons we'll discuss later (on page 249). However, you can only join SESAC and GMR if they invite you (which means their members are established writers, and which also means you'll most likely be joining ASCAP or BMI in the beginning).

Virtually every foreign country has an equivalent PRO for its own territory. Unlike the U.S., there's generally only one per territory, and most of those are government-affiliated, such as SACEM for France, GEMA for Germany, PRS for the United Kingdom, etc.

The societies go to each publisher and say, "Please give us the right to license performing rights in *all* your songs. We'll then go to the people who want to use them [radio stations, TV stations, concert halls, night clubs, etc.] and make a deal that lets them use *all* the songs of *all* the publishers we represent. For each license, we'll collect the fees, divide them up, and send you a share."

So publishers sign up with (known as "affiliating with") the PRO. If the publisher has a lot of writers, they affiliate with all of the PROs. These societies then issue licenses to the users, collect the monies, and pay the publishers. Got it?

Performance rights were a relatively staid business for the last hundred years, but as we'll discuss in a minute (on page 245), this area is on the verge of a massive trauma. Stay tuned.

Blanket Licenses

The license that the performing rights societies give each music user is called a **blanket license** because it "blankets" (i.e., "covers") all of the compositions they represent. In other words, in exchange for a fee, the user gets the right to perform *all* the compositions controlled by *all* the publishers affiliated with that society. The yearly fee can range from a few hundred dollars for a small nightclub to multimillions of dollars for television networks.

Separate Writer Affiliation

It isn't just publishers that affiliate with these societies. The writers also sign on, and even more importantly, *the writers are paid 50% of the money (the writer's share) directly by the society.* This means the writer's performance earnings are not paid to the publisher. Instead, the society bypasses the publisher and sends the checks to the writer. This is designed to protect the writer (which it does nicely) from flaky publishers who might steal their money.

By the way, writers can only affiliate with one society at a time in the U.S. (most of the other territories only have one, so it's not much of an issue there . . .) Historically, writers had only one society for the world, but there's a trend for writers with a lot of international success to divide the world (for example, they might affiliate with ASCAP or BMI in America, and the UK's PRO (called PRS) for the rest of the world.

Allocation of License Proceeds

So here are the societies sitting with squillions of dollars from their licenses. How do they know how much to pay each publisher and writer?

First, the monies are used to pay the operating expenses of the society. Then, at ASCAP and BMI, everything left over is divided among the participants, while at SESAC and GMR, they keep a profit before they distribute.

But how, you ask, do the societies know who to pay? Historically, it was all based on radio airplay and synch licenses, then extrapolated for everything else. But in the digital age, the data pool is far more detailed (and complicated), so they can more accurately allocate the money. (If you're really into 50 Shades of Performance, both BMI and ASCAP have the details of their calculations on their websites, so go on over and spank yourself to your heart's content.)

Generally, here's how it works:

1. **Radio.**
   Both ASCAP and BMI use media monitoring companies to scour radio stations across the nation, 24/7. They believe they cover about 85% of all the licensed stations, and from that, they extrapolate the rest.

2. **Television.**
   Television stations are required to keep **cue sheets,** which are lists of every musical composition used, how long it was played, and how it was used (theme song, background, performed visually, etc.). The cue sheets are then filed with the societies and there are specific dollar amounts paid for each type of use (theme, background, etc.). The amount also varies with the size of the broadcast area (local stations pay a lot less than networks), and the size of that program's audience. Both ASCAP and BMI supplement the cue sheet data with digital monitoring of broadcasts and also use independent information (essentially a gigantic TV Guide) to verify the data.

3. **Digital.**
   One of the advantages of digital delivery is that the service providers have precise data of what's been played, how often, and to how many people. The disadvantage is that they overwhelm the societies with megatons of data that some poor schlump has to sort out.

4. **Live Events.**
   The societies pay based on domestic live performances, but it's only for the top three hundred grossing tours as reported in a magazine called *Pollstar.* They pay based on **set lists**—lists of the songs played by the band involved—which they get from either the venues or artist's management.

   They also track sports stadiums and arenas, to pick up the songs that everyone claps along to.

   If you're performing in coffee houses and small venues, these aren't tracked separately, but both BMI and ASCAP have programs for you to submit your materials and get paid.

5. **Background Music.**
The fine music you find in elevators, grocery stores, and waiting rooms is also logged separately.

BMI and ASCAP both pay bonuses, from a pool they set aside for big earners. The amounts vary by category (pop, classic rock, classical music, musical saws, etc.), and also the number of performances. Both societies pay quarterly (four times per year), and both societies pay about nine months to a year after the quarter in which the monies are received.

Motion Picture Performance Monies

Due to some fancy footwork by the film industry a number of years ago, PROs are not permitted to collect public performance monies for motion pictures shown in theaters in the United States. There is no logical reason for this (showing movies is certainly a public performance); it's just historical and political. However, foreign territories have never bought into this nonsense, and motion picture performance monies over there are significant. The fees are collected by local societies, then paid over to the U.S. PRO.

Foreign film performance monies are a percentage of the box office receipts, which means they generate a good amount of green (or whatever color the local currency is). How much? Well, the composer of a major smash film score can earn hundreds of thousands of dollars in foreign performance monies alone.

Which Society Is the Best?

Hard to tell.

The best gauge is to look at cross-registered songs, which means a song that is registered with both ASCAP and BMI. This happens when a song is owned by an ASCAP and a BMI publisher—for example, if a song is owned 50% by a BMI publisher and 50% by an ASCAP publisher, it's registered 50% with BMI and 50% with ASCAP. (By the way, the shares of each publisher must match that of the writer; in other words, if $1/3$ of a song is written by a BMI writer and $2/3$ by an ASCAP writer, a BMI publisher must have $1/3$ of the publishing, and an ASCAP publisher must have $2/3$ of the publishing.)

With cross-registered songs, ASCAP collects its share of the song's performance monies and pays the ASCAP writer and publisher, while

BMI does the same for its writer and publisher on the same song. Since each society collects and pays independently of the other, we get to see who pays more. And the result?

In the comparisons I've seen, ASCAP seems to do a bit better in general, but for some types of songs, BMI beats them. Also, BMI pays more for certain usages under specific circumstances, and BMI changes its payment schedules periodically. Thus (unfortunately) there are no hard-and-fast rules.

As noted earlier, SESAC and GMR claim they pay better rates than ASCAP or BMI. The only information I have is not public, so I'm sorry but I can't comment. In the next section I'll explain why they are set up differently from ASCAP and BMI, and you'll see that they could pay more money.

PROs, Call 911

As I write this, the performance rights organizations (PROs) are going through some rough times. In part, their income is down because fans are moving from radio and TV to online, where the ad rates are less. That's a double whammy—the TV and radio people cry the blues because their revenue is down (so they want to pay less to the PROs), and the advertising online doesn't pay as well as TV and radio, so there's less performance money there. Also, the volume of transactions has gone way up, so ASCAP and BMI have to process massive amounts of data (tracking millions of streams), which makes their job more expensive than ever. And their accounting systems were built before the deluge of information.

All of these woes, however, are child's play compared to a threat the PROs are currently facing. One that could mean they might cease to exist. Or if they do, they may not look anything like what they do today.

Have I built up the suspense enough? Well, before I can tell you what's happening, we need a little history. Cue in the harps strumming from high to low as we go back in time, then play some tinkly ragtime music.

In 1913, the composer Victor Herbert was having a lovely dinner at the fancy-ass Shanley's Restaurant in New York City. Somewhere between the soup and the nuts, a group of singers and an orchestra performed two songs written by ol' Victor. According to legend, when Victor got a large bill for the food (probably $2 in those days), he supposedly said, "You're charging me a huge amount for the food, but you're not paying for my music." The waiter brought over Mr. Shanley himself, who gave Victor the 1913 equivalent of "buzz off." What he actually said was, "We're not charging admission to our restaurant, and the copyright law says you only get paid if there's a 'public performance for profit.' So we don't have to pay you."

Shanley was right about the copyright law—he only had to pay for public performances for profit—but Victor figured an expensive meal was making Shanley a helluva nice profit.

Well, Victor was no pussycat. He started on a crusade to license bars and restaurants, who in response ganged up and refused to pay. So Victor decided he needed a posse himself. He rounded up a bunch of his pals to start The American Society of Composers, Authors and Publishers (ASCAP) and went after those varmints.

About the same time, Victor personally filed a lawsuit against Shanley Co., the owner of that fancy restaurant, and the case went all the way to the Supreme Court. No less than Oliver Wendell Holmes himself wrote the opinion in 1917, saying, "Victor wins." The court ruled that a performance where someone is making a profit from ways other than just an admission charge (in this case, the food) is in fact a public performance for profit. So Victor 1, Shanley 0.

Then the copyright owners went on a roll: The courts said that radio broadcasters had to pay, as did hotels that played the radio over loudspeakers in their lobbies. As did dance halls playing music. Victor 3, Users 0.

In fact, they were on so much of a roll that the U.S. Department of Justice took notice (no doubt prodded by a few late-night phone calls from disgruntled radio stations). The feds started an antitrust investigation, meaning that they were looking into whether ASCAP had become so powerful that it was creating a monopoly and forcing its will on the users.

Things got really hot in 1940. ASCAP had always licensed individual radio stations, but it hadn't charged the networks that sent their signal to these little fellas. So ASCAP decided instead to charge the networks a lot of money and reduce the fees for the local stations. The networks were not amused. In fact, they were so *un*amused that they stopped playing ASCAP music and formed BMI (remember, the initials stand for Broadcast Music, Inc.), which was owned by the radio industry. BMI signed up a bunch of writers, and the stations only played BMI songs, public domain songs, some news, and a lot of Sunday preachin'.

ASCAP was feeling the pain. The antitrust charges had been quiet for a while, but if they were reactivated, it could shut them down. The radio boycott was hurting their revenues. Things got even worse when they tried to raise the price for movie theaters, who joined in the antitrust complaints.

Sparing you too much history, the courts found that ASCAP had become too much of a bully, and things only settled down in 1941 when ASCAP voluntarily entered into something called a **consent decree.** That basically said ASCAP could keep operating as long as they stuck to some very strict rules (and by the way, BMI got so big that they also had to sign a consent decree with essentially the same provisions). Under these consent decrees, which are still in effect today, Big Brother Uncle Sam gets to look over their shoulder and slap their hands (or possibly more vulnerable parts) if they get out of line.

The consent decree did a number of things to clip ASCAP's and BMI's wings, such as saying they can only take **non-exclusive rights.** That means the publishers always have the right to license public performances themselves. The consent decree also exempted movie theaters from paying for music, a huge blow that we talked about earlier.

Another part of the consent decree, and the biggie in the digital wars, says that ASCAP and BMI can't refuse to issue a license to someone who wants to use their music. In other words, if you want to use their songs, but you and ASCAP don't agree on the price, they still have to let you use the music while you fight about how much you have to pay. This fight happens in a federal court called a **rate court,** where a judge listens to evidence from both sides and then decides the price.

This system is inefficient, expensive, and generally a pain in the butt, but it hadn't been that big of a big deal until the digital age arrived. ASCAP and the digital service providers argued in rate court about a fair price for digital rights, and after many years, a decision came down that both ASCAP and BMI (and more importantly, the publishers they represent) didn't think was fair. So a major publisher, Sony/ATV Music (which also controls EMI Music), withdrew its digital rights from BMI and ASCAP (something the industry calls a **partial withdrawal,** because they left all their other performance rights there). Sony/ATV then went out to make their own deals with the digital services, and of course wanted a higher price.

One of those services, Pandora, took them to court, saying that Sony/ATV's withdrawal from ASCAP and BMI was illegal. Pandora argued that the consent decree said they either had to take out *all* of their performance rights (not just digital), or else they couldn't take out any of the performance rights.

To the surprise of most everyone except maybe Pandora, Judge Stanton in the Southern District of New York agreed that you can't take out just the digital rights. It's all or nothing. This decision is on appeal at the time of this writing, but it certainly put a hitch in everyone's git-along.

In response, the industry got in touch with the folks over at the Department of Justice, who are the ones that manage the consent decree. ASCAP and BMI both said the consent decrees don't work in to-day's world, and the Department of Justice (the DOJ) actually listened. They've been studying the issues for a while now, though at the time of this writing, they haven't come back with a recommendation (which then has to be approved by the federal rate courts). The handicapping is that they will allow partial withdrawal for digital rights. If they allow partial withdrawal, the major publishers will likely pull out their rights, make direct deals with the digital services, then hire ASCAP and BMI to administer these rights (in other words, the PROs would collect the money, then pay the publishers and writers, and take a percentage for doing that).

If the DOJ and the courts don't allow partial withdrawal, it is possi-ble, even likely, that the major publishers will pull all their performance rights from ASCAP and BMI. This would be a devastating blow to the PROs, as most of their income would disappear overnight. They would then only act for the smaller publishers, while the majors would have to figure out how to license bars, restaurants, local television stations, and the like.

If this happens, it's possible that the PROs would administer the performing rights for the majors, but it's not clear that's the case, or whether they can do it for enough profit margin to cover their costs. And however this shakes out, the PRO's structure for the last half-century could be turned on its head.

We were supposed to get a DOJ ruling in the summer of 2015, but it's been delayed because of an issue that set back the whole process. This is called **100% licensing.**

The DOJ is now considering whether each PRO is required to license 100% of the rights to a song, even if they don't control 100% of that song. For example, if a song is co-written by an ASCAP writer, a BMI writer, and a SESAC writer, any one PRO could license the entire song (rather than, as it works today, licensing partial rights from all three PROs). This sounds a little bizarre—how do you sell a horse you don't own?—so let me explain how they got there.

From a music user's point of view, it's a little more complicated to get licenses in multiple places. I'm guessing one or more of the users pressed the DOJ to say, "Let's make it simpler. We should be able to get a license from one place." Their legal argument why the PROs should do this it is twofold:

1. As we'll discuss on page 337, if there are multiple copyright owners, any one of them can non-exclusively license 100% of a

song. It then collects the money and has to account to the other owners.

2. The consent decrees require ASCAP and BMI to license "the works" in their catalog, which could mean 100% of the song, even if the PRO only has a small percentage of that work.

While this is appealing from a user's point of view, it causes enormous problems. First, none of the PROs have the right from any publisher to license more than that publisher owns. Second, this would be incredibly disruptive of the business. Using our example of a song that's co-written by an ASCAP writer, a BMI writer, and a SESAC writer, every user would take the position that they get 100% of the song from whichever PRO has the cheapest rate. Wouldn't you go for the cheapest price? Let's assume that's ASCAP. If ASCAP licenses 100% of the song, they have to pay all the writers. Well, ASCAP doesn't even have the addresses for the non-ASCAP writers, so how can they pay them? Maybe ASCAP could pay BMI and SESAC for those writers, but they'd be deducting ASCAP's overhead charges before the money goes out, then BMI would deduct their overhead before paying the writer, so the writer is hit twice. And making this tectonic shift in the industry could produce massive errors in accounting that take years to sort out. So I'm guessing this would mean the publishers withdraw their rights from the PROs.

If the publishers withdraw rights (partially or fully), the good news is that the publishers would not be subject to a consent decree. That means they can say "Stop using my music until we make a deal." That will lead to true, marketplace deals, which the music industry believes it has never gotten (though the service providers fear they'll get gouged, since the publishers could shut them down). Whatever deal gets made, that in turn becomes evidence in the rate court proceedings for all the licenses still subject to ASCAP and BMI.

This issue is important enough that I'm going to do something I've never done before. When it gets decided, and as the decision reverberates through the biz, I'll post an update on my website, www.don passman.com. So if you want to check on the latest, come take a look.

By the way, and importantly, SESAC and GMR are so small that they're not subject to consent decrees. Accordingly, they can actually threaten to withdraw their music, and arguably make better deals than ASCAP and BMI. Which is why they claim to earn more per writer, even though they take a profit.

So as you can see, we're in for a major roller-coaster corkscrew ride in PRO Land. Hang onto your hats, small children, and copyrights.

MECHANICAL ROYALTIES

As we discussed on page 229, mechanical royalties are monies paid by a record company for the right to use a song in records. The publisher issues a license to the record company that says, for each record manufactured and distributed, and each digital copy that's downloaded, the record company will pay a royalty equal to a specified number of pennies. Sometimes this rate is tied to the statutory rate (see page 231), and thus it increases if the statutory royalty increases. However, it's more commonly tied to *today's* statutory rate, meaning it's fixed in pennies and won't go up even if the statutory rate does. This is most likely when the songwriter is also an artist, for reasons we'll discuss later (on page 254).

The fixed rate can either be at the full statutory rate, or it can be a reduced percentage of that statutory rate. If reduced, it's called a **rate,** which means a mechanical royalty of less than statutory. Companies ask for a 75% rate (meaning 75% of minimum statutory) for mid-price records (see page 169 for what those are) and for compilation packages, and a 50% to 66.66% rate for budget records (see page 170). Artists ask publishers for a rate if they have so many songs on their album that they can't afford to pay everyone a full shot, as we'll see later (in the discussion of controlled composition clauses).

Harry Fox and CMRRA

Two major organizations are delighted to issue mechanical licenses for publishers. One is the **Harry Fox Agency,** which in the United States is the largest organization of its kind, and its Canadian counterpart, **CMRRA,** standing for **Canadian Musical Reproduction Rights Agency.** (There have been a few competitors over the years, but none has succeeded to any real degree.) Basically, these organizations act as a publisher's agent for mechanicals. They issue mechanical licenses for the publisher, police them (i.e., make sure the users pay), and account to the publisher. For their services, Harry Fox currently charges 11.5% of the gross monies collected, and CMRRA currently charges 8%.

Fox and CMRRA periodically audit record companies and the streaming services on behalf of all their clients, and then allocate the recovered monies among their clients in proportion to their earnings. This is particularly significant for a smaller publisher, as the cost of an audit for small earners is prohibitive. (Today, a typical publishing audit can cost $15,000 to $25,000 or more, and unless the recovery is likely to be several times this amount, it's not economical.)

For more info, check out their websites: www.harryfox.com and www.cmrra.ca.

It may surprise you to know that many midsize publishers (and some large publishers) use Fox and CMRRA, because the cost of hiring a staff to issue numerous licenses and police them is more expensive than the fees these organizations charge. Recently the trend is for the larger publishers not to use Fox, as technology has made it easier for them to directly license the record labels, and just as importantly, technology made it easier keep track of the thousands of licenses and make sure they get paid. However, some of their deals with the writers say they can charge an equivalent fee on mechanicals, even if they do it themselves.

Accounting

Unlike artists under record deals (who are paid twice a year), publishers get paid **quarterly,** meaning four times each year. They're usually paid forty-five days after the close of each calendar quarter, meaning forty-five days after each March 31, June 30, September 30, and December 31.

Reserves

In reporting mechanical royalties to publishers, record companies take substantially larger reserves than they do in accounting to artists for record royalties (see page 79 for what reserves are). And I mean *substantially* larger. Publishing reserves historically ran anywhere from 50% to 75% of the amount earned, as opposed to 30% to 50% for record royalties, though it's recently been trending downward. (As with record royalties, this applies only to physical goods. There are no reserves on digital sales.)

Why such a huge amount? Remember, as we discussed, that reserves protect the record company against overshipping (i.e., shipping more records than it can sell). If a company overships and therefore overpays a publisher, the only way it can get the money back is to offset the overage against future royalties for *that specific composition.* (Once, in 1911, a publisher actually repaid an overpayment, but he was executed by his fellow publishers.) This is different from record royalty overpayments, which can be charged against royalties on *any* records.

For example, suppose a publisher issues two licenses to the same record company, one for Song A and the other for Song B (written by two different songwriters). If the record company overpays on Song A, it has no right to offset this amount against royalties for Song B (though every once in a while they try). The reason is that, even though the overpayment was made to the same publisher, it's for a different song and there are different songwriters involved. This is not the case with an artist, where, if the record company overpays on the first album, it can take the excess out of royalties payable on the second, third, fourth, and later albums (because it's dealing with the same artist and one royalty account). Accordingly, a record company can take smaller reserves in record deals than it can on publishing licenses, because it has more ways to get back an overpayment.

CONTROLLED COMPOSITION CLAUSES

Congratulations! You now know enough to talk about **controlled composition clauses** in record deals. These clauses are one of the most significant provisions in your recording arrangement. I couldn't put this section earlier in the book because you needed to understand both record deals and publishing to get these concepts. Now that you do, let's boogie.

A **controlled composition** is a song that's written, owned, or controlled by the artist (in whole or in part). However, it's usually defined more broadly than that, and includes:

1. Any song in which the artist has an income or other interest. This means that, even if the artist doesn't own or control the song, if he or she wrote it or otherwise gets a piece of its earnings, it's a *controlled composition*.
2. The definition also often includes compositions owned or controlled by the *producer* of the recordings. You really have little, if any, control over a producer's publishing, and thus you should try hard to knock this provision out. (In a minute, you'll see why the producer won't like it.) It's hard to get rid of this, except at superstar levels, but do your best. I say this not only because it's difficult to get a producer to comply with it, but also because, if it's an important producer, you could end up blowing your producing deal over it.

The Controlled Composition Clause

The **controlled composition clause** (also known to its buddies as a **controlled comp clause,** although it has no "buddies" except record companies) puts a limit on how much the company has to pay for each controlled composition. See, unlike artist royalties, the companies don't recoup advances or recording costs from mechanicals (though they may try to claw back some things against mechanicals, like budget overages). But for the most part, this is money going out before they break even, and they're very touchy about how much they have to pay.

You have to be just as touchy about your mechanicals, because they may be the only money you're going to see for a while. As we discussed earlier, you only get artist royalties after you've recouped recording costs, video costs, etc. (which means they may never come, or if they do, it may be a couple of years). And as we'll discuss in Chapter 23, you won't be making any money from touring in your early stages. So take extremely good care of your mechanical royalties—they may have to last you through some cold winters.

Companies limit mechanical royalties in two ways:

1. **Rate per Song**
   The ink was hardly dry on the 1976 Copyright Act, raising the statutory rate from 2¢ to 2.75¢, when the record companies hit on the idea that they should require their artists to license controlled compositions at 75% of the statutory rate, with further reductions (to 50%) for record club or budget records. (Controlled composition clauses existed before the 1976 Copyright Act, but they didn't reduce the rate below statutory.)

   To a large degree, the companies have been successful in getting these 75% and 50% rates with almost all new, and many midlevel, artists. Even the biggest superstars have some form of controlled composition clause, although the "limit" may be 100% of statutory.

2. **Rate per Album/EP/Single**
   There is also a limit of ten or so times the single song rate for each album, five times for an EP, and two times for a single.

These issues are much more complex than they seem. So let's take an in-depth look. I promise to go slowly.

MAXIMUM RATE PER SONG

Because the maximum album rate is a multiple of the single-song rate, let's first look at what they do to you on each song. Here's the skinny:

Percentage of Statutory.   The first argument is to see if you can get more than the standard, off-the-shelf "75% of statutory." If you're a new artist, you probably won't. If you're midlevel or up, or if you have some bargaining power, try to get the percentage over 75%—anywhere over 75% would be nice. If you can't, one compromise is to ask for an escalation on later albums. For example, you might have a 75% rate on albums 1 and 2, an 85% (or 87.5%) rate on albums 3 and 4, and 100% after that. Or another possibility is an escalation based on sales: For example, you might get 75% for the first 250,000 (or 500,000) albums, 85% for the next 250,000 (or 500,000), and 100% thereafter.

Some labels offer an incentive for you to sign with their sister publishing company by increasing the mechanical rate to 100% if you give your songs to sis, or by waiving the 360 participation in publishing income if you do it (see page 102 for what a 360 participation is).

Minimum Statutory Rate.   The limit per composition is based on the *minimum* statutory rate. This means that all compositions are treated as if they are five minutes or less in duration, regardless of their actual playing time—in other words, there is no additional payment for lengthy compositions. For example, the current statutory rate for a seven-minute song is 12.25¢ (see page 231 for why), but under these provisions, you're only paid 9.1¢ if you get 100% of statutory, or 6.82¢ (75% of 9.1¢) if you have a 75% rate.

Changes in Statutory Rate.   As we discussed, the statutory rate has changed over time (see page 231). But controlled composition clauses set a rate that doesn't go up. Thus, even if you get a full statutory rate in your deal, it's normally locked to the statutory rate on a particular date, and there's no change if the statutory rate later escalates. This is tough to change, even for superstars.

The companies lock into the statutory rate in effect on one of these three dates: (a) the date of recording; (b) the date the master is delivered to the company; or (c) the date of first release of the master.

The general thinking (and historically this has been correct) is that the latest possible date is best for you—the statutory rate has never gone down, and thus the longer you wait, the more likely it may go up. However, with the abysmal performance of the music biz, there's been talk over the last few years of the rate going down, which would be the first time in history. So far, the publishers have squashed this, but if it happens, the silver lining is that the companies will have forever locked themselves into a higher rate. Shhhh. Don't tell them.

Free Goods, Real and Imagined.   The controlled composition clause will say that you get no mechanicals on free goods (see page 77 for what free goods are). Nothing wrong with that; the company isn't getting paid for them, so they don't pay mechanicals. However, the contract will also say that you're only paid on 85% of sales. And why is that? You high achievers, who read the historical royalty computations (on page 80), will know that record companies used to deduct 15% for phony free goods, and therefore only paid artist royalties on 85% of sales. Well, mechanicals were paid on this same 85% basis. When the companies switched over to paying artists on 100% of sales, without deducting anything for phony free goods, they adjusted their pricing and royalty structure so that they would pay about the same amount of dollars per album as they did before. In other words, the change-over in artist royalties didn't really change the economics—it just made the calculation simpler. However, if they paid mechanicals on 100% of sales, they couldn't adjust the pricing (mechanical rates are set independently of the record price), so they would have ended up paying *more* than they had in the past. To stay in the same place, they had to keep paying mechanicals on 85% of sales, which is what all these clauses say.

If you've got some clout, you can sometimes increase this to 92.5%, and superstars sometimes get paid on 100%. Variations include escalating to 92.5% (or 100%) at certain sales levels, or for later albums in the deal.

Multiple Uses.   Controlled composition clauses say that, if a particular song is used more than once on the same record, you only get paid as if it were used once.

Short Uses.   The companies don't want to pay for uses under ninety seconds, for **intros** (a little snippet before another song), **interludes** (a short piece between songs), or **outros** (which means either (a) a little snippet after a song, or (b) a belly-button that sticks out).

Reduced Rates.   The company typically asks for reduced rates on budget (50% to 66.66%), mid-price (66.66% to 75%), television-advertised packages (50%—see page 166 for what those are), and record clubs (50% of your normal rate).

Note, if you have a 75% of statutory rate on top-line product, you'll get a reduced percentage of that already reduced rate. For example, if you had a 75% rate on top-line, and a 50% reduction for budget records, you'd only get 37.5% (50% of your 75% rate).

These reductions are sometimes negotiable, but not very.

Public Domain Arrangements.   If a song is an arrangement of a public domain composition, the record company doesn't want to pay you for it. Your argument is that songs like "Scarborough Fair" were extremely successful public domain songs, and if you're brilliant enough to have this concept, you should be paid. (Sorry to use old stuff, but I can't think of anything more current.) The typical compromise is that you get a proportionate royalty for public domain material, in the same ratio that the performing rights organization (see page 241 for what those are) pays for the composition involved. In other words, if ASCAP pays you 50% of normal performance monies for the song, you get 50% of the mechanical rate. Everyone routinely accepts this.

Non-controlled Songs.   This is a particularly nasty piece of business. The rate limits may be imposed not just on controlled compositions, but on every composition in the album. Not all companies do this, but many do. If you're using **outside songs** (meaning songs that aren't controlled compositions), this may be impossible to deliver—the owner will tell you to get lost. Remember, you can't force an owner to license you for a first use, and even if the song was used before, the owner doesn't have to take less than the full statutory rate (see page 233). The only way to pay less for outside songs is to either threaten ("We'll drop your song if you don't reduce the rate") or grovel ("Please, I'm just a poor little singer"). But if you're dealing with major songwriters, you can forget it unless you sell a lot of records.

The real problem is not whether you can deliver the outside song at a reduced rate, because the record companies know there's a lot of times when you can't. The real problem is how the company punishes you when you don't. Essentially, if they have to pay more than your contractual limit because of outside songs, the company carves the excess out of your hide.

For example, suppose you just delivered an eight-song album, and you promised the record company they would only have to pay 75% of statutory for each song. Four of the songs are controlled by you, so no problem there. However, there are four outside songs. So you go to the publisher of the outside songs and ask for a license at 75% of statutory. The publisher tells you to blow it out your kazoo.

Here's what the situation looks like:

4 Outside Songs at Statutory (4 × 9.1¢)	36.40¢
4 Controlled Compositions (4 × 75% of 9.1¢)	27.28¢
TOTAL MECHANICALS PAYABLE	**63.68¢**
Maximum Allowed (8 × 75% of 9.1¢)	54.56¢
Less: Amounts Due Outside Songs	−36.40¢
MAXIMUM PAYABLE FOR YOUR 4 CONTROLLED COMPOSITIONS	**18.16¢**

As you can see, since you promised the record company that outside songs wouldn't cost more than 75% of 9.1¢, the excess comes out of your mechanicals on the other songs. In this example, the excess is 9.12¢, which is the difference between the 36.4¢ (4 × 9.1¢) due to the four outside-song publishers, and the allowable 27.28¢ (4 × 75% of 9.1¢). This 9.12¢ excess is deducted from your 27.28¢ for the controlled songs, so you get only 18.16¢ for your four songs (27.28¢ less the 9.12¢ excess). This equates to only 4.54¢ per song for you (18.16¢ divided among four songs), which is less than 75% of statutory (75% of 9.1¢ is 6.82¢). And if you don't have enough controlled songs from which to take the excess, it comes out of your record royalties or your advances.

By the way, "outside songs" don't just mean songs totally written by other folks. It can include songs you write with other people (the other writer's portion is an outside song) and samples you use in your own songs, which we'll discuss later.

Canada

There's no compulsory mechanical rate in Canada. Instead there's a contractual agreement between the Canadian Recording Industry Association and a number of major publishers setting the "industry royalty rate." Currently it's 8.3¢ for the first five minutes, plus 1.66¢ for each additional minute or fraction thereof (all in Canadian pennies).

Record companies, unable to restrain themselves, try to give artists three-quarters of this rate as well.

So now you're a master of the single-song limit. You're ready to conquer:

MAXIMUM RATE PER ALBUM, EPS, AND SINGLES

The maximum-per-album concept also applies to EPs and singles, but for simplicity, I'm only talking about albums here. EPs and singles are exactly the same computations, except that the limit is usually five times the single-song rate for EPs, and two times for singles.

Standard Clause. All controlled composition clauses impose a limit on the total mechanicals for each album, which is called a **cap.** It's usually ten times 75% of the statutory rate (or ten times the full rate if your per-song rate isn't reduced). This is known as a **ten times rate,** meaning you get ten times the single-song rate. Note this is *an added restriction,* which is independent of the per-song limit. In other words, you must deliver each song at the specified single-song rate, no matter what the total album limit, but you can't exceed the total album limit no matter what you pay for each individual song. This is to keep you from delivering, for example, fourteen songs at a 75% rate, which totals more than the company is willing to pay, even though you haven't exceeded your per-song limit.

The album limits are based on a multiple of the *minimum* statutory rate (the rate for songs five minutes and under), as we discussed on page 254.

Nowadays, it's not uncommon for albums to have anywhere from eleven to fourteen songs. So you should always try for more than a ten-times limit. New artists, get used to ten times, though it's gotten a little easier to get eleven times. With clout, you can easily get eleven, or edge up to twelve times, and occasionally a little more. If you can't do better at the beginning, then try to escalate your cap based on sales (for example, ten times for the first 250,000 albums, then eleven times after), or for later albums (like ten times for the first album, then eleven for the rest).

Wherever you end up, it's pretty easy to slide right over the limit. Lemme show you what happens when you do. Warning: Do not read this section alone at night.

Just for consistency in the examples, I'm going to assume that you have a maximum album rate of ten times 75% of statutory, or 68.2¢. Under the standard clause, if you deliver more than ten songs, or if you have outside songs that cost more than the 75% rate, the excess reduces the mechanical royalties on songs you control. For example, if you deliver twelve songs that are all controlled, the ten times cap means you only get 68.2¢ for all the songs. In other words, each song earns 68.2¢ divided by twelve, or 5.68¢ per song (instead of 6.82¢ per song, which is what you'd get if there were no cap). If you deliver twelve songs, and two of those are outside songs for which the company has to pay a full statutory rate, your ten controlled songs would only get 50¢ (68.2¢ less 18.2¢ [the 9.1¢ statutory rate for the two outside songs]), which means your controlled songs only get 5¢ per song (instead of 6.82¢).

No Limit on Noncontrolled Songs.   As your bargaining power goes up, you may be able to get a clause with no limit on outside compositions (other than statutory rate), even if you have a 75% statutory limit on controlled compositions. The catch is that you can't exceed the overall limit for the album (which in our example is ten times 75% of the statutory rate). This sounds a bit odd at first, but it's much better than a flat 75% of statutory limit on each composition (as in the example on page 256). The advantage is that you can now pay the outside publishers full statutory without reducing your royalties, because you're not limited on outside songs as long as you stay under the album limit.

Let's look at this using numbers. If you had a ten times 75% album rate, here's what happens to the example on page 256:

4 Outside Songs at Statutory (4 × 9.1¢)	36.40¢
4 Controlled Compositions (4 × 75% of 9.1¢)	+ 27.28¢
TOTAL MECHANICALS PAYABLE	**63.68¢**
Maximum Allowed (10 × 75% of 9.1¢)	68.25¢

Note that the amount payable (63.68¢) is less than the maximum allowed for the album (68.25¢), which is ten times 75% of 9.1¢. So you get the full 27.28¢ for your songs, which is 75% of statutory. This contrasts with the result under the clause discussed on page 256, where you only got 18.16¢ for the exact same album. And by the way, that extra 9.12¢ can add up to a hefty sum if you sell millions of albums.

On the other hand, if the mechanical royalties total more than ten times 75% of statutory under this clause, the excess comes out of your royalties. So if you pay outsiders at the statutory rate, you either have to put less than ten songs on your album, or else take a reduced rate on your songs. For example, if there were five outside songs and five controlled compositions, you would get less than 75% of statutory for the controlled songs under this same clause. This is because the maximum per-album rate applies to *all* the compositions on the album, not just the controlled compositions. Thus, in a sense, the company is imposing a rate on outside compositions under this restriction, even when there is none under the maximum-rate-per-song provisions. Take a look at the numbers:

5 Outside Songs at Statutory (5 × 9.1¢)	45.50¢
5 Controlled Compositions (5 × 75% of 9.1¢)	+ 34.12¢
TOTAL	**79.62¢**
Maximum Allowed (10 × 75% of 9.1¢)	68.25¢
Less: Amounts Due Outside Songs (5 × 9.1¢)	– 45.50¢
MAXIMUM PAYABLE FOR YOUR 5	
CONTROLLED COMPOSITIONS	**22.75¢**

So, for each of your songs, you don't get 75% statutory (6.82¢), but rather only 4.55¢ (22.75¢ divided among five songs).

No Penalty for a Limited Number of Outside Songs.   The next step up is to say that you can pay statutory rate for the outside songs, and that you're allowed to *exceed* the overall album limit in order to pay this to the outsiders. If you can get this, it's usually limited to one or two outside songs per album.

This concept is easier to understand with an example:

Assume your overall album limit is ten times 75% of statutory (68.25¢). If you have ten songs on the album, and two of them are outside songs licensed at statutory, you will exceed the maximum by the difference between the 75% limit and the full statutory amount (100%) that has to be paid for the two outside songs. (The difference is the 100% paid less the 75% maximum, or 25% of statutory, for each of the two songs.)

8 Controlled Compositions (8 × 75% of 9.1¢)	54.60¢
2 Outside Songs at Statutory (2 × 9.1¢)	18.20¢
TOTAL	72.80¢
Maximum Allowed (10 × 75% of 9.1¢)	68.20¢
EXCESS	**4.60¢**

If your clause allows up to two outside songs at full statutory, the company will pay the excess to the outsiders and won't take it back from you. Another way to look at it would be to say that the overall album limit is eight times 75% of statutory plus two times statutory, or 72.80¢. But this isn't really the case, because you only get the extra amount if you use two outside songs. If there was only one outside song, the maximum would be 70.52¢ (nine times 75% of statutory plus one times statutory), and if all ten songs on the album were yours, the rate would drop back to ten times 75% of statutory (68.25¢).

No Penalty for Any Outside Songs.   With still more clout, you can get a clause that allows you an overall album limit of ten times the full statutory rate, even though controlled songs are limited to 75%. This means you're not penalized at all for the outside songs (unless you exceed ten songs on the album, and/or unless you have outside songs over five minutes). Here's an example using five outside songs under this kind of clause:

5 Outside Songs at Statutory (5 × 9.1¢)	45.50¢
5 Controlled Compositions (5 × 75% of 9.1¢)	+ 34.12¢
TOTAL MECHANICALS PAYABLE	79.62¢
Maximum Allowed (10 × 9.1¢)	91.00¢

Since the maximum allowed (91¢) is now more than the amount payable for both outside and controlled songs, you get the full 34.12¢ (five times 75% of statutory) for your songs.

The Ultimate.   The ultimate is to say that the only limit is ten (or eleven or twelve, if you can get it) times statutory, and the only per-song limit (on either outsiders or you) is statutory. However, you still have to live with the *minimum* statutory rate, as described on page 254, as well as the other provisions in the section on per-song rate limits (rate lock-in, multiple uses, free goods, public domain songs, reduced rates for club, etc.).

Special Packages/Bonus Tracks.   It's become more common to do special packages exclusively for certain territories (like Japan), or for certain retailers (like Target or Walmart). In exchange for this exclusive product, the retailer gives the product a push (puts it in their brochure, better placement in the store, etc.).

These special packages usually have more songs than the normal album (usually two or three "bonus" tracks), and the problem is that there are mechanicals on these extra songs. Normally this is worked out at the time, but with enough clout, you can generally get something in your deal. Of course, as the writer, you want to be paid in full for the extra songs, but second place is to not be penalized on the original album mechanicals because of the extras. For example, if you had ten times full stat for the normal album, and they add two tracks, maybe you don't get paid on the extra tracks, but you don't want to be reduced by third parties who do get paid on them.

But be sure to raise these issues as soon as there's talk of extra tracks, because the standard controlled composition clause will clip your ponytail into a buzz cut.

Multiple Albums.   Most controlled composition clauses don't distinguish between normal albums and multiple albums (we discussed multiple albums on page 164). If you don't raise the issue, you'll have a ten-song mechanical limit on a multiple album that has twenty or more songs. If you ask, you may get more than a "ten times" limit, but it won't be "twenty times"; the companies will only increase the mechanical royalties in the same proportion that the wholesale price increases over that of a single-disc album. For example, if a single disc album is $10, and a double album is $11, you would get 11/10ths, or 110% (the ratio that $11 for the double album bears to $10 for the single album) of the mechanical royalties payable for a single album. (This formula is very similar to the one used for your artist royalties on multiple albums, which we discussed on page 164.) If there is no price increase, you won't get any more mechanicals in your contract, but you can often work it out when you start to record the multiple album (since you can't do a multiple without the company's consent anyway, this is one more thing to negotiate at the time).

This can be serious business if you have a lot of outside songs, because the outsiders will insist on getting paid (greedy pigs that they are), and it comes out of you. For example, if there are sixteen songs and six are outsiders, all six are in excess of the allowed ten and would be deducted from mechanicals (leaving only four songs' worth of mechanicals for your ten songs). And if you pay the outsiders full statutory, while your limit is ten times 75% of statutory, you're even further in the hole. So, if you have an attack of multi-album-itis, negotiate the mechanicals with your record company, and ideally get a reduced rate from the outsiders as well, before you start.

As noted before, box-set artist royalties are specifically negotiated when the package is put together, and you should negotiate the mechanical royalties at the same time.

Videos

The first draft of almost every controlled composition clause requires you to license your songs for use in videos, forever, for *free*. This may be overreaching, but it's hard to change. Let's look at two parts of it:

1. **Promotional usage.**
   I don't think it's unreasonable to give the company a free promotional video license. When it's using the video to promote your records, it's not making any money. However, the line about what's "promotional" gets blurry these days because the primary video outlets (YouTube and Vevo) generate money for the record company (as we discussed on page 150). In addition, some artists get money from sponsors that put products in their videos (as we discussed on page 192).

   As we'll discuss on page 278, the publishers get paid for streaming on YouTube/Vevo, so the only issue here is a synch license (which you don't understand yet, because we'll talk about it on page 265. Essentially it's a fee to put the music into the video, as opposed to a fee for streaming the video). Currently, the custom is not to push for a synch fee, since you're getting paid for the usage. But be careful in your deal.

Feel free to flip back here after you've read the synch section if this isn't clear (which it probably isn't).

2. **Commercial usage.**

When it comes to commercial usages, you should argue for some compensation. At present, the major commercial usage is streaming (Vevo, YouTube), which we just discussed, though some artists can still sell downloads and DVDs.

As noted in the prior section, the publishers get paid for streaming but there's a fight these days about **lyric videos,** where the record company produces videos that (not surprisingly) show the lyrics while the song is playing. Most publishers try for an additional royalty for lyric videos, and most of the labels are fighting.

For DVDs, independent publishers (those not subject to a controlled composition clause, who can charge what the market will bear) usually get in the range of 8¢ to 15¢ per song, though some get a percentage of PPD (6% to 8% or so). Also, there is almost always a 10,000–15,000 unit guarantee, meaning, for example, if you got 12¢ per unit and a 10,000 unit guarantee, you would get a $1,200 advance (12¢ × 10,000 units). In addition, they often get something called a **fixing fee,** which is a nonrecoupable payment for *fixing* the song in the video (basically, a synch license—see page 265 for what that is). These range from $250 to $500 per song.

It's very difficult to get compensation for DVD use if you're the artist, for the simple reason that companies don't like to do it. Remember, your video royalty as an artist (see page 169 for what that is) *includes* any publishing money, so in one sense you'd be taking it from yourself. However, publishing royalties are paid prior to recoupment, while video royalties aren't. So if you can get something here, it's worth the fight. But it's difficult. And if you do get it, it will be a reduced amount from the marketplace (maybe 6¢ to 8¢ per song if it's a penny rate, or 6% if it's a percentage of PPD).

We'll discuss what publishers get for video streaming on page 278, but the record company will want a free license to stream on their own website for promotional purposes.

Producers

When you hire a producer who is also a writer, you'll discover that the major producers don't want to be bound by your controlled composition clause and will insist on a full rate for their songs, no matter what. If you have enough clout, or if the producer doesn't, you can get them to go along with your controlled comp clause completely. Even if the producer has moderate clout, if your clause is reasonably favorable, you can often get them to sign off. If not, you're into a negotiation, and compromises can end anywhere along the spectrum. For example, if you have a 75% mechanical and a ten times cap, but twelve songs on the album, the producer might agree to a full mechanical rate with a cap of ten songs. Or they might agree to your 75% rate, but with no cap on the number of songs.

Postscript

Now that you've read it (I didn't want to prejudice you before you did), I can tell you that controlled composition clauses are among the most complicated critters in the music business (you probably figured that out on your own, huh?). This section is packed full of numbers and weird concepts, so it may take a few times through to get the flavor. Don't feel bad if you miss some of it the first few times—it took me years to get a decent handle on this stuff. But mechanicals may well be your only monies for quite a while (see page 252–53 for why), so it's worth taking time to understand these clauses.

DPDs

And now, for some really good news.

As we discussed earlier, in 1995 Congress added digital downloads (DPDs) to the compulsory mechanical license provisions. Your representatives also tossed in, at no extra charge, a provision that says any record contract made after June 22, 1995, *can't* reduce the mechanical rate that you (as author of the songs) get for DPDs. So controlled composition clauses (in deals made after that date) don't apply to DPDs, which means you get a full rate per song on downloads. This also means, as digital sales gobble up more and more of the market, that controlled comp clauses will become less and less important.

So be nice to your congressman.

17

Secondary Publishing Income

Now let's take a look at other sources of publishing income: synchronization, digital, print, and foreign monies.

SYNCHRONIZATION AND TRANSCRIPTION LICENSES

A **synchronization license** (also called a **synch** [pronounced "sink"] license) is a license to use music in "timed synchronization" with visual images. (Sometimes it's spelled without the "h" as **sync.**) A classic example is a song in a motion picture, where the song is synchronized with the action on the screen. It also includes television programs, television and Internet commercials, audiovisual streaming, home video devices, etc. Interestingly, it doesn't include radio commercials (since they're not synchronized with visuals). Radio commercial licenses are called **transcription licenses.**

Fees

The fees for synchronization licenses are really all over the board, and they vary with exactly how the song is used, which media you want, how long you want to use it, the importance of the song and the songwriter. (Also, keep in mind that this chapter is only talking about fees for the *song*. If the master is also being used, there's a separate fee for that, which is usually an equal amount).

An example of the lowest-end fee would be a ten-second background use of an unknown song in a television show (maybe being played on a jukebox while the actors are talking and ignoring it). A high-end example would be an on-camera, full-length performance of a well-known song in a major studio's high-budget film. And when we get into the realm of commercials, the fees go even higher.

Here's an idea of the range:

1. **Motion picture:**
   Major Studios. Motion picture synch licenses for a major studio film generally run in the range of $15,000 (for very minor usage of a song that's not particularly well known) to over $100,000. **Main title** usages (meaning over the opening credits) are generally from $50,000 to $300,000, and **end title** usages are more like $35,000 to $200,000 (why pay as much for a song that's played while everybody's walking out of the theater?). The end title song fees may also be lower if there is more than one song over the credits, which happens commonly these days. Of course, if it's an incredibly hot, recent hit song, and the film company is salivating over it, these figures can get very high into six figures.

   For these fees, the film companies want more than just the right to use the song in the picture. They also want **in-context advertising** (meaning ads that use the song exactly the same way it's used in the film—see the next paragraph for more of an explanation) and in-context **trailers** (those "previews of coming attractions" that you see online and in your local theater before the movie), clips, and promotions (like excerpts shown on talk shows while the film's stars are interviewed). Sometimes you can get an extra 10% of the synch fee (or more) for usage of your song in the trailer, since often it is not exactly in-context (more about in-context in a minute).

   In addition (and for which you should get extra money), the studios may want things like **featurettes** (short films, often showing behind-the-scenes footage that was taken while the film was being made; this is also called a **making-of**), playing the song over DVD menu selections, usage in deleted scenes, **sequels** (films that start where the last one left off), **prequels** (a film that takes place in time before the film for which the song is licensed), **spin-offs** (a film with the same characters in a different adventure), and on **out-of-context** uses, which are the opposite of the in-context uses we discussed in the preceding paragraph.

   Featurettes tend to run about 10% of the original synch fee, so if you got $100,000 for the film, you'd get another $10,000 for the featurettes. Sequels, prequels, and spin-offs are either left to future negotiation, or are the same price as the original synch fee, sometimes with a built-in uplift (say 10%).

As noted, in-context means the song is used exactly the same way it's used in the film. In other words, if it's playing in a scene where a couple is strolling on a beach, putting that scene in a TV ad would be an in-context use. So *out-of-context,* not surprisingly, means a use of the music differently from the way it's used in the film. For example, playing the song in a television ad while showing another scene from the film.

You get more dough for out-of-context uses, because they're no longer just snipping something from the film to entice viewers—they're using your song like a commercial. And that can mean a lot more money. How much more? For out-of-context instrumental background music (called **cues**), it's usually around $20,000. (By the way, we're talking here about cues from a licensed song. If it's a cue from the underscore that was written for the film, we'll cover that in chapter 30. Spoiler alert: The composer doesn't get any extra money). For licensed songs that are not in the film at all (but only, for example, in the trailers or ads for the film), the fees run anywhere from $25,000 to $150,000 or more, depending on the importance of the song and nature of the use. If the song is used in the film as well as out-of-context (meaning you're already getting a chunk of money for the in-context use), the out-of-context fee is usually cheaper, say around $25,000 to $100,000, but if it's a major song, it could go as high as $500,000.

Independent Films. For low-budget, independent films, the deals get much more creative. Funny how things always get more creative when someone doesn't have any money.

The fees are usually much lower, at least initially (as we'll discuss), and in part depend on the kind of indie film involved. Documentaries are the serious bargain basement, since they rarely make any money. Next step up are true indie films, with unknown directors, actors, etc. At the top are indie films that feature major stars and/or directors who are working as a labor of love. While this last category may be low budget, the publishers tend not to be so sympathetic because these films can have commercial success. Accordingly, these kinds of films often pay higher fees (sometimes as much as the major film fees discussed above), at least for important music.

If an indie film was made by producers who barely scraped the money together, and they don't even have a **distributor** (meaning a company to put the film in theaters and pay for advertising and marketing), the producers run around to film festivals with the reels tucked under their arm, trying to find someone to market their little baby. A typical synch deal is a cheap license that only allows them to show the film in festivals, and it's usually limited to a term of one year. For documentaries, the festival fee might be $500 to $2500, depending on the use and importance of the song, and there's often no deal beyond that. The idea is that the filmmaker looks for a distributor, comes back to the publisher if they find one, then gets a license for broader rights.

Non-documentaries pay a similar license fee for festivals, but they usually want options, at preset amounts, to move their film up in ranks. For example, an indie film might pay $1,000 for festivals only. Then, if it goes into theatrical release, there's a preset fee of $2,500 to $7,500 (there might be a smaller fee for "art house" releases, and a larger one for a mainstream release). The publisher would then get the same amount again if the film is released on television. And that amount again if it goes into DVD or is made available for video-on-demand streaming (like Netflix, Amazon, etc.). These are called **step deals,** because the money comes in steps.

There might also be **kickers** (additional fees) if the film achieves certain success. One recent deal for a very low-budget film paid amounts equal to the original license fee if the film had worldwide box office gross of $3,000,000, and additional kickers at every $3,000,000 increment, up to a maximum of four times the original fee. Other deals don't have a maximum, so the publisher can make out nicely if the film does well.

2. **Television:**
   Historically, television quotes were for limited rights, with options for the producer to pay set amounts for additional rights. For example, a TV producer might license a song for over-the-air TV broadcasts, **basic cable** (meaning advertiser-supported cable channels), and **basic satellite** (also advertiser-supported channels). They would then have the option (for additional money) to use that show on **pay TV** (HBO, Showtime, and similar services where subscribers pay an additional monthly fee for that channel), home video (DVDs or one of the streaming services like Netflix, Hulu, Amazon, etc.), foreign theatrical (sometimes movies shown on TV in the United States are released in foreign

theaters), and new media (Internet streaming, downloads, etc.). These licenses were also limited in time, usually five to seven years.

Well (except for the competition shows, which we'll discuss in a minute), that's all changed. Over the last few years, the usage of TV shows has multiplied like mushrooms in deep fertilizer. You can buy DVDs of an entire TV series, year by year. You can stream TV shows to your computer. Watch them on your cell phone. Download them to your iPod. Catch them at the hot-oil wrestling parlor (just seeing if you're awake). Slight problem with these new technologies: TV producers didn't have the right to use the licensed music in these new gizmos, since nobody even dreamed about these things back in the days of waiting for your TV set to warm up. Big Oops.

This meant the studios had to go back and license the music for all these new media, and the publishers weren't shy about how much money they wanted.

As a result, most TV licenses are now in perpetuity and include the rights to all media now or hereafter known (but excluding theatrical, as some TV shows get released in theaters, particularly outside the U.S.). The good news is that the license rates have gone up, since the rights are no longer broken down like a Chinese menu.

How much can you get? Around $10,000 to $50,000 plus, depending on whether they're licensing an obscure song or a well-known hit, and also how prominently it's used. If you're an indie artist looking for exposure—some artists have launched their careers by having music on a big TV show—you might give them a very cheap rate, meaning $1,000 or so, sometimes even less since they know they "gotcha." If you're a superstar who couldn't care less, you'll carve out their livers.

The only rights that are usually excluded from these licenses, and for which you can get more money, are the right to use your song in out-of-context ads (see page 266 for what that means). You can usually get around $1,500 to $5,000 per week for out-of-context promo uses, which is payable for as long as the promotion runs. (Unless you're a major player, you don't get any more money for in-context ads; that's always included in the price.)

The competition shows (*American Idol, X Factor, The Voice, Dancing with the Stars,* etc.) have gone back to the Chinese menu model, meaning they only pay for what they actually use. They then take options, for specific amounts, if they want more rights. All these deals are done on a **most favored nations (MFN)** basis, meaning they pay the same amount for every song on the show, no matter what. Because these shows use such a huge amount of music, they don't have time to negotiate every deal separately, so the publisher just decides if they're in or out. And because these shows are great promotion for the songs, the publishers are almost always "in."

The exact license fees vary from show to show, but if all rights were exercised, they'd be in the range set out above. However, they start with a small fee (which also varies amongst the shows, but it's several thousand dollars) that allows them to use the song for two to five years, in the United States and Canada only. For that initial fee, they get things like unlimited broadcasts (within the two- to five-year term), **recaps** (a program that features clips from earlier in the season), Internet streaming, and in-context usage for advertising and promotion. Some shows are even sophisticated enough to license the lyrics, in case the camera pans past a contestant who's reading the lyrics while singing.

If they want to go beyond those rights, they'll pay additional amounts for things like downloads of the program, territories outside the United States and Canada, and extending their rights to perpetuity. They also have to pay if they repurpose the original use, such as taking a clip from a TV show and exploiting it apart from the show online. Payment for this can be a flat fee, or sometimes a rolling fee based on the view count of a video (for example, $X for every 500,000 views). Sometimes there's a revenue share of the gross earnings, anywhere from 15% to 50%. The specifics depend on the usage, stature of the song, etc.

3. **Commercials:**

For commercials, a reasonably well-known song can get anywhere from $50,000 to well into six figures for a one-year national usage in the United States, on television, radio, and Internet. Really well-known songs in major campaigns can go higher, sometimes over a million for a classic, iconic song.

These figures get scaled down for regional or local usages, and for periods of less than a year.

Internet-only usage is on the rise, and the prices are rapidly going up for the simple reason that these ads reach a lot of people—particularly the younger demographic that advertisers want, who these days hardly ever watch television.

The issue of "territory" on the Internet is interesting, as the net is of course available worldwide. The deals require the advertiser to **geo-filter,** which means the commercial is only available to users in a particular territory. That works reasonably well, though I'm told it's not that hard for a die-hard to get around it.

A new twist that really scrambles your brain is the "repurposing of commercials for commercial use." Huh? Well, for example, you take an incredible Super Bowl commercial, put it on a YouTube channel or Machinima, and run ads around it (prior to playing the video, banner ads on the page, etc.). So you're actually making money running commercials, by running other commercials. At any rate, if this floats your boat, you need to pay more for the privilege, which would be an additional flat fee, or a share of the revenue (15% to 50%, depending on the usage and the stature of the song).

4. **Video Games:**

Video games don't generally pay royalties because they sell millions of copies and don't see any reason why they should pay a royalty. So you only get a flat fee for the use of your song. This can be anywhere from nothing (because a publisher wants kids to hear the song while they're trying to kill a flesh-eating zombie) up to $50,000 or so for a major hit. The norm is around $5,000 to $10,000.

If they want to use the song in a commercial for the video game, you can sometimes get up to an additional $10,000 to $100,000, depending on the extent of the usage, how widely the commercial will be shown, and the importance of the song.

As we discussed for masters, the only exception to the "no royalty" rule is for a music-based game, like SingStar or Guitar Hero. For these music-based games, the companies will pay a royalty for songs, and usually an advance. The terms are confidential, but it's a fraction of the statutory mechanical rate.

ELECTRONIC TRANSMISSIONS, INCLUDING DIGITAL DOWNLOADS, RINGTONES, WEBCASTING, SUBSCRIPTION SERVICES, AND PODCASTING

After years of wrangling, the industry has come to an uneasy resolution for most of these new businesses, all of which fall under the industry term **electronic transmissions.** However, many of the players are unhappy with some of what's happened, so look for more action.

The reason it's taken so long is that everyone knows this is the future of the business, and both record companies and publishers have been afraid they'll sell their rights too cheaply. Also, there's been a fight inside the publishing world: If you're a performing rights organization, everything looks like a performance, but if you're the Harry Fox Agency, which collects mechanicals, everything looks like a mechanical. For example, if you stream a song, ASCAP argues that it's a performance, just like hearing the song on a radio. No one really disputes that. However, Fox thinks it's also a mechanical use, which is a much trickier question. They say you need a license to reproduce the song on the server of the company doing the streaming, and that your personal computer has to make a copy in its cache for you to hear it, both of which are true. Since the right to duplicate a copyrighted work is separate from the performance right, they argue that you need a license from them. Conversely, if you download a song, ASCAP says you have to stream it over the Internet to deliver it, so it's also a performance. (There's a more detailed discussion of this fight below, in the section on webcasting.)

Essentially, both sides are struggling to fit these newfangled gizmos into boxes that were built before the technologies existed. The reality is that all these things are sort of performances and sort of mechanicals, though some feel much more like one or the other. Also, frankly, part of the fight is over who gets to collect the money and therefore keep a piece of it for their services.

We've finally come to somewhat of a resolution of this fight, as we'll discuss in a minute, but interestingly Europe worked this out some time ago. There most countries agreed that a download is 25% performance and 75% mechanical, while streaming is considered 75% performance and 25% mechanical. However, the UK splits 50/50 between performance and download, and in Switzerland and a handful of other countries, they don't recognize any performance right for a download.

Another brewing issue was started by publishers who directly collect mechanicals (in other words, they don't use the Fox Agency). Some of them are sniffing around the idea of also collecting performance money from the streaming services, cutting out the PRO. As we discussed on page 247, PRO deals are all non-exclusive, so the publisher is entitled to issue their own license. If your publisher is one of them, then *run* (do not walk, do not pass Go) to the section on page 176, about making sure they don't recoup advances from your performance monies in record deals and put a similar provision in your publishing deal.

Here's today's state of play in the United States, along with a current scorecard of mechanical versus performance:

1. **Permanent downloads.**

   Let's start with an easy one, permanent downloads (see page 146 for what that means), like the ones sold on iTunes. It's now well settled that these downloads are treated just like sales of CDs. That means you get a full mechanical royalty, and it's not a performance. (In a rate court decision a few years back, the performing rights societies argued it was a performance, but the court ruled against them, saying the test was whether you could hear it while it was being transmitted. So much for the European imports.)

   Ringtones are also permanent downloads (see page 150 for what those are), and as we discussed earlier, the mechanical royalty for these is now settled at 24¢. As we also discussed, ringbacks aren't downloads; they're stored on the servers of the mobile provider and just played to the caller, so they're considered a stream.

2. **Non-interactive audio streaming and satellite radio.**

   Non-interactive means someone else decides what you hear (as opposed to your choosing the music yourself). It's essentially a radio station that's delivered any way except over the air.

   It's now settled that the publisher only gets performance monies (from ASCAP, BMI, etc.), which is exactly what you'd get if an over-the-air station played your music. The rates are pretty complex, and they change over time, but in essence they're a percentage of revenue, with minimums (in case the user doesn't have much revenue). You can see the standard ASCAP, BMI, and SESAC licenses on their websites (www.ascap.com, www.bmi.com, and www.sesac.com).

   Monster streaming companies (Spotify, Apple Music, and the like) don't take these off-the-shelf licenses, in the same way that CBS television doesn't take an off-the-shelf performance license that's geared to local TV stations. Instead, the big guys negotiate their own specific deals with each performing rights society.

   For the technical freaks out there (the rest of you can skip to number 3 below), there's an important difference between Internet streaming and over-the-air stations. Before you can stream on the Internet, you have to make a copy of the song on your server, and two lawsuits have held that a server copy of a copyrighted song requires a license: *UMG Recordings et al. v. MP3.com, Inc.*, 92 F. Supp 2d 349 (2000), and *Rodgers and Hammerstein Organization et al. v. UMG Recordings, Inc., and the Farm Club Online, Inc.*, 60 U.S. P.Q. 2D [BNA] 1342 (2001). Note this server copy license is *in addition* to the performance license. A performance license lets you stream. The server copy license lets you make a copy. (Take a look back to our discussion of the various rights in a copyright on page 226. One is the right to perform, and the other is the right to duplicate. However, as industry practice, the publishers only require a performance license for non-interactive streaming.)

Over-the-air radio stations also make server copies of recordings for broadcast, but they're allowed to do this without a license under a specific provision of the copyright law (their server copy is an **ephemeral recording** under Section 112). Technically, this only gives them the right to make a copy of the sound recording, not the song, but if they have a performance license, they're good as a matter of industry practice.

Webcasters who are not over-the-air broadcasters wanted the same rights, and after some back and forth, industry practice was settled as we've discussed: Non-interactive services only need a performance license, and interactive services require both a performance and a mechanical license. Currently, there are rumblings that non-interactive streaming services should pay more than just a performance license, because some publishers argue that allowing users to skip ahead on songs makes them "interactive." But for the moment, they're only getting performance licenses.

3. **Interactive audio streaming (on-demand streaming).**
   Now for some tougher stuff.

   There are subscription services that give you interactive streaming, which means you can call up whatever song you want to hear, whenever you want to hear it. Examples are Spotify, Apple Music, Rhapsody, and Rdio.

   To understand what's happening here, we need to travel back in time, to the dark ages of the year 2000. That's when someone first got the idea that interactive streaming would be a cool thing, so they went to the music publishers and tried to make a deal. The publishers liked the concept but thought they should have a much bigger piece of the pie than the streamer had in mind. The two sides battered each other for a while, then made a temporary deal in 2001 to let the subscription services launch. Under that agreement, the streamers agreed to pay advances to the publishers, which would be recouped from royalties whenever they were determined in the future. The idea was to keep negotiating, and when the royalty rate was settled, the publishers would get royalties all the way back to the beginning. Everyone expected the streaming-on-demand royalty to be set within a year or two. In fact, they never got close to each other (except to put their hands on each other's throats).

Finally, they all gave up and turned the matter over to the Copyright Royalty Board (see page 232 for what that is). The CRB set rates for a number of uses, including interactive streaming. It's a pretty complex set of formulas, as they cover (a) subscription streaming services; (b) subscription streaming services that are bundled with other services (which we'll discuss in the next section); (c) portable services (meaning you can get the music on a portable device); (d) nonportable services (you can probably figure out what that is); and (e) non-subscription/advertiser-supported services. (Whew.)

But don't relax just yet. We have subcategories for the subscription services!! There are rates for services that only play when you're connected to the Internet, those that play both when you're connected and when you're not, and limited offering subscriptions, meaning you can only get a particular genre, limited playlist, or only preprogrammed playlists. Can you stand the excitement?

In a *very* simplistic form (and I use the word *simplistic* guardedly), the rate is the *greater* of:

(a) 10.5% of subscription fees paid by the consumer, or if the service is advertiser supported, 10.5% of gross advertising revenues (less only the cost of obtaining ads, not to exceed 15% of ad revenue); or

(b) either (i) if the record company pays the publisher, 17% to 18% of what's paid to the record company for the masters and publishing combined, or (ii) if the streaming service pays the publisher, 21% to 22% of what's paid to the record company for the masters alone (without publishing rights); or

(c) from 15¢ to 80¢ per subscriber per month (assuming, of course, there are subscribers, which there wouldn't be in an ad-supported service).

The exact percentages and pennies under (b) and (c) depend on the kind of service being licensed.

By the way, to be doubly clear, the rate in (c) is not 15¢ to 80¢ per *song* per month; that would bankrupt the digital service provider. It's a minimum figure that the service has to pay for *all* the songs used, divided among all the songs and their publishers. It's designed to keep the DSP from dropping its prices too low (or at least costs the DSP a bigger percentage if they do).

This license covers only mechanical rights (*not* performing rights). However, the above rates are a total of both performance and mechanical rates. So whatever is paid for the performing rights (currently a little over 5% of gross income) can be deducted from the above monies (though the minimum penny rates in (c) have to be paid for mechanicals, no matter what goes out for performance monies). In practice, the entity responsible for making publishing payments usually gets a license from the performing rights society, then deducts the performing rights payments from what's due under the above formula and pays the balance to the publisher.

The actual rates are way more complicated than I've made them sound (though I did a pretty good job of making them sound complicated, didn't I?). If you want more, the Fox Agency has slides describing these rates that you can access from a link on their home page (www.harryfox.com), right next the slides of Mr. Fox's last vacation in Schenectady. The link is called "Royalty Calculations Explained" and it's very helpful if you're into those things (much more helpful than the pictures of Schenectady City Hall).

And if you *really* want to understand it, you should read 37 CFR Part 385, which is published in the *Federal Register*, vol. 74, no. 15, p. 4529, as amended by *Federal Register*, vol. 74, no. 27, p. 6832, and further amended in 37 CFR 835, Subpart C. You might want to print a few copies and keep them next to your bed, in case of insomnia.

By the way, outside the U.S., there are no compulsory mechanical licenses at all. Instead, in many territories there are "published tariffs" set by the local societies or a government agency that everyone follows.

Now have we covered everything? Well, SoundCloud falls into a category pretty much all its own. It allows people to post music, share music, etc., and the major labels have used it as a discovery tool because there's a social aspect to it. However, SoundCloud has no ads and generates no money (at least as of this writing, though I'm told there are plans to monetize it). They also have no licenses from anyone, claiming they're entitled to let people post under the copyright law (see page 352 for a discussion of the DMCA's "safe harbor"). So to date, they haven't paid the record companies or publishers, but I understand there's a move to change this.

4. **Bundled services.**

As we discussed on page 151, a bundled service is one that puts together two or more products or services (Two For the Price of One!), like a music streaming service that comes with your mobile phone rate plan.

Under this new agreement, there are now two flavors of bundles: **mixed service bundles,** and just plain ol' **music bundles.** A *mixed service bundle* is the sale of a music product (like a streaming service, permanent download, or a locker service), along with a non-music service. For example, you get a music streaming subscription when you buy Amazon Prime. A *music bundle* is the sale of two or more music-only products together, such as a download code when you buy a CD; the only requirement is that they have to be different kinds of music products (for example, selling two ringtones together doesn't count).

If what's being bundled is a subscription, then the rates are similar to what's above. Specifically, you get the greater of (a) 10.5% of the music service revenue, or (b) the greater of (i) 21% of what the service pays for the masters and pays the publishing money separately, or (ii) 17.36% of the record company payments if the service pays both publishing and master monies to the record company, or (c) 25¢ per subscriber per month. These rates under (a) and (b)include the performance monies, but the rate under (c) does not.

If it's not a subscription that's being bundled, the rates are a little simpler because there's no penny minimum: The publishers get the greater of (a) 11% to 12% of revenue generated by the services, or (b) 21% to 22% of what the service pays the record labels for the master. Just like the rates for interactive streaming, the performing rights payments are deducted from the above.

For mixed service bundles, the rate is the greater of (a) or (b) in the prior paragraph, but is based only on the *music portion* of the monies, and not the cost of the other service or device.

Like I said, I'm way oversimplifying this to give you the general gist. Check on the Harry Fox website referenced above for more details.

5. **Locker services.**

We talked about these babies on page 151. Essentially they're a place to store your music in the sky and access it from any device you own.

As noted on page 151, the upload lockers (where you upload your own music) don't pay anybody. The full lockers (meaning services that let you access songs already on their server) set rates in the recently negotiated deal we just discussed (in the bundled services section above), and they pay the greater of (a) 12% of revenue, or (b) 20.65% of the amount charged by the record labels for the masters, but in no event less than 17¢ per subscriber per month.

Just like interactive streaming, the above amounts (other than the penny rate) include a performance license, so that's deducted (and paid to the PROs) before the mechanical portion goes to the publisher.

6. **Video streaming/Multi-Channel Networks.**

You may remember that there's no compulsory license for videos. That means the CRB has no jurisdiction over video streaming services like YouTube and Vevo, because the CRB only deals with compulsory licenses. And since the CRB doesn't have the authority to set a rate, the publishers can charge whatever they want. So this area has been like the old Wild West.

Here's what's happenin' down on the ranch.

For record-company-produced videos, the U.S. record companies make deals with the video DSP that cover both video rights and publishing rights. Under these deals, the record labels get about 70% of ad revenues and/or subscription monies (sometimes with a fraction of a penny as a minimum per-stream payment, or a minimum per subscriber payment, though that sometimes goes away for a service with a proven track record). Out of that 70%, they pay the publishers whatever deal they make, which isn't so uniform, but generally in the range of 10% of the ad revenues (a little under 15% of the 70% that the company gets).

Outside the U.S., with the exception of Canada, all the monies go to the mechanical and performance collection societies).

User-generated videos (the UGC we discussed on page 158) are handled differently. Since the record company isn't involved in making these videos, they don't handle the payments. So the licenses have to be done directly between the streaming service and all the individual publishers, or through the Harry Fox Agency. This is a serious problem, because there's no central place for the YouTubes of the world to make a deal for all their music (Fox doesn't represent all the publishers). It also means the publishers who don't use Fox have to do a lot of licenses for tiny money, and that the services have to do tons of licenses with smaller publishers.

After some amount of wrangling, the **National Music Publishers Association (NMPA)**—an industry organization that represents publishers in both lobbying and dealing with users—came to a settlement with YouTube, and this looks like it's going to be the norm (for a while anyway). A variation of this license is available to anyone who wants it, and it's administered by the Fox Agency. The terms are:

a. If it's a user-created video that includes a commercial recording of the song (remember, this doesn't include videos made by record companies, where the record company pays the publisher), the video streaming service pays the publisher 15% of net ad revenues.

b. If it's a new recording of the song (like Uncle Benny, the musical saw player in Picayune, Texas), the publisher gets 50% of net ad revenues. But if the uploader gets some of the ad revenue (for example, if Benny has a YouTube channel and gets a cut of ad money), YouTube deducts whatever it pays Benny from the publisher's 50%. However, this deduction is subject to a limit of 15%, meaning the publisher never gets less than 35% of net ad revenue.

For more details you can visit the ever-scintillating www.YouTubeLicenseOffer.com.

A real problem is that, while YouTube's content identification program does a good job of recognizing original sound recordings, I'm told it doesn't pick up live versions of UGC as well. So your publisher has to police this—yet another example of how complicated the world is becoming, and how difficult (and expensive) it is for publishers to make sure they get their share of the river of pennies (more accurately, "fractions of pennies").

The YouTube deal only covers non-commercial users who upload videos (meaning consumers), which means there's a hole in the system: It doesn't cover things like Vevo and other commercial channels (the multi-channel networks we'll discuss in a minute) that run through YouTube, and of course it doesn't cover any services outside of YouTube. This isn't a big deal for the major publishers, who have enough clout to make deals with everyone using their videos commercially, but it means all the little guys are left out of the system. In other words, they're not getting paid. And the money is so small for each indie publisher that it's not economical to chase giants to catch a gnat. However, the numbers are growing and a few services have sprouted up to help the little fellas (see page 282).

All the major record labels have negotiated deals with the NMPA and for the online use of videos produced by those record companies. The deal is called the **NDMA** (standing for **New Digital Media Agreement**), and it's similar to the YouTube deal, except that it's with a record company (not a digital service provider), so it only covers video material owned or controlled by that company (promotional videos, concert footage, etc.).

What do you get under an NDMA? Well, for digital music videos, the record company pays the publishers 15% of its revenue (in other words, 15% of the 70% that the record company gets from the DSP, as we discussed on page 158).

As noted on page 263, there is currently a fight over lyric videos, which are not covered by the NDMA. The publishers want a higher royalty for the use of the lyrics, on the theory that it's an additional grant of rights, but the record companies have resisted and the arm-wrestling continues at the time of this writing. So watch this space.

The NDMA also covers ringtones, for which the record companies pay the statutory rate (meaning the company gets a license and doesn't have to go through the compulsory license administrative hoops). It also deals with videomaster ringbacks and videomaster ringtones at 20% of wholesale, or 10% of the consumer price if it's sold directly to the consumer by the record company. Interestingly, as massive as YouTube is, the ad revenue rates around music, especially UGC (see page 158 for what that is) are pretty low. That's because the audience is so wide that it's hard to target ads—nobody pays much to advertise tampons to a sixty-year-old dude. So until this gets more efficient, the ad rates will stay low, and the money from YouTube isn't what it could be.

In response to this problem, **Multi-Channel Networks (MCNs)** came into being. MCNs are companies that license or produce content, then stream and sell ads around it. Examples are Maker and Vessel, and Vevo in the premium music video space. The MCNs package their materials and focus them on targeted demographics (for example, fourteen- to eighteen-year-old girls), where advertisers who want that audience will pay a much higher rate. And speaking of MCNs, the NMPA also sued Fullscreen and Maker Studios because they didn't have a license for the songs they were using. After some legal wrangling, the case settled with a revenue-sharing deal. The terms aren't public, though you can get them if you're a publisher affiliated with Fox. I'm told they're similar to the YouTube deal.

7. **Apps.**

By *apps* in this section, I mean the same kinds we talked about with masters on page 158 (apps that use music, but not apps that simply let you access streaming music, such as Spotify, Apple Music, or iHeartRadio, as those are covered by the streaming section).

The app deals are either a flat fee (the amount varies hugely, depending on how the music is used) or a share of revenue, and the publishers more and more insist on some kind of sharing. As a general rule, the record masters and publishers combined try to get 50% of the revenue. The publishers try for half of that, though they sometimes end up with more like 10% to 20% of the total revenue (20% to 40% of the 50% music revenue).

Some apps don't use the masters, so the publishers can get up to 50% of the revenue, depending on how important music is to the project. However, the norm is closer to 30%.

As we discussed when we talked about masters, the platform selling the app (e.g., the iTunes store) takes 30% off the top, so these percentages are applied to what's left.

App deals are all short-term (one year to eighteen months), so they can renegotiate if the app is a success.

There's a company called Songlily (www.songlily.com) that makes deals with the labels and publishers, then licenses the tracks to developers. The idea is to make the process simpler for everyone, especially developers who have little patience for these kinds of things.

8. **Podcasting.**
As we discussed under record deals (on page 152), people don't like putting music in podcasts, because it's too much like a free download. So if the publishers allow their music to be podcast at all, they limit each song to ninety seconds (which is viewed as promotional). The deals are small, and usually a fee or percentage of ad revenues.

As you can see, these models are not only complicated, but also require publishers to track usage all over the Internet. And while the bigger publishers have sophisticated tracking systems, what about the rest of us? Well, the Fox Agency offers these services, as do a number of competitors. For example, Songtrust, started by the people who run Downtown Music, helps songwriters and publishers track and collect all their publishing income, and they have partnered with CD Baby and The Orchard (who distribute masters for indie folks as we discussed on page 72) to deliver these services. They are located, not surprisingly, at www.songtrust.com. Other companies in this area are Audiam (www.audiam.com), started by the founder of TuneCore, and AdRev (www.adrev.net), which monetizes YouTube.

If you're on the *Fast Track,* go to the Bonus Section on page 296. Everyone else, onward . . .

PRINTED MUSIC

Printed music primarily means **sheet music** (printed music of a single song—the kind you stuff inside your piano bench) and **folios** (which are collections of songs, such as *Greatest Hits of the Eighties, The Complete Led Zeppelin,* etc.). Collections of songs by a number of different artists are called **mixed folios.** Another type is a **matching folio,** which has all the songs of a particular album (i.e., it "matches" the album). Matching folios are usually printed with the album artwork on the cover and various posed candid shots of the artist inside.

Royalties

The following royalties are what's paid to a *publisher* for physical (meaning printed on paper) print rights. We'll talk about what share of these monies the writer gets a little later, and we'll discuss digital print rights on page 285.

For single-song physical sheet music, the standard royalty is 20% of the marked retail price (currently most single-song sheet music has a $4.95 retail price, so the publisher gets about 99¢).

Royalties on folios are 10% to 12.5% of the marked retail price, and the current marked selling price of most folios is $24.95. A **personality folio** is one that has the picture of the performing artist plastered all over it, such as *Stevie Wonder's Greatest Hits*. (A matching folio [see the previous section for what that is] is also a personality folio.) For a personality folio, there's an additional royalty of 5% of the marked retail selling price for use of the name and likeness of the artist, and it goes to the *artist* (who may or may not be the same person as the songwriter). If the songwriter is also the artist, the publisher may get the extra 5% if their deal includes name and likeness rights.

Unless the folio represents the selected works of a particular songwriter and only one publisher, it will contain songs written and/or published by a number of different people. Thus, the royalties are pro-rated, in exactly the same way as royalties are pro-rated for records that have recordings by different artists (see page 160). For example, if there are twenty compositions in the folio, and you own ten, you would get 10/20ths (one-half) of the 10% to 12.5% royalty. When you negotiate a pro-ration provision, be sure to insist that the royalty can only be pro-rated on the basis of *copyrighted, royalty-bearing* works in the folio. Otherwise, your royalty gets reduced by "Mary Had a Little Lamb" and "The Star-Spangled Banner," even though the printer isn't paying anyone for these songs.

The balance of print music consists of things like instructional music (such as putting your songs in *How to Play the Nose Flute*), marching band arrangements, choir arrangements, dance arrangements, etc. The royalty for these is generally 10% of retail unless it's a folio of lyrics only, in which case the royalty is 5% to 7.5%.

Print rights also include reprints of lyrics in books, magazines, greeting cards, etc. For books, if it's just a snippet of the lyrics, the rate is around 1¢ per unit, with a $200 minimum. For more extensive reprints, or a use that's significant to the story, per-unit rate can climb to about 4¢, with an advance based on anticipated sales—for major book authors, the advance can go over $100,000.

For paper greeting cards (we'll discuss digital e-cards in a minute), the publishers get the greater of a penny rate (usually 12.5¢ to 15¢) or a percentage of the wholesale price (usually 5% to 8%). If it's a greeting card that actually plays the song, publishers also insist that their royalty can't be less than what's paid for the master.

Reprints of lyrics on clothing run from 8% to 11% of wholesale, depending on whether the goods are sold in high-end stores or through a **mass-merchandiser** (meaning a store like Walmart, which sells at deeply discounted prices in a no-frills environment). The mass-merchandiser's sales are at the lower royalties, because the discounted prices mean there's a thinner profit margin. Most other products are around 6% to 8% of wholesale.

Advertising uses (such as printing the lyrics in magazines, newspapers, and on billboards) are flat fees, and can run $25,000 or more for major uses.

Traditional lyric reprints on inserts in physical albums are customarily free.

Term

Licenses for print music (other than lyric reprints) are for limited periods of time, usually three to five years, during which the printer has the exclusive print rights. Because of the limited duration of their rights, you have to spell out what the printer can do with the stuff at the end of the term. (This obviously isn't a problem for digital print licenses.)

So what can they do when their rights expire? Certainly they can't manufacture any more inventory, but can they continue to sell what they have? Normally these licenses give the printer a right to sell their existing inventory for a period of six to twelve months after the term expires. These sell-off rights are *non-exclusive* (meaning someone else can sell the same materials at the same time). At the end of the six to twelve months, they have to trash anything left over. For mixed folios (because they're so much more expensive, and also because there are a lot of other writers involved), the printers try not to have any time limit on their sell-off rights, and in fact want the right to keep manufacturing them.

When you make these deals, make sure there's no **stockpiling, dumping,** or **distress** sales. *Stockpiling* is where the printer manufactures eight quadrillion units right before the end of the term, so that they have tons of your inventory to sell after the term. (Your new printer won't like it if the market is already flooded with the same books it's trying to sell.) You stop this by saying the printer can only manufacture enough to meet their reasonably anticipated needs during the term.

Dumping and *distress sales* mean the printer sells your inventory at less than customary wholesale prices. *Way* less. You don't want this because, if they end up with a ton of goods left over, they'll blow it out at whatever rock-bottom price they can get. (Since they have to destroy everything they don't sell, they use the age-old theory that it's better to get something than nothing.) This practice, shall we say, "perturbs" your new printer, who is trying to sell the same stuff at full price. You solve this by saying your materials can be sold only through normal retail channels, at normal wholesale prices.

Digital Print Rights

There are a number of players in the digital lyric space, including websites that post song lyrics without the music (like LyricFind, Musixmatch, and Genius), lyric videos on YouTube, and services like Spotify that synch lyrics when you listen to a song. The lyrics are usually available free to users, because the sites have advertising up the yin-yang, though some have subscribers. For allowing sites to reprint the lyrics, publishers get about 50% of the advertising revenue, often with a minimum amount per view, and (if it's subscription based) a minimum amount per subscriber.

We already talked about Youtube lyric videos, on page 262.

This space is still the Wild West, as there are tons of lyric sites that aren't licensed at all. At the time of this writing, there's a growing movement to shut them down.

E-cards, meaning those cutesy-wutesy pictures of snow falling on sleighs while music plays in the background, are another form of digital print. For these, the publisher gets the greater of 10¢ to 15¢ per unit, or 5% to 8% of the retail price.

Companies like Musicnotes.com and SheetMusicPlus.com sell downloadable sheet music, which is truly the equivalent of (and a substitute for) paper sheet music, while Tonara and Chromatik have apps for tablets and smartphones that have cool things like ticking metronomes and pages that turn in synch. The cost is about the same as physical print music, which is currently $4.95 per song. For these licenses, the publishers get 50% of the income—a big jump from the 20% they get on physical print.

If the music is used in an interactive game, or a musical instruction or notation app (such as one that that scrolls along as you play the song), the deals range from 15% to 25%, depending on how interactive it is, and whether it's really educational or just entertainment. If the master isn't used, the norm is more like 50%. The publishers know the app would have to pay 60% to both the master and the publisher if they did use the master, so they give a discount to 50% if they don't. That incentivizes the app developers to not use the master, and it gives the publisher more money. (This bleeds into the app discussion we had on page 281.)

Unlike physical print deals, the digital deals are *non-exclusive*, meaning the publisher can license the same rights to multiple users. This is a big shift in the industry. Historically, setting up a printing company, buying the presses, hiring a sales and warehouse force, and taking the inventory risk (which of course doesn't exist with digital) was so expensive that, as we discussed, the printers wouldn't put out a particular song catalog unless they had it exclusively. The publishers were fine with this, and not just because they didn't want to invest in setting up a print company—by making long-term exclusive deals, the publishers could get huge advances from the print company.

FOREIGN SUBPUBLISHING

Except for the worldwide conglomerates, publishers don't have branch offices in all territories. So how do they collect their money when your records sell in Abu Dhabi?

Well, they do it by making deals with local publishers in each territory to collect on their behalf. The local publisher is called a **subpublisher.**

Foreign Mechanicals

Before we talk about deals with the local publishers, you should know about an unusual creature that lives in most territories outside the United States. This is the *mandatory* mechanical rights collection society. It works like this:

Most countries have a mechanical rights collection organization (mostly government owned) that licenses *all* musical compositions (regardless of who owns them) used by *any* record company in that territory. It's like the Harry Fox Agency (see page 250), except that it's mandatory. (As noted on page 233, mechanical licenses are not issued on a per-song basis outside the United States and Canada. Rather, the entire record is licensed for a percentage of the wholesale price, regardless of the number of compositions. This greatly simplifies the process of putting all the monies through one organization.)

The society collects mechanical royalties from the record companies, holds them for as long as they can get away with it (they can earn interest on these monies and keep it for themselves), and finally sends the monies to the appropriate publishers. Just like ASCAP and BMI, they deduct their operating expenses before they distribute income, but they also deduct some things we don't have here, like cultural deductions and non-music-related investments. These societies are a bit on the murky side, as they don't allow people to audit (meaning come in and check their accountings), and their practices have stirred up concern in the last number of years. The mood of reform is in the air, but they're mostly owned by the governments, so we'll see how it plays out.

How do the societies know which publisher to pay? Under this system, each local publisher files a claim with the organization, saying it owns a particular song. It can either be a claim for the entire song, or a percentage share if the rights are split among several publishers in that territory. If a claim is contested (and in some territories even if it isn't), the publisher is required to file proof of its claim, such as a copy of the contract with the U.S. publisher.

Foreign Performances

All foreign territories have some sort of performance rights society, usually only one per country, and usually government owned. These societies pay the *publisher's share* of performance monies to local subpublishers. They pay the *writer's share* to the U.S. PRO (which in turn pays the writer), again keeping these monies out of the publishers' hands (as we discussed on page 242).

If there's no foreign subpublisher, the publisher's share will ultimately wind its way back to the U.S. publisher through the U.S. society. However, it takes substantially longer, and it's worth paying the subpublisher a piece so you can get it earlier. How much do the subpublishers want? Well . . .

Subpublisher Charges

The range of deals for subpublishing allows the subpublisher to retain anywhere from 10% to 50% of the monies earned, with the vast majority of deals being from 15% to 25%. The contracts are actually written the opposite way, stating that the subpublisher collects all monies and remits 75% to 85% of it to the U.S. publisher. The shorthand industry expression of these deals is "75/25" or "85/15" (referring to the percentages kept by each party). By the way, I heard of one deal where the local subpublisher kept no percentage whatsoever of the earnings (i.e., they remitted 100%). Can you figure out why anyone would do this? See page 295 for the answer.

Covers

It is customary for the local publisher to get an increased percentage for **cover records.** A cover record, also called a **cover,** is a recording of a U.S. composition by a local artist in the local territory. The subpublisher usually gets 40% to 50% of the earnings from cover recordings (meaning it remits 50% to 60%).

When you make a subpublishing deal, be sure to limit the subpublisher's increased percentage to the cover recordings' earnings only, or else you'll decrease your money on the U.S. version if the local publisher's nephew records the song.

By the way, you should try to make sure that any covers have a different title. Since it's often in the local language, that's not an issue, but sometimes it's in the original language. If it's the same title, it gets really difficult (if not impossible) to sort through which version earned what in the way of mechanicals and performances, so it's always a good idea to push for this.

Performance Monies

A number of subpublishers try to charge a bigger percentage of performance royalties than they do for other monies. For example, they may keep 25% of all monies except performances, but keep 50% of performances. Here is their argument:

Assuming the subpublisher gets 25% of all earnings other than performances, for every dollar of earnings it gets 25¢. The 75¢ paid back to the U.S. publisher includes both the publisher's share and the writer's share (as did of course the dollar paid to them in the first place), and thus their percentage applied to the total writer/publisher combination. On performances, however, remember that the writer's share is paid to the U.S. performing rights society, and not to the local subpublisher (see page 287). This means that, instead of getting the full $1 of performance monies, the subpublisher only gets 50¢ (the publisher's share).

Here's a chart:

	Mechanicals	Performances
Total Writer/Publisher Earnings	$1.00	$1.00
Amount Paid to Subpublisher	$1.00	$ .50
		(other $.50 paid to writer directly by society)
Subpublisher's 25% Share	$ .25	$ .125
Percentage of Dollar Earned	25%	12.5%

Accordingly, subpublishers argue, they're really only getting 12.5% of the performance dollar. Thus they should have 50% of performance monies, so they can get 25% of the full performance dollar and be in the same position as they are with other monies. This 50% equals 25¢ (50% of the 50¢ publisher's share of performance monies), or 25% of the total writer/publisher performance dollar.

This reasoning, while clever and not without merit, usually gives way to sheer bargaining power. If the subpublisher has enough bargaining power, they'll pull it off. Otherwise, the U.S. publisher simply says no.

Printed Music

For printed music, if the subpublisher actually manufactures and sells the stuff, it pays the U.S. publisher from 10% to 15% of the marked retail selling price, the norm being 10% to 12.5%. If the print music is licensed out by the subpublisher, the subpublisher keeps the same percentage it gets for all other monies (15% to 25%) and remits the balance.

Advances

It's customary for subpublishers to pay the U.S. publisher an advance against their ultimate earnings. This is basically a banking transaction — if the U.S. publisher's catalog has a track record, the subpublisher pays an advance based on historical earnings. It will vary, of course, with the size of the territory and the size of the catalog. The range of advances is anywhere from zero (for a new artist or a so-so older catalog) to millions of dollars for major catalogs in major territories. Again, as with all other rules, there are exceptions. For example, if the publisher controls a new artist whose record is doing extremely well in the United States, the advance can get driven up, despite the lack of historical earnings.

A deal with no advance is known as a **collection deal,** meaning the subpublisher merely collects on behalf of the U.S. publisher. Also, if there is no advance, the percentage kept by the subpublisher is lower, usually in the 10% to 15% range.

Advances are also affected by the currency exchange rates. When the dollar is weak, high U.S. dollar advances are relatively easy to come by; the opposite is true, of course, when the dollar gets stronger. In other words, the same number of English pounds equals more or fewer dollars at any given time, depending on the current exchange rate. When it equals more, you can get a larger dollar advance.

"At Source"

If your subpublishing deal isn't directly with the publisher in a particular territory (for example, you make a deal with a major U.S. publisher for all of Europe), one of the most important points to have in your subpublishing agreement is a requirement that all monies be computed **"at source."** This means the percentage remitted to you must be based on the earnings in the country *where earned*, which is the *source*.

So if you have an 85/15 deal at source in Germany, and $1 is earned there, you get 85¢. If you don't require this, you'll pay 15% to the local subpublisher in Germany, then another percentage to your U.S. publisher.

An extreme example of why your deal should be "at source" is this scam, which has been around for many years: A subpublisher in the United Kingdom makes a 75/25 deal with a U.S. publisher for all the territories of Europe. The subpublisher in Germany (owned by the U.K. publisher) collects a dollar, keeps 50¢ as its collection fee, then pays 50¢ to the U.K. publisher. The 50¢ received in the United Kingdom is then split between the U.S. publisher and the U.K. publisher.

Here's a play by play:

Earnings in Germany	$1.00
Less: German Company's 50% Share	− .50
Amount Remitted to UK	$.50
Less: UK Company's 25% Share	− .125
AMOUNT REMITTED TO U.S. PUBLISHER	**$.375**

It doesn't take a genius to see that the $1 earned at source (in this case, Germany, where the actual earnings were generated) gets dwindled radically before it finds its way into your pocket. And the 75% deal you thought you had becomes 37.5% (you only got 37.5¢ out of the $1 earned in Germany).

This scam is no longer played in the shadows, but right up front. If you don't say the deal is "at source," the publisher will take both the local share and its share. Of course, ultimately, it's only a matter of dollars: how much do you get, and how much does the publisher keep. But make sure you address this issue directly. Either the deal is "at source" or it's not; say so from the get-go.

If the publisher doesn't own the foreign affiliate, the local publisher's share doesn't go into their pocket, so you don't have the same argument. But you can argue that the U.S. publisher's share has to include the foreign publisher's fee. In other words, if the U.S. publisher gets 25%, it could pay 15% to a local publisher and keep the other 10%, so in effect you're getting 75% "at source." If you can't do that, then try to limit what the subpublishers can charge. For example, put in your contract that they can't deduct more than, say, 10% to 20% before sending the dough back to the United States. The result of this push-pull depends on bargaining power. However you dress it up, it's just a way of computing how much of each dollar you get.

Translation/Adaptation Shares

An interesting quirk of subpublishing deals is the **translator** or **adaptor** share. If your song is popular, many territories will want to release a version with lyrics in the language of that territory. This all sounds innocent enough, but it creates some problems:

1. First of all, the local lyricist automatically gets a share of royalties, which is paid by the local societies. Most societies require that the lyricist receive about one-sixth of gross (meaning combined writer and publisher shares) for mechanicals, and one-sixth of the writer's share only for performance royalties.
2. Subpublishers, naturally, want to charge you for this share. If you have sufficient bargaining power, you may be able to muscle them into absorbing it out of their percentage. As their percentage decreases, however, so does the likelihood of your making them eat it. So, more commonly, the translator's percentage comes off the top, which means you pay your share of it. In other words, if you get 60% of the earnings from covers, you are absorbing 60% of the translator's share, and the subpublisher eats the other 40%.
3. Always require that the translation be registered separately with the society (since it will have a foreign title, this isn't so dif-

ficult), and also require the publisher to make sure the translator doesn't get paid on the English-language version. This can be done in most territories, but some (notably Germany) insist on paying the translator on the *original* composition no matter what you do (in the case of Germany, however, the translator gets only a piece of mechanicals and not other income).

The upshot is that you should have the absolute right to approve whether the subpublisher can authorize a local translation. Apart from its taking money out of your pocket, you want to be sure you like what they're doing. Make them send you an English translation of the lyrics for approval before they can record. If you don't, your ballad may find itself associated with a number of perverse sexual practices, drugs, Republicans, etc.

The Black Box

Remember, as we discussed on page 286, that the societies collect mechanicals for *all* songs, not just those registered. But they only pay out for the songs that are registered. By now your sharp eye has probably figured out that there may be some songs not claimed by any local publisher. And you're right—there are always unclaimed songs. For example, through sheer inadvertence, a U.S. publisher may not have a subpublishing deal in a particular territory. Or maybe the rights are disputed in the United States and no foreign publisher has been given the rights.

These unclaimed monies are called **black-box** monies. In some countries (notably Germany, Italy, Spain, France, and Holland), if the funds aren't claimed after a set period of time (usually three years), they're paid to the local publishers. Each publisher gets a portion of them, based on the ratio that its earnings bear to the total earnings of the society, and also based on seniority. So if a publisher earned 100,000 drapkes and the society collected 1,000,000 drapkes, it might receive 100,000/1,000,000, or 10%, of the black-box monies, and perhaps another 3% because it's been around for twenty years. This can be a substantial source of additional revenue, and the local publisher keeps it all because the monies aren't earned by any particular compositions.

If you get into the "major leagues" of publishers, you may be able to get a portion of the black-box money. The usual formula is to take a proportionate amount of the black box, based on the ratio that your songs' earnings bear to the total earnings of that subpublisher. For example, if your songs earned a total of $200,000 for the subpublisher, and its total earnings were $1 million, you would get 20% of the black-box monies, because your $200,000 is 20% of its $1 million total.

In recent years, the societies have begun allowing electronic registration, which enormously simplifies the process, and makes it easier to register compositions around the world. Because of this, most songs are properly registered and the amount of money in the black box is dropping. But it's still around.

P & U

When I was a kid, pronouncing "P.U." with a Texas accent meant you'd just smelled something yucky. Not unrelated to this is the concept of **P & U,** which means **pending and unmatched** monies. There are a chunk of these sitting with the digital service providers, who are holding money because they don't know who to pay. Some of this is legitimate—there are conflicting claims to the same song—but a lot is because they're getting information that doesn't quite match from different people. For example, they get publishing information from a performance society, a record label, and a third party data management company. When they try to reconcile them, sometimes there are data conflicts. Or worse yet, they'll get the same information from three different places, each adding up to 100%, only to have their computer think someone has claimed 300% of the song!

When they have a data conflict, they usually don't pay anyone. And they don't bother to tell anyone, which means your money can sit there for years.

Most songs have multiple writers and publishers, so there's often an issue, and it can mean a lot of money. Hopefully this is a short-term problem, while the data gets digested by the beast, but it's very real today.

So make sure your publisher is on top of this.

By the way, record labels don't usually have this issue, because there is only one owner per master.

DART MONIES (AUDIO HOME RECORDING ACT OF 1992)

Congress passed the Audio Home Recording Act of 1992, not surprisingly, in 1992. This act is the DART (Digital Audio Recording Technologies) bill we touched on before, and it did two things:

1. It said that consumers who copy records at home for their private, non-commercial use are not committing copyright infringement. I'll bet you're sleeping much better now.

   Actually, this wasn't such a big deal. The legislative history accompanying the 1976 Copyright Act made it clear that home copying was not copyright infringement. (Note this doesn't apply to unauthorized copying off the Internet, which is a big no-no. Thank goodness no one does that.)

2. The DART bill imposed a tax on digital audio recorders and digital audiotapes.

   In other countries of the world (most notably Germany), there was historically a tax on recording media and devices, going back to blank tapes. The money collected was paid to the record companies, musicians, and songwriters who are deprived of income because of home taping, and it amounts to substantial sums of money. When we got to the digital age, Germany was ahead of the curve in taxing blank CDs and even computer hard drives.

   The DART bill was a step in that direction for the United States. However, it only applied to digital audio recorders and tapes, and in a gigantic "OOPS," the tax managed to miss computers. This is because the act only applies to machines made *solely* for the purpose of duplicating audio, and therefore blank CDs, CD burners, hard drives, and the like (which do much more than copy audio) have skated past, thumbing their noses at the musicians. (The only thing caught in the net was digital audiotapes, which I'm sure you buy on a regular basis . . .) This isn't likely to change, because computer companies (who now rule the world) don't like anybody telling them what to do. They figure, if consumers are willing to pay a few more bucks for their products (the tax), those bucks should go in their pockets.

   The DART taxes get paid out in various percentages to the record companies, featured artists, unions, songwriters, and publishers, all separately (actually, it pays the PROs for the writers and publishers, who then pass along the money). This would be a great thing if digital audiotapes weren't D.O.A. As of this writing, it's under $1M per year, and its high point was only about $3.5M per year.

   In 2014, however, the **Alliance of Artists and Recording Companies (AARC),** whose job is to collect DART monies, filed suit against Ford, GM, and two electronics manufacturers because some of their cars have devices that can rip music from CDs onto the car's hard drive. To the AARC, this is a device subject to the DART bill, but to the car companies, it's not. As I write this, it's winding its way through the court system, so if you want to catch the latest, go on the net and search for AARC vs. Ford.

Answer to question on page 288:

While it was a stupid business deal, the subpublisher's thinking was that (a) it would have a certain amount of prestige from having landed a major catalog (which prestige immediately vanished when everyone found out what an idiotic deal they made); and (b) even though the subpublisher kept no piece, it collected the monies and held them for a period of six months, which meant the company could earn interest on them (this was back in the days when interest actually meant something).

If you find someone ready to make a deal like this, give me a call because I still have that land in Florida for sale.

Bonus Section!

HOW TO SET UP A PUBLISHING COMPANY

I am now about to save you an enormous amount of time and frustration in setting up a publishing company. The tips I'm giving you here, revealed in print for the first time, were gained by yours truly through a series of hard knocks that will become obvious as you see the proper way to do it.

The Absolute First Thing to Do

Before you do anything, and I mean before you do *anything,* you positively must take this first step: *Affiliate your company with ASCAP, BMI, SESAC, or GMR.* The reason you have to do this first is because these societies won't let you use a name that's the same as (or similar to) the name of an existing company (to make sure they don't accidentally pay the wrong party). So you don't want to have label copy, printed music, copyright registrations, and everything else in the name of a company that can't collect performance royalties.

You can affiliate and secure your name by completing an application and giving the society three name choices, ranked in order. That way, at least one of the names should clear. If you're also a songwriter and haven't yet affiliated, you should affiliate as a writer with one of the societies at the same time (they won't let you affiliate with more than one as a writer). You'll have to affiliate as a publisher with the same society that you affiliate with as a songwriter because, as we discussed on page 244, the societies insist on having a song's publisher affiliated with the same society as the song's writer. And for the same reason, if you're going to be a "real" publisher (meaning you're going to publish other people's songs, as opposed to only your own), you'll need to have several companies, one for each PRO.

The publishing company affiliation forms are pretty straightforward; they ask you who owns the company, the address, and similar exciting questions. You also need to give them information about all the songs in your catalog (writers, publishers, foreign deals, recordings, etc.), so they can put the info into their system and make sure you're properly credited (read "paid"). You can get affiliation applications by contacting ASCAP, BMI, SESAC or GMR at:

ASCAP
www.ascap.com
1900 Broadway
(headquarters)
New York, NY 10023
(212) 621-6000
(212) 621-8453

Two Music Square West
Nashville, TN 37203
(615) 742-5000
FAX (615) 742-5020

7920 Sunset Blvd.
Suite 300
Los Angeles, CA 90046
(323) 883-1000
FAX (323) 883-1049

BMI
www.bmi.com
320 West 57th St.
(headquarters)
New York, NY 10019
(212) 586-2000
FAX (212) 489-2368

10 Music Square East
Nashville, TN 37203
(615) 401-2000
FAX (615) 401-2702

8730 Sunset Blvd.
3rd Floor
West Hollywood, CA 90069
(310) 659-9109
FAX (310) 657-6947

SESAC
[only by invitation]
www.sesac.com
55 Music Square East
(headquarters)
Nashville, TN 37203
(615) 320-0055
FAX 615-329-9627

152 West 57th St.
57th Floor
New York, NY 10019
(212) 586-3450
FAX (212) 489-5699
6100 Wilshire Blvd., #700
Los Angeles, CA 90048
(323) 937-3722
FAX 323-937-3733

GMR
[only by invitation]
www.globalmusicrights.com
1100 Glendon Ave., 20th Floor
Los Angeles, CA 90024

By the way, all of these societies have offices in other places, such as Atlanta, Miami, etc. You can get the contact info on their websites.

Here's a tip in picking a name. The more common your name, the less likely you're going to get it. So steer clear of names like "Hit Music" and similar choices that, because they're obnoxiously obvious, won't clear. Names using just initials, such as "J.B. Music," also seem to have a hard time clearing (so save that concept for your license plates). For some reason, many of my clients enjoy naming their publishing companies after their children or their streets, and these seem to clear routinely. (For the record, I once owned a publishing company, "Holly Kelly Music," that I named after my dogs.)

Also, get started early—it can take about five weeks to get an approval.

Setting Up Business

If you're not a corporation or an LLC that's using your corporation's or LLC's name as the publishing company name, the next step is to file what in California is known as a "fictitious business-name statement." This is a document filed with a county recorder and also published, and it has its counterpart in most states. It tells the world that you're doing business under a name that isn't your own and makes it legal to do so. At least in California, you need this statement to open a bank account and, even more importantly, to cash checks made out to that name. You can imagine the screaming phone call I got as a young lawyer when I learned this lesson.

Copyright Registration

Next, register the songs with the Copyright Office in the name of your publishing company (see page 365). If the songs were previously copyrighted in your name, you need to file an assignment transferring them to the publisher's name.

By the way, if you're thinking of using an LLC, corporation, or other legal entity, be sure you get tax advice first. There are some serious tax consequences to holding copyrights in these entities, and you should be sure it's cool for you.

Society Registration

To the extent you didn't do it when you originally affiliated, you need to register all your songs with the performing rights society. That authorizes them to license those particular songs, collect the money, and pay you. The societies will send you the forms, which are self-explanatory. You only have to register the songs as either the writer or the publisher, not both.

After that, you're in business. You can issue licenses to record companies and other users, as well as make foreign subpublishing agreements, print deals, and so forth. However, there's no particular need to rush into these deals, nor will anybody be interested in making them, until you have a record released. In fact, unless you've got a record coming out (or some other exploitation, like a film or TV show using your songs), the societies won't even let you affiliate, and frankly there's not much point in doing any of this. You'll just be all dressed up with no place to go.

18

Songwriter Deals

Now let's look at the terms of the agreement between the songwriter and the publisher. Remember, as we discussed, the songwriter signs a contract transferring ownership of the copyright in a musical composition to a publisher. In exchange for this, the publisher agrees to handle the business and pay royalties to the writer.

SONGWRITER ROYALTIES

The reason we first discussed publishers' receipts is because a songwriter gets a piece of the publisher's collections (with the exception of performance and DART monies, which are paid directly to the writer). The writer almost invariably gets 50% (except for print music in a few cases). Just to remind you, the monies kept by the publisher are called the *publisher's share*, while the monies that the writer gets are called the *writer's share*.

STANDARD CONTRACTS

For some reason, all songwriter contracts seem to be labeled "Standard Songwriter Agreement." However, I haven't seen any two Standard Songwriter Contracts that looked like they were even distant cousins, much less twins. So don't take any comfort from the words at the top of the page. Here's what to really look for:

"Catch-All."   Some contracts say the songwriter gets 50% of the publisher's receipts from "mechanical, synchronization, and transcription income," or words to similar effect. The problem is that the language is sometimes a limited list of monies for which the songwriter is

paid. This means that the publisher could be collecting monies that it doesn't share with the writer, and this is definitely something to avoid (if you're a songwriter).

This problem isn't cured by adding everything you can think of to the list. For example, even the most complete list of income sources in the 1950s wouldn't have included income from streaming, video games, and so forth, which not only didn't exist but weren't even contemplated. What you really need, at the end of the list of items, is a **catch-all.** This is a phrase that says the writer gets 50% of "all other monies not referred to in this agreement." Often, you'll find the contract states just the opposite: The writer is only entitled to a share of monies *specifically* set forth in the contract. So cross this out, and add your catch-all. (Tell them I said you have to have it.)

Share of Advances. Most contracts also say you don't share in any advances the publisher may get. Most of the time, this is fine—if the publisher gets an advance for its entire catalog of songs (of which you're only a part), you really have no right to share in that advance until your song has earnings that are used toward recoupment. There's no way to know whose songs will earn back the advance, and so there's no reasonable way to allocate the advance to a particular song until royalties are earned.

The exception is an advance paid specifically for your composition. One example is when a publisher issues a license at less than the statutory rate and gets an advance (or guaranteed payment for a certain number of units) for one particular song. (We touched on this on page 252.) Since this advance or guarantee is only for your song's earnings (and doesn't have to be repaid if there are no earnings), you should get your share when the advance/guarantee is paid to the publisher. So add language saying you *do* share in advances and guarantees that are specifically for your composition.

No Playing Footsie. If the publishing company is affiliated with your record company, you want to make sure they don't issue "sweetheart" licenses (i.e., licenses at less than customary rates) to their own record company. In other words, you don't want them playing footsie with their sister companies at your expense. For example, they might license your songs to their company at half the statutory rate. Sure, their publishing company makes less (it only gets its share of a smaller amount), but the record company more than makes up the loss, and you don't. This would also apply if they own a film company or any

other potential user. So add a provision saying that licenses to their affiliated companies must be on an arm's-length, customary basis.

As 360 deals spread, and some companies "encourage" you to make
a deal with their affiliated publisher, these issues becomes even more
important.

"At Source."   It's also important (and cheap insurance) to make sure
your publisher's deals with its subpublishers are all "at source" (see
page 290), so that the publisher's income (in which you share) is the
largest possible amount. Also, you should limit what the subpublishers
can charge to, say, 15% or 25% for third-party subpublishers, and maybe
10% to 20% for subpublishers owned by your publisher. The only exception might be a developing country with new copyright laws, where
the price of getting your money involves "tipping" the local warlord.
In that case, you might allow the subpublisher to get as much as 50%,
on the theory that your 50% is better than zero or a machete.

It's possible (although extremely difficult, and takes a lot of clout) to
have your *writer's share* computed "at source." If you do, then you still
need to limit what the subpublisher can charge.

PERFORMANCE MONIES

As we discussed on page 241, the performing rights societies pay songwriters directly (that is, they don't pay the publisher, who in turn accounts to the writer). In fact, the societies are so protective of a writer
being paid directly that (except for certain special circumstances, noted
below) they won't honor an assignment of performance royalties by the
writer. In other words, if the writer tries to sell his or her performance
monies, the society will simply refuse to pay the buyer and continue
paying the writer. (The exceptions are things like an assignment of
performance monies to a publisher who paid the writer an advance,
and assignments to a bank securing a loan, but these assignments are
limited to the amount of the advance or loan.)

Because the writer is paid directly, all songwriter contracts say the
writer doesn't share in any performance monies received by the publisher. Without this language, the writer would get all of the writer's
share (from the society), and a part of the publisher's share as well. It's
a good idea, however, to provide that, if a society no longer pays writers directly, or if a publisher directly licenses performance rights, the
publisher must share its receipts. You should also require the publisher

not to cross-collateralize these monies with advances under your deal, on the theory that the publisher never expected to have performance monies for recoupment in the first place. As we discussed on page 247, it is likely that the publishers will withdraw digital rights (and maybe even all rights) from the PROs. So this provision is now more important than ever.

PRINT MUSIC ROYALTIES

As we discussed on page 282, physical printed music consists primarily of single-song sheet music and multi-song folio books. Not surprisingly, the physical market is shrinking as the digital revolution takes hold. (We discussed digital print rights on page 285.)

Structure of Business

There are three major manufacturers of secular, physical printed music in the United States these days, namely Hal Leonard, Alfred, and Music Sales. This means that, unless your publisher is one of these companies, it will be licensing physical print rights to one of them. Thus, in songwriter deals with publishers who license out these rights to a printer, it would be eminently logical for the writer to get 50% of the publisher's licensing receipts. Logic, however, has never been a major impediment to the music business, and for some twisted historical reason (guess who it favors), print music royalties are expressed as either a percentage of the retail or wholesale price (on folios), or in pennies (for sheet music).

Sheet Music

When we get to single-song sheet music, we really enter the Twilight Zone. Historically, sheet music royalties have hovered in the range of 7¢ per copy. Occasionally some superstars got as high as 10¢ to 12¢, and the publishers acted like you were removing their eyeteeth. If you recall from our earlier discussion (on page 283), the publisher gets 20% of the marked retail price, which today is about $4.95, meaning the publisher gets 99¢.

I've been told by major publishers this practice persists because they have **favored nations** clauses (meaning a contract that says its rate goes up if anyone ever gets more) with a number of old writers, and that raising the pennies for the new guys would cost them money on the older deals. (*Favored nations* clauses can be in any kind of agreement, not just publishing.)

Over the last number of years, this practice has become less significant. Except for one major publisher, the penny terms now only apply to sheet music actually manufactured and distributed by the publisher. As noted above, most every publisher now licenses out their print rights, meaning the writer gets 50% of the money paid by the printer to the publisher, and not these stupid penny rates. In fact, some publishers are doing away with the penny rates altogether and splitting the licensed income, or paying the same royalty as they pay on folios (see the next section).

With respect to digital print rights, the publishers treat the income just like any other licensed income, and the writer gets 50%.

Folios

With regard to folios, remember the printer pays the publisher 10% to 12.5% of the marked retail price (see page 282). Most songwriter agreements pay the writer 10% of *wholesale* (you can kick it up to 12.5% with a bit of clout), which approximates 50% of the publisher's receipts. However, to my knowledge, none of the major print houses account to publishers on the basis of wholesale, so most publishers just split their income and call it good.

Remember to allow pro-ration only on the basis of copyrighted, royalty-bearing songs (see page 283).

Name and Likeness

In addition to the writer's portion, if you ask, most publishers will give you 5% of wholesale for use of your name and likeness in a personality folio (see page 283), which is about half of the publisher's receipts. You can sometimes hold out for the full 5% of *retail* that the publisher gets, arguing this payment is for your name and likeness, and the publisher shouldn't share in it.

Charges Against Royalties

Often a publisher pays the costs to create a **demo** of your song or, in some deals, pays you $600 or so for you to make one on your own. A *demo* is an informal recording made solely for the purposes of pitching a song to artists (similar to those for record deals, discussed on page 109). It's usually made by an unknown singer (or the songwriter), accompanied by one or two instruments (which, since the advent of synthesizers, can sound like the London Symphony Orchestra). The publishers try to charge 50% to 100% of the demo charges against the writer, though of course if you only wrote half the song, they'd only charge you half of those amounts. As your bargaining power increases, the amount they can charge decreases to as low as zero.

No songwriting agreement should charge you for anything other than the following: (1) demos; (2) subpublishing fees (see page 287); (3) collection costs, which means (a) monies spent by the publisher to collect your song's earnings, such as Harry Fox fees (see page 250) and (b) the cost of chasing deadbeats who don't pay; and (4) the cost of outside legal fees if there's an **infringement** claim against you (i.e., a claim that you stole someone's copyright). If you're in that kind of fight, the publisher will likely hire a **musicologist,** and you'll get charged for that as well. A musicologist is a music expert who compares your song against the one you supposedly ripped off, then says whether he or she thinks it's a copyright infringement or not.

All other costs of administration, copyrighting, advertising, etc., should be borne by the publisher. This is their cost of doing business and the reason they get 50% of the income. (When you share in publishing income, you're charged with these and much more. We'll get to that on page 317. As a writer, however, it should be limited.)

Accountings

Publishers typically account and pay within sixty to ninety days after the close of each semiannual calendar period (June 30 and December 31). Some superstar songwriters get **quarterly** accountings (meaning March 31, June 30, September 30, and December 31), but this is rare. If a publisher agrees to pay you quarterly, you don't usually get full accountings on the off-cycles (meaning March and September) because the publishing company systems aren't set up to do full accountings more than twice a year. Instead, you'll get an estimate of earnings for the March and September quarters, and, if it looks like you're owed money, they'll give you an advance. This is still worth trying for, as it means you'll get your money earlier, though it's hard to get without massive bargaining power.

Contracts typically limit the period in which you can object to your accounting statements, and most first drafts say you have to object within one year or else you lose your right to do so. You can usually get this extended to at least two years, and often three. Beyond that is rare.

The other considerations about statements, auditing, etc., are the same as record deals, which we discussed on page 177.

DART, WEBCASTING, AND INTERACTIVE STREAMING MONIES

As we discussed previously, DART monies are paid to writers and publishers based on the sale of digital audiotapes and recording equipment, and webcasting monies are paid for webcasts of their songs. As we also discussed, the PROs collect for the writers, so these monies are treated like performance monies and not subject to publishers' sticky fingers (see page 240 for why performance monies don't get to the publisher). However, as noted on page 245, publishers are more and more looking into direct digital licensing, so protect yourself on the performance monies, as suggested in that section.

The mechanical royalties paid for interactive streaming and permanent downloads (as we discussed on page 274) are paid to the publishers, and you get 50% of what they get.

ADVANCES

The advance for a single-song agreement is usually not very significant. It ranges anywhere from nothing (the most common) to $250 or $500, if we're talking about unknown songwriters and no unusual circumstances (such as a major artist who's committed to record the song, which of course changes the whole ball game). Major songwriters rarely sign single-song agreements other than for films (which are another story entirely, as we'll discuss in Chapter 29). If they own their own publishing, they keep the song, and if they don't, they're probably under a term songwriter's agreement.

There can be significant advances under term songwriter agreements, which by coincidence is our next topic.

TERM SONGWRITER AGREEMENTS

A **term songwriter agreement** is just like a record deal except that, instead of making records, you agree to give the publisher all the songs you write during the term. In a sense, it's also like a bunch of single-song agreements hooked together, because it's similar to signing a single-song agreement for each composition when it's created. The difference is that there's one overall contract that sets out the terms on which each song will be delivered, and of course the advances are recoupable from all of the songs on a cross-collateralized basis (see page 89 for what cross-collateralized means).

Term

The term of the agreement (the period during which you have to sign over everything you write) is usually tied to delivery and release of songs (we'll discuss *delivery* in detail shortly). Thus, the term ends after delivery and release of the required songs (like record deal terms). Sometimes deals are for specific periods, such as one year, with the publisher having two to four additional one-year options. And some deals are tied to your recording agreement (i.e., if it's with a publisher affiliated with your record company), meaning it has the same term as the record deal (two or more deals with the same term are called **co-terminous**).

Note that the term only denotes the period during which you exclusively agree to deliver your songs—the songs you deliver are owned by the publisher for the life of the copyright, which of course extends far beyond the term. (As we'll see on page 324, however, this is sometimes negotiable.)

Deals based on delivery of albums have an interesting way of exercising options in the publishing world. Instead of picking up your option within a certain time after delivery of your last album (like a record deal), publishers want you to deliver the *next* album to them (the one for which they haven't yet picked up their option) and give them some time (thirty days or so) to decide if they want to go forward. In other words, they get to test-drive the car before they buy it. If the publisher does pick up their option, it gets the new album and everything chugs along. If it doesn't, you get back the new album, tuck it under your arm, and look for greener pastures. Be sure to add that you also get back everything else you wrote after delivery of the prior album, or else they'll be keeping some of your songs without paying for them.

Tying the term to release of product has become an increasing problem for writers. The historical definition of *release* in publishing deals requires a physical (CD) release, and more and more product is being released only in digital. That means you could earn tons of money for the publisher but never have your deal end.

The delivery and release requirements are two of the most important terms of your deal, so we'll discuss them in more detail later.

Advances

Term songwriter agreements almost always require the publisher to pay advances to the songwriter. Historically, "true songwriters" (meaning songwriters who don't come with access to someone who uses their songs, as opposed to, for example, a writer who is also an artist who can record their own songs, or a writer/producer who can get songs to the artists they produce, or someone who writes regularly with well-known performers, etc.) received monthly advances. This is still the practice in Nashville, but it's not so easy for true songwriters to get these deals in rock 'n' roll. If you do get such a deal, new writers signing to a major publisher might get an advance in the range of $18,000 to $100,000 per year, and less if you sign to a smaller publisher. The advances are paid monthly, quarterly, or sometimes even annually, at the beginning of a contract year. (Don't get discouraged if you're a true songwriter—there's always a need for good talent. And there are true songwriters who make multimillions writing hits for other people.)

If you're an established writer, the advances are based on a historical analysis of your earnings—meaning they guess your future potential based on your past—plus whatever additional gouge factor you can leverage. These advances can range from $2,000 to several thousand dollars per month, and up. Some superstar writers get hundreds of thousands of dollars per year.

The trend these days is away from paying advances every month or so, and instead basing advances on songs that are recorded and released. (This is of course much more difficult if you're what's called a "true songwriter," since you don't have the ability to record [or produce] the songs yourself.) For example, if you're a songwriter and also an artist without a record deal, a typical deal might be $25,000 to $50,000 on signing, another $25,000 to $50,000 when you secure a record deal, and another $25,000 to $50,000 on release of the album. There are often further advances at certain U.S. sales levels, or reaching certain chart positions. For example, you might get an additional $25,000 at sales of 150,000 albums, and another $25,000 at sales of 300,000.

Under this kind of deal, if you don't get a record contract within a certain period of time (usually twelve to eighteen months), the publisher has the option to make you deliver a minimum number of songs (around ten to twelve) over the coming year, and it pays advances for these (in the range of $15,000 to $25,000 for the year, paid quarterly). If you do get a record deal, the advance on release of the first album is the amount negotiated up front (which we just discussed).

Another scenario, for bands already signed to a record company, is to base the advances on delivery *and release* of songs (we'll talk about the specific delivery requirements in a minute). A typical payment schedule is 50% of the agreed advance on signing (or on the publisher's exercise of its option for the next period of the term), 25% when you deliver and release half of that period's commitment, and the remaining 25% on delivery and release of the balance. So if the deal was $400,000 and you promised to deliver and release ten songs, you'd get $200,000 on signing, $100,000 on release of the first five songs, and $100,000 on release of the second five songs. The number of songs you're required to deliver and release is sometimes called the **Minimum Delivery and Release Commitment,** abbreviated as **MDRC.**

If you ask, you can often get a **formula** for future advances. The formula is a percentage of your prior earnings, and is similar to the formulas used in record deals. (See page 134 for a discussion of record deal formulas.) Unless you have a lot of clout, the only earnings that count for the formula are U.S. mechanicals and performance monies.

If you're an artist/writer, the formula would determine the advance for your next album. If you're not an artist who's releasing albums, it would determine your advance for the next contract period. For an artist/writer, the formula is usually based on earnings during the twelve months after release of your last album. If you're not an artist, it's usually based on your earnings during the twelve months prior to commencement of the contract period. Try to make the earnings period longer than twelve months (which isn't easy). The longer you make it, the more earnings you get to pump up your formula.

Here's a recent deal for an artist/writer where the advance for the second album was ⅔ of the earnings during the first year after release of the first album, less the unrecouped balance, with a floor and ceiling:

Formula: ⅔ of the year's earnings, less deficit, but not less than the floor or more than the ceiling.

	Floor	Ceiling
Album 1	$75,000	(Not applicable)
Album 2	$100,000	$200,000
Album 3	$125,000	$250,000

Under this deal, if the writer earns $60,000 during the first year, meaning only $60,000 of the $75,000 is recouped (and she is thus $15,000 unrecouped), the advance for the second album would be $25,000: ⅔ of $60,000 (which is $40,000) less the unrecouped balance ($15,000) equals $25,000. However, there's a floor of $100,000, so she gets a $100,000 advance (because the formula result is lower than the floor). If the earnings are $180,000 (and thus the writer recoups), there's no deficit to be deducted from the ⅔ of earnings formula, and she gets ⅔ of the $180,000 earned, or $120,000. If she earns $600,000 in the year, she'd only get the ceiling of $200,000 for album 2, because ⅔ of $600,000 ($400,000) exceeds the maximum ($200,000).

Under some deals, the unrecouped balance is deducted from the *floor*. Using the above example, suppose the writer only earns $15,000, and is therefore $60,000 unrecouped. In this case, the floor would be reduced from $100,000 to $40,000 (by deducting the $60,000 deficit from the $100,000 floor). When you have this kind of deal, be sure to ask for something called a **subfloor.** (This is a number you get no matter how badly you're unrecouped. We discussed subfloors under record deals, on page 101, and the concept is exactly the same.) For example, if the subfloor was $75,000, then even if the writer was $60,000 unrecouped, she'd still get $75,000.

As we discussed in the record section, new artists for whom there is a bidding frenzy can get deals that used to be reserved for artists with a sales history. The same is true for publishing. For example, when a writer is the fox with a pack of hounds snapping at their tail, you can get bids of $150,000 to $500,000 per album, and sometimes even more. With that much heat, the deal won't just be a songwriter deal—it will be a copublishing deal, or maybe even an administration deal (none of which means anything to you, because we haven't discussed them yet. Hang on 'til the next chapter).

Delivery/Release Requirements

There are two aspects of delivery/release requirements:

1. **What you must deliver to move the term of the deal forward.**

   Since term deals require you to deliver and release a minimum number of songs during each period (the MDRC we discussed a minute ago), you have to negotiate how many that is. Until you deliver them, you can't move to the next period of the deal's term.

2. What you must deliver to get your advance.

When advances are based on your delivery and release of a minimum number of songs, that number is not always the same as the number required to move past the current period of the term.

Let's consider these separately:

Moving the Term Forward. Similar to record deals, the term of a songwriter contract continues until you deliver and release a minimum number of songs (your MDRC). If you're a songwriter with a track record of hits, you may be able to simply say you'll give the publisher ten or so songs during each period of the term. Usually, however, the songs have to be commercially released in the U.S. on a major label (or major independent) before they count, though sometimes you can agree that only a portion of them have to be released. For example, if you have to deliver ten songs, at least five of them have to be commercially released.

If you're a **self-contained artist,** meaning you both write songs and record them, the term of your deal will usually be geared to the release of an album containing your songs. The publishers will want you to write 100% of the songs on each album, so those songs can be 100% owned by them. This is fine if you always write all your own songs. But if you write with others, or might at some time in the future write with others, or if you ever want to record songs written by someone else, you have to scale that back. You can easily reduce the 100% to 90%, and with some pushing, you can sometimes get it down as low as 50%. In other words, if there were ten songs on your album, only five would have to be yours to move the term forward. However, if you routinely write your songs with someone who isn't a party to your songwriting deal, then you have to cut those percentages by whatever the other person takes. For example, if you only expect to write 60% of the album (because co-writers normally write the other 40%), then you should only agree to deliver half of that 60% (30%) in order to move the term forward. Same idea if you're a hip-hop artist with lots of cowriters, not to mention samples up the ying-yang.

If you deliver less than the agreed minimum, the publisher will thank you very kindly, gobble up what you've given them, then take the next songs without paying any additional advance (i.e., no more than what is due for the first album). That's because the deal won't move forward to the next period of the term (and therefore won't entitle you to the next album's advance) until you deliver what you're supposed to for this period. So when you deliver the second album, you'll only get the advance due for the first, which means the publisher will get two albums for the price of one.

Let's take a look at this concept using numbers:

Suppose you had to deliver five songs on your first album to move the term and were entitled to a $100,000 advance when the album was released. If the first album only contained four of your songs, the initial period of your songwriting deal would continue until you released one more song on one of your albums, and you wouldn't get the $100,000 until then. Since you can't release the last song until your next album comes out, the first term continues until you've released that song on the second album. And even if that second album contains five of your songs, the publisher only owes you the $100,000 due on delivery of the first album, despite the fact that they got nine songs. (You need to give them ten songs to get the next advance.)

In addition to the number of songs, there is usually a requirement that you deliver a minimum percentage of statutory rate for each one. If you haven't signed a record deal when you make your publishing deal, the publisher will want you to deliver 100% of statutory rate, with a cap of say ten or eleven songs, and payment on 92.5% of sales (see page 253 for what all that means). With some pushing, you can get them down to 75% of statutory (with the same cap and percentage of sales). If your record deal is already made, the publisher will want whatever is in your deal (which may be better than 75%). The higher the rate you deliver, the bigger advance you'll get.

Another problem with song delivery deals is you might never satisfy the delivery requirements, and the deals would go on forever. For example, if you're an artist and you committed to deliver songs that you've recorded and released, and your record deal comes to an end, you're hosed. Or if you're not an artist but agreed that a certain number of your songs must be released on a major label, you could be stuck in the first period, despite giving the publisher hundreds of songs that were recorded on indie labels and made a ton of money. Or if you're getting songs released digitally only, or outside the United States only.

Most publishing deals still require a release to be on a CD before it counts toward the MDRC. They want to know that the company is serious about marketing the record, not just slapping it up on Spotify. This will have to change as CDs disappear, but as of today, it's still here and not as easy to change as you'd hope, if you can change it at all.

You should try for some way to move the term under all these circumstances. For example, if you're an artist and you lose your record deal, some publishers will agree that the deal restructures as a song-based term, though the advances will be lower. Or maybe a combination of delivering songs and a smaller release requirement. Or sometimes they'll agree that, if you don't get another record deal in say two years, the deal is over.

Another angle is to say that a song counts if it earns a minimum amount of money. For example, if you got a $100,000 advance and have a five-song MDRC, a song would count if it earned one fifth (because it's one of the five required songs) of $100,000, or $20,000. (If you only wrote part of a song, say half, then the threshold for counting that song would be reduced [$10,000 instead of $20,000 in our example] so it would count as delivering half a song). Your argument is that the only reason for requiring a major label release was to make sure the record had a shot at making money, and if you get the dough from an indie or a synch license, it's just as green as money from the majors. Maybe even better, since the major release could have been a dud. So you should push for a song to count against your delivery requirement if it earns a certain amount.

A variation on this theme is to count non-major released songs if they hit an album- or single-sales threshold (e.g., if it sells over 500,000 albums, it counts). However, in today's world, you're better off with a dollar figure than you are with sales, because the biggest money is now in performances and synch, not mechanicals from record sales and downloads.

If you have clout, you can sometimes get the publisher to move the term forward if you're recouped, even if you haven't delivered all the songs you promised. Your argument is that they've gotten back their advance and should therefore be happy and shut up. They don't always shut up.

If there's nothing in your contract to cover any of this, you'll have to come begging. The publishers aren't always sympathetic to these pleas, particularly if you got a lot of money when you signed the deal.

Advance Delivery Requirements. A similar requirement is that you must deliver a certain number of songs in order to get your advance. If you're self-contained, they'll want whatever maximum percentage of the album you normally write (in other words, without the cushion we just discussed to allow the term to move forward). So if you normally write all of your own material, you'll only get your advance if you deliver 100% of the songs on your album, even if the term moves forward when you deliver 50%. (If, when the publisher makes the deal, they know that you normally write less than 100%, that smaller percentage should be the criteria.)

You should build in protections for falling short. Otherwise, your advance will be "all or nothing" if you don't hit the target. For example, if you're supposed to deliver 100% of the album and you only deliver 75%, you should get 75% of the advance, not zero. The publishers will normally agree to this, but they'll insist on a minimum percentage minimum (usually 50% of the target) below which they won't pay anything. So if you normally write 75% of your albums, you'll get all your advance if you deliver 75%. If you deliver 37.5%, you'd get half. But if you only wrote 30%, which is less than 50% of the 75% you were supposed to deliver, you'd get nothing until you delivered more songs. (If you got money on signing, or at the beginning of the term, you would, of course, keep that. You just wouldn't get any more.)

As with the term delivery requirements, the advance may also be based on your delivering a minimum percentage of the statutory rate. For example, you not only have to deliver five songs, but they must all be licensed for at least 75% of the statutory rate. Similar to negotiating the minimum percentage of songs requirement that we just discussed, you should ask for a pro-rata reduction (as opposed to all or nothing) if you get less than 75% of statutory. For example, if you deliver a 50% of statutory rate, and you were supposed to deliver 75%, you should try to get ⅔ of the advance.

A new wrinkle in this area is the new and developing artist pricing we discussed earlier (see page 171), which is the practice of releasing new artists at mid-price or even budget levels. As we discussed in the controlled composition section (see page 252), you only get 50% of your mechanical rate for these low-priced records. So putting these concepts together, if your songwriting deal has a 75% of statutory requirement, and your company only pays 50% of that because your new-artist-priced album is released at a budget price, publishers sometimes say they don't have to pay the advance, or move the term forward, for delivery of those songs. Not so cool.

The publishers will of course count the songs against your advance and delivery requirement when the album is raised to full price. But the problem is, if it doesn't sell very well at the introductory price, the record company may never raise it to full price, and you'll end up stuck in the first period of your publishing deal (meaning they'll get another album for the same advance).

Note these two concepts can both hit you. In other words, you could be reduced for delivering less than the required number of songs, and reduced again for delivering less than the statutory rate.

In all these provisions, be sure to add a formula saying that fractional compositions count toward the delivery requirement in proportion to your ownership. For example, if you deliver half the publishing of a composition (because you wrote only half the song; see page 318 for an in-depth discussion of this), it should count as one-half of a song for your delivery requirements. Many forms don't provide this, and the net effect is that you get no credit whatsoever for fractional songs. Since these little guys earn money just like the others, there's no reason you shouldn't.

Prior Songs

Most "standard" term agreements have an innocuous-looking provision that quietly picks up all of the songs you have written before the term of the deal. Language such as all songs "written during or prior to the term hereof." Unless this is something the publisher specifically negotiated, resist such a clause, or at least get paid for these songs with an additional advance.

Note, by the way, that prior songs don't count against your MDRC unless that's specifically negotiated; the MDRC is almost always tied to songs written during the term.

Another way to handle pre-term songs is to say that the publisher can administer them during the term of your deal (we'll discuss "administration" in the next chapter, but basically it means the publisher can control the rights for a period of time without owning them). If you have massive clout, you can argue that the prior songs' earnings should not be cross-collateralized with the newly written songs, and that the prior songs come back to you at the end of the deal if they're not exploited during the term (if they are exploited, they fall under the overall deal).

Record Deal Tie-ins

As noted on page 122, more and more companies are trying to grab your publishing when they sign you to a record deal. If there's any possible way to resist this, I strongly urge you to lash yourself to the mast and hang on. If you're dealing with an independent record company, many times their publishing company isn't a real publisher, but rather just another way to make money from you. If you're going to give up your publishing, it should ideally be to a fully staffed publisher (see page 239). These folks can add real value to your songs, by teaming you up with creative co-writers, helping you write for existing artists, and otherwise forwarding your career. In fact, they can even help you get a record deal. On the other hand, the independent label publisher often just makes a deal with a major publisher, under which the major administers your songs (something you could do by making your own deal with the major, and for which the independent takes a nice chunk of change for being in the middle), or worse yet, they sometimes do nothing but sloppily collect your money. This scenario isn't always the case—sometimes the independent advances you its own money, helps you creatively, professionally administers your songs, and thus brings a real benefit to the party. But unfortunately this is the exception.

If you must give up your publishing to make a record deal, then in addition to the normal publishing deal points discussed in this chapter, ask for these:

1. Try to just give a passive 360 right, meaning you keep control of your publishing and merely pay them a piece of the income (see page 102 for a discussion of 360 rights).

2. Try to limit their participation to mechanical royalties from your recordings. This means they wouldn't share in performance monies, print, etc., and they wouldn't share in any money (even mechanicals) from recordings of your songs by other artists. This is very hard to get.

3. If you lose point 2, agree to let them share in all earnings (not just mechanicals), but only earnings from those songs recorded by you as an artist. Ideally, you should also limit them to the *earnings from your recordings* of the songs. In other words, if you record a song that becomes a hit, and it's then recorded by three other artists, they would share in the earnings from your version but not the other artists. (There are some complicated allocation problems connected with this, as we'll discuss on page 331.) If you can't get this, at least try to exclude the earnings of songs not recorded by you. This is also hard to come by.

4. No matter how you do with the above, try for all the points in paragraphs 1 through 4 of the next section.

Sometimes you may make a deal with a major and at the same time make a deal with its affiliated publisher. The majors don't usually require you to do this (though some will "strongly suggest" it), so you're only making the deal because you think it's good for your writing career. The following deal points are important for these kinds of arrangements, but they're applicable to independent record/publishing situations as well:

1. Try to get advances for your publishing in addition to your record advances.
2. Since their affiliated company will share in your publishing, ask your record company to pay you a full mechanical rate for your songs (see page 253). You should get some concession from a major (though maybe not full statutory), but the independents who aren't true independents will argue that the distributing record company forces a reduced mechanical rate on them, and they want the maximum mechanicals just like you. Both of these arguments are true, but try it anyway.
3. If they take publishing, don't give them a 360-right share of publishing income (as we discussed on page 102).
4. Be sure they can't exercise an option under your publishing deal without also picking you up as an artist. The argument is that you're only giving them publishing because they're offering you a record deal, and if that's no longer true, they should get their hands off your songs. (Of course, if you're getting fat advances under the publishing deal, you may not care if they pick up your publishing option and drop the record deal. But it's always better to make it your option rather than theirs.)
5. *Never* let them cross-collateralize your record and publishing deals (see page 89 for what cross-collateralization is). This is not customary, but it's done. Remember the language about cross-collateralizing "this or any other agreement" between you and the record company (see page 89)? It could pick up a publishing deal as well, because, with some independents, it's the same parties to both contracts.

Bluntly, if you're dealing with independents who can muscle your publishing, it means your bargaining power is close to zip. So there's not a lot of room. But at least give 'em a good fight, and *never* give up points 3 and 4. **NEVER.**

POP QUIZ

Now that you have carefully digested all of the above, here's a pop quiz: What is a major source of money that a publisher can't (normally) use to recoup its advances? (Answer on page 325.)

If you're on the *Fast Track,* go to Chapter 19 on page 326.
Everyone else, boogie on.

CO-WRITES
(SONGS WRITTEN BY TWO OR MORE WRITERS)

One provision that needs special care and feeding is the one that concerns your writing with other people (people you write with are called **co-writers** or **collaborators**).

Most of the older term songwriter agreements, and a good number of the ones currently used, take the position that the publisher gets 100% of the copyright and publishing (meaning both your share *and* the co-writer's share) of compositions you write with other writers. This is virtually impossible for you to do. It requires you to deliver rights from somebody you have no control over, and who may not want to be delivered. Even worse, it may be someone you can't deliver because they already gave the rights to another publisher. In fact, if your co-writer has this same requirement in their songwriter deal, *they* are obligated to deliver 100% of the composition (including your share) to *their publisher.*

Obviously two people can't each own 100% of the same horse. So as a practical matter, this gets worked out between the two publishers, usually by splitting the copyright and administration between them (see page 326).

Some contracts take a compromise position, requiring you to deliver no less than 25% of each song to your publisher. That works fine if you've written 25% or more of the composition, but it's not so hot if you've written less than 25%. In that situation, your publisher takes part of your *writer's* royalties to make up the difference in income between the publishing they actually get and 25%. For example, if you wrote 12.5% of a song and delivered 12.5% of the publishing to your publisher, your publisher would take *all* of your songwriter royalties. This is because 12.5% of the publishing, plus your entire 12.5% of the songwriting royalties, equals the same dollars the publisher would get if it had 25% of publishing at the outset.

This is easier to see using money: For every dollar received, 50¢ belongs to songwriters (the songwriter's share) and the remaining 50¢ belongs to the publishers (the publisher's share). Since your publisher has only 12.5% of the 50¢ publisher's share, it only gets 6¼¢. Your 12.5% of the writer's 50¢ is of course also 6¼¢. However, the contract says your publisher must get at least 25% of the publishing (which equals 25% of the entire 50¢ publisher's share, or 12½¢). Since it only has 6¼¢ (12.5% of the publisher's 50¢ share), the publisher takes all of your writer's share (which is also 6¼¢), to equal the 12½¢ (25% of the publisher's 50¢ share) that you promised. This means you will make little (or nothing, in this example) for your collaborative efforts. Such a situation does not make for a healthy career, and it certainly turns you off collaborating.

Because of all this, the most you should do is agree to deliver that percentage of publishing that equals your percentage of the writer's share. In other words, if you write 10% of a song, you should only agree to deliver 10% of the publishing; if you write one-fifth, 20% of the publishing, etc.

How Are Songs Divided?

Historically, 50% of a song went to the writer of the music, and 50% to the lyricist. No muss, no fuss. So if one person wrote all of the melody, and one person wrote all the lyrics, they each got 50% of the song. If two people equally wrote the lyrics, and one person wrote the melody, then the lyricists each got 25% of the song, and the melody writer got 50%. You get the idea.

Over the last few years, this has gotten fuzzed up considerably. The reason is that rap, hip-hop, pop. EDM, and similar music are as dependent on the **track** as they are on the melody and lyrics. The *track* is the background rhythm and instrumentation, on which the melody and lyrics are laid (the lyrics and melody are referred to as the **topline)**. Because tracks are so important to these songs, the people creating tracks also get pieces of the songs.

Unfortunately, there are no hard-and-fast rules about how a track gets treated. It's usually negotiated by the parties at the time, depending on their sense of who contributed what to the song, and the muscle of the person creating the track. I've seen deals where the track gets one-third, with the melody and lyrics each getting one-third, and I've also seen deals for important producers where the track gets half the song. At the other end, there are deals where the track shares half the song with the music/melody side of the equation. And sometimes, if the track contribution is minimal, and the person creating it doesn't have much bargaining power, it gets little or nothing.

There's an added twist when tracks contain **samples** (we'll discuss sampling in detail later, but basically it means the track incorporates somebody else's song into the new material). In this case, the sample owner gets a piece of the publishing, and that has to come out of someone's share. Logically, since the person who created the track added in the sample, you'd think that the sample's share of publishing should all come out of the track's share. However, the track owner argues that it should come out of everybody's earnings, on the theory that everyone benefits from the use of the sample. (The same issue comes up if the melody or lyric writer "borrows" from someone else.) Results vary in direct proportion to bargaining power.

So sit down, slug it out, and have the survivor call me.

Writing Teams

If you're in a band that writes together, or if you write with a partner on a continual basis, and a publisher is signing all of you, there are some special points of concern. (If you don't regularly write with others, or if you do but you and the others are signing to different publishers, you can skip to the section on creative control, on page 322.)

Just to make the discussion simpler, I'm only going to talk about a writing team of two people, but the same principles apply to bands that write together.

The writing team issues are:

Advances.   Despite what your first thought might be, the advances don't double for a writing team. The reason is rather simple—even though there are two of you, you're each only writing one-half of a song, and so the total output is the same as the publisher would get from one person.

Delivery Requirements.   By the same token, if you have a song delivery requirement, that shouldn't be increased, either.

Cross-Collateralization.   If the publisher hands you one contract for both of you to sign, listen up. You want to make *absolutely certain* that you each have a separate account for your earnings and advances, and that your two accounts are *not* cross-collateralized (see page 89 for a discussion of cross-collateralization). If you always split the songs 50/50, and get equal advances, this point doesn't make any difference— your earnings are going to be identical, as are your advances.

But since that almost never happens, look at the result of cross-collateralization in the following instances:

1. One or both of you may occasionally write songs without the other (in which case you'll want to be sure those earnings aren't used to recoup the other guy's advances).
2. You might stop writing in the same ratio that you get advances (e.g., you take the advances 50/50, but on some songs you split the earnings 60/40 or 75/25). This means the advances get recouped unevenly (see the example below).
3. You may break up as a team completely, and begin writing on your own, in which case you absolutely don't want the other person's advances charged to your account.

Here's an example: Suppose you and your co-writer, Louise, are each getting $10,000 a year under a songwriting agreement. At the end of year one you have written a number of songs on a 50/50 basis that have earned a total of $5,000, and each of you has been credited with $2,500 in royalties. This means you are each $7,500 unrecouped. Now you write a song by yourself, which earns $20,000 in royalties. If your accounts are not cross-collateralized, the $20,000 earnings will recoup your $7,500 deficit, and the publisher pays you $12,500. *If your accounts are cross-collateralized, the publisher will deduct not only your $7,500 deficit but also Louise's $7,500 deficit.* Thus, out of the $20,000 your song earned, you'd only get $5,000 ($20,000 less your $7,500 deficit and less your partner's $7,500 deficit). Since you didn't get the other $7,500 advance (your co-writer did), you will not be a happy camper. So separate your accounts. I'd hate to read about Louise floating up in the East River.

Separate Obligations. Another problem with signing one agreement is that you have to be sure your obligations are separate, and that you're not responsible for a breach by the other guy. For example, if your partner wrongfully terminates his or her agreement and walks out, you don't want to find your royalties being used to pay for the publisher's damages and/or legal fees in a fight with your co-writer.

These problems are easy to fix if you ask up front, but they can be an enormous pain if you forget. So don't.

CREATIVE CONTROL

Moral Rights

In a number of countries outside the United States, there is a legal concept known as **moral rights,** or by the snooty term **droit moral** (which in French means "moral rights," and in Czech means "no parking"). The concept (among others) is that an author can stop any mutilation of his or her work, even though they may have parted with it long ago. For example, the creator of a painting (even though it has been sold four or five times) could stop someone from cutting it into smaller paintings, drawing mustaches on it, etc. Similarly, the author of a musical work can stop substantial changes in the music or lyrics.

Contractual Approvals

The United States has never recognized a moral rights concept for music (although there is a limited one for paintings and fine art). Accordingly, to the extent you want any protection, you gotta put it in your songwriter/publisher contract. You do this by saying the publisher needs your approval before it can do things like:

1. **Make changes in the music.**
    The publisher will normally say that's fine as long as they don't have to ask about simple changes merely to conform to the mood or style of a particular artist.
2. **Make changes in the English lyrics.**
    Again, this approval right usually excludes minor changes for mood or style.
3. **Add foreign lyrics.**
    If you have enough clout, you may be able to approve translations. This is much harder to come by, but it's worth fighting for. Remember, it's also a financial issue—translations reduce your royalties (see page 291).
4. **Make changes in the title (in English).**
    Usually no sweat—just ask for this and you'll get it.
5. **Grant synch licenses.**
    If you have some bargaining power, you may be able to get consent to all motion picture synchronization licenses. (These are defined on page 265.) If you have a lot of bargaining power, you might also get approval of television synch licensing, but

this is much harder to get. The reason is that publishers often have to give a yes or no answer to TV studios within twenty-four hours, and they don't want to lose the opportunity because you're off sipping lemonade on your yacht. One compromise is to get approval of television licenses with the exception of a few things that the publisher can do without you, such as music-centric programs (like *The Voice* or *Dancing with the Stars*), current programs like *SNL* or *Entertainment Tonight*, or live, on-camera performances of the song.

If you can't get this, another compromise is to say the song can't be licensed for NC-17 or X-rated films, or for a scene in a film involving illicit drugs, sex, violence, or anything else that rings your particular bell.

6. **Use the song in commercials and print ads.**
   At best, you should have the right to approve any usage of your song in commercials and print ads (newspapers, magazines, Internet, etc.). (If you have approval of synch licenses, you automatically control TV commercials. But this doesn't cover radio commercials because radio recordings aren't made under synch licenses, as we discussed on page 265, and it doesn't cover using your lyrics in print ads.) If you don't have enough clout to approve all commercials, you can compromise by requiring your consent to certain categories, such as alcohol, tobacco, firearms, political candidates, and my personal favorite, sexual hygiene products.

REVERSION OF COPYRIGHT

Smile whenever you hear the words **reversion of copyright,** because this will always be good for you (unless you're a publisher, in which case you can scowl). This is different from the termination of copyrights under the copyright law, which we'll discuss later, on page 344, because reversion is a *contractual* provision, negotiated specifically. It means the publisher must give you back your song (copyright and all) at some point in the future.

Conditions of Reversion

What should trigger reassignment? The best (short of the automatic reversions discussed below) is that the song reverts to you if it's not recorded and commercially released. Be sure to require that the recording/release must happen within some time frame. Otherwise the publisher can keep each song for the life of copyright, telling you every week that a recording is just around the corner. If it's a single-song agreement (rather than a term deal), the publisher usually gets about six months to two years after signing within which to get the song recorded and released. Try to break this into two parts—it must be recorded within six months (or twelve months) after signing the deal, and released within six months (or twelve months) after that. This is better for you, because it comes back sooner if nothing happens.

For term writer deals, the period in which it has to be recorded/released usually starts at the close of the deal, although songs delivered in the later years sometimes have longer time periods (because the publisher hasn't had time to work them). A typical provision is two or so years after the end of the deal, but no less than three or so years from delivery of a song.

The smaller your bargaining power, the less likely you'll be able to pull off a reversion. However, even at the most modest levels, you should be able to get back your song at some point if it hasn't been exploited (say two to five years after the term, and shorter is obviously better). The theory is that the song is of no value to the publisher, but potentially could be valuable to you in a new situation. This gets more difficult if the publisher has paid you an advance, particularly one that hasn't been recouped (which is probable if the song is unexploited). However, you may be able to negotiate an option to get the song back by repaying the advance (be sure to say you don't have to pay back an advance that's been recouped). The publisher will sometimes put a time limit on this right to repay (say a year or two after the first date the song can revert), but even with this limit, the option is a plus.

Be certain it's your *option* to pay the money back. You don't want to be obligated to buy back your losers, because all that does is guarantee the publisher against a loss.

Reversion of copyright for non-exploitation is something you should *always* ask for. You may not always get it, but you should *always* ask for it. Is it clear I mean *always*? Did I say *always*?

Automatic Reversion

When you move into the super leagues, or if you are in a bidding war, you can ask for a reassignment of all compositions, whether or not they're recorded. Time frames on these usually run from five to fifteen years after the close of the exclusive term, with the majority in the seven-to-twelve-year range. This is usually tied to recoupment—for example, ten years after the term, the publisher will reassign only if you're recouped. In this case, (1) take the right to pay the unrecouped balance (remember to keep it at your option), in which case you get the songs back sooner; and (2) be sure you get the songs back if and when you do eventually recoup, even if it's five or ten years later. Don't assume the contract will say either of these if you don't ask, because it usually won't.

If they give you the right to repay and get back songs, publishers now ask for more than 100% of the unrecouped advance. For example, if they want 125% of the balance and you're $10,000 unrecouped, you'd have to pay them $12,500. Their reasoning is that, if they kept the song, they'd get the money needed to recoup your account *plus* their own share of those monies. So if they let you go early, they want their piece on top. Sometimes you can get this percentage down, to say 110% or so.

After you get your songs back, the publisher will want the right to collect monies while they owned the song for a period of one or two years after the term. This is called a **collection period.** In other words, if $100 was earned from downloads during the term, but isn't paid by the record company until six months later, the publisher gets to keep that. Of course, you want to keep the collection period as short as possible.

Partial Reversion

A step down from full reversion is to get a **partial reversion,** meaning that you get back the administration rights to your share of the song, but the publisher keeps the administration of theirs. For example, if you have half the publisher's share and all the writer's share, you have 75% of the song's income. A partial reversion would give you back the administration rights to your 75% share, but the publisher would keep administration of their 25%. This is called **co-administration.**

So how does it work if two people have administration rights to one song? Well, that just happens to be our next chapter . . .

Answer to quiz on page 317:

Performance monies (see page 240 for why) and DART monies (see page 293).

19

Copublishing and Administration Deals

This chapter discusses deals under which two or more people share the publishing of a song. The variables are:

1. Who owns a piece of the copyright (some may just have a right to income, with no ownership);
2. Whether there is a sharing of the administration rights (the rights to issue licenses, collect monies, etc., which we discussed on page 235); and
3. How long the deal lasts (life of copyright, or something less).

The most common deals are:

1. Copublishing agreements coupled with songwriter agreements (we discussed songwriter agreements in the last chapter). In other words, a deal under which you get not only your songwriter's share, but also a portion (usually 50%) of the publishing income as well. The contract is not usually a separate copublishing agreement; it's just a songwriter's agreement with copublishing terms baked in.
2. A situation where songwriters who are signed to different publishers (or songwriters who own their own publishing) write a song together. This kind of copublishing agreement (which is also called a **split agreement**) sets out how the money gets divided, and how the song is going to be administered. As we'll see in a minute, the administration can be done by only one party, or shared by two or more of them. If more than one party administers, this is sometimes called a **co-administration agreement**.

3. A publisher who is too small to hire a staff enters into an agreement for a larger publisher to administer their songs (also called an **administration agreement**).
4. A publisher hires a subpublisher in foreign territories (in other words, the subpublishing agreements we discussed in Chapter 17).

Unfortunately, the industry definitions in this area aren't very precise. So for our purposes, I'm going to use the term **copublishing agreement** to mean a deal that shares copyright ownership, regardless of how long the deal lasts. If only one publisher owns the copyright, and the deal is for someone else to administer the song, then I'm calling it an **administration agreement,** even if it lasts for the life of the copyright.

Because the labels are fuzzy, these are not universal terms. Some people refer to life-of-copyright deals as *copublishing agreements* even if they involve no copyright ownership, and others call co-owned deals that last only a few years *administration agreements*. However, we gotta start somewhere, so I'm using these terms only to make the distinction of ownership. This will keep us from getting lost in overlapping labels.

Let's start with copublishing (shared ownership).

COPUBLISHING DEALS NET

Publisher's Share

One of the first things to decide, of course, is how the money gets whacked up. Usually it's the same as the percentage as the copyright ownership, which is usually the same percentage of the song written by each writer. (For example, if Fred wrote half the song, and Sharon wrote the other half, their publishers would share the money equally. If Fred only wrote one-third, his publisher would have one-third. You get the idea.) However, if one party has more clout than another, or if one party pays money for the privilege, they can get a disproportionate share. For example, even if Fred wrote only 50% of the song, his publisher might demand (or buy) 75% of the publishing.

A songwriter/copublishing agreement is actually two deals in one. In theory, the songwriter portion of the deal pays the writer's share of monies to the writer, and the copublishing portion says that the writer owns a percentage (usually 50%) of the copyright, and gets that percentage of the publisher's share. In reality, it just pays 75% of the income to the writer and looks pretty much like a songwriter deal.

What gets divided up on the publisher's side is called the **net publisher's share.** It's defined as **gross income** (which is everything the publisher receives, meaning writer's and publisher's shares combined), less the following deductions:

1. An administration fee,
2. Expenses, and
3. Songwriter royalties.

Let's look at them separately:

Administration Fee.   The first deduction is an **administration fee**, also called an **admin fee**, which is a percentage of the gross income (writer's and publisher's shares combined), usually from 10% to 20%. It's always deducted first, because it's a percentage. (Let's repeat our golden rule: "One who gets a percentage applies it to the largest possible number.")

Sometimes the administration fee is based on the gross monies after deducting the songwriter's royalties (meaning it's applied against our old friend, the publisher's share). For example, 10% of $1 gross income is 10¢, but 10% of the publisher's share (gross income less the writer's 50%) is 10% of 50¢, or 5¢. This practice, however, is really just playing word games. It's the same as cutting the percentage in half (10% of the publisher's share is the same as 5% of gross), but cosmetically it sounds like the publisher is getting more. So it persists.

An administration fee is, in theory, designed to reimburse the publisher for its indirect expenses of operation—rent, secretarial help, telephone, utilities, executive salaries, etc. In reality, it's just a function of leverage, because it disappears as soon as the other party has any appreciable bargaining power. In fact, for songwriter/copublishing deals, the administration fees have become much less common over the last number of years.

Expenses.   The administrating publisher deducts its **direct expenses,** which are usually spelled out in a list that ends with something like "and anything else we can think of." *Direct* means the expense is a specific item relating only to this song, as opposed to a general, unallocated overhead cost (like rent, secretarial, etc.). To my mind, there are only a few legitimate direct expense deductions, and none of them amount to substantial monies. They are:

1. Copyright Office registration fees (see page 365).
2. The cost of making demos—informal recordings, not for commercial release, made to promote the song (as we discussed on page 304).
3. **Collection costs,** such as charges by the Harry Fox Agency, subpublishers' fees, and legal expenses to chase deadbeats. By the way, a number of publishers who don't use the Fox agency want to charge an equivalent fee for their own services in this area. Try to resist that if you've got some clout.
4. **Legal costs and expenses** if you're sued because someone thinks you ripped off their copyright. This also includes the cost of a musicologist (who we discussed on page 305).
5. The preparation of **lead sheets.** A *lead sheet* (pronounced "leed" sheet) is a piece of paper with the words and musical melody line of a song. Before the 1976 Copyright Act, the U.S. government required lead sheets to be deposited with the Library of Congress in connection with registering a song copyright (see page 365). Now that the Library accepts CD copies of songs, publishers have stopped going to the expense of lead sheets, so they've pretty well disappeared (except for the reference to them in songwriter contracts).

Beyond these, I don't think anything should be deducted, and I've been pretty successful in limiting costs to the above. The other items publishers try to charge you for are advertising, promotion, legal fees for contracts to exploit the songs, and "all other expenses concerning the composition." Hold firm against these, and don't wimp out.

Writer's Royalties.   In some deals, the publisher deducts your songwriter royalties in computing net publisher's share. If this is the case, the writer's royalties are computed as we discussed in Chapter 18. More commonly, if you're both the writer and the copublisher, there's no deduction of writer's royalties; instead, the administrating publisher gives you 75% of the net publisher's share (representing 50% for the writer's share, plus 25% for half the publisher's share). Of course, if there are third-party writers, their royalties would be deducted before you get paid.

Who Administers?

The next question is "Who administers the song?" It's usually done one of two ways:

1. **One administrator.**
   One party has the exclusive right to administer on behalf of all, and the other parties only have the passive right to be paid a share of income from the administrator, with no control. This is the most common arrangement for songwriter/copublishing agreements. In these deals, the publisher controls administration rights (just like a songwriter deal), and pays out your share.
2. **Everyone administers.**
   All parties have the right to administer their own share of the composition. This is the most common arrangement for songs co-owned by publishers of approximately equal status. The mechanics of co-administration work like this: Assume you and I are 50/50 owners of a song. Under a typical co-administration deal, I can issue a license for my 50%, but not for yours, and vice versa. This means that no one can use the song without getting a license from both you and me.

Expenses, Fees, and Writer Royalties in Co-administration Deals

Co-administration deals have some peculiarities in handling expenses. When one party administers the entire song, it simply deducts the expenses from gross income before paying everyone else. In co-administration deals, however, everybody is collecting their own money, which means there's nothing to deduct from. Accordingly, there is no administration fee, because no publisher touches any other publisher's share, so there's nothing from which to deduct the fee (taking it from yourself isn't much fun). Also in these situations, the writer's share isn't usually deducted. Instead, the full publisher/songwriter royalties are paid over to each publisher in proportion to their ownership of the song, and each publisher pays its own writer directly. (This isn't always true; sometimes one publisher collects its share of publishing plus the full writers' share, and that publisher pays all the writers. But that's rare.)

As to expenses (the copyright registration fees, demos, etc., we discussed a minute ago), the one who pays the costs sends a bill to the other publisher(s) for their respective share(s). For example, if a 50% publisher pays $400 for a demo, it sends a bill for $200 (50% of the $400) to the other 50% publisher. It's a good idea to require that costs can't exceed a certain dollar amount (say $500) without the consent of the other party, and be *absolutely sure* that the publisher isn't taking these costs twice. I say this because, as we discussed on page 304, demo costs (and every once in a while, other costs) are sometimes charged against *songwriter* royalties. If so, they shouldn't also be charged against copublishing royalties. Observe: If a publisher pays $500 for a demo and charges it against the songwriter, it should not also charge it to a copublisher in computing the net publisher's share. However, many agreements would allow the publisher to do exactly this, which means it not only charges $500 against the writer, but also charges $250 against a 50% copublisher. Thus they would collect $750 for a $500 expenditure. A bit hard to justify on the grounds of fairness, but a good business to be in.

Shhh . . .

And now, an Industry Secret: Most of the time there is no agreement signed by the major publishers when they co-own a song with other publishers. Some years ago, they found that writing and negotiating these deals was so burdensome that they decided to rely on their rights as co-owners under the copyright law (which we'll discuss in the next chapter) and industry custom (which is true co-administration). But between co-writers who own their own publishing, these deals are still around.

ADMINISTRATION AGREEMENTS

With enough clout, you can go to a publisher and not give them any ownership, but instead merely give them the right to administer your songs, which is what I'm calling an **administration agreement.** The party getting the administration rights is called the **administrator,** and I'm going to refer to the party granting these rights as the **original publisher** (not an industry term).

This is a common deal for small publishers that don't have a staff, and for writers who own their own publishing (which is the case with most superstars these days), to make with a larger publisher. The subpublishing deals we discussed in Chapter 17 are also administration deals.

Usually these contracts are for a short period of time (three to five years or so, often with extensions if you're unrecouped). And because the publisher gets only a small piece, and only for a limited time, these deals have more modest advances (or no advance at all).

By the way, the difference to you of transferring copyright ownership and getting it back in, say, five years, as opposed to an administration deal for five years where you keep ownership, isn't terribly significant. There might be some tax issues, and there are some things under the copyright law that a co-owner can do that a non-owner can't, but these can be covered in your contract. From the publisher's point of view, they really want ownership because it makes them eligible for awards they can't get as administrators. And since publishers love lining their walls with plaques, they're often willing to pay more for ownership deals.

Administrator's Share

Under an administration deal, the administrator takes an administration fee, reimburses itself for any direct expenses, and pays 100% of the balance to the original publisher. The administrator customarily (but not always) takes care of paying the songwriters and any other participating publishers. These monies are of course deducted before paying the original publisher.

Administration fees range from 10% to 25% of the *gross* dollars (writer's and publisher's shares combined). Note (as we discussed on page 328) that a percentage based on the gross dollars is equal to double that percentage of the publisher's share alone. This means that an administrator taking a 20% administration fee is in reality getting 40% of the publisher's share of income. In other words, if a dollar comes in (including writer and publisher money), the administrator gets 20¢, which equals 40% of the 50¢ publisher's share. The original publisher gets the balance, less the songwriter royalties. It looks like this:

Gross	$1.00
Less: Administration Fee (20%)	−.20
Less: Writer's Share (50% of the $1.00)	−.50
ORIGINAL PUBLISHER'S SHARE	**$ .30**

Here's another way to look at what everybody gets out of the $1 in this same example:

Each Party's Share

	Administrator	Publisher	Writer
Original Dollar Amount	20¢	30¢	50¢
% of Gross	20%	30%	50%
% of Publisher's Share	40%	60%	0%

As noted above, any direct costs are deducted "off the top" and are therefore borne by the administrator and original publisher in proportion to their share of publishing (60/40). If the writer has a separate deal with the original publisher, and that deal allows recoupment of certain costs, then any recouped costs shouldn't be deducted in computing the publisher's share. But if the writer and publisher are one entity, these costs usually come off the top.

As discussed in subpublishing deals (on page 287), the administration fee on performance monies is sometimes doubled.

Cover Records

Many administration deals give the publisher an incentive to go out and get **covers**. As we discussed, a *cover* is a recording obtained by the administrator, and the incentives can be one of several:

1. **The administrator gets an increased percentage on covers.**
   For example, if the administrator has a 15% administration fee, this might increase to a 25% fee on income from cover recordings. This is the fairest approach, because it rewards the administrator's efforts directly. But it's not as simple as it looks. If the cover isn't the first recording of a work, you can't always tell which version of the song is generating the money. It's easy enough for mechanical royalties and digital exploitations—the royalty statements list the company and specific recording. But when it comes to nondigital performances (like radio and television), the songs are only listed by title, and there's no way to know which version was played on the radio (the original or the cover?).

   The best solution is to say they only get an increased percentage on mechanicals, which you can sometimes pull off. If not, there needs to be some allocation between the cover version's earnings and the original's. We used to deal with this by using a formula based on the ratio that the mechanical royalties from the cover version bear to the mechanical royalties from other versions. For example, if the cover version earned $100 in mechanical royalties and all other versions earned $200 in a particular period (total of $300), then one-third (100/300) of the performance monies are treated as being earned by the cover. In today's world, with mechanicals dropping and performances surging, this doesn't work as fairly. Because there's no easy way to handle it, most people don't bother beyond language saying you'll make a "reasonable allocation" between the cover version and the original. And some deals don't say anything at all.

2. **The administrator gets an increased percentage of all income.**

   Another possibility (although I don't like to agree to this) is that, if the administrator gets a cover, it gets an increased percentage of *all* earnings of the composition, not just those from the cover version. This eliminates the allocation problem, but it gashes your pocketbook.

3. **The administrator retains administration rights to the covered song for an additional period of time.**

   For example, if the administration term is three years, the publisher might continue to administer covered compositions for a period of five years from a particular date (the start of the deal, the date of the cover recording, the end of the deal, your mom's birthday, etc.). I don't particularly like this, because it breaks up your catalog and makes it difficult to move the songs away. This of course is precisely why publishers like such a clause (as well as the fact that it gives them a longer period to participate in the money).

4. **The administrator gets copyright ownership or life-of-copyright administration for covers.**

   Getting a cover may even mean the administrator gets copyright ownership (usually 50%), or the right to administer the song for the life of the copyright. If you do this, try to make sure it's an extraordinarily successful cover record. For example, require that it reach a certain level on a major chart, or that it earns a major dollar amount. (See the next section for more on this.)

5. **Any combination of 1, 2, 3, and/or 4.**

6. **None of the above.**

What's Really a Cover?   You want to be very careful about how a "cover record" is defined, because, as you just saw, the consequences are significant. If the only result is an increased percentage of income from the cover itself, it's not such a big deal—either it's successful and you both make a lot of money, or it's dead and buried. However, if a cover means the publisher gets copyright ownership, or an increase on non-cover earnings of the song, you gotta be tough about how a cover is defined. Certainly you don't want the publisher's aunt Esmerelda singing into her computer to be considered a cover. But under many definitions, it would be, because the contract simply says "a recording." (Aunt Esmerelda's recordings are available over the Home Shopping Network, between the cubic zirconia and the porcelain carousels that play "Somewhere, My Love.")

The first test should be that the cover is actually procured by the publisher (called a **procured cover**). In other words, they went out and got it, as opposed to the artist calling up and asking for it. This clause isn't as easy to get as you think, because the publisher doesn't want to argue about who actually made it happen. They will also say that if they raise your stature to the point that everyone wants your songs and starts hounding them, they shouldn't be penalized. But with enough clout, you can pull it off.

Second, you want the recording they procure to be a commercial one, and it must be released (it's amazing how many people neglect these simple criteria). If possible, you should add that the release has to be on a major record company label, and you should try to require that (a) the recording features a major artist (which you should define as an artist whose last album was gold, platinum, or better); and/or (b) the release itself must achieve a certain chart position. As to chart positions, the higher you get, the better—Top 5 or 10 is ideal, but even the Top 30 or 40 isn't bad. Make sure this is on a national chart such as *Billboard*, and not some schlock local station chart. Ideally it should be a singles chart (which means airplay and streaming), but album charts are second best. And it should be on a mainstream chart, not country, gospel, etc.

NOW LOOK WHERE YOU ARE!

Here you are, only partway through the book and you already know enough to answer the final homework assignment I gave after my nine-week music business class at USC Law School. Very impressive!

Try your hand at this:

You are a record company and have just been delivered an album by Freddy London, produced by Marvin Lester. Freddy is signed exclusively to Warner/Chappell Music as a songwriter, and he wrote eight of the ten songs on the album. The other two were written by Marvin, who owns his own publishing under the name Marvelous Music.

1. Each time an album is sold, who is entitled to a payment from the record company? (Ignore any recoupment.) Clue: There are five parties, but you won't know the last one if you're not on the Expert Track.

2. Freddy makes a promotional video of his single, which he wrote by himself. Who gets paid when the video is played on YouTube?

Answers to quiz:

1. Artist; producer; publisher (Warner/Chappell), which includes Freddy's songwriter royalties; publisher (Marvelous Music), which includes Marvin's songwriter royalties; and unions (see page 168).
2. The publisher and writer get public performance/mechanical monies (see pages 240 and 250). The record company gets a share of advertising monies, which it shares with the artist.

If you're on the *Fast Track,* and if you're in a group,
go to Part IV (Chapter 22) on page 371.
If you're on the *Fast Track,* and you're not in a group,
go to Part V (Chapter 23) on page 395.
Everyone else, read on . . .

20

Advanced Copyright Concepts

WHO OWNS THE COPYRIGHT?

Copyright ownership is pretty easy to figure out if you sit down with your accordion and knock out a little ditty by yourself. You, of course, are the owner, since you created it. But we lawyers wouldn't have much to do if it were all that simple, so let me show you how we've managed to fuzz it up over the years.

How About Two People Writing a Song Together?

Suppose you and your cousin Louie write a brilliant work together. Which one of you owns it?

As you probably guessed, both of you do. But there's more to it than appears at first glance:

Who Controls the Song?   Suppose you want to put the song on your next album, and Louie wants to save it until he gets a record deal. Can he stop you?

The copyright law, in Section 201(a) of the Copyright Act, spells this out pretty clearly. It says that you and Louie have created a **joint work,** meaning it was created jointly by the efforts of two or more people. When you have a joint work, either of the authors/owners can deal *non-exclusively* with the *entire* composition, subject to the obligation to pay the other person his or her share of the proceeds. That means you can give all the non-exclusive licenses you want to record companies, film companies, etc., subject to paying Louie for his share of the song. And Louie can do the same.

What Do You Own?   How about this one: You and Louie sit down to write a song. You write only the music, and Louie writes only the lyrics. Suppose you don't like Louie's lyrics, so you take back your music and ask somebody else to write new lyrics. Can you do that and cut out Louie?

My mentor Payson Wolff once told me that creating a joint work is like adding water to a ball of clay and squishing it. My partner Bruce Ramer uses the analogy of scrambling the white and the yolk of the egg. So as you may be starting to guess, the law isn't what you would intuitively think. It says that, even if two people create separate, distinct parts of a work, they each own an interest in the *whole copyright*, not just their own contribution. Thus, Louie owns half the music and half the lyrics, and so do you. You can't just pick up and leave each other. Even if you add new lyrics, Louie has a percentage of the song.

Does this sound like an absurd result? To some extent, yes; but if you get into dividing up works where the contributions aren't so easily defined as music and lyrics (which is most of the time), the alternative is even more impossible. Think, for example, about all the elements that go into making a film. What part is the screenwriter's? The director's? The producer's? The wardrobe designer's? Or what about a song where three people work on the lyrics, while two work on both music and lyrics?

What Makes a Joint Work "Joint"?   By now you're beginning to see that this is more complex than it first appears. But we're just getting warmed up. Try this one: A songwriting team consists of one person who lives in California, and another who lives in New York. The California writer, totally on her own, writes a piece of music and emails it to her friend in New York. A few days later, the guy in New York sits down and writes the lyrics. Is this a joint work? Did these two people create the composition together?

The law says, to have a joint work, you only need an author who *intends*, at the time of creation, to merge his or her work with someone else's. In other words, when the musician wrote the music in California, did she intend to have lyrics written for it? That's certainly the case in our example, even though the lyricist never physically got together with the melody writer. (It's almost always true that a lyricist intends to merge the words with music, since he or she probably has little call for poetry readings.) So, to have a joint work, you don't need to be in the same room (or on the same planet), and you don't even have to know each other, as long as there is an intent to merge the work at the time of creation.

If you want to see this principle carried to extremes, get a load of this one. In the 1940s, a guy named Ernie Barnett wrote the melody of a song, and his wife, Maybelle, wrote the lyrics. They sold the song to a publisher who thought Maybelle's lyrics were pretty awful (a lot of "moon" and "June," I'll bet). So the publisher tossed out Maybelle's words and had a new set of lyrics written by a total stranger, George Norton. The result was a song called "Melancholy Baby."

Based on these facts, a court held that "Melancholy Baby" was a "joint work," and that George was one of the joint creators. Even though Ol' George came along after the song was supposedly finished, he was still a joint author because, when Ernie wrote the melody, he intended to merge lyrics with it. The fact that the lyrics were ultimately written by someone Ernie never met was irrelevant. Moreover, the new lyricist had an interest in the music (although the case didn't deal with that issue). Nice coconuts, eh?

For the legal freaks, the case is *Shapiro Bernstein v. Vogel*, 161 F.2nd 406 (1947).

WORKS FOR HIRE

When Teddy Kennedy was at Harvard, he hired someone to take an exam for him, and it caused a big stink. Well, the copyright law is one place where this is perfectly legal. It's done with **works for hire** (technically known as a **work made for hire** in the copyright statute). A *work for hire* happens when you hire someone else to create for you. If you observe the technical formalities, the employer actually becomes the author of the work insofar as the copyright law is concerned. And when I say "the author," I really mean *THE* author. It's as if the person you hired doesn't even exist (in the eyes of the copyright law), and indeed their name doesn't even have to be on the copyright registration form.

I suspect (but I really don't know, and would hate to disillusion myself by researching it) that the "work for hire" concept was developed to cover such things as fabric companies that print copyrighted designs on their cloth. They wanted to be sure that the company (not the backroom dork who actually designed the pattern) was the owner of the copyright. Seems reasonable enough.

But for showbiz . . .

Application to the Entertainment Industry

Here's an example of works for hire in the entertainment world. Suppose you are Walt Disney Pictures and you hire someone to write the theme for *Snow White*. (I picked the example of a motion picture for a particular reason, as you'll see on page 341.) In this situation, Walt Disney Pictures (the corporation) becomes the author of the work, and the person hired to write it disappears. Does this mean the writer won't get his or her name listed as the writer of the song (e.g., on sheet music, in the film, etc.)? Usually not; the real creator customarily gets credit. (But sometimes, for example with jingles written for radio or television commercials, a creator doesn't.) Also, the amount of compensation paid to the real creator isn't usually affected by this type of arrangement—most of the time they're paid exactly the same money, whether or not the work is "for hire." However, a number of important rights in works for hire are drastically different (as you'll see later, on page 344), so whenever you're creating a work for hire, be alert to the consequences.

Technical Definition

A work for hire can be created under the copyright law in only one of two ways, which are a bit technical. They're set out in Section 101 of the Copyright Act. (You can skip to the "Duration of Copyright" section on page 342 if technical things make you squirmy. But try it first.)

1. If the work is made by an *employee* within the *scope of employment*, it's a work for hire. An example of this is the fabric designer I mentioned before.

    The test of whether there is "employment" is not the one used for the income tax laws, or in fact for any other type of laws. The law says the only employment situations that count are those where the employer is actually "directing, or supervising the creation of the work, in a very specific way." (The major case in this area is *Community for Creative Non-Violence v. Reid*, 490 U.S. 730 [1989], in which the Supreme Court held that a Vietnam memorial sculpture was not a "work for hire" because the people who paid to have it created didn't exercise control over the details of the work, didn't supply the tools, had no ongoing employment relationship, etc.).

    Normally (although not always), a songwriter is given quite a bit of latitude in his or her creation, so it would fail the employment test. I suppose, if a songwriter is given very specific instructions, and is supervised during the process, he or she might be considered an employee under the copyright laws. But that's very rare. The most common works for hire in the music area are those that fall under the next section.

2. If not created by an employee within the scope of employment, a work can only be a work for hire if it meets *all* of the following criteria: The work must be (1) **commissioned** (meaning created at the request of someone); (2) created under a written agreement that specifies it's a work for hire; and (3) created for use in one of the following:

  (a) A **motion picture or other audiovisual work.** This is the most common area where songs are treated as works for hire. It includes musical scores, title songs written for films, etc. Remember, these songs do not have to be written by employees. There only needs to be a written agreement saying they are works for hire, and that they are commissioned for use in an audiovisual work.

  (b) A **collective work.** A *collective work* is a collection of individual works, each of which is independently capable of copyright. Examples are an anthology of short stories; a magazine containing copyrightable articles; an encyclopedia; etc.

  (c) A **compilation.** A *compilation* is a work made by compiling a bunch of things, and thus it includes collective works (where the parts are separately copyrightable). However, it also includes works where the compiled materials are not separately copyrightable, such as a reference index to the Bible.

  (d) A **translation of a foreign work.** *¿Qué pasa?*

  (e) A **supplementary work,** which is a work supplementing another work (clever definitions, these copyright guys, eh?), such as an introduction to a book.

For a brief period in 1999, master recordings were added to the categories listed above (in other words, the Copyright Act said they could be a work for hire). However, the artist community went ballistic, and after a battle royale, Congress reversed itself and took out "masters." Nonetheless, record companies take the position that an album is a "collective work" and therefore think they have the right to treat masters as works for hire anyway. Some view otherwise.

Before we can discuss the consequences of something being a work for hire, you need a few more concepts. So, plug it into your memory bank (or put a Post-it on this page if your memory is like mine), and we'll get back to it later.

DURATION OF COPYRIGHT

Remember we said (on page 225) that a copyright is a *limited duration* monopoly? The next logical question is, "How long?"

Funny you should ask . . .

History

Prior to 1978, the United States had this bizarre copyright concept that was adopted in 1909 and not changed for almost seventy years. I tell you about it because (1) it's still relevant for older copyrights; and (2) I had to learn it, so why shouldn't you listen to it?

The main thing to know about these old copyrights is that they used to last for a period of twenty-eight years from publication of the work. (I could spend an entire chapter on what *publication* means, but I'd like you to finish my book awake, so I'll skip it. Basically, it means "distributed to the public.") These copyrights were then renewable for an additional twenty-eight years (total of fifty-six years). (For your purists, I'm aware that some copyrights could be obtained without publication, but none of this stuff is the law anymore, so let's not get carried away with too much detail.) By the way, it used to be the law that, if you forgot to renew, your copyright was gone after twenty-eight years. However, in 1992, Congress passed a law stating that the renewal is now automatic, so there's no loss of copyright if you forget.

Thus, the maximum copyright protection was fifty-six years. If you wanted to sell your copyright, you could sell the full fifty-six years' worth. You were, of course, free to sell much less, but the number of buyers dropped radically. Even if you sold the whole fifty-six, however, there was one way you could get back the second twenty-eight years. If you signed an agreement transferring all fifty-six years, you automatically got back the second twenty-eight years if you did one little thing during the first twenty-eight—die. (It's not for everyone, but it's had its fans.) If the author of the work died before the second twenty-eight years started, then the transfer was nullified and the author's heirs got to renew the second twenty-eight years for their own benefit. If you didn't die, you were stuck with whatever stupid deal you made when you first sold the work.

In 1976, Congress did a major, seventy-thousand-mile overhaul of the copyright laws. The 1976 Copyright Act (which wasn't effective until January 1, 1978, because the revisions were so extensive that Congress gave everyone a year to study it) dumped the old twenty-eight plus twenty-eight nonsense. Instead, it said that the duration of copyright for works created after January 1, 1978, was the life of the author plus fifty years (many other countries have used the lives of the authors to measure copyright for years). Congress also extended the old fifty-six-year terms (for works created before January 1, 1978) by nineteen years, for a total of seventy-five years.

In 1998, the congressional folk got together and, in memory of congressman and croonster Sonny Bono, slapped on another twenty years. That extended the copyright term for pre-1978 songs (if they were still under copyright) to a total of ninety-five years, and for stuff created after January 1, 1978, to life of the author plus seventy years (we'll get more into this later, in Chapter 21).

When a copyright expires, the work goes into the **public domain** (also called **p.d.**), which means anyone can use it for free.

This new system (life of the author plus seventy years) sounds a lot simpler than that old system of renewals, publication, etc., right? Well, how about:

1. A work written by two people. Whose life do you use to measure the copyright duration?
2. A work written anonymously or under a phony name (called a **pseudonymous** work). How do you know whose life to check on?
3. Works for hire. Remember, the author is the employer, who could be a corporation. And some of those suckers live forever.

Rest comfortably, dear friends, because all of these have been handled. They work like this:

1. In the case of a joint work, the copyright lasts until seventy years after the death of the last survivor. So write all your songs with your five-year-old son.
2. Anonymous (no name) or pseudonymous (phony name) works last the sooner of ninety-five years from publication, or one hundred twenty years from creation. *Creation* means the first time it's fixed in tangible form (written down or recorded). *Publication*, as I said, is a tricky little devil, but for our purposes just assume it means distribution to the public.
3. Works for hire are the same as anonymous.

RIGHT OF TERMINATION

One of the best goodies that authors got in the 1976 Copyright Law is the **right of termination.**

The termination provisions say that, even if you make a bonehead deal, the copyright law will give you a second shot—thirty-five years later. In other words, thirty-five years after a transfer, you can get your copyright back. And under the 1976 law, you don't even have to die. Big plus.

By the way, this termination is only for the U.S. copyright. You're stuck with whatever deal you made for the rest of the world, because the U.S. is the only country where you get a do-over.

The exact mechanics get a bit technical, so I've stuck them back on page 356, in a section for the real die-hards.

Termination and Works for Hire

Now you know enough to understand the consequences of something being a work for hire (see page 339 for what that is). With works for hire, there are *no* termination rights, because there was no transfer in the first place, and therefore no transfer to terminate. Remember, the creator never existed in the eyes of the copyright law—the person or company commissioning the work owns it as if they had created it themselves. So with works for hire, there's no copyright coming back to you and your kiddies. Bummer.

Be very aware of this consequence when you create a work for hire.

Sound Recording Copyright Terminations—
Be Afraid. Be Very Afraid

The right to terminate transfers of sound recordings, which started coming up in 2013 (thirty-five years after the 1978 act), is going to spawn some massive fights. The record companies will argue that these are works for hire (see page 339), for which there is no termination right, because they are contributions to a collective work (an album), and for various other reasons they're still cooking up. If that turns out to be wrong, meaning the transfers can be terminated, the question becomes, "Who is the author of a sound recording?" That sounds like an easy one—the artist, right? Well, not necessarily. Especially in cases where the artist didn't write or produce, but just showed up and sang. And even assuming the artist is an author, it's possible that the producer is also an author under the copyright law, and potentially others who contributed significantly to the work. Also, if an artist is a group, there could be an issue between the band members as to which one or more of them was really an author.

As a result of all this, the U.S. rights may be co-owned by several people, each of whom would have non-exclusive exploitation rights in the master. And each will have to figure out what percentage their contribution is worth. The answers to all these questions will be partly legal, but also very fact specific. Translation: "Messy." Further translation: "Expensive."

I suspect it will take years (and millions of dollars in litigation) to sort this out. For that reason, unless the artist is truly hell-bent on recapturing ownership, I suspect that most of these will get settled by making a new deal with the record company. But we'll see . . .

DIGITAL PERFORMANCE OF MASTERS AND WEBCASTING

As we discussed earlier (on page 176), public performance of masters was first covered by the **Digital Performance Right in Sound Recordings Act of 1995.** Those folks in Washington sure know how to put a sexy title on something, huh?

The Digital Performance Act did two things that are interesting to the music business:

1. The act extended the compulsory mechanical copyright license (see page 229 for what that is) to include the digital distribution of records. In other words, when records are sold by downloads over the Internet, telephone lines, satellite, waffle irons, etc., the act makes sure that the companies selling these transmissions have the right to use the songs (though not the masters) in exchange for a compulsory license fee. We discussed this on pages 229–32.
2. For the first time in U.S. history, it created a right for the *artist* and *record company* to be paid when records are performed (As you know from the publishing section, songwriters and publishers have been paid for this all along).

Let's take a closer look:

Public Performance Right for Masters

Until 1995, the United States had no public performance right for *masters*. Quite the contrary, when it passed the antipiracy law in 1972 (which we'll discuss on page 362), Congress specifically said that it *wasn't* creating a right for the artist or record company to be paid when the recordings were played on radio or TV. This was true even though the owner of the *song* is paid.

As we discussed on page 176, other countries of the world have paid artists and record companies for the performance of their records for many years, and it can mean substantial money. Because the United States had no such right, most other countries felt no need to pay Americans for overseas performances of their records, under the age-old government theory of "Why should I pay foreigners when I can have more money for my citizens?"

Digital Performances of Masters

The United States first put its toe in the water of master public performance in 1995 by amending Section 106 of the Copyright Act. You get paid for performances of your master if all of the following apply:

1. It must be a *digital* public performance. And what's digital? Digital is music made by computers, as opposed to *analog*, which is FM and AM radio.

   In the last few years, many over-the-air radio stations have converted their signals to digital (HD radio). So it sounds like you'll get performance monies when they play your masters over the air, right? Well, not so fast . . .

   Turns out the broadcasters have a lot of friends in Congress. In a nice little lobbying move, they managed to exclude digital over-the-air broadcasts from the definition of digital performances. The only exception is when an HD radio station **simulcasts** its signal over the Internet (meaning it streams the signal on the Internet at the same time that it broadcasts over the air), in which case you get paid for the Internet streaming portion (but not the over-the-air part).

2. It must be an *audio-only* sound recording that's performed (meaning the artist doesn't get paid for performances of a master in films or TV shows).

So to break it down, the only digital performances that fall under Section 106 are audio-only transmissions that don't go over the air. That means satellite radio services (like Sirius XM), digital cable and satellite television audio music channels (e.g., Music Choice), non-interactive webcasters (including originally programmed "Internet-only" services and retransmissions of FCC-licensed radio stations on the Internet), services streaming to commercial businesses (like Muzak, which is now called Mood Media), streaming to mobile devices, and other assorted digital weirdos.

If a broadcast qualifies for a performance royalty under this criteria, you get paid one of two ways:

1. In 1998, Congress followed up their 1995 performance with the **Digital Millennium Copyright Act** (also known as the **DMCA**). This baby set up a *compulsory* license for webcasting, which means that, under certain conditions (which we'll discuss in the next section), the owner of the recording *must* allow its performance for a set fee. (Remember, as we discussed on page 228, that without a compulsory license, the copyright owner can stop someone from using their work.)
2. If the broadcast doesn't qualify for a compulsory license, and that includes Spotify, Rdio, and the other interactive services, the sound recording owner gets paid whatever they can gouge out of the digital service provider (DSP). If they're not happy with the money, they can stop the DSP from using their master at all.

Compulsory License.   How does a broadcaster qualify for a compulsory license? The rules are found in the riveting Section 114 of the Copyright Act. There's a whole slug of requirements to get the compulsory license, but it boils down to making you act like a noninteractive radio station. For example, you can't announce your playlist in advance, there are limits on how many songs you can play in any three-hour period from a certain artist, or from a certain album, and things like that.

If a broadcaster qualifies for a compulsory license, if files papers with the Copyright Office, then pays statutory license fees to an outfit called **SoundExchange**. SoundExchange is a nonprofit organization whose board is made up made up of record company people, artists, and artist representatives. Essentially, it acts like ASCAP and BMI (meaning it collects fees and pays its members), except it collects for performances of masters instead of songs.

SoundExchange is starting to get some serious money. In 2104, they collected $773 million dollars, which was a little over 11% of the entire U.S. record business. SoundExchange divvies up the dough as follows: 50% to the record companies, 45% to the featured artists, and 5% to a fund controlled by the American Federation of Musicians (for non-featured musicians) and AFTRA (for nonfeatured vocalists) (see page 57 for who AFM and AFTRA are).

The statutory rates are set by voluntary industry negotiations, or, if the two sides look like they're going to bloody each other, it's decided by the Copyright Royalty Board. Which is basically what happened—before the two sides tapped out, the CRB came down with a set of rates that neither of them liked. So they got Congress to pass the Webcaster Settlement Act, which allowed the industry to privately negotiate their own rates for webcasting. The catch was that they had to make those rates available to anyone who wanted to do streaming, just as if the user had a compulsory license (except of course they got the privately negotiated rates).

So . . . you now get the choice of the CRB's rates, or the private deal made by the music industry players, whichever you think is better for you.

The rates are incredibly complex. They vary with whether you're a **commercial webcaster** (an FCC licensed station that puts its signal on the Net), a **pureplay webcaster** (someone who's only business is streaming on the Internet), an **educational webcaster** (like a college radio station), or a **non-commercial webcaster** (a charity, NPR, and the like). Then within these categories, we have **small webcasters,** meaning a webcaster who earns under a specified revenue amount, or one that has less than a certain number of **Audience Tuning Hours** (also called **ATHs**), which means one listener for one hour. There are even **micro-webcasters,** who are so little that they have (seriously) no more than four or five listeners at any one time. Go click on one and increase their listenership by 25%.

Got all that? Good, because there's more.

At the higher end, there are **SDARS,** which sounds like a lung disease epidemic but in fact means **satellite digital audio radio services** (like Sirius XM); **BES,** meaning **business establishment services** who pump music into restaurants, hotels, and tropical fish stores; **CABSAT,** standing for **cable/satellite services** like Music Choice, who deliver music over cable or satellite to your TV or set-top box; and **PES,** which means **pre-existing subscription services** that were in existence prior to July 31, 1998. Because the older subscription services have been around a while (and because they have strong lobbyists and lawyers), they get a senior citizen discount and pay about half of what others pay for the same service. The record companies are not exactly thrilled . . .

Depending on where you fall in this lineup, you'll pay something different. And as I said a minute ago, you get to choose between the rate set by the CRB and the rate negotiated under the Webcaster Settlement Act, whichever you think is more favorable. Also, the rates change every year (unless you're a micro-webcaster). Have I gotten you excited yet?

Essentially, other than Public Television or NPR, there's a minimum per year, ranging from $500 for micro-webcasters; to $500 *per channel*—with a cap of $50,000 per year—for bigger webcasters; to as high as $100,000 per year for the CABSAT/PES folks. Most of the bigger pureplay webcasters have minimums of $25,000 per year.

These minimums are advances against fractions of pennies for each performance of a master (for example, under the Webcaster Settlement Act rates, a commercial webcaster paid $0.0021 [that's 0.21¢] for each performance in 2013, which means they paid a little over one cent for every five performances). While this sounds like really small stuff, it adds up fast, and the revenue is really growing. In 2005, SoundExchange distributed about $20 million to its members, and in 2014 they distributed over $770 million.

If you really want to know the details of the rates (though I can't imagine why), head over to SoundExchange's website (www.soundexchange.com), click on "Service Provider," then click on the tab to the left that says "2016 Rates" (I'm sure the exact clicks get changed now and then, but I'm guessing you can figure that out). When you've had your fill, be sure to "Like" them on their Facebook page.

Voluntary Licenses. If a performance doesn't fall within the statutory license (primarily this means performances on interactive services), then the record company doesn't have to allow the master to be performed at all. This is a good thing if you're a record company, because it means you can charge whatever the traffic will bear. However, since the record company (the owner of the master) holds the rights and makes the deal, unlike the compulsory license, the law doesn't require the artist and non-featured musicians to be paid anything directly. This means the record company will keep all the money unless you have a provision in your recording contract that says you get a piece. So add one.

As we discussed previously (on page 155), the current industry custom is for the record companies to get about 60% of the webcaster's revenue, and (as we discussed on page 275) the publishers get around 10%.

There are some legally interesting in-between types of services that are arguably interactive and arguably non-interactive. For example, services like Pandora let you tell the website what kind of music you like, then they customize a stream for you. You can also tell them whether or not you like each song they stream, and the more feedback you give them, the better they get at pleasing you with their choices (at least in theory). So you sort of control the content, but not exactly—you can't tell them to play a specific song at a specific time, but you can shape what's coming at you. The record companies argued that this made these services interactive, and therefore they had to get a voluntary license (which is much more expensive than a non-interactive license). The services had a very different opinion, saying they were non-interactive and therefore entitled to a compulsory license. This led the major record companies to sue a company called Launchcast for copyright infringement.

All of the record companies settled this case except Sony, who took it to trial in New York. The trial court ruled in favor of Launchcast, saying their service wasn't interactive, and Launchcast won the appeal as well. So for now, these services are non-interactive.

By the way, the owners of *songs* have always had a right to get paid for using their music on the Internet, and there is no compulsory license (other than for digital downloads, as we discussed on page 230). As a practical matter, this is handled by the performing rights organizations, though as noted earlier, this might change if the publishers pull their digital rights away from the PROs and do direct licenses.

Over-the-Air Master Performances

At the time of this writing, there's a bill in front of Congress (and there have been others in the past that died painful deaths), which would pay money for the use of masters in over-the-air radio broadcasts (also called **terrestrial radio broadcasts,** to distinguish them from satellite and streaming). Historically, the radio broadcasters (who are very powerful in Washington) have fought this, and interestingly, so did the publishers who feared that a royalty for the master would reduce what the publishers get for broadcasting songs. The broadcasters were delighted to see the record companies and publishers squabbling, because they knew that no law would get passed if the music business was fighting with itself. However, the bill that's now getting kicked around seems to have both publishers and record companies on its side.

It's actually two bills: one sponsored by the RIAA (the record company lobbying group) and one sponsored by the publishers. They dovetail together like this:

1. The RIAA-sponsored bill creates a terrestrial radio performance right for the first time, and leaves the question of what it will cost up to the Copyright Royalty Board (CRB) (see page 232 for what that is). The bill also has a provision that says this payment can't reduce what songwriters get, and as teeth for that provision, it says the CRB can't consider the songwriter payments in setting the rate. The broadcasters are fighting this bill, but inside baseball says they may support it if they get a break on the rates for digitally streaming their signals.

   The bill also sets a rate for pre-1972 masters (you may remember that there is no copyright in pre-1972 recordings).

2. The songwriter bill, called the Songwriter's Equity Act, goes the other way, and says that the CRB *can* look at what the masters get paid in determining how much to pay for digital broadcasting (which today it is prohibited from doing—under Section 114 (i) of the Copyright Act). It also changes the standard for setting mechanical rates, moving to a "willing buyer/ willing seller" model. These two things are more important than they sound, as they could jack up the rates for the publishers.

My guess is that neither of these bills will get passed in the near future, given the complicated maneuvering around them and, oh yeah, the fact that Congress can barely pass a budget for the federal government.

A company named iHeartMedia, the largest owner of radio stations in the U.S., and also the owner of the digital service iHeartRadio, has made deals with some of the independent record companies to pay for over-the-air broadcasts in exchange for a lower rate on webcasting. As of this writing, the only major label to make this deal is Warner Music, though a number of independents have done it. This is somewhat controversial, because everyone assumes that webcasting revenue will grow, while terrestrial radio will shrink, so the amount they'd be giving up on webcasting may not make up for what they get on terrestrial.

Stay tuned (so to speak).

Video Streaming

There's no compulsory license for video streaming, whether it's in-teractive or not. So the companies charge whatever they can extort. We covered the rates that publishers and master owners get earlier (on pages 278 and 158).

Many record companies have made the same kind of deal for use of their masters in User-Generated Content (like a homemade YouTube video of some old lady dancing to a Prince song), though there's still a lot of haggling over that one. The problem with UGC is that it could be anything, and both artists and companies are sensitive to how their master is used—for example, it may be linked to drug use, a political campaign, or some college girl stripping (which, depending on your image, might be a plus). So most of these deals between the record companies and YouTube have **take-down rights**, meaning the company can require the site to pull down certain videos at their request.

The DMCA and Its Not-So-Safe Harbor

An important issue in the video world is the **safe harbor** rule of the DMCA (see page 347 for what the DMCA is).

To understand what this is about, think back to our earlier discussion, where I said that one of the rights you get under copyright is the right to distribute your work. That means, if someone creates an infringing work, and someone else distributes it, you can go after both of them (one sleazo infringed the duplication right, while the other one infringed the distribution right).

Under the DMCA (section 512 of the Copyright Act), there's an exception to this distribution liability. A digital service provider is not liable for distribution of infringing material if it didn't create it, post it, or know it was infringing. However, once you give the DSP a notice that says it's distributing infringing material, if it keeps doing it, then you can sue them for copyright infringement.

That all sounded innocent enough when it came into being, but then along came YouTube, distributing millions of videos, and a lot of those infringe somebody's rights (for example, fans routinely put up an entire album, with the cover artwork). So a record company or publisher sends them a notice that says, "Knock it off," and they stop. Easy, right? Well . . .

What actually happens is what we in the industry call "Whack-A-Mole." As soon as YouTube takes down a particular post, hundreds of others appear. So the copyright owners send out hundreds more notices. YouTube takes those down, and thousands more appear. No matter how many notices they send, the lemmings keep coming.

Viacom sued YouTube over this, claiming that videos on You-Tube were infringing a massive amount of Viacom content. Viacom's claim was that (a) YouTube was chock full of infringing material, which it was; (b) YouTube knew it was infringing; and (c) YouTube could stop it if they wanted to. YouTube basically said, "Under the law, we don't have to stop, and we don't want to." After some wrangling, the court agreed with YouTube, but the fighting went on hot and heavy. Finally, the case was settled. (There's a reported appellate decision: [*Viacom International v. YouTube*, No. 10-3270, 2012 WL 113085 (2d Cir. Apr. 5, 2012)] for the technical freaks), but there was a lot of action before and after that in the lower courts. If you're interested, you can Google the case and get much more information—there's some irony in that, since Google owns YouTube).

Anyway, to date, no one has found a way to stop this practice, so the industry decided to make the best deals they could (we discussed earlier what they're getting paid), figuring it was better than the zero they were getting before that. The music biz is not happy, as they think they're getting way too little. They believe that if they had the legal right to stop YouTube, they could make a marketplace deal for a business that is largely built on the back of their music. But since they can't stop them (so far), they don't have that much leverage in the negotiations. So I don't see any major shift on the horizon.

If you're on the *Advanced Overview Track* and are in a
group, go to Part IV (Chapter 22) on page 371.
If you're on the *Advanced Overview Track* and you're not
in a group, go to Part V (Chapter 23) on page 395.
Experts, keep rollin'.

21

Even More Advanced Copyright Concepts

I GOT YOU TWENTY, BABE

As we discussed briefly in the last chapter, in 1998, Congress passed the **Sonny Bono Copyright Term Extension Act.** Basically, this added twenty more years to the term of a copyright—it now lasts for the life of the author plus seventy years for works created after January 1, 1978, and ninety-five years from publication for earlier works.

This "life plus seventy" idea brings the United States in line with the European Union, whose copyrights have lasted this long for quite a while. Without ol' Sonny's bill, U.S. copyrights would drop out of European protection much sooner, because of something called **the rule of the shorter term.** The *shorter-term rule* says that, even though U.S. copyrights are protected in Europe for life plus seventy, if they go into the public domain earlier in the United States, the European copyright disappears at the same time. For example, if an author died in 1970, her copyright could last until 2040 in Europe. However, if the work went into the public domain in the United States in 2020, the European protection would also end that year.

But now that's all behind us, and we're one big harmonious family. The 1998 act also:

1. Gave libraries and archives the right to make copies of works during their last twenty years of protection (under certain restrictions);
2. Created a new termination of transfer right, and expanded the old one (these are discussed on page 356); and
3. Strongly suggested that motion picture studios and talent get together and agree how to divide money earned by films and TV programs during the twenty-year term extension.

The act only applies to works still protected by copyright on October 27, 1998. In other words, it doesn't go back and re-protect works that were in the public domain on that date. So works published between 1904 and 1922 still belong to you and me.

This copyright extension didn't come without a hefty price tag. The lobbyists for stores, restaurants, and bars got together and persuaded Congress to pass the **Fairness in Music Licensing Act of 1998,** in exchange for supporting the twenty-year copyright extension. Just hearing the name lets you know this isn't going to be good for the music biz, huh? I mean, anybody who has to tell you how "fair" they're going to be . . .

Anyway, this little piece of handiwork says that playing a TV or radio broadcast in stores, restaurants, and bars under a certain size (2,000 square feet for stores, and 3,750 square feet for restaurants and bars) doesn't require a license to perform music. Larger stores and restaurants are also exempt if they have limited pieces of equipment (like no more than six loudspeakers, no more than four TV screens, no more than one TV screen per room, and similar titillating criteria). So if the store, restaurant, or bar fits under this limbo bar, they can use your songs for free. (For more details, take a look at Section 110 (5) of the Copyright Act, or watch it on one of the four TV screens at Hooters).

An interesting twist is that the World Trade Organization (known to its friends as the WTO) determined that this U.S. small business exemption violated an international treaty. (For technical folks, it violated Article 11 of the Berne Convention, which was made enforceable by Article 9 of the TRIPS agreement.) The Europeans cried foul because the small businesses were no longer paying for their songs, and they asked the WTO to fix it. To the United States' surprise, the WTO agreed with the Europeans and said the treaty didn't allow us to exempt the little fellas. So the American government coughed up $3 million in penalty money, in essence paying the Europeans' lost earnings with your tax dollars. At the time of this writing, nothing else has happened, and no one really expects another shoe to drop.

As you can see by the Europeans' reaction, the small business exemption is serious stuff, and it will cost copyright owners a fair chunk of change over the years. Hopefully the extra twenty years will make it up.

Now speaking of those extra twenty years . . .

In a lawsuit that went all the way to the U.S. Supreme Court, a group of folks challenged the constitutionality of the extra twenty years. As you might remember, the Constitution authorizes a "limited duration monopoly" for copyrights. Well, this lawsuit argued that the latest extension went beyond any reasonable definition of "limited duration" that was contemplated by our founding fathers. And the Supreme Court found the question interesting enough to take the case.

Under the surface were a lot of political issues. On one side were the free-speech folk, who believe things should dump into the public domain as quickly as possible. On the other were (1) the creators (or more likely their heirs, since this is old stuff) arguing for their livelihood; (2) the millions of dollars that the United States collects in taxes on copyright royalties; and (3) monies that come from overseas based on uses during these extended periods (which would disappear along with the U.S. copyright, under the rule of the shorter term we just discussed).

Anyway, the Supreme Court ruled that the twenty years were okay—basically, they said Congress was being reasonable when it extended the term. So your copyrights are safe. For now. (If you want to look up the case, it's *Eric Eldred v. John Aschroft*, 537 U.S. 186 [2003]).

And the beat goes on . . .

HOW TO TERMINATE A COPYRIGHT TRANSFER IN YOUR SPARE TIME, FOR FUN AND PROFIT

As noted on page 344, the 1976 Copyright Law lets you undo any deal (for songs created on or after January 1, 1978) thirty-five years later (we'll talk about the pre-1978 songs later, on page 357). So if you sell your song to a publisher, you can get it back after thirty-five years by merely sending a notice. Here's how to do it.

You can give a notice of termination no less than two years, nor more than ten years, before it is to be effective, and the effective date must fall within five years after the end of the thirty-five-year period. To be more precise, if the grant of the work covers publication, which it almost always does, the right to terminate is effective on the sooner of forty years from the grant, or thirty-five years from publication. This protects you even if the work is never published.

This is easier to understand if we use some actual years. For example, if a copyright was transferred and published in 1990:

Year of Publication: **1990**	Years in Which Termination Can Be Effective (5 Years After 35 Years from Publication): **2025 to 2030**
First Year That Notice Can Be Sent (10 Years Before First Possible Effective Date): **2015**	Last Year That Notice Can Be Sent (2 Years Before Last Possible Effective Date): **2028**

If you really want to know the details, take a look at Sections 203 and 304 of the Copyright Act.

The Sonny Bono Copyright Term Extension Act, which we discussed in the prior section, added some frills to this. They are:

1. Previously, only a living author, surviving spouse, or surviving children or grandchildren could exercise the right of termination. Now, if none of them are alive, the author's estate can do the honors.
2. There's a second bite at termination rights for pre-1978 copyrights, which I'll go over in a minute.

Remember, as we discussed previously, this termination only applies to U.S. rights. If you sold off your copyright in foreign territories, you're stuck with the deal.

Attempts to Avoid Termination

As much as the publishers would love to avoid termination, Uncle Sam said no. The copyright law says that nothing you do with the termination rights is valid until you actually have the rights back—in other words, you can't sign them over to anyone until you actually have them in your fist. The only exception is that you can deal with the guy who has the rights about to be terminated (but no one else) after you've sent the notice, but before you get the rights back. In other words, if you send a notice to the publisher saying the termination is effective three years from now, you can make a new deal with that publisher during the three years, and it's enforceable. This gives the current publisher a head start, because they can make a deal (and pay you for the rights) before anyone else can.

EXTENSION RIGHTS

Extension Recapture

So Congress took care of folks who wrote songs after 1978, by giving them the right to get out of a stupid deal after thirty-five years. But what about the oldsters who made stupid deals? There's a transitional quirk thrown into the 1976 Copyright Act that takes care of the pre-1978 copyrights. (If you weren't writing prior to 1978, or aren't the heir of such a writer, you can skip to the Digital Samples section on page 360. This isn't mandatory; feel free to read this for your general education, but I don't suggest driving or operating heavy machinery afterward.)

Pre-1978 copyrights lasted for a period of fifty-six years (remember the twenty-eight plus twenty-eight discussed on page 342?). The 1976 act extended that to a period of seventy-five years. (And, as noted above, this has now been extended to ninety-five years. But for now, let's just look at the 1976 act.) In other words, the 1976 act added nineteen years to the fifty-six years that already existed.

In addition to extending the life of the copyrights, the act gave the author (or his or her heirs) the right to take back the new nineteen years. The recapture procedure is similar to that for termination rights of post-1978 copyrights (the right to terminate after thirty-five years, which we just discussed in the prior section). It's done by a notice given no sooner than two years, and no more than ten years, before the beginning of the nineteen years (i.e., before the end of the fifty-sixth year).

Here's an example: If a song was first published in 1970, the fifty-six years expire in 2026. So, beginning in 2016 (ten years before the end of the fifty-six years), and ending 2024 (two years before), you can give a notice to be effective in 2026. After the effective date of the notice, the nineteen years added to the copyright (the extension from 2026 to 2045) belong to the author, or his or her heirs.

A few years ago, publishers began scurrying around to buy these extended terms from the authors or their heirs, and it looked like it was going to be a nice business. However, Congress gave the original owners (i.e., the original publishers) a nice perk, which is similar to what publishers get under the post-1978 copyright transfer termination provision. The law says that, before the extended term actually comes into effect, but after giving a termination notice, the person who got the original grant can make a new deal for the extra years. So the original publisher has the ability to buy the rights at least two years before any outsider, and therefore has an advantage in getting them. Unless the publisher has really been a jerk during the first fifty-six years (which is no small "unless"), it can usually keep the copyrights.

Now enter the Sonny Bono Copyright Term Extension Act of 1998, which added twenty years to the copyright term and made the extension period thirty-nine years after the original fifty-six years (a total of ninety-five years). They also threw in (at no extra charge) an added bonus: If your right to recapture came up before October 27, 1998, and you forgot to send the termination notice, you got another bite. At any time within five years after expiration of the first seventy-five years (the old fifty-six, plus the nineteen you blew), you can get back the newly added twenty years.

The Mills Music Case

Another quirk of the termination/extension rights is that the original publisher can continue exploiting derivative works (see page 227 for a definition of *derivative works*), but it can't license any new works. This derivative work exception looked like it was going to be a loophole you could drive a truck through, based on a U.S. Supreme Court case involving the appropriately titled song "Who's Sorry Now." (If you want to look it up, it's *Mills Music v. Snyder*, 105 SCT 638 [1985].) In this case, the publisher (Mills Music) acquired the rights to "Who's Sorry Now" from Ted Snyder and two other writers. Snyder went to that Great Songbook in the Sky, and in 1978, his heirs exercised their right to terminate the last nineteen years. (So much for my theory that the initial publisher can hang on to the songs.)

After termination, Mills Music argued that all of the *records* it had licensed were derivative works, and therefore it had the right to collect mechanical royalties for sales of these records after termination. As you can imagine, Mr. Snyder's heirs took a contrary view. They felt these rights should come back to them, so they could then license the record companies (and get all the money). The decision flipped back and forth until it came to the U.S. Supreme Court (known to its friends as "the Supremes"). In a closely divided decision (five of the nine justices in favor, four opposing), the Supreme Court found that indeed the records were derivative works, and that the money from them went to Mills Music, the terminated publisher. Mr. Snyder's heirs had the right to money from future recordings, but not the existing ones. Sorry, all you little Snyders.

After *Mills Music*, two other cases further defined the scope of a publisher's right to hang on to derivative works. The first was *Woods v. Bourne Co.*, 603 F.2d 978 (2d Cir. 1995), where the terminated publisher argued that every piece of printed music was based on the original lead sheet, and therefore the right to put out sheet music forever belonged to the old publisher (see page 329 for what a *lead sheet* is). The court kicked their butts on that one, holding that new versions of printed music weren't derivative works and therefore belonged to the new publisher. Next came *Fred Ahlert Music Corp. v. Warner/Chappell Music, Inc.*, 155 F.3rd 17 (2d Cir. 1998), where the court made the derivative work exception even narrower by saying that the reissue of a master recording with a different catalog number was not a derivative work, even though it was the same recording. Accordingly, the new publisher of the song could issue the mechanical license (and get the dough).

So, as you can see, the sentiment in the later cases is to expand the rights of the person getting back their copyrights. Stay tuned to this channel; as the older copyrights tick on and terminations become more prevalent, there may be some more interesting law.

DIGITAL SAMPLES

Sampling is the art of taking any sound (whether it's a full master recording, or just a drum sound, synthesizer riff, voice, etc.), and making a perfect digital copy, which you then incorporate into your own masterpiece. Unless you've been living in a moon colony for the last few years, you know that every rapper on the planet samples freely from other people's works.

In the beginning, everyone groped around for what kind of deals to make. In fact, a lot of sampled records were released before anybody even tried to clear the rights, and the artists and companies often had an attitude along the lines of "If they catch me, I'll make a deal." When they did get caught, they threw around a few bucks and bought out the rights.

Can you guess whose rights had to be bought out? The obvious one is the record company owning the sampled recording. But they aren't the only one whose rights you need. You gotta also take care of the publisher of the sampled musical composition.

This "catch me if you can" attitude came to an abrupt halt after the case of *Grand Upright Music Limited v. Warner Bros. Records, Inc.*, 780 F.Supp. 182 (S.D.N.Y. 1991), which involved the rapper Biz Markie sampling Gilbert O'Sullivan's "Alone Again (Naturally)." See if you can guess how the judge ruled in this case by reading the first line of his opinion:

"Thou shalt not steal."

The Honorable Kevin Thomas Duffy of the federal court for the Southern District of New York not only slapped the hands of the sampler, but referred the matter to the U.S. Attorney's Office for possible *criminal* prosecution! (As you'll see on page 367, intentional copyright infringement is a criminal offense.) End of the days of casual sampling.

And if that wasn't enough for you, check out *Bridgeport Music, Inc., et al. v. Dimension Films et al.*, 383 F.3rd 390 (6th Cir. 2004). This case held that *any* sampling of a master, even if it's *unrecognizable*, is an infringement of the copyright. (Note the court only dealt with infringement of the copyright in a master recording, not the infringement of a song. The court said there could be a different analysis for the song, which wasn't part of this case. So it's not clear how broad this rule will be.)

At any rate, the decisions are scary enough that everyone now handles the clearance of samples with white velvet gloves. Record companies won't release a record containing samples without assurances that the samples have been cleared, and you as an artist should want the same thing. Clearing samples is a major pain in the butt, because there's nothing in the law that requires anyone to let you use a sample, and thus any record company or publisher is free to make you pull it off your record. Moreover, you can't clear the sample until you finish the track—the publisher and record company want to hear exactly how the sample is used before they'll tell you how much they want to charge, or whether they'll let you use it at any price. That puts you in the position of having to record the sample before you know whether you can use it. If you're on a tight schedule and/or if it ruins your song to take out the sample, you won't be a happy camper.

Suppose you don't actually sample, but just duplicate the track by playing it in the studio. Does that solve your problems? Well, only half. You've just created what we call a **replay.** *Replays* eliminate the need to license the master, but you still need to license the song.

As noted previously, since there's no compulsory license for samples, you have to make whatever deal the rights owners decide to bless you with. If the usage is minor, and it's a little-known song, it will of course be smaller than a major use of an important song.

For the master, a record company will always want a royalty, which was historically in pennies (3¢ to 8¢), payable on worldwide sales. As the business is moving to streaming, pennies don't work so well, so they converted the royalty to a PPD equivalent (about 2% to 8%), or a percentage of the artist royalty (20% to 50%). The exact amount depends on the usage, importance of the sample, and how desperate they think you are to use it. The sample owners also want an advance of however much they can squeeze, usually based on past sales of your records.

Publishers almost always insist on owning a piece of the copyright, and the same share of songwriting royalties and publishing income. The percentage varies with how significantly the sample is used in your record. If you've lifted an entire melody line, or their track is the bed of your song, they might take 50% or more; for less significant uses, the range is 10% to 30%.

A particularly fun thing happens with multiple samples. I've seen several situations like this: Your song has three samples. Publisher X wants 40%, Publisher Y wants 40%, and Publisher Z wants 30%. If you do some quick math, you'll see that's 110%. So every time you sell a record, you get to write a check out of your own pocket. By the way, don't assume the publishers will be the least bit sympathetic. Their attitude is usually something like "Those other publishers are pigs. But my share is really worth 40%, so go squeeze the other guy."

Even when you get past all these hurdles, the publishers (and some record companies) often limit the usage of their sample to just your records and promo videos. Also, the publishers will want to co-administer their portion of the composition (see page 330 for discussion of co-administration). All this means they have the right to stop you from granting a particular license—for example, you couldn't license the song in a film or a commercial without going back to the record company and publisher, getting their consent, and paying them for it. So when you sample, you can lose control of your own song.

The lesson in all this is that putting a sample in your record is serious business. So think carefully about what it means. A moment of pleasure can mean a lifetime of pain.

SOUND RECORDING COPYRIGHTS

It may surprise you to know that, prior to 1972, the United States had no copyright protection for a sound recording itself. I'm now talking about the physical, master *sound recording* (not the musical composition). Here's what happened:

The Age of the "Lawful Duplicators"

Prior to 1972, nothing in the U.S. copyright law made it illegal to duplicate a master recording (other than the fact that permission was required from the owner of the musical composition, who was almost never the owner of the sound recording). Thus, to take an easy example, suppose a group made a recording on Elektra Records of "My Country, 'Tis of Thee" (or "God Save the Queen," if you're British), which is, of course, a public domain song (see page 343 for what public domain is). Prior to 1972 it was perfectly legal to set up a machine in your garage and begin manufacturing records from that recording without anyone's permission, and more importantly, without paying the artist or the record company who invested the money to create the recording. (As a note for you purists, I am of course assuming that the group making the original recording did not create such an unusual arrangement of "My Country, 'Tis of Thee" to be copyrightable as a derivative work [we discussed derivative works on page 227]. If this were the case, then the composition would have to be licensed from the publisher. Also, I'm assuming there's no trademark infringement, such as knocking off the Elektra Records name or logo.)

Avoiding the Wrath of Publishers

As you can imagine, there wasn't much demand for knockoff recordings of public domain songs—people were much more interested in the Beatles, the Rolling Stones, and other bestselling groups of the day. So how did the pirates get around infringing the copyrights in the songs? Since the artists often controlled the publishing, and they weren't getting any royalties from the sale of these rip-offs, they certainly wouldn't give the pirates a mechanical license. So the duplicators used our old friend, the compulsory copyright license (see page 229).

Remember, once a composition has been recorded, the publisher *must* issue a license to anybody who wants to use it in phonograph records. So the pirates went to the publishers, asked for a mechanical license for their unauthorized duplications, and, when they were turned down (which was the case with legitimate publishers), they simply got a compulsory license and proceeded to pay the publisher. Under this guise, and seeking to slip through a loophole in the copyright law, the pirates blossomed into a multimillion-dollar industry at the expense of the recording artists and record companies who had invested substantial monies in making the recordings. Many of these sleazebags used names like Pirate Records, or had a logo with a skull and crossbones, a pirate with a patch and a cutlass in his teeth, etc. Real class. (If you were going to give the music business an enema, this would have been the place.)

Antipiracy Legislation

This smelled like thievery (which it was). The companies stopped the pirates by suing under the laws of individual states, since there was no federal law, and they were doing pretty well, but it ultimately took an amendment to the copyright law to nail the coffin shut. In 1972, Congress enacted a full-fledged, legitimate copyright law provision dealing with piracy (which is now Section 114 of the Copyright Act). This prohibits the unauthorized duplication or dubbing of a sound recording that was created on or after February 15, 1972, by creating a copyright in the actual recording. (This is in addition to a separate copyright in the musical composition.) It is imaginatively called a **sound recording copyright,** and is represented by the symbol ℗ Look for it on CDs in your collection, assuming you still have any CDs.

One of the most interesting aspects of this sound recording copyright is what it did *not* protect. While it's clear you can no longer duplicate records without consent, the sound recording copyright doesn't prohibit a "sound-alike" recording, no matter how closely you duplicate the original. In other words, nothing in the sound recording copyright stops you from hiring a singer to imitate the original artist, or hiring a band that sounds just like the original recording, regardless of how close you come. Of course, you must license the song, and you must disclose that the recording is not the original. If you didn't label your record as an imitation, you would run afoul of various trademark and unfair practices laws, which deal with the proper labeling of goods (and thus stop you from defrauding the public into thinking they're getting the original when they're not). These are the same laws that stop you from calling a cereal Grape Nuts if it's not made by Post, even if it has exactly the same ingredients.

THE COPYRIGHT NOTICE

The copyright notice is a © followed by the year of copyright (the year that the work was first fixed in tangible form).

Copyright notices are much less significant under the 1976 Copyright Act than they were under the old law, because the consequences of leaving it off, or making a mistake in it, are no longer very serious. (Under the old law, you could lose your copyright.) It's not worth getting into all the niceties, but nowadays a notice basically just protects you from someone saying they had no idea the materials were copyrighted—in other words, they can't say they were an "innocent infringer." (You don't get a free pass if you're an innocent infringer, by the way, but it could affect how much you have to pay if you get nailed.)

If you want to do a notice, and I think it's a good idea:

1. For songs, the copyright notice is primarily significant for printed music. This is because you can only put a notice on "visibly perceptible copies" of something. Since you can't "see" a song by looking at a CD or digital file, there's no need to have a copyright notice for the song.
2. So why do you see copyright notices on albums? Good question! The reasons are:
    (a) sometimes the lyrics are printed inside, and since they are "visually perceptible," you need a copyright notice;
    (b) there is a copyright in the album cover artwork; and
    (c) there is the sound recording copyright ℗ notice we just discussed.

REGISTRATION AND DEPOSIT

The Myth

As we discussed, the myth that you get a copyright by sending something to the Copyright Office is just that—a myth. You get a copyright by fixing the work in tangible form.

Registering a copyright with the Copyright Office gives you certain legal remedies you don't otherwise have, and so you should always do it if you're going to commercially exploit your work. However, the failure to register doesn't affect the validity of your copyright and, if you're a beginning songwriter, it's probably not worth the money until someone bites.

The old trick of mailing a copy of the work to yourself actually accomplishes something. However, it has nothing to do with securing a copyright, and the name "poor man's copyright" is incorrect. The only thing it does is clearly establish a date on which you created your work. So if someone rips it off at a later date, you can prove your work was created before theirs. If you're going to do this, send it by certified mail and don't get excited and open it when it arrives; store it in a safe place, and let a judge open it if someone ever gets cute.

Having a date-stamped digital file accomplishes the same thing, though I'm told (anecdotally, not reliably) that digital dates may be manipulated. If that's true, then this isn't as strong a protection.

Penalties for Failure to Register

If your work is going to be commercially exploited (recorded on re-cords, used in a film, a commercial, etc.), you should register with the Copyright Office. If you don't, the following penalties apply:

1. You can't collect compulsory license royalties (see page 229).
2. You can't file an infringement action (**infringement** means someone ripped off your copyright) unless you've first regis-tered the copyright. That means you can't recover damages or stop someone from using your song (see pages 367–68) until you've registered. You're allowed to wait and register just before you file the lawsuit, but it's a better idea to take care of it as soon as you know there's going to be a recording (because of num-ber 4 below).
3. If you don't register within five years after first publication of the work, you lose the legal presumption that everything in the registration is valid. This legal mumbo jumbo basically means that if you do register within the five years, a court will assume that everything in your registration is correct, and the infringer has the burden of proving it's not. If you don't, you have to prove it's correct.
4. You can't recover attorney's fees, nor can you get statutory damages (see page 367) unless you registered before the in-fringement happened.

You can get the forms you need to register (and in fact register electron-ically) at www.copyright.gov, unless that's now become a porno site.

If you prefer snail mail, feel free to write the Copyright Office at:

Information and Publications
Section LM-455
Copyright Office
Library of Congress
Washington, DC 20559

Deposit

A separate requirement from registration is the obligation to deposit copies of "the best edition" of your work within three months after publication. If you don't, there's no loss of copyright, but there are penalties and fines. The purpose of this is to keep the Library of Congress overflowing with tons of crap that nobody has ever heard of, and the system works quite well. You can deposit CDs or sheet music for songs, or if your work is unpublished, or published only in electronic form, you can deposit electronically.

WHAT YOU GET WHEN SOMEONE RIPS OFF YOUR COPYRIGHT

When someone steals your song, they have **infringed** your copyright (meaning they've used it without your permission). Some of what you can get is peculiar to the copyright (and also trademark) world. Here's how it works:

1. **You get the fair market value.**
   of the use they made. For example, if they rip off your song in commercial, and that use of the song is worth $25,000 in a marketplace deal, you can get $25,000.
2. **You can recover the infringer's profits.**
   This is not a common remedy and is extremely valuable. It means that if the sleazeball made a profit using your work, you can recover his profits, which may be more than the fair market value of the usage. (If you pick this remedy, you don't also get fair market value.)
3. **You can get an injunction.**
   That means the court **enjoins** (prohibits the infringer from using) the infringing work. If they continue to use it anyway, they're subject to substantial fines, and sometimes even jail.
4. **You can recover statutory damages.**
   Statutory damages are a real copyright original. This is where you can't prove actual damages—for example, your infringer was not only a thief, but also a bungling businessman, and he lost money with your rip-off. Or maybe his profits are so well hidden that you can't find them. In this case, the court can give you anywhere from $750 to $30,000 for a single infringement (this is per act of infringement, not the number of copies actually made; for example, putting out 100,000 CDs with your song is still only one act of infringement). The judge can raise this to $150,000 if it's a willful (intentional) infringement, and can lower it to $200 for an "innocent" infringement.

5. **The court can order destruction or seizure.**
   The court can grab, or make the sleazebag destroy, all the infringing copies. This is also not a common remedy outside the copyright area.
6. **If the infringement is willful, there are criminal penalties.**
   An interesting bit of history is that the Marx Brothers stole some poor schlub's copyright for a radio show and were convicted of criminal copyright infringement.
7. **You can get your costs.**
   You can get back your court costs and, to a limited extent, you can recover your **attorney's fees.** The latter is unusual, because you normally don't get attorneys' fees even if you win a lawsuit.

If you're in a group, keep straight ahead.
If not a group, but you're using a professional name that
isn't your own, go to What's in a Name, on page 382.
If you're not a group and you're using your own
name, skip to Touring, on page 395.
If you're bored, take a nice walk around the block.

PART IV

Group Issues

22

Groups

If you're a member of a group, everything in this book applies to you. But you also get a whole set of goodies that don't concern individual artists. Let's take a look at them.

GROUP PROVISIONS IN RECORD DEALS

When you're a group, there's a whole section in your record deal that's not in a solo artist's contract. It spells out what happens if the group breaks up, or if one individual (a prima donna or the only rational member, depending on your side of the fence) decides he or she no longer wants to play with the others.

Key Members

Most agreements will say that a breach of the record deal by one member of the group is treated as a breach by all members of the group. This, in effect, means that if one member refuses to record with the others, the entire group is in breach. This is not such an unreasonable position if we're talking about the lead singer or main songwriter or key instrumentalist, but it's not so hot if we're talking about a percussionist who neither sings, writes, nor knows what state he lives in.

To handle our percussionist friend, we who represent artists gave birth to the concept of a **key member.** Under this system, certain individuals are designated as *key members*. If a key member leaves the group or otherwise breaches the agreement, the record company can treat the event as a breach by the whole group and exercise its various options (which we'll discuss in a minute). If anyone else screws up, it can't.

This is something you have to ask for—no company uses a key member concept in its form agreements. Also, as you might imagine, working this out has been known to break up bands, because the people who aren't named as key members tend to get their noses out of joint. It also puts the lawyer/manager in the position that non-key members may feel their representatives are "playing favorites." However, as you'll see, it isn't always so great to be a key member.

The Company's Rights to Leaving Members

What can the company do if a member (key or not) leaves the group?

1. All companies provide that, if a member leaves a group, the company has the option to get his or her services as a solo artist (and as a member of any other group). This is reasonable enough—without it, you could get out of your record deal just by leaving the band.

   Even when you have a key member concept, however, the company will want the right to pick up *all* leaving members, key and non-key alike. I like to argue that the company has no business (or usually interest in) keeping the services of non-key members, such as our percussionist. (This is also how you sell the percussionist on not being a key member—if he decides to leave the group, he can split from the record company and make his own deal, while a key member can't. But if the company insists on the right to pick him up as a soloist, even if he's not a key member, it scraps this argument.)

2. The company gets the option to keep the members who *don't* leave the group (assuming, of course, there's not a total breakup).

3. The company has the option to terminate the members who didn't leave, since the group is no longer the one they signed. Note this means, if they don't exercise their option for the leaving member, that the deal is over. So make sure that only a key member's leaving can trigger this right.

Leaving Member Deals

The person leaving the group is cleverly called a **leaving member.** The terms of a leaving member's solo agreement are spelled out in the group's deal and are almost always less favorable than the deal for the group. The record company's position, which is understandable, is that the soloist is an unknown quantity, whereas the group was the reason for making the deal. Success is by no means assured—there are many cases of soloists who have left groups to fall flat on their faces (as well as those who have been more successful than the groups they came from). If the group is important enough, the soloist's royalty may be close to or the same as the group's, but the advance is almost always substantially less, and the commitment is usually for one album at most (sometimes only demos). As your bargaining power increases, so does your ability to negotiate these clauses, particularly if a member of a group has been emerging as the star, or had an earlier solo career.

TRIVIA QUIZ

Name the lead singers who have had solo careers after leaving the following groups:

1. The Police
2. White Stripes
3. Destiny's Child

Name the groups from which the following soloists came:

1. Justin Timberlake
2. Neil Young (*not* Crosby, Stills, Nash & Young)
3. Eric Clapton

(Answers on page 391.)

Deficits

What happens to the group's deficit (unrecouped balance) when a soloist sets out on his or her own (see page 86 for what a deficit is)? Suppose a group breaks up and is $500,000 unrecouped. The company then picks up one member as a soloist, who sells millions of albums. Can the company take his or her solo royalties to recoup the group's $500,000 deficit? Conversely, if the group was recouped but the soloist is a flop, can the company use the group's royalties to recoup the soloist's deficit?

Many companies, at least in their first contract draft, take the right to do both these things. If you ask, however, they will generally agree that only a pro-rata share of the group's deficit can be charged to the soloist. For example, if there are five members of the group, only one-fifth of the deficit ($100,000 of the $500,000 in the above example) can be carried over to a solo deal. Conversely, if you ask, they'll also agree only to charge the soloist's pro-rata share of *group* royalties with the *soloist's* deficit. The company will sometimes agree not to charge the soloist's share of group royalties with a deficit under the solo agreement, but this takes more bargaining power.

You should be careful to provide that, if the group continues to record without the soloist, no *future* group deficits can affect the soloist's new account. Also, make sure this deficit can't affect his or her share of group royalties. It's not uncommon for a successful group, after a key member leaves, to record several dud albums, which then eat up all the old, successful albums' royalties. If they also eat up the ex-member's royalties on these successful albums, he or she will be, shall we say, perturbed.

For example, suppose Harvey leaves the group after making four successful albums. Because the group did well, it's fully recouped, and Harvey retires to that dream house in Elk's End, expecting to live on his royalties from future sales of these four albums. The group, without Harvey, then goes into the studio and runs up $1,000,000 trying to make the next *Sgt. Pepper's Lonely Hearts Club Band*, which sells three hundred copies. If you don't change the form, the company will take Harvey's royalties from the four successful albums and use them to get back the $1,000,000 it spent on the flop. Harvey will not be pleased.

Most companies will agree not to charge future costs against a person who has left, because the leaving member doesn't participate in the future records' royalties and thus shouldn't bear the costs. But you gotta ask.

INTERNAL GROUP DEALS

Why You Need an Internal Contract

When two plumbers in Pacoima decide to go into business together, they know enough to have a lawyer write them a partnership agreement. Or at least go to the supermarket and buy a printed form. On the other hand, groups earning tens of millions of dollars sometimes never get around to formalizing their relationship. And, every once in a while, this neglect bites them in the butt.

The time to make an agreement among yourselves is *now*, when everybody is all friendly and kissy-face. When you're fighting with each other, particularly if there's a lot of money on the table, you may find yourself killing the goose that lays the golden eggs, as well as supporting the Retirement Fund for Entertainment Lawyers.

One of my early experiences as a music lawyer was trying to solve the problems of a major group who had never formalized their relationship. One of the two key members got pumped up by a relative, who told him he was the real star of the group (even though he didn't sing or write). So he tried to stop the other guy from using the group name. Because they were set up as a corporation, with equal votes, they got so deadlocked that they couldn't agree to pay the phone bill. We had to go to court and ask the judge to appoint a neutral third director to break the tie. The court chose a crusty ex-judge, who wore a three-piece suit with a watch chain. He'd done this for many bitterly fighting corporations and was supposed to be the tie-breaker that allowed the corporation to finally move forward. Well, His Honor lasted about three months, saying, "I've never in my days seen anything as nasty as this," before disappearing into the sunset, leaving behind a large bill.

The upshot was that the litigation lasted more than nine years and cost the parties more than a million bucks in legal fees. The group of course was killed early in the process, and the fellow who started the fight ended up broke. All of which could have been avoided with a simple agreement and a few hours of planning.

So pay attention and take care of it now. I know, nobody likes to talk about negative stuff (like breakups) when everything is working well. But, believe me, when everything is going well is *exactly* the time to discuss it, because you can do it in a friendly way. It's like insurance— you may never need it, but you'll sure be glad you have it if you do. Find a third party (like a lawyer) to blame for raising the issue, so you don't have to take the heat. (I routinely say that I'm the jerk insisting on this, so you can be a good guy.)

But enough fatherly advice. Here's what you should do. (I'm referring to folks as "partners" in this discussion, though there may be a different legal structure, as we'll see later.)

The Most Important Asset

Can you guess what your most important asset is?

Apart from your good looks, charm, and talent, your most important asset is the group name. So, whatever else you do, by all means figure out what to do with your group name if there's a fight. In fact, if you only deal with your name in a written agreement, I will be happy (but not ecstatic; to get me there, you have to deal with everything).

You have to think through everything about the group name, such as what happens if:

1. The lead singer and songwriter leave the group.
2. The drummer who doesn't write music or sing leaves the group.
3. Three out of five members leave to form another group.
4. The group breaks up and everybody goes back to Waxahachie.

Obviously, there are about ten thousand other possibilities, but all of them can be covered with a few general rules. While you can do anything you want, the most common solutions run along these lines:

1. No one can use the name if the group breaks up, regardless of how many of you are still performing together (short of all of you, of course).
2. Any majority of the group members performing together can use the name. For example, if there are five people in a group that breaks up, any three of them together can use the name.
3. Only the lead singer, Sylvia, can use the name, regardless of who she's performing with.
4. Only George, the songwriter who founded the group and thought of the name, can use it, regardless of who he's performing with.
5. George and Sylvia can use the name as long as they perform together, but if they don't, no one can use it.

If one or two people really created the unique sound of the group, I've always thought they should have the right to use the name, because the others alone wouldn't truly represent the group to the public. On the other hand, many groups operate on a "majority rule" principle, regardless of that spirit. So anything you can imagine is okay as long as everyone agrees, and it has some rational basis that a judge can understand. Just do *something*.

What happens if you don't do anything? As you can gather from my previous horror story, the law is not very helpful. In fact, there is very little law on the subject (surprising as that sounds). This is because most disputes are settled privately, even though they may start as lawsuits. The cases that have gone the distance turn on the question of whether the performing members are deceiving the public. The argument is that one or more key people are the "essence" of the group, and anyone using the name without them defrauds the public. And that gets decided by a judge whose favorite singer is probably Wayne Newton.

If you think this sounds messy and expensive to resolve, you're right. So solve it yourself. *Now!*

Percentages

The next important thing to decide is everybody's percentages. It may surprise you to learn that there are many bands who, despite laughing, giggling, and slapping each other's tushies onstage, are in fact owned or controlled by one or two people, and everybody else is merely a hired hand. Being a hired hand doesn't necessarily mean you're on a salary—you can be a hired hand and get both a salary and a percentage of the profits. It does, however, mean you serve at the will and pleasure of the employer, which actually makes for a rather pleasant band atmosphere—somehow the knowledge that you could be out on the street tomorrow keeps people's attitudes a lot healthier than if they think they have a lifetime gig. (Hiring people usually isn't practical for new artists, because you don't have any money to pay them a salary. So everyone works for a percentage of the future pie.)

Assuming you're all going to be partners, how should the profits be shared? Again, there are no rules, and you can do it any way that makes you happy. The simplest way, of course, is to split things equally—if there are five of you, everyone gets one-fifth, or 20%. This is common in new bands, but it can become a source of irritation if some members work harder or contribute more than others (such as handling all the media interviews). Another approach I've seen (with a band that was built on a core of two people who were together for a number of years before the others joined) gave the two founders bigger percentages than the others. And frankly, even when everyone has been together from the beginning, there may be one or two key members who deserve more than the others.

By the way, nothing says you have to use the same percentage for all areas. Sometimes bands split evenly on concert monies (on the theory that everyone is out there sweating together) but have different splits for records, merchandising, television performances, etc.

Control

Just as ownership doesn't need to be equal, neither does control of the band's decisions. Normally you vote in proportion to your percentage of profits, but this is not carved in stone. So even if your percentages are equal, one or two key members may control the vote—for example, they may have two votes where everybody else has one. Or it can be set up so that the group can't act without one of the key members agreeing, regardless of how many people want to do it. The possibilities are endless, depending only on your desires, but they need to be thought out carefully. For example, try not to have an even number of votes, because this allows a **deadlock** (meaning an equally divided vote where nothing can be done). At worst, have a third party like your manager break the tie, but it's way better to do it inside the group.

Other Issues

Here are the other major issues in a partnership agreement:

Firing.   What kind of vote does it take to fire a member? Majority? Unanimous of everyone else? (Unanimous of everyone doesn't work, since the guy being fired usually votes the other way.)

Hiring.   What kind of vote is required to take in a new partner? Or to hire a lawyer, agent, or manager? Majority? Unanimous? When my son Danny was twelve, we came back from vacation to discover that his band had hired a manager and keyboard player without even asking him. It ultimately broke up the band. Yours could be next.

Quitting.   Is everyone free to quit at will? Note this only concerns leaving the other band members. You're not free to quit under your record deal (see page 371), and if you're in the middle of a tour, you're not free to walk out on the concert promoters without getting the teeth sued out of your mouth.

Since slavery was abolished, there's no way to force someone to continue working with a group. But it is possible to stop him or her from working as a musical artist after quitting, to require the member to pay his or her solo earnings to the partnership (meaning the other group members get a piece), and to require him or her to pay for any damages caused by their leaving. These are the real means to enforce such a provision. On the other hand, I've always been in favor of letting people go if they're unhappy, as long as they don't walk out in the middle of a tour or otherwise leave some third party hanging.

Incurring Expenses.   What kind of vote do you need for the group to spend money?

Contributions.   What kind of vote do you need to make partners contribute to the partnership (translation: put in money)? For example, if the group needs dough to buy equipment, cover unexpected expenses, etc.?

Amendment of Partnership Agreement.   What kind of vote does it take to change the terms of the partnership deal? For example, can a majority vote reduce your percentage? Or does it take your consent?

Death or Disability.   What happens in the event of your death or disability? The one sure thing is that your partners don't usually want your surviving spouse or parents voting on partnership matters (not likely they'll get onstage and sing). For this reason, there is normally a buyout (see the next section), and you're treated as if you had quit the partnership or were terminated.

Ex-partners.   What happens after you're terminated as a partner, or after you quit? Do you keep your same percentage level for past activities (almost always "yes")? For future activities (almost always "no")? Do you get bought out of your share of assets of the group, and if so, at what price and over what period of time?

Buyouts

Here's a buyout provision used by one of my clients for leaving partners:

Price.   The price of the buyout equals the leaving partner's percentage of all "hard" assets owned by the partnership. "Hard" assets mean things that you can touch (sound equipment, instruments, cash, etc.), as opposed to "intangibles" (such as the group name, recording contracts, etc.). Thus, if the assets are worth $100,000, and the partner had a 25% interest, his or her value of the assets would be $25,000. This is usually done on a "value" as opposed to "cost" basis, because used equipment is generally worth less than the cost. It can also be done on something called "book value," which is an accounting concept meaning the "value" on the books of the partnership. *Book value* is typically the original cost minus some scheduled factor of depreciation that is worked out by your accountant. Of these three methods, book value is likely to be the lowest, although it's possible the real value could be less. Cost is the least accurate measure of anything.

I specifically provide that there is no value given to any intangible rights. First of all, I think they're impossible to value, and second, the value may be different after someone leaves the group. (For example, if the lead singer/songwriter goes, the group name and record deal may be worthless. Conversely, a new lead singer might join and make things a lot more successful than they were with the old one.) Finally, I think the leaving member's contingent payout (discussed in the Contingent Payout section below) compensates for this.

You should know that not everyone agrees with this approach to intangibles. There are certainly situations where a name is worth a lot of money after the group has broken up. For example, the Beatles, the Doors, and Led Zeppelin still generate tons of dough from the use of their names in merchandising, and it's not illogical to give an ex-member some reduced piece of materials created after the member has left. (Note that if the band breaks up, everyone continues to own their shares of the name.) Despite all that, and despite the fact that it could arguably create an unfair result, I still like my way. You can't know in advance what a particular member will really contribute to the value of the name, or how much value will be added or lost after that member leaves. And figuring it out after the fact makes lawyers rich.

Cash Payout.   The value of hard assets is paid out over a period of two years, at the rate of 25% each six months. Thus, in our $25,000 example, $6,250 would be paid six months after termination, $6,250 paid twelve months after, and so forth. Because the total isn't paid up front, a leaving partner usually gets interest on the unpaid balance.

The reason for structuring a payout over time is to protect the remaining members from having to come up with a big chunk of cash (which they may not have). Also, it's not uncommon to provide that the terminated partner can look only to the assets of the partnership for his or her buyout payments. That means the other individual partners aren't responsible if the partnership tanks and has no money to pay.

Contingent Payout.   The leaving member(s) get their continuing percentage from activities of the partnership in which they participated. This means royalties from records they played on, monies from merchandise using their names or likeness, concerts and TV shows in which they performed, etc. (Remember, there are special record contract provisions about leaving members, which may affect their continuing royalties. See page 372.) In this deal, the leaving members don't get any portion of group earnings from performances and other activities that happen after they leave.

Legal Ethics

You should be aware of a common ethical problem that groups have. As we discussed on page 53, a lawyer who represents a group and draws up a partnership agreement has a built-in **conflict of interest.** A conflict of interest, called in shorthand a **conflict,** means the lawyer represents two clients whose interests are adverse to each other. So if a lawyer represents the partnership, he or she can't take sides and represent any one of you against any other of you. However, this is exactly what making a partnership agreement requires, because your best interests aren't the same. For example, extra chunks of money going to Sylvia have to come from the other members, whose best interests are to keep them. Same with voting percentages. (A manager, business manager, or agent who counsels you about group matters also has the same conflict.)

This situation, of course, happens every day, so those of us in the industry are used to dealing with it. And all ethical lawyers will advise you of its existence. You can do one of two things:

1. Each member can get independent counsel (which may or may not be affordable) to negotiate the agreement among yourselves. This also takes a long time and can be destructive if anyone decides to be a hero. However, it's the best way to do it.
2. Far more commonly, the lawyer explains all the issues to you openly, and then lets you decide among yourselves how you want to resolve them. In this case, the lawyer doesn't represent any of you, but rather just acts as a "secretary," writing down whatever agreement you reach on your own. If you use this route, your lawyer will ask you to sign a conflict waiver, which says he or she has explained the conflict to you, and you're going ahead anyway.

Corporation versus Partnership

Once you've decided all these issues, how do you set yourself up? The choices are a partnership, LLC, or corporation, and the major differences (as we discussed on page 203) are the tax-planning aspects (which could be a book in itself), the liability limitations, and the fact that corporations are more expensive to set up and run. By *liability limitations,* I mean that corporations limit the assets that can be grabbed by someone suing you. In a corporation, if you handle things properly, they can only get the assets of the corporation. With a partnership, however, they can grab both the partnership's assets *and* the personal assets of *every partner* (that means you). While these are nice benefits of corporations, they're offset by the increased cost of setting up and running the suckers, so it's marginal in your early stages.

A **limited liability company,** or **LLC,** is basically a partnership, but it provides the limited liability of a corporation. Because it's as cheap and easy to use as a partnership, it's the vehicle du jour for many groups.

The mechanical difference between these entities is that, if you want a partnership, you should have a written partnership agreement, and if you want a corporation or LLC, you need two agreements instead of one: (1) a written agreement (meaning an agreement among the shareholders of a corporation, or the owners of the LLC, who are called **members**), and (2) employment agreements between yourselves and the corporation or the LLC. If you go the LLC route, however, you may be able to get by with just a membership agreement.

If you don't have a written agreement, most states have laws that spell out what happens—generally everybody owns everything equally and has an equal vote—which may not be what you want. So I highly recommend that you do your own. As you'll see there are complicated issues to solve, and you'll be WAY better off doing it yourself rather than leaving it to the ding-a-lings in your state capitol.

WHAT'S IN A NAME?

We talked before (on page 375) about group members' rights in your name. Now let's talk about how to protect your name from people outside the group.

Rights in a Name

A number of years back, a band named Green Jellö changed its name to Green Jellÿ to avoid a dispute with the owners of the Jell-O trademark. While the group ultimately got some good publicity from all the flap, having a name that steps on somebody else's toes can be a serious problem. The most common problems don't come from naming your band after snack foods, but rather from another group that used the name before you did.

Your group name is protected by a **service mark,** which is similar to a **trademark**—a trademark is a name used for *goods* (like Heinz ketchup, Kleenex tissues, etc.) and a service mark is a name used for *services* (like

Delta Air Lines, Visa Credit Card Services, and Tommy's Dry Cleaners). The rule is that you get rights in a mark by actually using the name and having it associated with you in the mind of the public. So if the fans think of you when they hear your group name, it's yours and no one else's.

In fact, you can even stop names that are different from yours but are similar enough to confuse the public. For example, there's a famous case from the 1920s where Charlie Chaplin stopped someone from using the name "Charles Aplin," and there's an even more fun case where the Dallas Cowboy Cheerleaders stopped the porno film *Debbie Does Dallas* from calling its star an "X Dallas Cheerleader." (For you research freaks, the case cites are *Chaplin v. Amador*, 93 Cal. App. 358 [1928]; and *Dallas Cowboy Cheerleaders, Inc., v. Pussycat Cinema, Ltd.*, 604 F.2d 200 [2d Cir. 1979].)

By the way, your association with the group name doesn't have to be nationwide—it can be only in your hometown. Suppose you live in Tulsa, Oklahoma, and like the name Pukeheads. Using this name, you start playing locally in August 2014, and build up a major buzz and fan base. Then one day in 2015, a friend tells you about a new download on iTunes by a group from New York called Pukeheads. What can you do?

Actually, you may be able to do quite a bit. If you were a Pukehead in Tulsa before the New York guys used the name *in Tulsa* (the date you started using it is key—you have to be first), you can stop them from performing in Tulsa, and likely stop them from distributing downloads in Tulsa. Even if they used the name first in New York, if you were first in Tulsa, that town is yours. (They could, however, stop you from using the name in New York if they used it there first; and if they distributed their album first, they could hassle you in Tulsa. This gets pretty complicated and depends on the specific facts in each case, including the genre of music each group performs. But let's assume you own Tulsa.) Since it's impossible for a record company to skip a specific market when it delivers music on the Internet, if you own the name in Tulsa, you can effectively block them from using it for downloads or streams in the United States. This is a joyful result if you're the band from Tulsa, but nosedive downer if you're a Pukehead from New York.

Note that your rights come from *using* the name, *not* from registering it. ("Registration" means filing a public notice in the U.S. Patent & Trademark Office that tells the world you claim a particular name, and you get some major rights if no one opposes you and the Feds okay your registration. More about this on page 388.)

The reason usage is so important is that, when you use a name, the public begins to associate it with you. And if someone else uses the same name, the public could be fooled into thinking it's you or a spin-off group, which is a no-no. (There's one exception to this, called an **Intent to Use**, which gives you rights *before* the date you actually use the mark. More about this in a bit.)

Another important area in trademark is something called **dilution.** Historically, you only got trademark protection in the specific area where you did business. In other words, if you were a phone company named Presto, you probably couldn't stop a massage parlor from using that name, since people wouldn't think their massages were coming from your phone repairmen. Nowadays, there's a law that says using a famous name in another area *dilutes* the value of the original trademark, and it may be possible to stop the massage parlor. So, even though the Beatles don't have a record label under that name, you couldn't get away with using the name Beatles Records.

Check It Out

So how do you stop from being a New York Pukehead? You have to make sure no one else used the group name before you did, which is a bit of a pain (I'll tell you how in a minute, although there's no way to ever be 100% sure). It becomes an issue as soon as you post a page on Facebook, SoundCloud, Bandcamp, FanBridge, or some other similar site, and it gets more serious when you get ready to release records, or have your music available nationally for streaming or download, or start touring over a broad geographic area. Before you really roll out under that name, the most trouble you'll likely get is a snippy letter from someone else using the name, and you can usually work it out (see page 387 for how things get worked out). However, changing a name once you've built up a local following is not a happy event, and if you really have some momentum, you may want to check out the group name before you get too far along.

If you're about to sign a record deal and someone can stop your label from putting out records or downloads (as in our Tulsa example), it could cost the label a lot of money. And if it does, the record company will turn to you with a handful of "gimme"—every record deal makes you guarantee that they can use your name without any legal hassles, which means you have to pay for the mess if there is one.

After being stung by a few of these situations, most record companies now check the names of new artists before they put out their records or downloads. They use several common sources:

1. **The Internet** is a great way to do your preliminary searches.

   a. Try looking up your name on a search engine, like Google or Bing, to see what comes up. Also try social networking sites, like Facebook, SoundCloud, Twitter, Bandcamp, FanBridge, Billboard.com, or Last.FM. Look for You-Tube videos and also check some of the music websites like Amazon.com, iTunes, Spotify, Apple Music, Vevo, Allmusic.com, and Artistdirect.com. However, this is only a starting point: Finding your name doesn't mean the other band is still around using the name (bands break up regularly, in case you didn't notice), and just as importantly, not finding your name doesn't mean it's clear.

   b. Look for your name at www.whois.com, which is a registry for websites. Try combinations like pukeheads.com or pukeheadsband.com or pukeheadsmusic.com, and so forth. This could not only lead you to another band with your name, but also let you know whether you can get a domain name registration for your website.

   c. It's a good idea to lock up your domain names before you become popular. If you don't, the pirates will swoop down as soon as your name means something. More about this on page 390.

2. The U.S. Patent & Trademark Office has a website where you can search federal trademark applications and registrations. Go to http://www.uspto.gov/trademarks-application-process/search-trademark-database. Searching there can get awkward (what government procedures aren't?), but this can be a good jumping-off point.

3. California and many other states have a website that lets you check public records for corporations and limited liability companies that might have names similar to yours (in California, it's http://kepler.sos.ca.gov/). Because so many groups seem to hang out in California, it's not a bad idea to take a quick look even if you're in another state.

4. The U.S. Copyright Office also has a searchable catalog for copyright registrations from 1978 to the present. This can be another source for locating names of groups. Go to the following link: http://cocatalog.loc.gov/cgi-bin/Pwebrecon.cgi?DB=local&PAGE=First. When you get there, search under "Title." However, if your group name is a common word, this might be

a waste of time because you could come up with a lot of irrelevant information.

5. If the record companies don't find anything in the above sources, they order a **trademark/service mark search** to look for registrations (both state and federal), as well as other listings (known as **common-law references**) of the group name and anything similar. It currently costs about $400 for a preliminary search, and about another $1,000 to $2,000 for an in-depth one, which is cheap insurance in the long run. There's an even more extensive search known as a Music Media search, which is offered by Thomson CompuMark, whose address is listed below. That is an excellent search if the bucks are available. (Whichever search your label uses, it's recoupable from your royalties; see page 86 for what that means.)

These searches are conducted by independent search companies and by lawyers who specialize in trademarks. (If you use an independent search firm, it's a good idea to have the report reviewed by a trademark attorney who can advise you whether anything you found might be a problem.) Here are a few searchers:

Thomson CompuMark
22 Thompson Place
Boston, MA 102210
(800) 692-8833
www.compumark.thomsonreuters.com

Corporation Service Company
2711 Centerville Road
Wilmington, DE 19808
(800) 927-9800
www.cscglobal.com/global/web/csc/trademark-search.html

Fross, Zelnick, Lehrman & Zissu [a law firm with a lot of music experience]
866 United Nations Plaza, 6th Floor
New York, NY 10017
(212) 813-5900
email: fzlz@frosszelnick.com

CT Corsearch
111 8th Street
New York, NY 10011
(800) 732-7241
www.corsearch.com

As noted above, searches can never be 100% foolproof (for example, there may be a local band like the one in Tulsa that hasn't registered a service mark but has acquired rights in the name by performing), but it's the best you can do.

IMPORTANT NOTE: The record company is doing this to protect itself, not you. Also, their goal is to sell music, so their search will focus on recordings and music group names. But if you plan to use your name in another product category—headphones, perfumes, hamster earmuffs—they're not likely to search those areas. So the record company might consider it safe to use your name for their purposes, but not all the uses you may want. And, if they screw up the search and something goes wrong, it's your rear end that's on the line.

If you find a group using your name, or using a name that's similar to yours, you have to deal with it. (If you find a name that's similar, you'll need a legal opinion as to whether or not it's too close—the test is whether the public is likely to confuse the two groups.) Most of the time you can contact the other group and work out a deal. If you find them and discover that they broke up or abandoned the name, they may have lost their rights and you don't need to worry about them. If they're still using the name, and if they're willing to change it, they'll want to get paid. The most common deal is the payment of a lump sum in exchange for their drifting into the sunset (usually in the range of a few thousand dollars to maybe $20,000 or so, though it can get into six figures if they smell blood).

If you do make a deal, you'll need a knowledgeable lawyer to draw it up because this is a very tricky area. *Never* try to handle this kind of deal by yourself. And by the way, making a deal doesn't assure you of total peace. For example, you might buy out the New York Pukeheads, only to find there were Pukeheads in Seattle that you never knew about, and that they came before the ones in New York. Or there might be Pukeheads in Düsseldorf. In that case, you're back to square one (minus several thousand bucks).

Occasionally, bands in this position think they've got you by the squeezable parts, and they hold out for enormous sums of money. When you get one of these, or if you come across a band that simply won't sell the name, you have to change yours. Sometimes you can keep part of the name by adding something to it, but you need to add something distinctive that clearly separates you from the others. For example, if you were using the name Silver and found that it was taken, you might call yourself Denver Silver. (I always think of that great scene in the movie *Spinal Tap* where they talk about having been called the Originals, only to find another group had that name, so they called themselves the New Originals.) But this procedure is tricky, and you'll need legal help.

Registration

At some point in your career you want to file a **registration** of your service mark. *Registration* tells the world that you're using a particular name (or more accurately, it tells everyone in the United States; foreign protection is a different story, as we'll discuss on page 389). Registration also establishes a date on which you are using the name, and creates a **legal presumption** that you own it nationwide (not just where you used it). (A *legal presumption* means that other group has the burden of proving you *don't* own it; without the presumption, you have to prove you *do* own it.) Also, in addition to this basket of legal goodies, a registration makes sure that you will show up in any search that somebody else does (see point 5 on page 386).

If you're only operating in one state, you're only allowed to register in that state. If you're operating in more than one state (and being on the Internet qualifies), you can (and should) register with the federal government, so that you have a national notice. You can get federal applications from the incredibly sexy website of the U.S. Patent & Trademark Office, at www.uspto.gov. You can also call them at (800) 786-9199, or email them at usptoinfo@uspto.gov.

While I hate to tell you this, you can file an application online. I really don't recommend it; this area is very tricky and technical. I strongly suggest that anything having to do with these rights be run through a trademark lawyer—even with my experience in music law, I wouldn't do it myself.

You're on your own to find out where to file in each state. Try the governmental listings in your capital city or you can check online by searching "Secretary of State" followed by your state name and "trademarks" in the search box.

If you're a group, or if you're thinking of having a company hold your service mark (rather than you holding it personally), it's really important to get that nailed down before you file an application. The applicant has to be the owner of the mark (meaning the one who controls the use of it), and if you use the wrong applicant, your application is worth less than a guitar pick. So if there's any disagreement over ownership, get it sorted out before you file.

Do You Have a Reservation?   Since 1989, it's been possible to reserve a name before you actually use it. This was a major change from the prior law, which said you could only get rights by using the mark. You reserve the name by filing something cleverly called an **Intent to Use** federal service mark application, and all you need is a serious desire to use the name in the not-too-distant future. If you're the first one to file with your name, then even if someone else uses the name before you do (but after you file), you can stop them after your registration is issued.

You can turn the *Intent to Use* into a real, live registration application by filing evidence that you've actually started using the name. The evidence only needs to be something that shows you've used your name in interstate commerce (meaning across state lines). If you don't file this evidence within three years after the government okays your application, then your application is declared invalid, turns into a frog, and you have to start all over.

This "interstate commerce" requirement is pretty easy to pull off. For example, it's enough if you make your music available on the Internet, or if you send out a multistate email blast.

After filing your application, it can take a year or more to get the registration. And that's if everything goes smoothly (your tax dollars at work). First, the guys in the federal Patent & Trademark Office check around to see if someone already has a registered mark that they think is too close to yours. If they do, your application gets bounced, and you can start squabbling with them. If you get past these guys, they will then publish your name in the U.S. Official Gazette (so if you haven't made it anywhere else, at least you can happen there). This is so that anybody who reads the Gazette (don't you and all your friends?) can object to registering your name because it's too close to theirs.

Once you're registered, you have to continue using the name in order to keep up your rights. In fact, there's a legal presumption that you've abandoned the name if you haven't used it for three years. (*Presumption* means that you have to prove you didn't abandon it, as opposed to the other guy having to prove you did.) However, if you use a name continuously for five years after your registration is issued, you can file something called an Affidavit of Incontestability, which is fancy talk for saying that no one can ever come along and claim they had the name before you did (actually, they can still give you a hard time, but it's really tough for them). If you're happening big-time, this is a good idea.

Foreign Registration.   Many countries of the world have a registration system similar to the United States', but I doubt you could stay awake through a discussion of different territories' intricacies. This is only meaningful when you're having success on an international scale, but at that point you should start registering in foreign places (at least in the major territories such as Australia, Canada, Japan, and something called a **CTM registration,** which is a single registration that covers all twenty-seven countries of the European Community, including the United Kingdom and Germany).

Unlike the United States, some countries have a **first to file** rule, which means that someone who has never used the name could file ahead of you in a particular territory, then stop you from performing there. Since only a moron would rip off the name of a dud group, this isn't usually important until you're having some success. But when you do, start registering pretty quickly.

Domain Name Registration.   Once you're committed to a name, it's a good idea to check if anyone else owns that domain name. (See the discussion of using www.whois.com on page 385.) Be sure to check ".net" and ".org" as well as ".com," not to mention the newbies like ".biz" and ".porn." If the name is clear, it's usually worth the money to register it as a domain name, so you can set up a website at some point in your career. You may also want to register on the major social media sites (Facebook, Instagram, Twitter, YouTube, SoundCloud, Tumblr, etc).

All these "dot whatevers" (.com, .net, etc.) are called **top level domains (TLDs).** (The full name of each website (like www.pukehead .xxx) is called a **URL** [meaning **Universal Record Locator**]). There are now so many TLDs that it's cost-prohibitive to buy up your name in every one of them (I wasn't kidding about .porn, and there are tons of others that you can find by Googling "TLD list." Some pretty weird stuff in there, like .boo, .plumbing, .rehab, and so forth). Because the TLDs are endless, the best you can do is grab the ones you think are most important to what you're doing, and when you're really famous, steel yourself against the inevitable pirates who will grab some of the others. Most artists let the pirates do their thing as long as it doesn't create confusion with your fans (meaning the pirate site doesn't look like it comes from you). If they go over the line, you can look into stopping them, but that's not cheap.

In any event, owning a URL is nothing like a federal trademark registration, and doesn't give you any trademark rights. It's more like a telephone number—useful to have, but without the other protections, not much more than a locator.

Logos.   Some artists come up with a distinctive logo. That gives you another level of identification with your fans, even beyond your name (for example, the Rolling Stones's lips with the tongue sticking out). If you want to use a logo, all the same rules about searching and registering your name as a trademark also apply to registering your logo. And you have to register the logo separately from the name (meaning add more expense).

In addition, the artwork in your logo (if it's original enough) is protected under the copyright laws, which means you want to copyright it as well.

If you didn't do the logo artwork yourself, then the artist who created it would own the copyright. You can argue it's a work for hire (see page 339 for what that means), but as we discussed earlier, that's not so simple without a written agreement. So always get the artist to sign a written transfer of the copyright to you. And do this even if your best friend created your logo—friendships have a way of fraying when there's a lot of money involved. I strongly recommend you get a lawyer to help you with this one, because it's is a tricky area.

So, to recap: **Group names are a very complicated legal area, requiring careful analysis of your specific facts. If you have any problems with your name, no matter how small you think they are, you MUST get a lawyer. Do not ignore the problem—it will only lie there sleeping until you're successful, at which point it will wake up and chomp a large gash out of your rear end.**

Answers to quiz on page 373:

Groups:

1. The Police—Sting
2. White Stripes—Jack White
3. Destiny's Child—Beyoncé

Soloists:

1. Justin Timberlake—NSYNC
2. Neil Young—Buffalo Springfield
3. Eric Clapton—Cream; Derek & the Dominoes

PART V

Touring

23

Personal Appearances—Touring

Now let's see what happens when you hit the road, to get up close and personal with your fans.

ROLES OF TEAM MEMBERS

Here's what your team does when you tour:

Personal Manager

As the chief executive officer of your professional team, the personal manager is in charge of the tour. He or she is the one who decides which tour is the right one for you; ensures that your agent is bringing you the best touring options and making the best possible deals for you (read "hounding the agent on a regular basis"); and once the tour is set up, mechanically makes it happen. He or she has to coordinate and supervise:

1. Transportation of people and equipment.
2. Overseeing rehearsals, hiring band members, watching the finances.
3. Hiring and smooth functioning of crews.
4. Booking hotels.
5. Collecting money on the road.
6. Dealing with the **promoters** (the people who hire you, rent the hall, advertise the event, etc.; see page 400 for more about promoters).
7. Coordinating advertising, marketing, and radio and Internet promotions, both in advance and while you are in each city.

8. Handling day of show activities, such as interviews, meet and greets, etc.
9. Putting out whatever fires crop up (such as missing equipment, improper advertising, dates that aren't selling well, lapses in security, etc.).
10. Dealing with illness, cancellations, or other assorted disasters. When these happen, the manager and agent have to reschedule the dates and sometimes refund money to fans. And by the way, no one gets paid for any of this, since you're losing money.

With bigger artists, many of these duties are delegated to a tour manager and/or tour accountant. But the personal manager is ultimately responsible, and the buck stops with him or her.

Agent

The agent, in conjunction with your manager, books the tour. He or she makes the deals with the promoters (which includes picking promoters that will produce the show professionally and not disappear with your money). At the early stages of your career, they will be pounding promoters to book you. At the later stages, they will be pounded by promoters to book you.

Agents also put together **packages,** meaning shows with two or more artists playing together. When done right, this grows your audience, and even if you're established, it can expose you to different audiences who wouldn't have come if you weren't touring with that troupe of dancing donkeys.

Your agent and personal manager also make the following decisions about your tour:

Itinerary.   Your **itinerary** is your tour routing (which cities and in what order) and the halls you play in. If you're the opening act for a major tour, setting the itinerary means you show up when you're told. If you're headlining, the itinerary becomes critical. Proper routing can save or lose you a bundle of money. While it may seem obvious, the tour has to be planned so you don't end up going from New York to Oregon to Florida in a four-day period. However, concert halls are not available at all times (not just because they're booked by other rockers, but because they have hockey games, circuses, etc.), and the juggling act is quite a sight to behold.

Image.   How does the tour work with your image? This is twofold:

1. If you're an opening act, is the headliner compatible with your audience? If you're a heavy metal band, for example, you probably shouldn't open for the Osmond Family Reunion tour.
2. What venues are you playing? It says one thing if you play a brand-new 5,000-seat amphitheater in a high-end neighborhood, and it says something else if you play an older, 3,500-capacity hall with no seats, on the funkier side of town.

Skating Through the "Radio Promotion" Jungle.   Ever notice how many radio stations either "present" a concert, or else have concert tie-ins, ticket giveaways, live reports, etc.? That's because radio exposure is a critical element of selling tickets. And radio promotion never happens by chance; it's always very carefully planned. Apart from just picking the right station, it has to be done in a way that doesn't upset the other stations in the market (who will promptly drop your record). For that reason, it's almost always coordinated with the radio promotions people at your record label.

When to Put the Tickets on Sale.   This is something that varies from market to market. People in some markets buy tickets way in advance, while others mainly **walk up** (meaning the bulk of the audience "walks up" on the night of the show and buys the tickets). Also, it's crucial to put tickets on sale the right amount of time before the show—not too late and not too soon. You have to be careful that you're not going on sale the same day as a major tour that's blitzing the market (or maybe they have to be careful of you!).

The timing of ticket sales also varies with your kind of music. Classic rock acts go on sale earlier than anyone else, because people who buy their tickets are willing to fork over the dough way in advance. Tickets for urban/rap/pop are much more time sensitive. They usually go on sale when their record is hot and they're getting the most publicity.

Pricing of Tickets.   Although your first reaction may be to "grab all the gusto you can" by charging the highest ticket prices the market will bear, this decision isn't so black-and-white. Many managers and agents are squarely within this camp, and their thinking is persuasive: Nobody knows how long things will last, make hay while the sun shines, get 'em while you're hot, etc. On the other hand, many respected managers and agents take a different view, feeling a lower-priced ticket draws more people, creates a bigger buzz, makes the show accessible to people who couldn't otherwise afford to go, and in the long run is a better career-building move. Also, some successful bands keep a low ticket price as a commitment to their fans before business, or because they want to attract a younger audience who can't afford expensive tickets. (Keep in mind, when you're setting prices, that ticketing charges [like Ticketmaster] get slapped on top, and these can be as much as 40% of the price.)

This pricing debate is also related to what sort of audience you appeal to—for example, as we just said, young kids have more trouble with an expensive ticket than an older audience. In addition, the answer varies with where you are in your career—if you're an established artist, you needn't worry as much about building for the long term. Anyway, feel free to join the debate, because your guess is as good as anybody else's. (We'll discuss more details of ticket pricing on page 406.)

Most popular artists actually straddle this pricing issue at the same event: They **scale** their tickets (*scale* is an industry term for setting ticket prices) to charge more for up-front seats, and less for the back of the house, so that all kinds of fans can afford to come. And by charging more for upfront tickets, they also take a bite out of the scalper business (which of course means the artists make more money rather than have the scalpers grab it). We'll talk more about this on page 407–8.

Sites like StubHub!, SeatGeek, ScoreBig, eBay, Craigslist, Razorgator, and TicketsNow have become important sources for tickets. This is known as the **secondary market,** meaning a place where tickets are resold after their first sale. Ticket brokers (the ones you see advertising hot tickets at outrageous prices) are also players in the secondary market, but the Internet ticket sites have kicked them back quite a bit. Over the last few years, some artists have taken a number of their tickets and put them through a secondary player like StubHub! for the *initial* sale. The theory is that the true value of prime tickets is not the face value, but rather what someone is willing to pay in the secondary market. Why shouldn't the artist have those monies, rather than some yahoo who makes a business of buying tickets and reselling them?

It's also common for artists to hold back a number of tickets and sell them through their fan clubs, usually before the public on-sale. This makes sure the real fans get a shot at the best seats, and it's also an incentive to join the fan club.

Another trend is for credit card companies (like American Express and Citi Card) to offer a certain number of tickets to their cardholders in advance of the public. This seems to work best with classic artists, whose fans are older (and have credit cards). In exchange for access to the tickets, the credit card company puts up money for advertising, and sometimes pays a "bounty" for each ticket they sell (meaning money on top of the ticket price).

Deposits.   Agents are also responsible for collecting **deposits,** which are amounts paid in advance by the promoters. In order to hold you for a particular date, the promoters historically paid 50% of your fee, about thirty days ahead of the performance. It's a way of ensuring that you don't get stiffed (at least completely). So, for example, if your deal is $10,000 for a show, the promoter would pay $5,000 in advance. These days, promoters try to pay much less (10% or so), and they only want to pay three to five days before the date. This obviously increases your risk of getting stiffed, so artists don't like it. Whether you can get the money earlier depends on your bargaining power, the size of the guarantee (the larger it is, the less they like to pay up front), and whether it's a first-time promoter, or a promoter who hasn't worked with that agent or artist before. If it's a new promoter, I've seen deposits of 100% of the money, to make sure the artist gets paid.

Deposits are held by the agent and paid to you when you perform the gig (after deducting their commission).

Business Manager

The business manager is in charge of all financial aspects of the tour. This job begins way before the tour starts, by forecasting (a fancy accounting word for predicting) the income and expenses, and projecting how much you're going to make or lose. If you're a new band, this information lets you go to the record company and beat them up for tour support (see page 196). At all levels, it helps avoid unhappy surprises.

When the tour gets going, all your road personnel (the people who set up the equipment, supervise your crew, etc.) are on payroll, and the business manager is in charge of getting everyone paid. He or she also makes sure your performance fees are collected from the promoters (which is physically done by a tour manager, if you have one) and that all bills (travel, hotels, food, etc.) are paid. They deal with withholding taxes (both by states and foreign countries) and file tax returns in all those places. It's also the business manager's responsibility to make sure the tour doesn't run over budget without an alarm being sounded in advance, while there's still a chance to fix it.

Tour Manager

If you have a tour manager (and if not, your personal manager should be doing the job), he or she is responsible for everything running smoothly on the road. They make sure that your hotel reservations are in fact there, that your airline tickets are confirmed, that the bus is where it's supposed to be, that you are on the bus when you're supposed to be, that only certain groupies get through security, etc. It's the tour manager who's responsible for collecting the money after each show, reviewing the promoter's accounting on the night of the show (called **settling the box office** or, as a noun, the **settlement**), and depositing the dough in the right place. (As you move up the ladder, you'll have a tour accountant doing the money part of the job.)

Promoter

Promoters are the people in each market who hire you for the evening. They can be "local" (meaning they work only in one city or area), regional (several states), national (covering the entire United States), or international. (National promoters also book regionally as well as nationally.) Promoters book the hall (which means they owe the rent even if nobody shows up), pay for advertising the concert, and supervise the overall running of the show.

Promoters actually have a tough time. If they lose, they can lose big, but as acts get more successful they squeeze them and limit the promoter's upside (as discussed below). The result is a friendly game of "hide the pickle" that promoters routinely play in stating their expenses. But I'm getting ahead of myself, because we're going to talk about this later (on page 409).

Two companies, Live Nation and AEG, are international promoters, who purchase entire tours. In other words, they make a deal to promote every date. These deals have their own complexities, which we'll discuss when we get to promoter deals on page 410.

Over the last few years, **venues** (meaning the owners of the physical buildings—the amphitheaters, arenas, etc.) have begun buying shows themselves. Deals for these are imaginatively called **venue deals.** As we discussed above, promoters traditionally rent the buildings from the owners, then turn around and make the deals with the artists. Under venue deals, the building owners contract directly with the artists, in effect acting as promoters themselves, and in fact competing with the promoters who rent from them.

Sometimes the venues will pay artists more than promoters will pay. This is partly because they've eliminated the middleman, but more importantly, it's because they have income from parking, food, beverage sales, and other areas that promoters don't share.

Another alternative is what you might call "invisible venues" (not an industry term). By "invisible" I mean you can do an entire tour in these places and none of your friends will ever know about it. I'm talking about casinos, state and county fairs, and **performing arts centers.** Performing arts centers are small theaters (1,200 to 2,400 seats) that put on all kinds of entertainment for their local community, such as dramatic theater, classical symphonies, family shows, well-known speakers, and music. For the right kind of act (usually an older demographic, country, Christian, etc.), these invisible shows can be very profitable.

MARKETING

The biggest change in the concert business over the last few years has been the way concerts are marketed. Traditionally, it was all about advertising in newspapers, on radio, and (for really big tours) on TV. These days, most of the marketing happens over the Internet; at the time of this writing, more than 85% of all tickets are sold over the Internet. Accordingly, your visibility and presence on the Web (your website, social media, blogs, email blasts, tweets, etc.) go a long way toward bringing warm bodies into seats.

As discussed previously, credit card companies are sometimes involved in marketing, in exchange for the ability to sell tickets to their card members on a preferential basis.

PERSONAL APPEARANCE DEALS

It's difficult to make much money touring until you're a major star. In the traditional music biz, you didn't put a lot of tushies into concert seats until you'd sold a lot of records. Until then, you were touring to create a buzz, get a deal, and sell records, so you could tour profitably.

As the record side of the biz continues to nose-dive, people are less certain that record sales are crucial to a strong touring base. There are (and always have been) artists who sell relatively few records but pack concert halls. Conversely, some artists sell millions of records but can't fill a high school auditorium.

Some bands can tour locally and regionally, build a base of 500 to 1,000 people per night, sometimes even filling 3,500-seat theaters, all without a record deal. This seems to work best for DJs, rockers, jam bands, and digital stars (like YouTube phenoms) who can build a huge audience that wants to see them in person. We talked before (on page 14) about the ways new artists can build a buzz through direct contact with their fans, and if it works, it spreads by word of mouth, particularly over the Internet (like through people who go *Hey, dude, check this out!*, then email the bands' SoundCloud link to all their friends). Groups like this can make money and develop a cult following, which can lead to a healthy touring career and a record deal (if they want one).

In the beginning, unless you're one of these phenoms, you will most likely lose money on touring. You'll also get stuck opening for another act, in uncomfortable dressing rooms, with food left over from last night's headliner. And you'll be regularly humiliated, playing to half-empty concert halls, since the audience is coming later to see someone else. Also, the people who show up early will be buying beer, talking loudly during your ballads, and chanting the headliner's name if they don't like your show.

Ready to sign up? Let's look at the anatomy of personal appearance deals:

NEW ARTISTS

You first goal as a new artist is to play as a headliner in clubs (meaning venues of 100 to 1,500 people or so). In the very beginning, a lot of clubs will only take you if you buy a certain number of tickets to your show, which you then have to re-sell (or eat). If you can't sell enough tickets to cover yourself, then a good way to build a buzz is by playing local clubs that have themed nights of cool music from unknown acts (for example, in L.A., a club called Bardot's has "School Night" each week, which is a lineup of developing bands). Assuming the club has enough credibility, there'll be a built-in audience, and hopefully taste-makers show up who will blog about you, or at least be a loudmouth to their friends.

If you're signed to a record label, you might get a gig as the opening act on a big tour. How you get to be the opening act on a major tour is very political. If your album is only doing so-so, and there are several other groups in your position, then it depends on the clout of your manager and agent—it's that simple and cold. If you're selling a lot of albums, have a hot video or single, or generating big numbers on social media, you'll have an edge in the political process, but it's still political. The exception is where you're really exploding out of the box. In this case, the headliners may be clamoring for you. For example, a well-known headliner may not be selling tickets very well and wants a hot new opening act to bring people in.

There's also something called a **buy-on**, which means you get the opening slot on a major tour by paying money to the headliner. The theory is that you're getting so much exposure on a major tour that it's worth it to you (or more likely, worth it to your record company) to fork over some bucks. Sometimes these monies are paid directly to the headliner as a "marketing fee." Sometimes they disguise what's really going on by making you buy a certain number of tickets, or maybe pay for newspaper ads.

If you can build enough of a profile to get yourself booked there, **festivals** (meaning all-day or multi-day events, like Coachella, Bonnaroo, etc.) are a terrific place to push your career ahead. Even if you end up playing at 11 in the morning to about 100 hungover people, the fact that you were on that festival can parlay into booking another festival or getting a support slot on a tour. And if your performance sets off an Internet buzz, it can truly move the needle. Of course, everyone's vying for these festival slots, so getting one takes serious momentum, usually coupled with an aggressive manager or agent.

Fees

If your record is beginning to make some noise, or you've got a local following, you can get fees in the range of $250 to $1,500 per night, either from clubs or opening slots. If you're really big in the local/regional scene (like we discussed above for jam bands), and can draw 1,000 or so per show, you can get $5,000 to $10,000 or even more per night.

Splits/Guarantees

Some clubs will pay you no front money, but will give you a **split** of the **gate** (meaning a share of the money charged for admission). The splits run from 20% to 60%, depending on your stature and the number of other acts. For example, if there are three acts, you might divide up 60% of the gate. If your band is the biggest **draw** (meaning you draw in the biggest crowds), you can ask for more than an equal share. Sometimes you can even get 100% of the gross after the promoter gets back his or her expenses for the evening (advertising, sound, lights, etc.), and with a lot of clout, you can get 100% of *all* gross (the promoter makes money selling beer to your fans). This is most common when the promoter is also the club owner and is happy to break even on the door charge just to get thirsty mouths into the seats. As to the accuracy of the club's count, you'll have to rely on the club's reputation or else have Bruno, your 300-pound roadie, stand at the door and check.

If you're really hot locally, you might get a minimum guarantee of $100 to $250 or so against your share of the gate. Or you may just take a higher fee, of say $500 to $800 per night (with no share of the gate). (I'm basing the numbers in this section on the club scene in Los Angeles, because it's the one I'm most familiar with. These are also based on a ticket price of about $10 to $12. I'm told the basic pattern holds true for most major cities.)

Expenses

The *minimum* cost of putting yourself on the road is the money to rent a van you can use to carry equipment and sleep in, plus three meals a day at McDonald's. And you'd better get along really well with each other, or else expect some violent crimes.

The next step up (three or four to a room in cheap motels, slightly better meals, and maybe someone to help move the equipment) gets a lot more expensive, as you can readily see. But if you watch it carefully, you can get by cheap enough to play the independent circuit and make a few bucks.

If you're headlining larger clubs, or if you're the opening act on a tour, the minimum cost of putting a four-piece band on the road can run around $10,000 per week, broken down roughly as $1,000 for crew, $2,000 for food and hotels, $2,500 for equipment and personnel costs, and $4,500 for insurance, commissions to managers and agents, equipment repairs, etc. With travel, setup, etc., you can't really do more than five shows per week, and you don't need to be a math genius to see that you're going to lose money. Five nights at even $1,500 per night is only $7,500, which is $2,500 per week less than it costs you to be there. And the longer you stay out the more you're going to lose.

So where does this lost money come from? (See page 196 if you don't remember the answer.)

MIDLEVEL ARTISTS

Let's assume you're past the new-artist level, and are selling 250,000 to 500,000 copies of your albums, or selling the equivalent in single-song downloads, or have tons of streaming activity. You now have the option, in addition to opening for a major artist or playing clubs, of headlining small venues, such as 1,500 to 2,500 seaters.

At this point, you should at least be able to break even, and you may be able to take home a nice profit. If you're playing small venues (1,500 to 2,500 seaters) or if you're going out as an opening act, you should be able to make about $5,000 to $50,000 per night. If you're headlining small **amphitheaters** (meaning venues of about 5,000 seats), you can get anywhere from $20,000 to $100,000 or more per night, depending on the ticket pricing.

As we touched on earlier, many artists like to keep their tickets cheap (in the range of $20 to $35 per ticket), for their credibility and/or the fact that nobody will come if they raise their prices. If this is you, because of the expense of being on the road, you'll break even or make a small profit. However, if you're able and willing to charge $40 plus per ticket, you can make a tidy profit. And if you can get a $50 to $60 or higher ticket price, you could get $250,000 or more per night! Note also, because your expenses are fixed, the first $10 to $15 per ticket covers them. Thus, almost every dollar of increase (which isn't exactly true because the promoter, manager, and agent take a part, as we'll discuss in more detail in a minute) goes directly to your bottom line (meaning into your pocket).

At midlevel you can also get into **splits,** which is usually 85% of the profits. (We'll discuss splits in detail under superstars, so I won't ruin the surprise. But see the superstar section if you like ruining surprises.) The only difference is that the guarantees against splits at this level are of course lower than the superstars' (midlevel artist guarantees are in the range of $7,500 to $25,000 per show, or more if you raise your ticket price).

HERITAGE ACTS

Heritage acts are classic artists of the 1960s, '70s, '80s, '90s, etc. that once filled **arenas** (12,000+ seaters), but no longer sell huge numbers of records or draw big crowds. They've settled into a comfortable touring groove that keeps them on the road for most of the year and makes them a good living. Other than the obvious superstars from these eras (Paul McCartney, Madonna, U2, etc.), their deals fall somewhere between the high end of the midlevel deals and the superstar deals of the next section. They play amphitheaters, festivals, fairs, performing arts centers, and casinos, and generally stick to comfy places with plush seats because most of their fans are older (despite what the band may think). The plus side of an older audience is that they have more money, so the acts can charge more for a ticket—after all, it's not just a show, it's a trip back to their youth (well, musically, anyway).

A lot of the heritage dates are something called a **soft ticket,** which means that people come for reasons besides the show. For example, casinos give free tickets to their high-rollers; performing arts centers have season subscribers; and fairs draw people who may catch the show after a day of deep-fried Twinkies and pig races. (**Hard tickets** mean just the opposite; it's a show where people only come to see the act, such as an arena.)

Because the heritage bands are on the road a lot, and therefore hit the same markets frequently, they often package themselves in a double-header. That's to keep people from saying, "I think I'll pass because I saw them last year."

SUPERSTAR TOURING

Now we get into some real fun. And some real money. If you pay close attention, I'll tell you how to put a lot more bucks in your pocket. If you choose not to listen, don't get mad when your agent, personal manager, and other team members have more money than you at the end of the tour.

Splits

First let's look at the money you can earn. Here's how the deals work when you're a superstar: Instead of being paid flat fees, you get a **guarantee** against a percentage of the **net profits** or **gross** of the show. (As with the new and midlevel deals, your share is called a *split.* These deals are also known as **versus** deals, because you get a guarantee *versus* a percentage, whichever is higher.) This guarantee works exactly the same way as an advance against your record royalties (see page 86); if you don't make any profits, you still keep the guarantee. If you do make profits, the promoter deducts the guarantee and pays you the excess.

These numbers are not chopped liver. Major artists in arenas (meaning venues of 12,000 to 20,000) get guarantees in the range of $100,000 to $500,000 plus per night, sometimes as high as $1,000,000 or more. Also, major artists can often sell multiple nights in the same venue, which can be a substantial savings of costs—you don't have to move the equipment, yourself, or your crew every night, and you can get a better rental rate for the concert hall when you're a "long-term" tenant.

The usual split is from **90/10 to 85/15,** meaning the artist gets 90% (or 85%) of the net profits of the show, and the promoter gets 10% to 15%. Superstars sometimes push promoters even further (e.g., 92.5/7.5, or even 95/5), but that takes a *lot* of clout and it only kicks in after the promoter has gotten back all their money. For example, there might be a 90/10 split until the promoter breaks even, 92.5/7.5 to a certain level above break-even, then 95/5 after that. (There are also deals based on *gross*, which we'll discuss on page 410.)

Here's an example: If a date has gross ticket sales of $250,000 and the promoter's expenses are $150,000, there will be $100,000 in net profits ($250,000 income less $150,000 expenses); 90% of this, or $90,000, is paid to the artist. If the artist got a $60,000 guarantee, this is deducted from the artist's share. Thus the artist gets an additional $30,000 (the $90,000 share of profits less the $60,000 guarantee):

Gross Ticket Sales	$250,000
Less: Promoter Expenses	−$150,000
Net Profits	$100,000
Times: 90%	×90%
Artist Share:	$90,000
Less: Guarantee	−$60,000
PAYABLE ON NIGHT OF SHOW	**$30,000**

The sensitivity of profits to ticket pricing, which we covered in the previous section for midlevel artists, is even more dramatic when you get to the superstar level. As we discussed, once you've covered expenses, most of the increase goes directly into your pocket. Accordingly, adult-oriented acts sometimes charge as high as $400 per ticket and occasionally even more (though the norm is $75 to $175). At this level, especially when they're playing large venues, the artists can walk away with truckloads of money.

A new trend in ticketing is called **flexing the house,** which means you vary the ticket prices based on demand. There are normally two, but sometimes up to four, levels of pricing: from **P1** (meaning **Price 1,** the most expensive), down to **P4** in the nosebleed section. The gray areas between these sections (for example, the last row of P1 and the first row of P2) are called **flex.** So if the front orchestra is selling well, the promoter may expand P1 to include more of the middle/back orchestra. If demand dies down, those seats drop to a P2 price.

There is also something called **platinum ticketing** that some artists use. It's a program through Ticketmaster that takes some of the best seats in the house and sells them at whatever price people are willing to pay. The theory is that, if these tickets get into the hands of scalpers, the price they'd get is the true market value. So the artist and promoter should share in that true value.

Computation of Net Profits

Let's look at some of the finer points in computing **net profits.** *Net profits* are defined as "gross receipts less the promoter's expenses." The calculation looks like this:

Gross Receipts.   *Gross receipts* means gross monies from ticket sales, less selling costs (such as ticket fees), taxes, and facilities charges. That's pretty straightforward, but your team should go to great lengths to make sure you get an accurate accounting. For example, some of my clients have their tour accountant "count the house" (meaning they actually count the number of seats and people in them) and/or (especially in dates where there are no seats) stand at the door with clickers and count the number of people that come in (in response to which one promoter opened three other entrance doors without telling us).

Also included in gross receipts are the monies from **VIP Ticketing**, which I'll talk about in the next section. Sometimes **sponsorship** money is also included, which is discussed in the section after VIP Ticketing.

Expenses.   From the gross, the promoter deducts every expense he or she can possibly think of. The major ones are:

1. Advertising. It's obvious when you think about it, but not until then, that the more important an artist you are, the less advertising money the promoter has to spend. One or two announcements of a major show usually does it. So watch this expense. On the other hand, major stars don't want the promoter to

underspend, either. Advertising can be a cross-promotion for a current album, and your tour should be perceived as an "event."

Some of the larger promoters own their own advertising agencies, and the ad agency charges 15% on top of the advertising monies paid to Internet sites, radio stations, newspapers, etc. For example, if the promoter spends $10,000 on radio ads, their ad agency would charge an extra $1,500 (15%), for a total of $11,500 in computing your profits. The promoters argue that if they used an unaffiliated advertising agency, they'd have to pay this 15% (which is true), so why should you get a break? You say that the promoter owns this agency, so the money is only moving from one of the promoter's pockets to another. If you have enough clout, most or all of the 15% disappears.

2. Rent for the facility
3. Personnel (box office, cleanup, ushers, ticket takers, door-men, etc.)
4. Rental of equipment (PA [public address system], lights, pianos, etc.)
5. Insurance
6. Security
7. Stage crew
8. Ground transportation for the artist and entourage
9. Catering for artist and crew
10. Public performance license for the music (see page 241 for what this is)
11. Medical
12. Elvis impersonators (just seeing if you're paying attention)

Over the years, as promoters got more and more squeezed (or in some cases more and more greedy), they developed systematic ways of "adding" to the expenses. Crasser promoters have been known simply to create phony invoices for various items. A more sophisticated example is where the promoter advertises so much on the local radio station that they get a rebate at the end of the year. In other words, if they spend $100,000 for ads on a radio station, the station gives them back $5,000 at year end. This doesn't show up on each individual invoice, and thus the shows are charged for the full amount. Another example is a rebate that promoters get from Ticketmaster and certain venues, which they also don't share.

The interesting part is that everyone knows what the promoters are doing, and thus there is this little "waltz of the toreadors" while your agent negotiates how much the promoter can steal from you (using much more civilized terms, of course). Because everyone knows what expenses really are, there are accepted amounts of stealing, and it's bad form for (a) the promoter to steal more than is customary; or (b) the artist to "catch" the promoter and not allow the accepted level. So in this bizarre nether land, everyone reaches a happy compromise.

Promoter Profit Deals

In a **promoter profit deal,** a promoter's profit is added as an expense, which has the effect of delaying your split of proceeds until the promoter gets a negotiated amount of money. For example, if the gross from a particular show is $100,000 and the expenses are $60,000, the net profits would be $40,000 ($100,000 minus $60,000). If your deal is 90/10, you would get 90% of $40,000, or $36,000. However, if the promoter negotiated for a profit of $10,000 to be added as an expense, the net profits would only be $30,000, because the expenses are now $70,000 (the $60,000 actual expenses plus the promoter's $10,000 profit). Thus you would get only 90% of $30,000, or $27,000, instead of $36,000. (In other words, you got $9,000 less because you are paying 90% of the $10,000 profit.) As your bargaining power increases, the promoter's ability to add a profit disappears.

These deals are also called **split point deals.** That's because adding a promoter profit raises the *point* at which you *split* the net. Using the above example, if there were no promoter profit, you would split monies after $60,000 of gross income (when the gross equals the expenses). In a split point deal, you wouldn't start sharing until the gross equals $70,000 (expenses plus a $10,000 promoter profit), so $70,000 becomes the split point.

Splits Based on Gross

Some superstar acts get a percentage of gross income. (In these deals, the expenses are of course irrelevant.) The range is 65% to 70% of gross, and the artist can get even more when the ticket prices are high. Remember, the expenses are fixed, so that as gross income (i.e., the ticket price) goes up, expenses become a smaller percentage of the gross. Which means the artist can get a bigger and bigger piece of it. For example, if the expenses were $50,000 and the gross was $100,000, the expenses are 50% of the gross. But if the gross was $200,000, the $50,000 expenses would only be 25%. So the higher the ticket price, the bigger the artist's share of gross.

Actually, these deals are not based strictly on "gross," but on something bizarrely called **net gross**. *Net gross* means the promoter's gross income, less surcharges (amounts the building adds to the ticket price and keeps for itself), ticket fees, parking (if parking is part of the ticket price), and taxes.

VIP TICKETING

Another profit center for big tours is **VIP Ticketing.** These are P1 tickets (the most expensive tickets) packaged with a value bonus. The bonus can range from a basket of goodies (signed photo, signed poster, special T-shirt not otherwise available), to a special area in the venue with drinks and maybe food, to a meet and greet with the artist after the show. Some VIP packages let you get into the venue early, to watch a **soundcheck** (essentially a rehearsal where the artist does a few songs onstage to make sure the sound is right in the arena), often followed by a question-and-answer session with the artist from the stage.

If you're doing a national tour with one promoter (more about that later, on page 415), VIP Ticketing is usually built into the overall deal. If not, there are companies that specialize in VIP Ticketing who will handle this for you—they put together the packages, sell the tickets, make arrangements with the venues, manage the fans when they get there, etc. The VIP Ticketing companies charge 20% to 30% for this, which includes all the costs (the merchandise, customer service fees, building rentals, etc.).

SPONSORSHIP

Major tours can do deals with sponsors for the tour, though this has become less common over the years. The terms of the deals vary massively, depending on the stature of the artist, the length of the tour, and the rights the artist is giving to the sponsor. For example, is it just a tour sponsorship, or is the artist also doing a commercial? Are they the only sponsor? If not, are they the main sponsor, or are they an "also presents"?

I've seen deals from as little as $10,000 for a baby band, up to seven figures for major stars. I know that's not particularly helpful, but it's a little like trying to answer the question, "How much is a car?"

The major deal sponsorship points are:

1. How many dates are they sponsoring?
2. In what territories?
3. What is the exclusivity? In other words, if a soft drink is the sponsor, what products do you have to avoid besides soft drinks? It's almost always bottled water, but it could be liquor. Sometimes the soft drink company owns other companies that make random things like computers, so they don't want you endorsing those either.
4. Is the artist doing a commercial? If so, in what media, and in what territories? And how long can they run it?
5. Can they use your music in their ads? If so, who is paying the record company and publisher?
6. Do they get free tickets? The right to purchase tickets before the public gets them?
7. Will there be a "meet and greet" with the artist for the sponsor's guests? If so, how many guests, how many shows, and where?
8. How will the sponsor's name be positioned on tickets, and in tour ads?
9. How will the sponsor's banners be positioned in the venues?

I'm only scratching the surface, because these deals are pretty complex, but you get the idea.

HALL FEES

Over the last few years, agents have become responsible for negotiating hall fees. A *hall fee* is the amount charged by the building for selling merchandise (T-shirts, posters, etc.), and it's a percentage of the gross sales. This is discussed in detail in the next chapter, so hang loose 'til then.

RIDERS

The actual contracts for each appearance are customarily handled by the agency. At lower levels, they're merely AFM printed forms, though most agents have standard forms they attach to this. As you hit midlevel to superstar, they're the same printed forms with an attached **rider** (an addendum that *rides* on top of another contract). Your attorney (together with your manager and agent) puts the rider together for you, and it's the guts of the deal. The contract itself is only one or two pages, spelling out the specific terms (dates, guarantee, hall size, splits, etc.). Riders typically run thirty pages or more.

Here are the major points covered in your rider:

Expenses.   If your deal involves a split of profits, the promoter's expenses should be listed separately, with *maximum* amounts for each category. (Sometimes this list is in the contract itself.) In other words, the rider says you can only be charged for the actual expense, or the maximum in the contract, whichever is *less*. The rider should also spell out your right to verify expenses by examining invoices, checks, etc.

Free Tickets.   You want to have a certain number of free tickets (called **comps,** an abbreviation of *complimentary*) to each performance for yourself (usually fifty to one hundred, though that varies with the size of the venue). You also want to limit the amount the promoter can give away without your consent (usually twenty-five or so). (Remember, most of the revenue lost to free tickets comes out of your pocket, because 90% of the lost ticket money would have been yours.) If you have a tour sponsor, you may have to give and/or sell tickets to them, and the rider would cover this as well.

Free tickets are usually a minimal item, and not a big deal. However, some artists may not do so well in certain cities, and the promoter sometimes gives away as many tickets as humanly possible, to make the house look full. This is called **papering the house,** and it's done very quietly. (If you find a lot of police officers, firefighters, city councilors, and similar folks boogying and/or holding their ears in your audience, there's a good chance you've been papered.)

I use an interesting clause that says the promoter's free tickets can't be in the first ten rows. Can you guess why? (Answer on page 419.)

Billing.   You of course want 100% headline billing, and you should have the right to approve the presence and size of anybody else's name in the same advertising, publicity, or sign.

Recording.   The rider should have strict prohibitions against recording your performance in any way, whether audio and/or visual. And it should require that each ticket states the show can't be recorded. A poor-quality (or even worse, a good-quality) bootleg recording is a serious rip-off of your professional life, not to mention a possible violation of your record deal. I put in extraordinarily tough language, including high damages for a violation.

With the advent of smartphones, it's impossible to keep audience members from photographing or recording shows (unless you hire storm troopers to goosestep through the auditorium). However, you can print on the ticket that they can't use professional equipment, or commercially exploit what they record, and your contract should make sure that neither the promoter nor anyone working at the concert records anything.

Merchandising.   Your merchandiser will require you to include specific language giving them the exclusive right to sell merchandise at your concert. (Merchandising is discussed in Chapter 24.)

Interviews/Promos.   Be sure the promoter can't commit you to any interviews or local sponsors without your consent.

Catering.   I have so much fun reading the catering requirements of riders that I've made it a hobby. Many riders have three or more full pages of food and drink that the promoter has to provide for the artist and the crew. They range from mundane foods for the crew to true exotica for the headliner. (I always get a kick out of artists who require whole-grain macrobiotic food, together with six cases of beer and two gallons of tequila.) Here are some of the better items, actually lifted from various riders over the years:

Turkey (white meat only; never rolled or pressed)
Gourmet-grade coffee—no canteen type
Lactaid nonfat milk
Shelled red pistachios
M&Ms, with the brown ones removed

Technical.   You need to have very specific technical specifications for your show, such as size of stage, what equipment the promoter must supply, power requirements, exact security needs, dressing room facilities, sound check (meaning the time you can come into the actual venue and set the levels of your sound equipment), etc. Sometimes this is in a separate tech rider.

Legal.   Riders have a lot of legal sections regarding cancellation, bad weather, riots, mechanics of payment, insurance, etc.

I'LL TAKE THE WHOLE THING . . .

As I said earlier, a number of artists are selling their entire tours to one promoter. These deals look very similar to single-night deals, except of course they cover all the dates. The major economic difference is that all the dates are *cross-collateralized* (we discussed this concept in record deals on page 89). For tours, it means the promoter gets back their losses on turkeys from successful shows. This of course isn't good for you as an artist—without cross-collateralization, you'd get paid on the good dates, and the promoters would eat the bad ones. On the other hand, you can usually get a larger overall guarantee in these deals, because the promoter is hedging their risk.

Sometimes you can get a limited cross-collateralization. For example, the six major market dates are crossed with each other, but not the other dates; the eight secondary market dates are crossed with each other, etc.

These deals are easier administratively, in the sense that you only have to do one contract and negotiate one rider for the entire tour, as opposed to separate negotiations for each date. But since you're dealing with a huge promoter, and gargantuans like to flex their muscles, you don't have as much leverage.

As discussed on page 411, when you're doing one of these deals, the issue of VIP ticketing comes up. The national promoter wants these rights as part of the package, and their guarantee is priced to include that income.

The major promoters have a division that does VIP Ticketing. There are also independent companies that will handle it for you, but if the promoter allows you to use one, it will want the income put into gross (which means they can use it to recoup their guarantee). You can sometimes make a deal up front to keep this income yourself, but it will mean less of a guarantee.

The national promoters also want to share in any tour sponsorship income. Their argument is that it's an element of the tour, and they're helping facilitate it. But this is negotiable. Some deals include sponsorship if the promoter finds the sponsor (for which they'll want a 20% fee off the top, before putting the money into gross). With enough clout, and if their advance offer wasn't based on getting tour sponsorship money, you can keep at least a portion of the sponsorship income outside the pot. Certainly they shouldn't share in the money for a commercial that has nothing to do with the tour.

There's some controversy over what these one-promoter tour deals mean for the agents. Some people argue that, since you only have to make one deal (instead of the usual multiple deals for a tour with different promoters), maybe you don't need an agent. On the other hand, someone needs to supervise the national promoter, make sure you get an honest count, make sure the promoter is making the best deals with the venues (in fact, some of these promoters own the venues, so you have to be especially careful how they deal with themselves), etc. So arguably these big promoters need even more supervision—you're dealing with one powerful source, rather than a number of smaller players.

Good, bad, or ugly, these deals are becoming the norm for major acts. However, as the promoters consolidate into bigger and bigger chunks, more little seedlings wind their way to sunlight through the cracks. In other words, alternatives to the big players are starting to grow up as real forces in the marketplace. These are the "invisible venues" I described on page 401, meaning fairs (it may surprise you to hear that fairs pay big money for artists, because it brings people in to see their prize cows and spend money throwing darts at balloons), casinos (similar idea of luring in spenders), and performing arts centers, which are theaters of about 3,000 to 4,000 seats that traditionally put on classical symphonies but have found they can make money booking pop artists, particularly those with an older demographic.

LINING YOUR POCKETS WITH MORE GOLD

And now to my promised method of making you more money. Let me first say a couple of words about money in general.

More Income versus Cutting Expenses

It's more expensive to put another dollar of income in your pocket than it is to put a dollar of coast savings in your pocket. This may sound a bit weird, so let me explain.

For every dollar of income you make, you have to pay your manager, agent, and perhaps business manager and/or lawyer (if they're on a percentage) out of it. This will leave, for example, only about 65¢ to 75¢ to go into your pocket. On the other hand, for every dollar of expense you save, the whole dollar goes in your pocket because you've already paid the professionals on the money that would have been used to pay the expense.

Let's look at an example: Suppose your tour grosses $1,000,000, and your professional team's fees total 35% ($350,000). This means that you have $650,000 after commissions, out of which you must pay

$400,000 in expenses. Thus, your net after everything is $250,000 (I'm ignoring income taxes).

Had you earned another $100,000 on the tour, 35% would have gone off the top to your professional team, leaving you $65,000. Since your expenses are already covered, the full $65,000 would be in your pocket. Thus, your net after everything is $315,000 ($250,000 plus the $65,000). On the other hand, if you didn't earn another $100,000, but instead saved $100,000 in expenses, the picture looks quite different: Instead of deducting $400,000 in expenses, you'd deduct only $300,000, and your net after everything would be $350,000. You thus keep the full $100,000 by cutting expenses, *which is almost 60% more than the $65,000 you would put in your pocket by earning another $100,000.*

Here's a chart:

	Example	EARN $100,000 more income	SAVE $100,000 expenses
Earnings	$1,000,000	$1,100,000	$1,000,000
Less Commissions (35%)	−$350,000	−$385,000	−$350,000
Subtotal	$650,000	$715,000	$650,000
Less Expenses:	−$400,000	−$400,000	−$300,000
NET	**$250,000**	**$315,000** ($65,000 more in your pocket)	**$350,000** ($100,000 more in your pocket)

If you add another zero or two to these numbers, they get even more impressive.

What to Do

How do you pull off this minor miracle? It's pretty simple, but you may not like the answer:

Spend less.

Here are the biggest areas of abuse:

Salaries.   Watch carefully how much you're paying your band and crew, and really think about how many of them you need. This is primarily your manager or tour manager's area of expertise, and you obviously don't want to scrimp on essential personnel. But you don't always need to carry as many people as you think, or to pay them as much as they demand. And it's not just salaries—it's hotels, transportation, food, etc.

Be extra careful with friends and relatives. Hiring "pals" with little or nothing to do is not only wasteful, it's demoralizing to the people who really work.

Stage, Sound, and Lights.   Your stage, sound, and lighting systems have to be up to your level; anything less cheats your audiences. On the other hand, these expenses can eat up a large chunk of your profits. And the costs aren't just the obvious ones of building fancier sets. Larger staging means you need to hire more trucks to haul the stuff around, hire more folks to drive those trucks, and hire more crew to load, unload, set up, and tear down.

Remember, your fans are there to see you perform, and if you need an array of trapeze artists and rocket ships to keep their attention, either something is wrong with your show or you're being insecure and hiding behind the hoopla. (You're better than that—you wouldn't be where you are if you weren't.) Of course you should do something innovative and spectacular, but be practical as well.

Travel.   You can save a lot by traveling light. This means two things:

1. Almost nothing I know of (except non-income-producing real estate and owning a restaurant) eats money like chartering (or heaven forbid, owning) your own jet. As you reach a certain level, it makes economic sense (or at least not a significant difference) to begin chartering planes. But for the most part, flying commercial is feasible and substantially less expensive. I know it's more inconvenient—the hassles of the public in the airport and on the plane, delayed flights, missing flights, etc.—but every major celebrity and political figure has at one time or another flown commercial, and all survived the experience. Remember, it's *your* money.

2. Try not to **hub.** *Hubbing* means you base yourself in a central location (say, Dallas–Fort Worth) while you play venues within a short flight from that city (other parts of Texas, Oklahoma, and Arkansas). When you stay in one place like this, you double your mileage—every day you not only fly to the gig, but you have to fly back. And most artists like to hub out of expensive cities, which increases your hotel/lodging bills.

Catering. Some artists are particularly notorious for having lavish spreads backstage, much of which is never eaten by them (or even touched by human hands). Or, worse yet, it's eaten by the hangers-on who show up to see what they can scam. (I said that to make you mad; but it's true.) Because these goodies are supplied by the promoter as part of your deal, it feels like the promoter is paying for them. But the truth is that 90% of this expense is yours. Remember, as you get into the major leagues, you make only a portion of your money from the guarantee. A nice chunk of it comes from the profit split, which is usually 90/10 (see page 406 for a description of profit splits). Thus, every dollar spent on food for scavengers is 90¢ less you put in your pocket. So ditch the imported caviar and order in from Burger King.

Just Watch It. The above isn't exhaustive; there are many other ways to cut expenses (and I'm always surprised that people find even more innovative ways to spend money). I know the road is a hassle and you want to be comfortable. There's nothing wrong with that. But be mindful of your expenses and keep them down. You'll be glad you did when you get home and count your take.

Answer to question on page 413:

Nothing is as much fun as playing your heart out to a standing, screaming audience, only to have a bunch of coat-and-tie zombies sitting in the first ten rows looking at their watches.

PART VI

Merchandising

24

Tour Merchandising

So now you're famous, and kids can't wait to plaster your face on their backs, fronts, bedroom walls, etc. And bootleggers can't wait to rip off your picture with illegal merchandise (more about bootleggers later).

How do you make money from your face? Selling products (posters, T-shirts, bumper stickers, etc.) with your name or likeness on it is called **merchandising** (which is also called **merch**), and there are two basic kinds:

1. **Tour merchandising.** This is the stuff sold at concert venues, for prices you would never pay anywhere else, so you can prove you were there.
2. **Retail merchandising.** This is basically the same stuff (without tour names or dates), but it's sold everywhere *except* concerts, like retail stores, Internet, mail order, through fan clubs, etc.

Of the two types, tour merchandise is by far the more significant moneymaker (assuming, of course, that you're touring; otherwise, it doesn't mean much). While retail merchandising may be more visible, it doesn't create the same sales frenzy as concerts do, for the obvious reasons—people are all pumped up by the show, they want a souvenir, etc.

So let's discuss tour merchandising first, and we'll deal with retail in the next chapter.

MERCHANDISERS

Merchandising at concerts (and also at retail) is handled by licensing the right to use your name and likeness to a **merchandiser.** A *merchandiser*, very much like a record company, manufactures the goods, oversees the sales at your concerts, and pays you a royalty for each sale.

ROYALTIES

The computation of merchandising royalties is a lot easier than record royalties. For the most part, they're just a percentage of the **gross sales.** *Gross sales* is a term of art, meaning the selling price to the public, less only taxes (sales tax, value-added tax, excise, and similar taxes), and credit card fees. **Value-added tax,** or **VAT** to its pals, is something we don't have (yet) in the United States, but it's common in other countries. VAT is a tax on goods at each stage of creation, based on the "value added" at that point. For example, there's a tax on the lumber mill as it cuts down a tree and turns it into lumber (adding value); a tax on the furniture manufacturer when it turns the lumber into furniture (more value added); a tax when the upholsterer does its thing, etc. The tax gets bigger at each stage, but through a system of crediting back (which I have never had any need to fully understand, so I don't) each guy gets a credit for the tax paid by the previous guy: But it pumps up the price to the consumer.

The range of royalties, for sales at concerts in the United States and Canada, is generally 30% to 40% of gross sales (though recently, Canada has been running 3% or so less than the United States). There are higher deals for superstars. It's not uncommon to escalate your royalties based on sales, which can either be on a per-night basis, or a cumulative basis for the entire tour. This is a good thing to remember if you're getting stuck with a low royalty.

The souvenir programs sold at concerts are also based on a percentage of net profits, regardless of how everything else is calculated. In other words, the merchandiser takes the gross selling price, deducts the cost of the goods, etc., and divides up what's left. This is because the merchandisers finally figured out they weren't making much (or any) money on programs, but were paying the artists a lot of royalties. Programs are expensive—they have to be designed, laid out, set up for printing, etc. Thus the profit split evolved, and it's now the norm.

Foreign royalties run somewhere around 80% of the U.S. rate, but if your U.S. royalty isn't that high, you can try for the same foreign royalty. However, you're probably going to end up around 80%. More and more, foreign deals are moving toward a split of net profits, and the usual split is somewhere between 75/25 and 85/15.

Stadiums and festivals are also starting to be profit splits. This is because merchandising at stadiums is more expensive to set up and service, and also because festivals don't sell as much individual artist merchandise (because people want an "event" T-shirt—for example, a

Coachella shirt, as opposed to T-shirts of the specific performers). For stadiums, the artist usually gets around 80% to 85% of profits, and for festivals, about 70% to 75%.

Artists of major status will sometimes have **designer goods,** e.g., an expensive ($60 plus) sweatshirt, or a $100 plus leather jacket. Because a designer is paid a fee (or royalty) on these goods, your royalty is negotiated separately and is lower. Usually it's around 70% of net profits.

HALL FEES

As artists pushed royalties higher, the merchandisers started building in limits on **hall fees.** We touched briefly on hall fees in the last chapter (on page 412), but now let's take a closer look.

Your merchandiser doesn't usually hire people to sell products in each of the venues. Instead, they make a deal with the hall to supply the personnel, display racks, etc. (Actually, as we noted in the prior chapter, it's the artist's agent who makes the deal with the hall, though the merchandiser may help.) It works like this:

The merchandiser pulls up its truck early on the day of the show, checks in a certain quantity of merchandise to the hall personnel, and at the end of the evening gets back the unsold merchandise plus payment for what's been sold or otherwise disappeared. From the money that's turned over, the venue keeps a percentage, and this is the *hall fee*. It covers the cost of hiring the people to actually sell the crap, plus the venue's profit. It often includes a charge (usually 1% of gross) for bootleg security (more about that in a minute). (By the way, not all venues actually supply the merchandise personnel themselves. There are a couple of companies that contract with venues to supply the vendors. In that case, the independent company gets a percentage of the hall fee from the venue.)

A standard hall fee is from 25% to 30% of the gross monies collected for the merchandise, and superstars can sometimes knock it down even lower. So if you sold $10,000 of merchandise, the hall would keep 25% to 30% ($2,500 to $3,000) and pay the balance to the merchandiser. These are U.S. numbers. You can sometimes get lower fees (around 20%) in foreign markets. You can also negotiate a lower fee (10%) for CD sales, if you sell your CDs in the venue.

The buildings like to stick a 5% credit card fee on top of the hall fee. The merchandiser will want to deduct it from your end, but try to either get the building to lower the fee, or take it "off the top" from both you and the merchandiser.

Historically, the royalties paid by merchandisers to the artist were based on gross sales without regard to hall fees. So the hall fees never affected the artist. However, as artists demanded higher merchandising royalties, the merchandisers had their profits squeezed so tightly that they began making artists responsible for hall fees above a certain percentage. So today's deals almost always set a limit on the hall fees, and if you go over it, the excess comes out of your royalties. For example, a merchandise deal might say that you have a royalty of 37% and that the hall fee cannot exceed 30%. Under this deal, if your hall fee for a particular date was 35% (i.e., 5% more than the allowed 30%), the extra 5% would come out of your royalty, and instead of 37% you would only get 32%.

By the way, unless you ask, you won't get any part of the savings if you're able to push the hall fees below the maximum level. So in the above example, if you got the hall fee down to 25% (i.e., you saved 5% below the 30% maximum), you'd still only get 37%. If you do ask, you can usually get a percentage (50% to 75%) of the savings. So in this example, if you got 50% of the hall savings, when you push the hall fee down to 25%, your royalty increases from 37% to 39.5% (the 37% royalty plus 2.5% for 50% of the 5% hall fee reduction). Your argument to win this point is that if you don't share in the decrease, you don't have any incentive to do it.

Another deal that's becoming more common is for merchandisers simply to pay the artist a combined royalty/hall fee percentage of, say, 65% to 70%. Under a 65% deal, for example, if the hall fee was 30%, the artist would get a 35% royalty; if the hall fee was 25%, the artist would get 40%; etc. In other words, the artist gets 100% of the hall fee savings, as well as 100% of the burden for higher fees.

Of course, in a profit split deal, the hall fee is just one more expense, so you and the merchandiser are proportionately bearing it.

As noted above, hall fees are negotiated by the artist's agent (at the same time they make the overall deal for the guarantee, splits, etc.). Ironically, the agent doesn't get paid for this—the agent's commission is based on the artist's earnings from the performance only, and not from merchandising. So the agent is in the position of negotiating a part of the deal that gives him or her no benefit. However, their incentive goes way up when the artist glares daggers at them, and so they have gotten quite good at muscling down the hall percentages.

ADVANCES

As you learned from record and publishing deals, where there are royalties, there are advances. And merchandising is just such a place. Unfortunately, they're not nearly as favorable as record and publishing advances, because they're almost always **returnable** (meaning you might have to pay them back), and they sometimes bear interest. We'll discuss that in a minute.

Merchandising advances are usually paid over the course of a tour. For example, if your merchandising advance is $250,000, you might get $50,000 when you sign the deal, $100,000 one-third of the way through the tour, and the balance two-thirds of the way through. As your bargaining power goes up, you get more of the advance sooner. A lot of artists use their merch advance to pay for the startup costs of a tour: Before you go on the road, you buzz through a fair amount of money to buy equipment, rent a rehearsal hall, hire crew, and (for bigger artists) build a set, put together sound and lights, or hire dancers, jugglers, and mimes.

The size of the advance is based on a projection of your gross sales times your royalty rate. It will therefore be bigger for larger tours—the more bodies you play for, the more merchandise you can sell. Advances will also be higher if the deal includes retail merchandising (which we'll discuss in the next chapter). Because they are so deal-specific, it's hard to give you any hard-and-fast numbers. The broad range is anywhere from nothing to $10,000 or $20,000 for a baby act, to several million for a superstar.

Because the advances are returnable, a number of artists opt for a better royalty rate and less of an advance, particularly bigger artists who don't need the money. If you're with a good merch company, you can often make much more money this way.

TERM

The term of most merchandising agreements is one album cycle, or until the advance is recouped, whichever is *longer* (note this means the deal could go on forever). An album cycle is usually defined as beginning on the date of release of your album, and ending sixty days prior to release of the next album. If you have this kind of deal, you'll want to add an outside date of, say, two or three years, in case there never is a "next album." (The three years would be extended if you're unrecouped.) If the deal isn't based on an album cycle, it'll be based on your tour cycle, which means it continues until the end of the tour (or until recoupment, if longer).

When you're negotiating, try to get the right to repay the advance and terminate the deal during extensions for nonrecoupment, so that you don't find yourself with a perpetual merchandiser. For example, if you have a tour cycle term with an extension until recoupment, and at the end of the cycle you have recouped all but $10,000 of a $200,000 advance, it means you've done pretty well. However, if you don't have the right to repay, the term would continue until you recoup. Thus, the merchandiser would get your next tour automatically, for no advance. If you have the right to repay, however, you can write them a check for $10,000 (which should be more than covered by the advance you'll get for your next tour), and move on. Or more commonly, you rattle your sabre by threatening to repay the advance, which brings the merchandiser to the negotiating table and gets them to pay you an additional advance to make a new deal. (This payback right can only be good for you. If the unrecouped amount is very large, it means something is seriously wrong and you won't leave because no one else wants you; if it's a small amount, you want the ability to pay them off or renegotiate the deal for the next tour. For this very reason, this provision is also getting harder to come by.)

ADVANCE REPAYMENT

As noted above, unlike record and publishing deals, tour merchandise contracts require repayment of the advance, generally with interest. This is triggered by things like:

1. The tour doesn't start on time.
2. You're disabled or otherwise unable to perform all or part of the tour. This is based on the same theory as the tour not starting on time, and also protects them from the possibility that you might not tour for years, after which the public has forgotten you exist.

When you negotiate these provisions, make sure you don't have to pay back more than the unrecouped balance. A lot of deals talk about paying back "the advance," so be sure this isn't yours.

EXCLUSIVITY

Tour merchandise deals are of course exclusive, as the merchandiser doesn't want anyone else selling stuff with your name or smiling face on it. The usual restrictions say you can't sell your merchandise within two miles of a concert site, within forty-eight hours prior to the show.

Be sure you exclude retail sales from this restriction (otherwise, you'll be in breach of both your concert and your retail sales agreements). You should also exclude any record company promotions (such as T-shirt or poster giveaways to promote your album) and any merchandise the record company has the right to make (see page 195).

If you have a tour sponsor or have done a commercial, and they have the right to give away or sell merchandise, you have to deal with this specifically in your merchandising agreement—and your merchandiser isn't going to like it very much. So be extremely careful in giving these rights to a sponsor. The usual compromise is to limit the amount of merchandise the sponsor can give away in that city for a number of days before the concert, which is in both your and the merchandiser's interest. (If the sponsor gives all your fans a T-shirt just before the show, your concert sales won't be so hot.)

CREATIVE CONTROL

You should have the right to approve the design, artwork, photos, drawings, layout, etc., used in all merchandise, as well as the quality of the goods themselves. For the most part, merchandising companies give you creative approval without much of a fight (in stark contrast to the wrestling match you have with your record company over these same issues).

Speaking of photos, you'll often have to go back to the photographer before you can use your photos in merchandise. The same might be true of an artist who created unique artwork for your album cover, or who designed a special font, etc. The reason is that, when record companies hire photographers and artists, they only pay for the minimal rights they need to use the material in connection with your records. That means the photographers and artists keep all other rights. It also means you don't have the right to put their work on your merchandise.

So you have to go to the artist/photographer and say, "How much?" The answer is usually a flat fee that varies with the stature of the photographer/artist who created the work, and the rights you want. Occasionally (rarely), they get a royalty.

It's essential that you clear the merchandising right *before* you use the materials, or else the photographer/artist will have you in a squeezy-squeezy and demand a seriously huge amount of money. By asking early, if you find out that the rights aren't available at a reasonable price, you can use something else.

If you have a federally registered service mark for your name (see page 382 for what that is), you need to approve the merchandise quality in order to preserve your mark's legal status. Even if you haven't registered your mark, however, you should still insist on approving quality for purposes of maintaining your rights in the name, as well as keeping up your image.

SELL-OFF RIGHTS

At the end of the term, the merchandiser wants the right to sell off any remaining merchandise, usually for a period of six months. They should have no right to *manufacture,* only to sell whatever is on hand. The merchandiser will ask for the right to sell it through wholesale (meaning retail) outlets, since there won't be any concerts. You get a royalty for these sales, which is the same as if they were sold under a retail deal (see the discussion of retail royalties on page 434).

Here are some other things to ask for, which are very similar to the sell-off rights under print music deals (see page 284):

1. Before they can sell anything after the term, you should have the right to buy the remaining merchandise at their cost, plus some percentage (usually 5% to 15% of the cost). *Never* take the *obligation* to repurchase; if they can't sell this crap, why would you think you can? *Always* take the *option*—if you're successful, your next merchandiser may want it, or you may want to sell it online.

    If you buy your inventory, the merchandiser would of course have no sell-off rights. If you don't buy it, the merchandiser gets a sell-off period (usually six months), and you should restrict what they can do by asking for the following:
    (a) Their sell-off right must be totally non-exclusive, so it doesn't interfere with your making a deal with a new merchandiser.

(b) The merchandiser can't **stockpile** goods. This means it can't manufacture a ton of goods right before the end, so that it has a lot of leftovers to sell. You should get language that restricts manufacturing to "only such quantity of goods as is necessary to meet reasonably anticipated sales requirements."

2. State that your merchandiser can't do **distress sales,** meaning they can't sell your goods at low prices just to get rid of them. (This practice is also called **dumping.**) Otherwise you'll be adorning a lot of 99¢ Store shoppers and swap-meet fans. It also perturbs your new merchandiser, who's trying to sell your stuff at full price. However, this has become extremely hard to get over the years, as merchandisers' profits have been squeezed, and their tolerance for dining on leftover goods has been stretched to the regurgitation point.

3. At the end of the sell-off period, they should again offer you the remaining merchandise at their cost plus 5% to 15%. If you decide not to buy it, they should have to destroy it, or else donate it to a charity.

BOOTLEGGERS

Merchandisers want the right, and you should encourage them, to chase **bootleggers.** Bootleggers (as the name implies from its original usage during Prohibition, where bootleggers sold illegal booze) are people who, without any authority, manufacture merchandise with your name and/or likeness on it, and sell it outside the venues. Legitimate merchandisers are always inside the facility; bootleggers are the guys who hit you on the street or in the parking lot. (One of their better tricks is to hire college students for $100 or so per night, so the vendors look wholesome, clean-cut, and somewhat innocent, while the manufacturers stay out of sight.) Not only are these people costing you money because you don't get paid for the merchandise, but their goods are usually of inferior quality. And guess who gets the complaint letters when some Tucson fan's T-shirt shrinks to fit her Barbie doll?

The legitimate merchandisers have been relatively successful in dealing with these pieces of slime, and have discovered that in many cases they are large, sophisticated operations (one even owned its own T-shirt factory). Through means I'm not free to tell you, the merchandisers have been able to track the bootleggers down, and then get the courts to stop them. (The laws abroad aren't always so hospitable.) The merchandisers will ask you to pay part of the money to chase the pirates, but if you have some clout, they'll front it and charge it back to you, either out of any money recovered from the bootlegger and/or from your other royalties.

25

Retail Merchandising

Retail merchandising means all the non-concert ways of selling merchandise—retail stores (poster shops, Walmart, H&M, Zara, Gucci, etc.), mail order, Internet, fan clubs, etc.

A retail merchandiser acts not only as a manufacturer/distributor (as you would expect), but also as a middleman between you and other merchandisers. There are tons of small companies that specialize in particular areas (posters, buttons, belt buckles, stickers, patches, trading cards, condoms, etc.), and it's better to license some of these rights to an expert. Also, it's not economical for the merchandisers to engage in all these areas, since they're not great profit centers compared to clothing. However, there are some really meaningful licenses, such as liquor deals and slot machines.

So, retail merchandisers are only apparel manufacturers, and they **sublicense** these other rights (meaning they re-license the rights to someone else). The merchandisers keep a percentage of the license income, ranging generally from 15% to 25%. In other words, they make a deal with a company to manufacture and sell bumper stickers with your name, then pay you 75% to 85% of the royalties and advances they get from the sticker company. In exchange for their percentage, they negotiate and sign the license agreement, and afterward police it (read "make sure you get paid"). Because entering into a number of the small licensing agreements yourself is best described as a "pain in the butt for small money," paying this percentage is usually worth it. And even on the big deals, if they deliver you a major opportunity, and use their expertise to maximize it, they bring value to the table.

As you move further into the superstar realm, you may want to make some of these deals directly. However, unless it's a big deal (like liquor or a slot machine), it's not usually worth the aggravation.

By the way, because many of these license deals are such little money, and the merchandise can be on the cheesy side, a lot of artists don't do them at all. They think it hurts their cachet, and in the long run, that affects their overall value in the market. So however you handle this, make sure you have approval of all the licenses.

ROYALTIES

The royalties you get when merchandisers manufacture the goods themselves (as well as the royalties they get when they license someone else to do the manufacturing) are generally in the following range (for the United States). This includes T-shirts, sweatshirts, hats, posters, buttons, cards, bumper stickers, belt buckles, etc.:

1. **Retail sales:** 15% to 25% of the wholesale price for top-line re-
    tailers, depending on bargaining power. For the midlevel stores
    (JCPenney, etc.) you'll get 75% of these rates, and for mass-
    marketers (Kmart, Walmart, Target) you'll get 50%. The reason
    for lower royalties is simple: Stores that push out tons of mer-
    chandise have a lot of clout, and they beat up the merchandise
    distributor to give them lower prices (which means there's less
    profit for the merchandiser, so they can't afford to pay a full roy-
    alty). It's just like that great schoolyard tradition: He who gets
    beaten up, turns around and beats up the next smaller person.
2. **Internet sales:** 25% to 35% of the *retail* price, less sales tax, ship-
    ping, credit card fees, and the like. These royalties are higher
    because the merchandiser is the actual retailer selling directly
    to the public, and there is no distributor taking a profit in the
    middle. Thus they get more for the goods than when they sell
    them to a wholesaler.

Foreign royalties are roughly 80% of the U.S. rates.

OTHER DEAL POINTS

When you make a retail merchandise deal, most of the considerations are exactly the same as tour merchandising deals, such as:

1. Approval of the merchandise items
2. Approval of your likeness
3. Approval of the designs and layout

4. Restrictions on sell-off rights

5. Right to purchase merchandise at the end

In addition, there are a couple of points peculiar to retail:

Approval of Sublicenses. As we discussed, you want the right to approve all agreements that your merchandiser makes with sublicensees (see page 433).

Cross-collateralization. If your retail agreement is with the same company that has your tour merchandise (which it almost always is), you have to deal with whether the advance under the tour agreement is cross-collateralized with the retail deal (and vice versa). (For a discussion of cross-collateralization, see page 89.) Cross-collateralization is never good for you; allow it only if they offer you a humongous amount of money that you can't get any other way.

If you're on the *Fast Track* and you're interested in Classical Music, go to Chapter 26 on page 439.
If Classical music puts you to sleep, saunter on over to Motion Picture Music in Chapter 27 on page 445.
If you answered "None of the above," *Fast Track* to the Conclusion on page 495.

CAUTION

Before you tackle the rest of the book, be sure you have a pretty good understanding of record and publishing basics in Chapters 7, 8, 15, 16, and 18. If you skipped ahead and don't already know this stuff, I suggest you go back. Even if you're reading straight through, you might want to review those chapters quickly. The areas we're about to discuss are a bit complex, so be sure you have a solid grasp of the basics before attempting them.

Keep your arms and legs inside the car at all times.

PART VII

Classical Music

26

Classical Music

I shall now tap my baton on the music stand to politely engage your attention, as we move into the world of classical music. Please do not applaud between movements, and speak only in quiet, mellifluous tones for the duration of this chapter.

The principles of royalty, advance, etc., are the same for classical as for rock and all other kinds of music. In particular, **crossover** artists like Andrea Bocelli (*crossover* meaning their appeal extends beyond the classical market) have deals that are virtually identical to the contracts we've discussed for pop artists. At the other end are the traditional, pure classical deals, which look quite different. These "classical" classical deals have become rare over the last few years for one simple reason: Their economics suck. Classical records are very expensive to make and have limited sales potential. So unless you're a major-name classical artist, record deals are very hard to come by, and the ones that do get made have very modest terms.

TERM AND PRODUCT

Because classical artists don't generally compose the material they record, and because their recordings are in essence "live performances," they can make records much faster than pop artists. Also, since the compositions already exist, the recordings can be planned very far in advance, which is not generally possible in the pop world. So for both of these reasons, classical artists can record several albums per year. Historically, classical deals would commit the company and artist to two or three albums per year, and the term of the deal would be for several years, firm. However, as the classical market continues to shrink (or at least not grow), and costs continue to rise, multi-album commitment deals have dropped off radically and are rare except for very significant artists. Instead, similar to pop deals, the record company commits to one album at a time, with options for more.

ROYALTIES

As noted above, the economics of classical music are quite different because the potential sales are so much smaller, and the costs of recording can be quite large. For example, the cost of recording with a full orchestra can run $150,000 to $400,000, and typical album sales are in the 5,000 to 10,000 unit range *worldwide* (the sales levels that we've been using for pop artists are only for the United States). In fact, a "big seller" classical album is 50,000 worldwide.

In light of the low sales levels, you won't be surprised to hear that royalties in the classical world are also lower. The good news, however, is that you're paid on every record sold, meaning the company eats all of the recording costs. In other words, the only thing recouped is the advance you put in your pocket. As you've seen, this is a radical difference from the pop world, where the company will recoup anything that crawls (remember, in this section, we're talking about the traditional classical deal, not crossover artists whose recording costs are recouped just like pop artists).

How much lower are the royalties? A typical deal is in the range of 7.5% to 10% (See page 93 for the range of pop music royalties). However, classical artists' royalties aren't "all-in" (see page 96), which means you aren't responsible for a producer, and thus you keep all of the royalties (though you often have to share them, as noted in the next paragraph).

In classical, unlike pop, albums are often amalgamations of several artists. This means the royalties get spread around. Important guest soloists get a royalty, and so do both major conductors and very successful orchestras. In fact, it's sometimes difficult to tell whose album it is. Take, for example, an album on which Leonard Wheezebottom, violin virtuoso, performs with the Tarzana Symphony (Lil Wayne conducting). Is that a Lil Wayne, Tarzana, or Wheezebottom album?

Just like joint recordings on the pop side (see page 161 for what those are), the royalties are allocated among the participants in an agreed proportion. While there's no hard-and-fast rule, a principal soloist might get 4% to 5%, a conductor 1% to 2%, a guest soloist 2% to 3%, and a well-known orchestra 1% to 2%.

ADVANCES

As noted above, a typical classical release sells far less units than a typical pop release (or at least far less than what the pop company hopes to sell). So because of this, advances are much smaller, typically in the range of $5,000 to $10,000 per album. If an artist has "marquee value," meaning that his or her name is recognizable (e.g., Yo-Yo Ma, Plácido Domingo, John Williams, etc.), the advance is generally from $15,000 to $50,000.

The size of an advance also depends on:

1. The extent you participate in the recording. If you're only guesting, for example, your advance will be lower than if you're the principal soloist.
2. The expense of the recording. If you're the principal piano soloist on a recording, for example, you'll get a lower advance for an orchestral recording (which is expensive) than you will for a recording of piano solo works (where they just set up a microphone and drop a few bucks in your brandy snifter).
3. And lastly, your advance depends on that common denominator of all business: clout.

MECHANICAL ROYALTIES

Much of classical music is in the public domain, which means that no mechanical royalties are paid for the music (see page 343 for an explanation of public domain, and page 229 for a discussion of mechanical royalties). However, some of the compositions may be more recent, or even contemporary, and the record company has to pay mechanicals to the publishers of these works. Also, as we discussed, arrangements of public domain works are copyrightable if they have enough originality, and these also bear mechanical royalties.

When a company has to pay mechanical royalties, there is often a reduction of your royalty. You're usually charged about half of the burden, although this is negotiable, and it's not always as simple as I've just stated. For example, sometimes the contract just says that your royalty rate goes down a point or two if the company has to pay mechanicals. By an amazing coincidence, this also results in your eating about half of the mechanicals.

MARKETING TIE-INS

Because of the limited market for classical recordings, the companies look for alternative ways to market their albums. For example, a great way to move product is for you to appear in a public television special, perform a concert tour, etc. If you have some clout, you can get the company to commit money to these ventures. For example, you might get tour support (which we discussed on page 196). Or they might help pay for a PBS special. While TV shows move records nicely, they're very expensive—public television only pays $50,000 to $100,000 for their programs, while the costs can easily run $500,000 to $700,000 or more. (You might get some money back from selling the show to foreign television, or DVDs, but it's not usually much.) So the rest has to come from somewhere—guess where? If the record company picks up the shortfall, the amount they spend (or only 50% of it, if you push them) will be recoupable from your record royalties.

If you're on the *Fast Track,* and you're interested in Motion Picture Music, go to Chapter 27 on page 445.
Otherwise, *Fast Track* to the Conclusion on page 495.

PART VIII

Motion Picture Music

27

Overview of Motion Picture Music

Congratulations! You are now in graduate school. To understand music in films, you need a complete knowledge of the music business (records, copyrights, and publishing), as well as a knowledge of the film business. I couldn't have put this chapter earlier in the book, because you wouldn't have been ready for it. But now you are, so let's go.

INTRODUCTION

I have seen music screw up more motion pictures than bad directors. This is because music is a stepchild in movies. Its budget is small in comparison to the budget of the film, and as you'll see, music in films is really complex. It's normally left until the last minute, at which point there's a massive panic and very little time to get it together properly. Often this is for a good reason—it may not be possible to record the music until the studio knows exactly what the picture looks like—but many times it's simply a matter of neglect. As music supervisors became more important in the industry (more about them later), this seems to have changed (a little). However, there are always panicked emergencies, no matter what.

ONE SONG—EIGHT DEALS

One of the main difficulties is that film people, by and large, don't fully understand music (not that they should—their expertise is in making films). And it doesn't help that film music is complicated. For example, for every song going into a film, there are always deals to be made with at least three, and often up to eight, different folk:

1. The performer (singer/instrumental)
2. The record company to whom the performer is signed
3. The record producer
4. The songwriter
5. The publisher to whom the songwriter is signed
6. The owner of a master recording that's sampled in the song
7. The publisher who owns a song that's been sampled
8. The record company putting out the soundtrack album

If you have several songwriters signed to different publishers, several performers signed to different record companies, and a number of samples, you can get up to fifteen or twenty deals for just one song!

Now if any of these balls drop while you're juggling, or if any of the rights under one agreement don't match those required by another, the song may have to be trashed. And film producers on a tight delivery schedule with a multimillion-dollar film at stake don't like to be told that a song is holding up their picture (would you?).

For all these reasons, the music supervisors/business affairs/lawyers/ studio executives in charge of film music have extraordinarily difficult jobs. If they deliver the music and pull off a minor miracle by balancing all the competing interests, it was expected and they're lucky to get a thanks. However, if something goes wrong and the film producer can't use the song, they're the villains. Wanna sign up?

To sum it up, clearing music for films is (as we say in Texas) like being a one-legged man in an ass-kicking contest. But it's fun and satisfying when it works, and if you're strong of heart, come along and I'll show you this side of the business.

THE RIGHTS INVOLVED

Film music rights fall into two categories:

Acquisition of rights for the picture. These are deals to put music in the film, meaning deals with:

1. Performing artists
2. Songwriters, composers, publishers
3. Record producers
4. Record companies (both for use of existing masters or samples in the film, and for clearing the right to put new recordings of their artists in the film)

Licenses of rights from the picture company to others. Once the film company acquires the rights, these are the deals to let other people use the music. Specifically:

1. A deal with a record company to release a soundtrack album
2. Licensing film clips for music videos
3. Possibly a publishing administration deal

28

Performer Deals

OVERVIEW

The deal for an artist to perform in a film consists of two distinct parts. One is to perform in the picture itself (which is pretty straightforward), and the other is to use the performance on a soundtrack album and/or single (which can be horrendous).

PERFORMANCE IN THE FILM (NO RECORD RIGHTS)

The deal for an artist to perform a song in a picture is usually for a flat fee. No muss, no fuss, no complications. However, as we discussed on page 185, most record deals say that the record company owns all "recordings" made during the term, and that language is broad enough to include film recordings. Also, home video devices and electronic transmissions of the film require the record company's consent, because these are treated as "records," as we discussed on page 73. So the record company becomes a cozy partner in these deals, usually wanting a nice chunk of the fee. Often they'll want all of it, but will graciously apply half against your account. However, this is negotiable.

Since you can't make this deal without the record company's consent, you have to involve them as soon as a proposal comes up. So, before you even start negotiating, *you must clear the deal with your record company.* In case you didn't hear me, *Before you start negotiating, you must clear the deal with your record company.*

Today, the major film companies have been stung enough to make sure the artist's record company has blessed the deal. But minor and independent film companies may not be so careful, and in the rush of the moment, anyone can slip in a puddle of *oops*. Also, there are sometimes missed signals and miscommunications. For example, a manager might think he's cleared the rights with the record company, and indeed he has (sort of). He may have discussed it with the company, and the company said it "sounds okay." However, the record company meant their approval was subject to working out a deal to compensate them, while the manager believed they had approved without qualification. So the moral is: Have the film company talk directly to the record company.

Of course, if you can build an exclusion for soundtracks into your record deal at the outset (see page 183), you don't have to worry about this. But most of the time you can't. And even if you have an exclusion, you may not want to use it for this film. (If the record company agrees to a particular soundtrack, you might want to save the exclusion for a time when they don't.) Or you may have already used the exclusion—the exclusion may only allow one cut every album cycle or so, and there may be a second film you want to do. Or the film company may require more rights than your exclusion allows. So be sure everyone knows what everyone else is doing.

Fees

The artist's fee can range anywhere from union scale (see page 88 for what that is) up to $400,000 plus for a major artist. The norm is about $5,000 to $10,000 for a minor artist, escalating to somewhere around $15,000 to $25,000 for a midlevel artist. Superstars tend to be in the $100,000 to $200,000 range, with some occasionally going higher if the film company is hot for them and the star is playing hard to get. Title songs (i.e., songs played over the opening or closing credits) pay better than background music. If the artist is also giving the film company soundtrack record rights and songwriting services, big names can get $200,000 to $400,000 plus.

Featured instrumentalists (for example, a solo violinist playing over the titles) get fees in the range of $10,000 to $20,000 for lesser-knowns, and sometimes as high as $100,000 for big names.

There is a recent trend to bring in specialty vocalists the same way that featured instrumentalists are brought in—sort of like being a "vocal instrumental." Usually it's someone well-known in their particular genre, like opera, Native American chanting, fraternity songs, etc. These folks usually get a fee of about $10,000 or so per track. It can go much higher if they're well-known and their vocal might help sell records.

If you're getting the high end of these fees, they're often all or partly treated as an advance against your royalties (we'll discuss soundtrack record royalties in a minute).

All-in Deals

Some artists prefer to negotiate an all-in type deal with the film company. For example, for a total of $75,000, they'll record and deliver a completed track. In this case, the artist pays the recording costs out of the $75,000, then keeps the difference as a fee.

Unless the fee is extraordinarily high, and the artist produces himself or herself, I generally don't like to do this. Directors are fussy about what goes into their films, and you don't want to be in the position of having to re-record it several times at your expense. Also, if the artist is not the producer of the recording, you have to pay a producer's fee to someone else, which can be an unknown variable. I much prefer just having the artist show up, sing, and leave.

Credit

The other major negotiating point is credit. Unless you have the main title song (which I'll talk about in a minute), you won't have much to say about credit. Just make sure your credit is no less prominent than any other artist's, both as to size and placement in the film. In reality, this means you'll be included in the **crawl,** which are those credits resembling an eye chart that roll by at the end of the film after everyone's left the theater. (Everyone except me, that is, because I always stay to see who did the music. Half the time I can't read it because it goes by too fast.)

If you do the **main title song** (meaning the song at the beginning of the picture, as opposed to the **end title song,** which is, not surprisingly, the song played over the credits at the end), you can sometimes negotiate a credit in the **main titles.** *Main titles* are where the director, writer, and stars are credited, and are usually, but not always, at the beginning of the picture. Whether or not you get main-title placement, a title song performer should be able to get a **single card** credit (meaning no other credit is on the screen at the same time as yours), or at least a card shared only with the songwriter. Other folks who will want to be on that card are your music producer and your record company.

You should also ask for your credit to be the same size as the director's, writer's, and (film) producer's credit.

RECORD RIGHTS TO FILM PERFORMANCES

When we move into records, things get more complicated. *Way* more complicated.

First, as with your performance in the film, you must clear things with your record company. This is doubly important when the film company wants record rights, which is directly in their backyard.

Assuming you get your record company to go along, you then need to negotiate a deal both for the use of your recording in the film (remember, your record company may try to grab a part of your fee, as we discussed on page 449), and for the use of your recording on the soundtrack album. There are seven aspects to the album part of this:

1. What's your royalty?
2. Is your royalty paid to you (rarely) or to your record company?
3. What can the company distributing the soundtrack album recoup against your royalty?
4. What can your record company recoup against your royalty?
5. Exactly what record rights does the film company get?
6. Does your label get the right to use the master, and if so, how can they use it?
7. Who is responsible for what in connection with music videos?

Let's take these in order:

Royalty

Artists' royalties on soundtrack albums generally hover in the range of 12% to 14%, all-in (i.e., including the producer), and if you're a new artist, it's sometimes lower. Animated films like to pay even less (pretty much for everything, by the way, since the star is often a singing weasel). If you're midlevel and up, this is lower than you would get in the marketplace (because the film company takes part of the royalties). Also, this royalty is pro-rata (see page 160), which means you only get a small piece of the royalty (because you will only have one or two cuts out of the ten or more on the album).

If there are a number of artists on the album at about the same level, the 12% to 14% pro-rata is pretty fair. However, if you're the only star on the record (such as an album whose other cuts are minor artists, or if you're the only song on an album of **underscore** [meaning the orchestral score], or if you're the only superstar among a bunch of midlevel artists), you should definitely get more. In these cases, you're justified in asking for a much higher royalty, say in the 16% to 18% range—sometimes more if you've really got clout. You might also ask for a **floor,** meaning that no matter how many tracks are on the album, your pro-rata royalty will be no less than say ¹⁄₁₀ (or ¹⁄₁₁, or ¹⁄₁₂, depending on your bargaining power) of the total royalty. For example, if you had a 10% royalty and a floor of ¹⁄₁₀, you'd get 1% on the album even if there were fourteen masters. Still another technique is to get a non-pro-rated royalty, of say 1% to 1.5% on the entire album. The companies will kick and scream, but if you have enough clout, you can pull it off. And if you're a big enough artist, try for a higher royalty on single song downloads and streaming of your song.

It's also possible to get escalations based on sales of the album.

An exception to all this is where the soundtrack album is on your own label. In that case, you should get no less than the royalty you get under your record deal.

For a featured instrumentalist or a featured vocalist (which we discussed on page 449), royalties are in the range of 9% to 10%, pro-rated based on the number of album cuts, and further pro-rated if you're performing with another royalty artist (for example, if you sing with an orchestra that gets a royalty). In other words, where there are two or more royalty artists on a track, it's treated as a joint recording (which we discussed on page 161).

The Record Company Piece

Record companies want to collect all the royalties you get from soundtrack albums and singles. They normally keep 50%, as a cost of waiving your exclusivity and allowing your recording to be released on somebody else's label. If you have an enormous amount of bargaining power, you may be able to beat them down below 50%, but it's getting tougher to pull this off. However, if your company happens to be distributing the soundtrack album, you should ask for 100% of the royalty, because you're not being released from any exclusivity.

The companies normally treat your share of royalties exactly the same as all other royalties under your deal. That means they use your share to recoup your deficit, or else pay it to you on your next accounting statement if you're recouped. Sometimes you can get half or all of your share paid to you even if you're unrecouped. The ability to do this varies directly with your bargaining power.

If you get an advance against your royalties, the record company will also want a piece of that.

Recoupment

Unlike record deals, where everything is recoupable, in films you can often knock out a good portion (sometimes even all) of the costs. Let's look at them individually:

Recording Costs. You can sometimes make all or a portion of the recording costs nonrecoupable. You do this is by arguing that the costs of recording are really costs of the film, which they would incur even if there were no album, and thus it's not fair to charge them against record royalties. If you're a superstar, you can pull it off; if you're not, you'll end up with anywhere from 50% to 100% of the costs being recoupable.

Artist's Performance Fee. Another question is whether any of your fee to record for the film is recoupable from your royalties. Again, you can take the position that this is a fee to perform for the film, not on records, and so they shouldn't recoup it. If you have some bargaining power, you can pull this off; otherwise, a part of it may be recoupable. (As a negotiating ploy, if you want to increase your fee and are getting nowhere, try making a portion of the increase recoupable. But use this as a last resort.)

Sometimes, soundtrack albums are financed by a record company that pays for the music and gets the right to put out the album (we'll discuss these deals in Chapter 33). The monies paid by the record company are advances against the soundtrack album royalties, and because the film performers' fees come out of these advances, all or a portion of the fee is often treated as an advance against the artist's royalties.

Conversion Costs. As good as all this news sounds, there are other costs recouped under film deals that aren't chargeable under record deals. They're not charged under record deals for a simple reason: They don't exist in record deals.

These babies are known as **conversion costs,** a name I take credit for inventing. (I'm really a pretty modest guy, but every once in a while something gets the better of me.) *Conversion costs* are the costs of converting a film recording to a master that can be used in a record. For example, the recording for the film might only be thirty seconds, but you need a three-minute version for the album. The conversion costs are the costs to do this, and they include the kind of costs you'd expect, such as remixing, editing, overdubbing additional instruments (called **sweetening**), and sometimes even totally re-recording the song. But they also include something you haven't seen before, called:

Re-use Fees.   Whenever you take a recording made for one medium (in this case, a motion picture) and use it in another (like records), the union charges you a fee. These fees are called **re-use fees** or **new-use fees** because they are charges to re-use an existing recording in a different way (a new use). (Re-use fees are also payable when you go the other way around—taking a recording made for records and using it in a film—and in other situations like going from television to records, records to television, records to commercials, etc.) The reasoning is that, when you use an existing recording, you don't have to hire the singers and musicians you would have needed to re-record the song. Since you're putting union members out of work, the unions allow you to do this only if you pay them an amount listed on a schedule (which is close to union scale for the missed sessions).

The re-use fees charged for a particular recording are directly proportionate to the number of performers on the track. Thus, a three-piece band is cheap, and the Los Angeles Philharmonic Orchestra is not. Indeed, for a fully instrumental, orchestral soundtrack album, the re-use fees can run $90,000 or more.

Conversion costs are almost always recoupable from your royalties.

What Rights Are Granted

If you can help it, you don't want to give the film company any more than the right to use your master in the film, on the soundtrack album, and on a single. This means you're excluding things like compilation albums, licenses for commercials, licenses for other films, etc. You and your record company should control these other rights, although they're often restricted (as we'll discuss in a minute).

Unless you have very little bargaining power and are up against an obnoxious film company (or unless you are dealing with an animated film, where they dig in no matter who you are), none of this should be a serious problem (although the usual form contract gives them all rights unless you change it). The usual restriction required by the film company is that you can't issue a synchronization license for the master (meaning you can't license the master to another film or television show, or a commercial) for a number of years, if not forever. The theory is that they don't want someone else getting the goodwill of a song closely identified with their picture. The other kicker is that some film companies require the right to use your recording in sequels and remakes of the film, as well as ancillary uses such as studio tours. You almost always have to give up these rights, but sometimes you can get an additional fee for the use. Either it's a set fee per use, which the film company pays according to a schedule, or sometimes, with a lot of clout, you can leave it to be negotiated in good faith at the time of the use (with the provision that you can't stop them from using it; you just get to argue about the size of the fee).

Another issue is **co-promotions.** That's where the film company ties into an advertiser (such as McDonald's, Pizza Hut, Burger King, Le Sex Shoppe, etc.). These folks do things like give away plastic cups and toys to promote the movie, hang posters in their stores, hype the film in their advertising, write the film's name on their men's room walls, etc. As part of this package, the film company will want to use your master in radio and TV commercials that promote both the advertiser and the film, and that's a source of negotiation. You may well object to having your voice on a commercial for something besides the film—certainly without getting paid, and maybe altogether if it's inconsistent with your image. Also, if you're a superstar, the right to use your voice in a commercial is a serious exploitation of your persona.

This is usually resolved by bludgeoning you into submission, since the film companies fight hard for these rights—co-promotions can mean millions in advertising for the film. If you have a lot of clout, you may be able to get a prenegotiated additional payment, or even prohibit some or all co-promotions without your consent (which means you can make a deal later, if you're willing to allow it). Another compromise is to limit how the song is used in the co-promotion (for example, it can only be used to promote the film itself, not to promote the product). You may also be able to get category restrictions for co-promotions, though they usually give you things that wouldn't likely sponsor the film anyway, like tobacco or firearms. Alcohol may be an issue if the film wants to go after that demographic, but if you have a personal concern about association with liquor, they'll usually respect that.

Re-recording Restriction. Just like your record deal, soundtrack deals include a re-recording restriction (see page 183). The period is usually five years, but the date can be from recording, from release of the picture, or release of an album or single. If the date is measured from anything except the date of recording, be sure the restriction period someday expires. Also, even during the restriction, try to exclude live streams, festival broadcasts, TV appearances, and the like.

Singles. Another major point of contention is the question of whether there will be a single, and if so, who can put out a single with your performances on it. (We touched on this on page 184.)

The "whether" question depends on scheduling. Singles are the most helpful to the film if they're hits right when the film opens. So if you've got your own single on the radio, your record company won't want a competing single out there fighting for airplay. If that's you, then Presto, Change-o, no single.

Assuming there's going to be a single, the next question is which company can put it out. Historically, the company with the artist's exclusive agreement never parted with singles rights, but this is no longer a hard and fast rule.

Can Your Record Company Use the Master?

One nice goodie you can sometimes get is the right to use the recording on your own records. If the film company allows this, they'll limit it to one album, or maybe one studio album plus one Greatest Hits. They'll also say you can't put it on your record for a period of somewhere between six months (if you've really got clout) to two years, with the norm being around nine to twelve months. The period before you can release the master on your record is called a **holdback.** The clock may start at release of the picture, release of the soundtrack album, or release of your recording as a single. Whatever you do, make sure the date someday arrives. For example, if you measure your period from release of the soundtrack album, and the album is never released, you could never use it. If you ask, the film company will usually agree to an outside date after which you can use it no matter what.

The holdback effectively means the soundtrack recording will end up on one of your Greatest Hits albums, because it's going to be stale by the time they let you use it (especially if it's released as a single in conjunction with the film). Sometimes your record company wants to put the cut on your own album at the same time as the soundtrack album is out (in other words, there's no holdback). The film company (and especially the record company with the soundtrack album) won't like this at all. But if you're important enough, and it's the only way they can get you, they may go along.

In recent years, with rare exceptions (like *Frozen*, for example) soundtrack album sales have been abysmal, so there's been a trend for many pictures not to have a soundtrack album at all. In that case, the only records with the soundtrack cut are the artist's own, and there's obviously no holdback in these situations.

The film company may ask for a piece of your royalty if you use it on your record, and my response is to tell them to stuff it. So far, they've generally stuffed it.

Music Videos

If there is going to be a music video, the record and film company usually share the cost 50/50, and the film company customarily supplies footage from the film (at no cost) to be included in the video.

In the beginning, film companies turned these videos into long previews of the movies. This worked terrifically until the TV broadcasters figured out they were giving away free advertising for the film, at which point the practice came to an abrupt halt. This is less of a problem in the streaming days (though MTV, VH-1 and other TV broadcasters still object), but the film companies now limit use of the footage because of issues with their unions. Basically, they can only use film footage to promote the film, which means it can only be in the song video around the release of the film in theaters, and around the DVD release—if you're not in those time frames, you can't show the video. So as the result of this, there is limited footage from the film in the music video, and there's always a second version without any film footage to be used when you can't use the first one.

The record company will want to recoup some portion of the video costs from your royalties. Remember, in normal record deals, 50% of the video costs are recoupable (see page 157). In this case, however, the record company is only paying 50% of the costs, and thus there is a strong argument that none of it should be recoupable. The outcome depends on your bargaining power.

29

Film Songwriter Deals

TERMINOLOGY

Let's now look at film songwriter deals. By songwriter deals, I mean deals for *songs* (both music and lyrics, or sometimes instrumental only) written for the film, as opposed to what's known as the **score** or **underscore,** which is background music underneath dialogue, action, etc. (We'll deal with underscore in Chapter 30.) Also, this chapter deals with *creating* a song for the film, as opposed to licensing an existing song (not written for the film). (Licensing songs is covered in Chapter 31.)

DEAL POINTS

When you write a song for a film you typically get a fee plus songwriter royalties. If you're a songwriter of even modest stature, you may be also able to keep a piece of the publishing.

Fees

The range of songwriting fees is anywhere from zero to $100,000 plus for established writers. There are occasionally deals even higher in the stratosphere, but they're rare. Zero is even rarer, usually a low-budget film with no music budget, and the songwriter keeps all the publishing (see page 244, where we talked about the fact that songs in films can earn substantial performance monies in foreign territories, as well as on television here). The vast majority of deals fall in the range of $25,000 to $50,000 for major studio films. Whether or not the writer gets a part of the publishing also affects the size of the fee. You can sometimes get additional monies (called **kickers**) based on the success of the film. For example, you might get more dough if the film does $100 million U.S. box office gross; another kicker at $150 million, etc. There can also be kickers based on album sales and/or single chart performance, and sometimes an advance against mechanical royalties.

By the way, a film company will never obligate itself to use a song. The most it will do is agree to pay the fee, which is known as **pay or play** because it can either use you (play) or pay you to go away. This is similar to the pay-or-play provisions in record deals, which we discussed on page 107.

Step Deals

Songwriter deals are sometimes done on a **step** basis, meaning the deal is done over a series of "steps." The steps are:

1. The writer creates the song and gives the company an informal demo recording. They only get a small amount of money for this.
2. If the film company doesn't like it, the company either passes or goes to step two, which requires the writer to rewrite the song for a small additional fee (or maybe no more money). If the company then likes it, it's a firm deal; if not, the deal is off.
3. Once the film company is happy, it goes forward on a prenegotiated deal to use the song. At this point the deal is the same as the songwriter deals we just discussed, although I like to ask for more money because we've covered their downside.

All of this is a fancy way of saying the writer does it **on spec** (meaning "on speculation"; i.e., he or she writes the song without a commitment from the film company to pay a full fee). The deal may be completely on spec, meaning a film company pays nothing or perhaps a few bucks for the cost of a demo. Sometimes the film company pays a small fee (usually in the range of $2,500 to $5,000, sometimes as high as one-half the normal fee) for writing the song, then has the option to go forward if it likes it (by paying the rest of the full fee)

If you're a major songwriter, you should do very little on spec, because you don't want to spend your time working on a project that will pay you half your normal fee. Also, rejection is not good for your self-image, unless you get your full fee. (It's not great even then, but at least you didn't totally waste your time.)

If you're doing a step deal, try to get your song back if they don't accept the demo. The studio will only be out a few bucks, and they shouldn't get ownership rights. Another way around this (*shhh*—don't let them know I told you) is to simply not sign anything until the demo is accepted and the deal is firm.

Rights Granted

Music written for films is always treated as a work for hire (see page 339), so your contract will have the magic language that makes it so. The film companies insist on this because, if it's not a work for hire, you (or your heirs) could terminate the copyright assignment after thirty-five years (see page 344). If you terminate, you might stop them from exploiting their film, or demand a percentage of the gross national product to let them continue. (As we discussed on page 344, there's no termination right for works for hire.)

With respect to usage, the film company wants the right to use your song not only in the film, but also in sequels, prequels, spin-offs, trailers (see page 266 for what all that means), advertising for the film, co-promotions (we discussed co-promotions on page 455), and the like. Over the last several years, film companies have radically expanded the list of things they can do with your song, all without paying you: studio tours, theme parks, live entertainment (like Broadway shows, ice shows, etc.), storyteller and sing-along records, a TV series based on the film, film-themed video games, merchandising, DVD menus, outtakes (scenes deleted from the film), making-ofs (behind the scenes footage of filming), and whatever else they can throw in the soup. You usually have to give up these rights, but with some clout, you can get more money for them—either by increasing your original fee, or getting additional monies if the song is used in one of these categories (you either get a prenegotiated amount or a requirement to pay you a "customary fee" that you can argue about later). If you have a *lot* of clout you can sometimes prohibit some or all co-promotions, or at least limit how the song is used in the co-promotion (see page 456 for the limitation on masters; you can get the same things for the song).

As we'll discuss in more detail in the next chapter, there are also some categories for which the film company gets paid by third parties and still doesn't pay you. In other words, they treat your fee as having "bought out" these usages, even if they get paid.

Publishing

Historically, writers got no share of publishing on film songs. These days, with some clout, you can get from 25% to 50% of the publishing income, and usually the same percentage of copyright ownership. If the song is based on music in the underscore (see the discussion of underscore on page 463), getting a share of publishing is trickier. As you'll see in the next chapter, underscore composers don't get a share of publishing in the score. Thus, since the song includes underscore, the composer won't have a piece of the publishing. By contrast, a lyricist brought in to write the words can get a share of publishing.

If you're the underscore composer, and the song is separately identifiable from the underscore—in other words, if it has a distinct name and lyrics—you should argue for a share of publishing on the song, even though you don't share in the same music when it's used in the underscore. We'll discuss this more on page 463.

Also, if you're the underscore composer and you write a song that is *not* based on a theme in the underscore, you may—if you have enough clout—get a percentage of that song's publishing.

If you do get publishing, the studios want the exclusive administration rights (see page 235 for a discussion of administration). If you've got clout, you may be able to keep co-administration (unless it's the title song, where the studio feels it's so identified with the film that they have to keep control). (Co-administration is discussed on page 330.) Even with co-administration, however, there will be restrictions on synch licenses, as we discussed in connection with masters on page 454 (e.g., you can't license to another film, TV show, or commercial).

If you don't get co-administration, you may still be able to approve certain types of synch licenses (such as commercials), just like in any other songwriter deal (see page 322), but this takes muscle. At a minimum, try for consultation rights on commercials, which means they have to discuss proposed uses with you, but they can make the final decision. Also, try to get paid directly by the record company for mechanical royalties, and by your performing rights society for performance monies, so you don't have to wait for the money to go through the film company.

Some small-budget films will license songs for very little and let the composer keep all ownership, administration, and income from the songs. However, they will restrict synchronization licenses, as we've discussed.

Credit

The other provision negotiated in a songwriter deal is credit. Normally, unless you write the title song, and it's performed by a major artist, you get a credit in the "crawl" (see page 450). If this is the case, there's not much to say except that your credit shouldn't be any less prominent than anyone else's. If you do write the main title song, and if a major artist performs it, you may be able to get credit on a **single card** (meaning no one else's is on the screen at the same time), or on a card shared only with the artist performing the song. However, unless you're the performer as well as the writer, you don't usually get a single card—at best, you share credit with the performer, in a form such as "Title song performed by X, written by Y." Possibly you can get your card in the **main titles** (meaning those listing the stars, director, etc.) and, if so, you should ask for the size to be no less than that of the writer, director, or producer.

If you're a really major writer, you may be able to get credit in the **billing block** of paid ads for the film, but this is extraordinarily hard to come by. (The billing block is that microscopic box of credits down at the bottom of movie ads.) If you do get the credit, it will only be in ads where the writer, producer, and director are credited, since some ads only list the film title and the big stars. A compromise is to get credit in full-page ads in New York and Los Angeles only (which is great, unless your mother lives in Des Moines). You may also be able to get credit in full-page **trade ads** (meaning entertainment industry ads, such as *Variety, Hollywood Reporter*, etc.), so at least people in the industry know what you did.

Top-level writers may also get a credit in ads for the soundtrack album in *Billboard* and other trades.

30

Composer Agreements

Composers are the guys and gals who write the **underscore**. *Underscore*, also called **score,** is the music underneath the dialogue, action, transitions, etc., that you're not supposed to notice. If you've ever seen a film without music, you know how stark and empty it feels. A good underscore can radically increase the impact of a movie, just as a bad one can make a movie feel weird and cheap. (For an example of a bad underscore, watch any porno movie, though I'm told that even they've figured that out and done away with the music.)

You may be surprised to hear that most film scoring is no longer done by a full orchestra sitting in a recording studio, watching film clips on a giant screen. Nowadays, most films are first scored electronically (meaning with just a synthesizer), so the director and producer can approve the music. If it's a small-budget film, that electronic score may be it. For bigger budget films, once the electronic score is locked, the composer brings in an orchestra, clamps headphones over their ears, and has them listen to the electronic score while they overdub their parts (meaning they replace the synthesized violins with real ones, add acoustic instruments, etc.), or in some cases, the composer replaces the electronic score with an orchestra.

With the exception of a few old-school composers, many of whom don't "do" electronics, the studios now expect demo recordings of the score in advance of the finished product, so the director can see the music in context and give it a thumbs up or a thumbs down.

DEAL POINTS

Deals for composers are similar to those for songwriters, except that a composer almost never gets any share of the publishing.

Other than extremely low-budget films (where the composer might keep publishing in the score to compensate for getting little or no fee), the only exception to the publishing ban is where a portion of the underscore is used in a song written for the film (we touched on this on page 461). For example, if you're a composer, and the studio hires a lyricist to write words for one of your underscore themes, you might get some of the publishing for that song. But you only get it if the stars line up correctly, meaning: (1) the music and lyrics constitute a "real song," with its own title, and (2) the lyricist is getting a piece of the publishing on that song (if the lyricist isn't getting a share of publishing, it's much harder for the composer to get any). Assuming all that works out, and you get a publishing piece, it will only be for that melody when it's used in the song. You won't share in the publishing of that melody when it's used in the underscore.

The fee for writing and conducting a major studio theatrical motion picture underscore ranges anywhere from a low of $50,000 to a high of $1,500,000 plus for the superstars. The normal range is from $300,000 to $700,000, though lower-budget independent films are less.

With the downturn in the film biz, and fewer films being made overall, there are less superstar deals, so most top out in the $700,000 to $800,000 range, with the electronics included. The really big deals are reserved for **tentpole** pictures (basically meaning the massive releases, like *Fast and Furious*, *Avengers*, *Iron Man*, etc.) or big budget animated films.

The tentpole and big animated films pay fees to the composer, with the recording costs on top, but for everything else (and sometimes even for the big movies), many studios want to do **package** deals (meaning a lump sum that covers both the fee and recording costs). If you can avoid a package, you'll be better off, though that's not always possible. As we'll discuss in a bit, packages can do some serious damage to the composer's pocketbook if things don't go well.

As composer prices have slid downward, more and more studios are open to the idea of bonuses based on box office gross. For example, you might get $50,000 for every $25 million of box office. Historically, the bonuses were based only on U.S. box office, but now you can get kickers for worldwide box office (usually excluding China, because the studios don't consider the numbers there to be reliable). By the way, you can only get this kind of deal from a studio that owns the international distribution of the film. Studios sometimes sell off foreign rights to independent distributors (for large guarantees that help finance the film), and in those cases, the studio makes little or no additional money from the foreign grosses, so it will only base your bonus on U.S. earnings. In that case, the box office figure should of course be less.

The size of each bonus, and the levels where you kick in, are very deal specific, depending on the budget of the film, the size of your fee, and that ever-present factor, your clout.

Most of the issues we discussed in Chapter 29 concerning songwriters also apply to composers. However, there are some weird twists that live only in composer deals, so let's take a walk down that crooked path.

Delivery Date. Interestingly, composer deals have no term. They go on until the composer delivers, which could mean the composer works on the score for four or five months, sometimes even years. The process starts with **spotting,** which means the composer and director determine precisely which "spots" need music, as well as the exact length of each piece needed (measured in tenths of seconds). (It's interesting to note that a change of even one second in a scene may require a total rewrite of the music. This is because a well-written score moves precisely with the action on screen, and even a slight variation throws everything out of whack. It's like a marching band doing an extra half step between beats.)

Historically, spotting happened only when there was a **final cut** of the film, meaning there wouldn't be any more changes. With animation, and with films that add a lot of special effects after they've been shot, it's not uncommon for the composer to get chunks of the film over time. In this case, they do the spotting and writing for the pieces as they come. And, whether the film comes to the composer in pieces or one big glorious package, it's common for directors to keep making changes in the film, meaning the music has to adjust. (By the way, a good music editor can sometimes creatively edit existing music so the composer doesn't actually have to re-write every time.)

Anyway, because there's no end-date, you could be tied up for a *looooong* time. Which brings us nicely to our next topic:

Exclusivity. Composer deals used to be exclusive until delivery of the score, which meant you couldn't do anything else during that time. Since the studios no longer limit how long they can keep you working, you have to say that your deal is **non-exclusive** (which means you can do anything else you want, as long as you perform on time). However, the studios all require exclusivity from the time you actually start recording the score until you finish.

Payment Schedule. Historically, before you got any money, the studios made you sign something called a **Certificate of Authorship**, also known to its friends as a **C of A.** This is a one-page document that says they own everything you do, and confirms the deal points of your (still being negotiated) composer deal. However, more and more studios have now adopted a policy of not paying any money until the full contract is signed. Because these deals can be pretty complex, this policy can seriously delay your money. If you're working for one of these studios, it's a good idea not to do too much work before the contract is signed.

Composers normally get their fees in either thirds or fourths. If it's in thirds, you usually get one-third on spotting, one-third on commencement of recording, and one-third on completion of services. If you're paid in fourths, expect one-fourth upon spotting, one-fourth on commencement of recording, one-fourth on completion of recording, and the balance on completion of services. "Completion of recording" is almost always the same as "completion of services," but occasionally you have to stick around and help with dubbing the music into the picture, editing for the soundtrack album, sweeping the floor, etc.

Major composers can speed up the payment schedule a bit. One recent deal was as follows (it's in thirds and sixths, but it could also be fourths as well): one-third on commencement of services and execution of the agreement, one-third on commencement of recording, one-sixth on delivery of the score, and one-sixth on completion of all services.

The studios that pay based on a C of A will hold back some money until signature of the full agreement, which may be well after the services have started (or finished). The range is from 10% to one-third of the total fee.

Orchestrations. It may surprise you to know that many composers don't have the ability to write musical parts for each instrument in their orchestras. (In fact, some composers don't even read music, although this is rare. These guys are known in the trade as "hummers.") Most of us assume that all film composers are like John Williams, who is a premier orchestral arranger, and who understands the subtleties of every instrument. However, many composers only write the melody line for the underscore, then give it to an **orchestrator,** who writes out the parts for the trumpets, oboes, clarinets, violins, etc. Next time you see a film, look for the orchestrator's credit buried among the assistants, makeup people, grips, and gaffers (whatever they are).

Orchestrators aren't used only by composers incapable of writing their own instrumental parts. Quite the contrary, virtually all composers use orchestrators, if for no other reason than to save the time and/ or tedium of mechanically doing it themselves. However, classically trained composers often sketch out the parts pretty thoroughly, and the orchestrator then becomes more of a copyist. (By the way, I know of one situation where a composer, under extreme time pressure to finish a film, hired three orchestrators at the same time to crank out the parts.)

The orchestrator is of course paid for his or her services. If it's the composer, or a primary orchestrator, they get a negotiated fee, usually in the range of $80 per page of score. Second and third orchestrators are generally paid union scale, but the better-known ones can get more. Scale for orchestrators varies with the size of the orchestra and number of pages of music. As a rough guideline, at the time of this writing, the price for *simple* orchestrations is roughly $400 per minute of music (e.g., thirty minutes is $12,000). Complex orchestrations can exceed $30,000 for a film.

An important part of the deal is whether your composer's fee includes orchestrations. Even if the film company knows you aren't capable of doing this job, you may be responsible for paying the orchestrator out of your fee. Conversely, you may be perfectly capable of doing orchestrations but (a) your time doesn't permit it; or (b) you're only willing to do the orchestrations if you're paid additional money for the trouble. You should make sure the orchestration fees are on top of your composer fee (if you don't raise this issue, the film company may try to deduct the cost of orchestrations from your money), unless of course you're doing a package that includes everything (as we'll discuss in a minute).

Record Royalties.   A film composer, being a songwriter and not a performer, doesn't automatically get record royalties. Underscore royalties are paid only for (a) conducting the orchestra; and/or (b) producing the recordings, neither of which may be done by the composer. Let's look at them separately:

Conducting royalties.   When conducting, the composer becomes (in a sense) a recording artist by leading the orchestra. The customary range of these royalties is 6% to 10% (though some studios won't go beyond 9%), pro-rated by the number of cuts (see page 160 for a discussion of pro-ration), and further pro-rated for royalty artists on any particular cut (see page 161 for a discussion of joint recordings).

In actuality, many composers don't really conduct. Instead, they hire a conductor and "buy out" his or her royalties for a fee. Thus, the composer steps into their shoes and gets the conductor royalty.

Producing royalties.   If you produce the recordings (see page 125 for what producing is), you can get 3% to 4%. (Note this is independent of conducting royalties; you can produce even if you don't conduct, or vice versa.) Like other producer royalties, these are usually retroactive to record one after recoupment (see page 127 for a discussion of retroactivity). Historically, "producing" didn't mean much more than remixing the masters, since no one really "produced" music that had already been recorded for the film. However, since a lot of scores are now electronically pre-recorded (as we discussed on page 463), composers are in fact doing more production—they handle production of the pre-recorded synthesizer score, then after the orchestra overdubs the pre-record, they produce and mix the final product.

You can usually insist on producing the underscore for records, but composers have had singularly bad luck imposing themselves as producers of *songs*. This is because artists may simply refuse to work with them. The best you can do is say that the film company must use you as the producer of all songs if the artist and record company approve. Sounds great, eh? Unfortunately, it's almost meaningless, because most artists don't want a film composer producing them. (If a composer is a producer of note in his own right, that's of course a different story.)

The studios will insist on reducing your royalty if you produce and then another producer reworks your cuts. Try to have this only happen with your permission, and in any event try not to go below 50% of your producing royalty.

Floors.   Major composers can sometimes get a *floor*, meaning that if you do absolutely nothing on the record, you still get a royalty. Usually it's a guarantee of one or two cuts on the album, although they don't really guarantee to include your cuts. They only agree to pay you as if your cuts were included. In other words, if you have a 10% royalty, and there are ten masters on the album, you would be guaranteed 1% or 2%, even if you don't have any recordings on it. You should also argue for an imputed mechanical royalty on the tracks, since you would have been paid one if the tracks were actually included.

This point is relatively easy to get when the album is mostly underscore, but it gets difficult to impossible if you're working on a film with a number of pop songs (like a Quentin Tarantino movie). The reason is obvious—the company has to pay royalties to a lot of expensive outside artists, and there's no assurance of how many score selections you'll have on the album (if ny).

Some major composers get a guarantee that there will be a score album released (many films don't release score albums, even if they release song albums). In recent years, this has been extremely hard to come by, since there are so few soundtrack albums being made.

Recoupment.   With composers, the record company normally recoups only conversion costs. (Conversion costs are discussed on page 453.) The issue becomes what they're recouped from, and the larger the royalty rate, the faster you'll get paid. The best is the gross royalty payable to all participants, and the worst is your artist/conductor royalty. On the other hand, most deals say you won't get paid until the film studio has recouped everything charged against *their* total royalty, which could be huge advances that will slow you down quite a bit. When they do recoup, your royalties will be payable from the time the conversion costs are recouped—in other words, once they're recouped, you'll get paid on all sales other than those used to recoup conversion costs (this is similar to the concept of retroactive producer's royalties, which we discussed on page 127).

Try to get the *record* company to pay your royalties directly to you once the conversion costs have been recouped. The studios don't like to do this, so you'll have to fight. Your argument is that most of the studio's advances were used to pay artist advances and recording costs, and therefore the studio will be able to recoup those costs from the artists' royalties. Accordingly, it's not fair for them to take these advances and costs out of the overall royalties before paying you. Sometimes you can pull this off, and sometimes the studio will agree only if the record company agrees.

Credit

1. **Credit in the Film.** Composers normally get main title, single-card credit. (See page 450 for a discussion of film credits.)
2. **Paid Ads.** All composers can get credit in paid ads where the full billing block of film credits appears. Midlevel to major composers can get credit in ads even if the only credits are the writer, film producer, and director. (See page 462 about paid ads.)

3. **Soundtrack Album Credit.** Composer credit on soundtrack albums is a hot issue. As we discussed, the composer isn't really an "artist"—he or she only wrote the music, and maybe conducted it or produced the record. So it's not a foregone conclusion that the composer will get credit on the soundtrack album. Which means you gotta ask.

Ideally, you want credit on the front cover of the soundtrack album. The film company will argue (correctly) that it doesn't control this; it's up to the soundtrack album record company. So you'll probably end up with a commitment for the film company to use its "reasonable efforts" to get you front-cover credit.

Whether you get front-cover credit (and the digital equivalent credit) also depends on the nature of the album. If it's a compilation of songs by major artists, you're not likely to get credit on the front cover—bluntly, your name won't sell as many records as the names of the artists. However, if it's a 50% or more score album, front-cover credit shouldn't be too difficult.

You should always insist (and the film company should have no trouble agreeing) that you get credit on the back cover of the album, and anywhere else that the songwriters and artists are credited.

The exact credit can sometimes be a tussle as well. Composers want the credit "Music by," but if there is other music in the film, the studios want to say "Score by" or "Underscore by" or "Flowers by" (OK I made up the last one to see if you were paying attention). The composers fight hard for "Music by."

Other Uses. As we discussed earlier, film companies take the right to use music in more than just the film for which you're hired. As the composer, you pretty much have to go along, but the question is whether you can get more money for any other uses.

As noted in the last chapter, with enormous clout, songwriters can sometimes get paid for sequels, prequels, and spin-offs. However, composers normally don't get additional monies for that or anything else, even in situations where the film company gets money (see page 460 for a laundry list). One exception, if you ask, is for ringtones and mastertones (see page 150 for what these are) *if* the film company gets paid. For those, you can get a songwriter royalty (50%) of the ringtone mechanicals, and a record royalty (whatever percentage you negotiated) on the mastertone sales. However, you won't be paid for promotional uses—if the film company doesn't get paid for these, neither do you.

The other area coming down the pike is the whole business of streaming and downloading motion pictures. What if anything will composers get? So far, the answer is zippo, on the same theory that composers aren't paid on DVDs of the movie.

Travel Expenses. It's not uncommon for composers to travel to places where it's cheaper to record (to places like England, Ireland, Czech Republic, Germany, or Canada, or the slightly less exotic Seattle and Salt Lake City). In this case, you should negotiate for reimbursement of your expenses. On a high-class, big-budget picture, this is usually business-class travel (unless you're Godzilla, or unless it's a very long flight, in which case you can sometimes pull off first class), plus something in the neighborhood of $2,000 to $3,500 per week for New York or London. Sometimes you can get first-class accommodations plus $100 to $150 per day for all expenses besides the hotel (this is called a **per diem,** which I think is Latin for *per day,* but it may be Slovakian for *pay my expenses, cheapskate*). For low-budget flicks, you'll get Greyhound tickets and Motel 6 vouchers.

If you're going to a foreign country, it's important to get your expense money in the local currency, as you don't want to be in the business of speculating whether the dollar is going to be worth more or less than the peso. For example, suppose your London hotel room costs £100 per night, which at the time of your deal is $150. If your deal is $150 per night in dollars, and if the dollar drops against the pound so that your $150 only equals £90, you're in trouble. The room is £100, but you only get £90 for your $150. So you'll be coming up £10 short. If your deal says you get £100, you're covered. For this reason, it may be better to get the studio to cover the hotels and give you a per-diem on top.

PACKAGE DEALS

Some composers are asked to do **package** deals, especially in television and low-budget or independent films. A *package* is very much like a fund in record deals (see page 97 for a discussion of funds). In other words, the composer agrees to deliver a completed score for a set fee, and the fee includes both the compensation for the composer's services and the costs of recording the score.

Not surprisingly, most package deals are done by composers who create electronic scores. In other words, they use a small number of musicians (sometimes only the composer) to create music on a synthesizer (which, these days, can sound like the Academy of St Martin in the Fields).

There are some score package deals that use real orchestras, but they tend to be for really big money (we'll discuss how big in a minute). In these deals, the composer gets the film's entire music budget, less only an amount the studio thinks it'll need to license existing songs and recordings, and/or to create new songs and recordings.

There is also a hybrid package, which consists of synthesizer recordings mixed with orchestral recordings (see the next section).

Package Prices

The price of packages can be anywhere from $50,000 for a low-budget film up to $1,500,000 or even $2,000,000 plus for a mainstream, big-budget feature (though packages in big-budget films are rare; they are mostly low-budget creatures). Pure electronic scores (or electronic scores with up to maybe ten musicians in a package) for major studio films run around $100,000 to $400,000, sometimes a bit higher for top-level folk. The hybrid packages described above (both synthesizer and score) have funds of $50,000 to $250,000 for the synthesizer portion, on top of which the composer gets a market-rate fee for conducting the orchestra. The costs of the orchestra are paid in addition by the studio—in other words, they're not part of the package.

At the other end of the scale, I've seen starving composers do low-budget film scores for a $5,000 to $10,000 package price. In this case I always try to keep the publishing, and sometimes you can get the soundtrack album as well. At the very least you should get a nice chunk of the income from publishing and records, since you're taking so little up front.

Exclusions

If you're going to make a package deal, you have to worry about exactly what's in the package. Most contracts just require you to deliver "all music," and the trick is negotiating what's *not* included. This turns out to be more complicated than you'd think, and through the courtesy of my friend Michael Gorfaine (one of the most experienced film music agents in the business), I bring you the following list of exclusions:

Licensing of Outside Music (i.e., songs not written by the composer for this project). Since most contracts say you must provide "all music," I've seen film companies license an expensive outside tune and expect the composer to pay for it. You can't control the costs of outside songs (indeed, one license could eat half your package fee), so never agree to this.

Note this exclusion is stated as "songs not written by the composer *for this project*." Some composers have a "library" of cues they've previously written, and there's an issue whether those should be excluded from the package price. We'll discuss these babies on the next page.

Recording Costs of Outside Music. If the sessions for outside music can't be scheduled during the normal scoring sessions, their costs shouldn't be included in the package.

Re-use Fees. (See page 454 for a discussion of re-use fees). Not your problem.

Re-scoring. This is one of the most important and trickiest areas. The concept is to save your rear end if the director says he wants bands of angels accompanying his scene, which you record and deliver, only to have him decide later that he really meant heavy metal. In other words, if the film people require you to re-record for reasons totally beyond your control (as opposed to your screw-up), it should be on them.

Lyricist Expenses. If the studio wants a lyricist to write words to your music, it should be on their nickel.

Vocalist Expenses. As with lyricists, if the company wants somebody to croon your newly created song, they should pay.

Music Editor Fees. The music editor's fee should be a film cost, not a package cost. A **music editor** is to film music what a film editor is to film. In other words, he or she is the technical person responsible for getting all the music in the right places. They will create the **spotting notes** (which are detailed notes, down to a tenth of a second, as to where music goes), edit music to fit a scene if the film has been cut, help with any technical difficulties, etc.

Mag Stock and Transfer Costs. **Mag stock** is the actual soundtrack imprinted on the film, and **transfer costs** are the costs of transferring the music from the recording studio to the film. The purpose of this exclusion is to clarify that you only have to deliver a standard audio recording, and that the cost of physically putting the music into the film is a motion picture cost, and not a package cost.

In truth, with digital sound, there are no more mag stock or transfer costs, but everyone still excludes them from the package, and the words sound so cool that I've left them in the book.

Pre-records. This is music recorded before shooting, to be lip-synched and/or danced to in the film. Note these are not demos of themes prior to writing the score (those are customarily included in the package), but rather cuts of finished songs that will actually be in the film.

Since the on-camera action has to precisely follow the recording, these cuts have to be done in advance. A package should include the cost of pre-records only if it's specifically negotiated up front.

For purely electronic scores, pre-records are usually included.

Sidelining. This is a situation where a musician either gets on camera and pretends to perform, or actually performs. Film companies have been known to charge this cost against the package, which again is a matter of negotiation. It's usually easy to exclude if you ask, because the musician is paid through SAG (Screen Actors Guild) as an actor, and this isn't a music cost.

Excess Musicians. It's a great idea to limit the number of musicians you're required to supply. For a television package, this is usually small—in the range of four or five at the most—and the limit gives you ammunition to ask for more money if the director has a sudden attack of orchestra-itis.

Library Music. As noted above, there's an issue over licensing music that was written by the composer, but not written for the film. For example, many composers have built up "libraries" of music that they own and license to films. If you have such a library, you should try to exclude this music from the fee (meaning you can charge them extra if it's used in the film).

The studios don't want to pay anything for your library music; they say they should get it as part of your fee. Their argument (not without merit) is that they're paying you to create new music, and if they give you extra money for old stuff, you're likely to toss in a lot of it. The usual compromise is to say they won't have to pay for preexisting material unless it's used at the film producer's request.

Of course, any of the above exclusions may be included in your package if it's negotiated up front and you budget for it. But be sure they're only in there when you expect them, or you may be paying the film company for the privilege of using your music.

CREATIVE FINANCING

In today's world, there are a number of films that use something known loosely as "creative financing" (not really an industry term). That's where an independent studio (or a major studio for that matter) doesn't have the budget to hire the composer they want, and instead comes up with creative ways to snag their dream person for a lower fee. These are things like:

Back-End Participation. The composer gets a piece of the film's profits, or built-in bonuses at certain box-office levels (the "kickers" we discussed earlier).

If it's a piece of profits (maybe you'll get 1% or so), that looks great on paper. Unfortunately, the reality is that you're not likely to ever see any money. Film company accountants are far more creative than record company accountants, and film profits are defined in a way that makes them virtually nonexistent. Still, if the best you can do is a share of profits, try to get the same profit definition as the director or producer, and hope they had enough clout to get something decent.

Because of this little accounting game, you'll be better off with box office bonuses, which we discussed on page 488. The advantage of box office bonuses as compared to a share of profits is that box office numbers are specific figures, published in industry trades, so there's no question whether or not you're entitled to the money.

Percentage of Publishing. As we discussed, film companies normally own all the publishing for the underscore. In these creative deals, the composer might get ownership and/or administration. Or if not, certainly a share of the publishing income. Sometimes the composer gets a large percentage of publishing until they make a certain sum, then a lesser amount for a while, maybe dropping to zero at some earnings level.

Soundtrack Record Goodies. The composer gets a higher than normal record royalty, or a higher guaranteed number of cuts, or sometimes the right to own the soundtrack album itself, subject to paying the film company a small royalty. If you own it, try to keep all non-film rights, such as ringtones, commercial licenses, etc.

Adding the Advance. The composer's fee or package price is increased by some or all of the advance (less conversion costs) that the film company gets for the soundtrack album, or for its publishing. In these deals, the additional monies are almost always recoupable from the composer's record royalties (for a soundtrack album advance), and sometimes even the mechanicals.

If the composer gets several of the above goodies, there's often a ceiling on the dough. For example, once the composer has made $1 million from all sources (including the fee), the participations drop out. However, the improved record provisions usually go on forever.

TELEVISION COMPOSERS

Television composers live in a different world from film composers. The time they have to compose and deliver is shorter because, as I'm sure you know, television programs are knocked out like little pancakes right before they go on the air. Also, the budgets to produce TV shows are substantially lower than motion picture budgets, so the TV music budgets get squashed down along with everything else. Thus the composer's fees and the money available for recording costs are much less than those for theatrical films.

The good news is that, even though the fees are lower, the performance monies generated by television programs (see page 241) can be substantial—much more than for films—because programs may be shown over and over, forever. And remember that you get performance monies each time your music is played on television. (By the way, when I say "forever," I really mean "forever." My kids watched some of the same shows I did when I was a kid, although they thought the old *Superman* half hours were stupid. I love them.)

Background Score

Because of the short time frame and lower budgets, television music is tailor-made for electronic score packagers (the folks who get an all-in amount that includes both their fee and the recording costs, as we discussed on page 471). In fact, almost all television deals are packages.

Typical package fees (which include recording costs) are around $2,000 to $5,000 for a half-hour television episode, with a few going as high as $7,000. One-hour programs are from $12,000 to $22,000, but the higher end is only paid for shows with really big budgets and lots of music, or shows that have been on the air a long time (the longer they're on the air, the more money the networks pay for them). If the composer is hired for the series, there's usually an annual adjustment of about $200 per episode for half-hour shows, and about $500 per episode for one-hour shows. A two-hour movie-of-the-week package is about $35,000 to $90,000, though for major composers it can be a fee of $25,000 to $90,000 plus recording costs.

With respect to a **pilot** (meaning a single episode of a TV show that is produced as a demo, in hopes of selling the show to a network), and something called a **sales version** of a show (which may only be a ten-minute pitch, never intended to be aired, and which is becoming more and more common), studios pay a very small fee (from $500 for 30 minutes, to as much as $5000 for 60 minutes, including all recording costs and musicians). For these Dollar Store prices, they get a quick electronic score, or cues from the composer's library. For a fully scored pilot, before it's sold as a series, the package fees are between $3000 and $6000. Even though the fees are low, the producers insist on owning any new material created for these programs (though they shouldn't own any preexisting library material).

If the series is picked up by a network, usually one of two things happen.

1. The producer gets additional money for reshoots and additional material to be added to the presentation package. In this case, the total package fee is about the same as, or a little less than, the episodic fees we just discussed.
2. The composer is hired to do the full season of the series, and the pilot becomes one of those episodes. In this case, the composer gets an episodic fee for the pilot (actually, she gets the difference between the fee for the sales version and the episodic fee).

Some composers have started hiring their own music editors. In this case, they include the cost in their package, and typically raise the per-episode fee by $2,000 to $4,000.

Very few TV projects use an orchestra anymore, so the above package fees are for a synthesizer score. If there is an orchestra, it's usually a big-budget production, and the deal is structured as a fee (in the range of $25,000 to $35,000) plus recording costs. In the case where there's a package that includes an orchestra, the orchestra will usually be only a percentage of the music (for example, half of the music) and the package fee will of course be higher (in the range of $45,000 per episode). But this is rare today, probably less than 10% of the television music.

Miniseries deals are mostly done for a per-episode fee (rather than a total amount for the entire series). If it's a package, the fee is about the same as the sixty-minute episodic package fees we talked about. If they're done as a fee deal (with the producer paying the costs on top), the range is about $30,000 to $50,000 for the entire series (divided by the number of episodes if it's paid per episode). If there's a package for the whole series, it's in the range of $100,000 to $300,000, with the higher numbers being for a series with more episodes.

If you want to give somebody a good chuckle, just ask the TV people if you can have a piece of the publishing. In the television industry, the producer's commandment to hold on to publishing isn't just carved in stone, it's tattooed on their foreheads. (Remember all that lovely performance money? The TV guys figured that out, too.) The only exceptions are a few non-studio shows (miniseries, HBO, TNT), where, if you have major clout, you can sometimes get a piece of the publishing income (and rarely a piece of the copyright), though usually not any administration rights.

If you think it's bad enough that the television people want to take your publishing, get a load of this. Some of the smaller TV producers, including cable networks that produce their own shows, are not only getting publishing, but are also taking your *writer's* share of royalties. And every now and then, even some of the bigger players try to do this as well. Under these deals, you don't get any of the performance monies I talked about in the previous section. In fact, you don't get any money for *any* use of the score (besides your fee). And by the way, the fees for these deals aren't any higher than the fees for deals where you keep your writer's royalties!

BE VERY WARY OF THIS. Sometimes you don't know that's what they want until the contract arrives, so you have to be clear up front that you expect writer's royalties. If they absolutely refuse, it may be worthwhile to give up writer's royalties when you first get started (to get credits under your belt), but as soon as you have any clout, fight hard to hang on.

Other deal points are the payment schedule (usually all the money is paid on completion); record royalties, which are usually left to good-faith negotiations, unless the producer knows in advance there will be a record; and credit. Prominent credits are getting harder to come by, but give it a whirl. A half-hour show credit is usually in the end title crawl no matter what. For one hour or more, try for a main title or Act One credit, single card, shared only with the theme composer, though the recent trend (if you can get a single card at all) is for the card to be in the end titles. (See page 450 for what all this credit stuff means).

TV Themes

Composers sometimes write the main title theme for a television show (meaning the theme at the beginning of the show). This is usually done as a package.

If it's instrumental only, the package is in the range of $10,000 to $25,000. Sometimes you can get up to $40,000 or more, if you're a superstar.

For both the music and lyrics of a theme, the package price is more like $30,000 to $60,000.

Studios won't give up publishing on TV themes, but sometimes non-studio players will.

Occasionally the producers hire a Big Name Writer to compose the television theme, and someone else (cheaper) to write the weekly score. Big Name gets the high end of the scale we just discussed, plus a royalty on records close to what film composers get (see page 467).

There's also a trend for producers to license a well-known song for a theme. We discussed those rates on page 266.

If the composer is doing the underscore, the fee usually includes writing an end title theme.

VIDEO GAME COMPOSERS

In recent years, a number of composers have written scores for video games. In days past, these video game scores were predominantly done on a synthesizer. Nowadays, some of them use live orchestras.

Unlike films, where the action moves linearly, video game composers have to pick the right music for every possible twist and turn in the game. In addition to all this juggling, the composers have to write a lot more music. A typical film score has thirty to forty minutes of music, while a typical video game has more like eighty to a hundred minutes.

These deals can look very much like the deals for motion pictures—the music is written as a work for hire, the composer usually gets songwriter royalties, etc. Unlike films, however, there are very little performance monies, for the simple reason that video games aren't played on television or in theaters. However, as games have moved to the online and mobile environment, this may be changing.

Some game companies take a much tougher stance and refuse to pay writer royalties at all (though the writer can collect performance monies from the performing rights societies). Others take a little softer stance and agree to pay the writer a share of mechanicals (not for video game sales; only if the song is exploited on records). However, they won't pay the writer for anything else, even if the game company licenses the songs (and gets money) for third-party uses.

Fees for video games were historically smaller than film fees because the video game budgets are much smaller than film budgets, but as film fees drop, they're getting closer together. While a few deals are the composer's fee plus costs, most of them are done as packages (meaning the fee includes recording costs). These deals are sometimes a flat fee for the entire game, but they're usually done as a dollar amount for each minute of music. It's typically $1,000 to $2,000 per minute, though for big names, it can get up to $3,000 or more. The packages typically include all music costs except third-party music licenses, rescoring after delivery, and any musicians requested by the game company (for example, if they request an orchestra, that would be a separate budget and fee).

If you're on the *Advanced Overview Track*,
go to the Conclusion, on page 495.
Experts: Onward!

31

Licensing Existing Recordings and Existing Songs for Motion Pictures

This chapter deals with licensing existing masters and songs (records and songs *not* created for the film).

MASTER LICENSES

Record Company Masters

Most of the master licenses are, not surprisingly, from record companies. The rest are individual owners of recordings, which we'll deal with a little later. With record company masters, you'll only be involved in the deals as a secondary player because the contracting parties are your record company and the film company, who make a deal with each other. The money is paid to your record company, who promptly pockets half and treats the balance as artist royalties under your deal.

If your record contract says they need your consent to license masters into films (see page 163), they'll call up and ask you to bless the deal. If the record company doesn't need your consent, they may not even call you, although most will as a courtesy. (By the way, even if you don't have the right to consent in your record deal, if you wrote the song and control the publishing, you can block the deal—remember, the right to use the master is only the right to use the physical recording itself. The record company can't give a film company the right to use the musical composition [they don't have these rights], so the film company has to make a deal with *both* the record company and the publisher to get a full set of rights. So, if you're the publisher, you can control the deal through the side door even if you can't do it through the front door. We'll talk about publishing deals in a minute.)

Because you may be asked to consent to these deals, and because you share in the income, you should know how they work. So let's take a look.

A record company/film company master license has two main elements:

1. How much is the fee to synchronize the master in the film?
2. If the master is also going on a soundtrack album, what's the royalty?

Master License Fees

The fee to use the master in the film varies directly with the importance of the song in its own right (was it a number-one single, or an obscure album cut?), the stature of the artist, and how it's used in the film (is it on a radio in the background for ten seconds while people are talking, so that you need a truffle-sniffing pig to even know it's there, or is it played in its entirety, maybe even integrated with the onscreen action, so that it takes on dramatic content and moves the story forward?). Obviously, there are all shades of variations in between, and sometimes it's just a question of how much the producer has fallen in love with a particular cut. The range of fees is the same as what's paid for use of the song in the master, which we discussed on page 300.

You should always ask the record company to pay through your half of the fee if you're unrecouped, on the age-old theory of "Hey, no harm in asking." Most of the time you won't get it, so don't let that affect your self-esteem.

Royalties

If the deal also grants record rights, the range of royalties paid to the record company is 11% to 14% pro-rata (see page 160 for what pro-rata means). You'll get half of this, unless you can bludgeon more out of them. Of course, if your record company is releasing the soundtrack album or a single, you should get 100% of your normal royalty.

If your master is the key master in the album (meaning, for example, it's the only song in an album of underscore, or it's the only hit in an album of obscure toads), then the royalty should be higher, as we discussed for artists (in Chapter 28). In addition, your record company can usually get a **favored nations** treatment for the master (meaning no one gets a higher royalty), at least insofar as other *existing* masters are concerned. The film company usually wants the right to pay higher royalties for recordings that are created for the film.

Since the film company didn't pay the recording costs, the only things that can be recoupable are the union re-use fees (see page 454), and this too is negotiable. The fee paid to use the recording in the film or television program should *not* be recoupable under any circumstances, although film companies sometimes pay a small advance for the record use.

Other Master License Deal Points

The other deal points are about consent: the AFM (American Federation of Musicians) and you.

AFM Consent. There is an obscure rule in the AFM labor agreement that requires not only the payment of re-use fees, but also the consent of the AFM to put existing masters in a motion picture or television program. The theory is that the union won't put musicians out of work (i.e., by not requiring a new recording session) unless it's such a unique master that a new recording won't do justice to the film. An example would be a Buddy Holly master, which can't be duplicated since Buddy isn't available. In actual practice, however, I've never seen the union object to any licensing—in fact, this rule is almost always ignored and no one even asks. If you do ask, their consent is a rubber stamp.

You. Since the licensing deal is between your record company and the film company, you're not directly involved. But once the deal gets under way, the record company will call up your manager and ask if you're okay with the use of your master in a particular film. How do you evaluate this?

On the financial side, you should review the deal and decide if you think it's fair. The above criteria should give you a pretty good feel for it. If the deal sounds okay, then proceed to the next step, which is just as important as checking the financial terms, but often overlooked: You should find out precisely what's going on in the film when your song is being played. I have avoided a number of disasters with this simple question. For example, a film company once wanted to use a recording of one of my clients during a scene where a number of kids were shooting drugs. Or perhaps it's a graphic sexual sequence (which, depending on your image, could be a plus). Remember, it's your music and your career, so be careful about the creative aspects.

Non–Record Company Masters

As we discussed in the section on record deals, artists don't usually end up owning their own masters, and even when they do, they often license the rights to a record company for a number of years. On the other hand, there are artists whose careers are, shall we say, "taking a holiday"—they might have been huge in the eighties or nineties, but they don't mean as much today. Often these artists are "between deals" and have recorded stuff that they own. The same holds true for other artists whose deals have expired, and they've decided they can make more money by recording and distributing their own records. When these artist-owned masters are licensed for movies, the deals are pretty much the same as those outlined above, except of course there's no record company in the middle.

Another type of license is made by composers who have built up a library of instrumental song masters that they license into small films (who then hire someone to sing over the track). This is similar to the underscore library music we discussed on page 474, but they are more than instrumental cues—they're actual song masters without the vocals. These library songs go for anywhere from $500 to $5,000.

LICENSING EXISTING MUSICAL COMPOSITIONS FOR FILMS

As we just discussed, the money paid to use a master goes to your record company. This means two things:

1. Right off the top, they get half of it.
2. If you're unrecouped, you never see the other half.

Not such an appetizing proposition. But remember that the film also needs a synchronization license for the *song* in the master. So if you wrote the song and own the publishing, they now need to make a deal directly with you, and this side of the equation looks very different in one aspect:

You keep all the money.

No minor distinction.

Fees

We discussed the fees for synchronization licenses on page 265.

FILM MUSIC QUIZ

You are the representative of an independent film company, which is producing a teenage motion picture. The music supervisor called Capitol Records and got a license to use the Beatles recording "She Loves You" in the film, for a payment of $10,000. The license is fully signed, the money has been paid to Capitol, and the master has been dubbed into the film.

Assuming you're now aware of everything that's been done, are there any problems in going forward and distributing the film? If so, what?

Answer to quiz:

Here's what's wrong: They haven't licensed the *song* for the film, only the recording. Thus they can't use the track until they make a deal with the publisher. (See page 265 if you want a refresher.)

Also, the Beatles haven't licensed anything for $10,000 since 1962.

32

Music Supervisors

ROLE

A **music supervisor,** as the job title implies, coordinates the music for a film. They primarily focus on the choice of songs, though they may be involved in the underscore as well.

First, he or she sits down with the producer and director to work out the type of music needed, ideally before production. If the film is a musical, or one that relies heavily on music (such as a dance film), the music supervisor *must* be involved in advance. This is because songs performed on camera have to be **pre-recorded,** meaning they're made in a recording studio before commencement of photography of the film and merely lip-synched or danced to on film (we discussed pre-records in the section on composer packages, on page 474). As you can imagine, it's difficult to dance to a song not yet recorded.

Actually, I was once involved in a situation where the opposite happened. A dance scene had been shot to a specific song, but after the film was finished, the writer of the song refused to make a deal with the film company, and the song had to be scrapped. A client of mine then wrote a new song for the dance sequence (obviously having to match the beat precisely), which ended up being a number-one hit.

After meeting with the director and producer, the music supervisor comes up with suggestions for artists, songwriters, composers, etc., for the film. The director and producer make the final decisions, then the supervisor oversees the process of making it happen, often in conjunction with the studio's music department. He or she contacts the creative people, arranges for meetings with the film personnel, negotiates and structures the deals (or oversees the negotiation and structuring, depending on the supervisor and the film company), and supervises the recording sessions.

Done properly, being a music supervisor is one of the most difficult jobs on planet earth. Let me count the ways:

1. Other than pre-recorded music (which we discussed above, and which is a tiny fraction of film music), most of the music can't be finalized until the film is complete (see page 465 for why). The studio has millions of dollars riding on a specific film release date, and music is at best considered a minor element in the overall production, even if it's a central element in the film. (The cost of a *major* music budget is maybe $1,500,000, while most major studio films run $40 million to $100 million, not to mention the multimillions for advertising and marketing. And $1,500,000 is a huge music budget. More typically, music budgets for major films run about $500,000 to $1,000,000.)

2. Most studio executives (with a few outstanding exceptions) don't understand music nearly as well as they understand films (which is why they're film executives instead of music executives). This can make it very difficult to conclude a deal—the executives think the prices demanded by the music people are outrageous (which they often are), and they have no patience for the complexity of a bunch of little deals.

3. Each piece of music in a film can represent eight or more deals (see page 445 for what they are), and because music comes in last, complicated deals have to be made under enormous time pressure, which geometrically increases the likelihood of mistakes.

It's the music supervisor's job to keep all these competing interests satisfied and to ensure a happy ending. So good music supervisors are worth their weight in gold (maybe platinum). They call on their relationships to pull favors and smooth out difficult situations, getting music into pictures that couldn't be there any other way. Music supervisors are in a sense "marriage brokers." They creatively marry music and films, which is no easy process, as well as marry the two industries on a business level (which is even more difficult).

Unfortunately, because the film industry went into distress and the number of films being produced dropped radically, the number of music supervisor jobs shrank as well. There was a double whammy: there aren't very many films with a big enough music budget to afford a supervisor, and a lot of this work went in-house (meaning studio employees now do the work) because it's cheaper. But there are still music-intensive films that have supervisors, even smaller budget ones, and television shows with heavy music (like *Empire*) use them regularly.

The supervisors that are working, however, still get paid nicely. How nicely?

FEES AND ROYALTIES

Music supervisors can get fees of $25,000 to $100,000 per picture (sometimes even more). The top supervisors also have royalties on the soundtrack album, usually in the range of 1% to 2% non-pro-rated. There may also be escalations of .25% or .5% at 500,000 and 1,000,000 units. These royalties are payable prospectively after recoupment of all costs, at the same time the film studio recoups.

In addition, there may be box-office bonuses based on the picture's gross, just like the deals for composers that we discussed on page 475.

TELEVISION SUPERVISORS

Over the years, a few television shows have licensed extensive amounts of existing music to create a "cool vibe" for the show. Because of the rushed production time frame in television, and the smaller budgets, and the fact that television producers' music departments simply aren't equipped to deal with the complicated clearance issues we've just discussed, this is a tough thing to pull together.

Stepping in to save the day are music supervisors who work on television shows. The fees are pretty small—$3,500 to $5,500 for a half-hour episode, and up to $8,000 for an hour. If there are records, downloads, or streams, supervisors can get a royalty of about 1%, sometimes with sales escalations.

A recent trend in this area is for music supervisors to troll indie labels, music blogs, YouTube, and similar sites, looking for unknown artists with cool material. They then approach the artist or label and say, "We love your song. We'd like to put it on a TV show, which is a great way to promote your career. And if you wrote the song, you'll even get performance money when it's aired. Oh, by the way, we pay almost nothing."

The artists are usually thrilled, because it can mean massive exposure for their material.

33

Soundtrack Album Deals

As an artist, you have nothing to do with the deal to distribute a soundtrack album—not even consent or consultation. These contracts are made between the film company and a record company, and in a sense are "none of your business." However, they affect the types of deals you can make with the film company, so you should know about them.

Once the film company has acquired the bundle of rights we discussed in Chapters 27 through 31, they turn them over to a record company to put out a soundtrack album. There are two different kinds of soundtrack albums—score albums and song albums—and the type you're dealing with radically impacts the deal.

SCORE ALBUMS

A score album is an album wholly of underscore (i.e., with no songs), often because the only music in the film is underscore. Unless there's something extraordinary about the situation (for example, the film looks like it's going to be huge), the soundtrack album deal is relatively modest or, more commonly, nonexistent. The reason is simple—pure underscore albums don't usually sell very well (anything over 10,000 copies is unusual). Many record companies aren't interested in this product at all, and will only put out a score album if someone forces them. (For example, a film company may put out a score album just to satisfy the ego of a film producer or composer.) However, there are a couple of companies (like Varèse Sarabande, or the classical divisions of major companies) who specialize in score albums.

Assuming someone is interested, the deal for pure score albums is usually an advance equal to the re-use fees, though sometimes there is no advance at all (which means the film company has to pay the re-use fees). (For a discussion of re-use fees, see page 454.) The royalty on these albums also tends to be lower than for the song albums, usually in the range of 17%, to 18%, but it can climb higher for major event films.

SONG ALBUMS

At the other end of the spectrum is an album of songs by major artists, usually a combination of preexisting songs and songs written for the film. The deals for these albums are bigger if the new songs (a) are completed before the soundtrack album deal (so the record company can hear them); and (b) sound like hits. For these albums, the price escalates dramatically. If a lot of companies are chasing the deal, these song albums can command advances up to $500,000 (sometimes even more if the record company is really frothing at the mouth), but usually the advances are in the range of $100,000 to $300,000. (These prices include re-use fees.) The royalty on song albums is also higher, usually in the range of 18% to 20%, and sometimes with escalations to 21% and 22% at sales levels of, say, 1 million and 2 million albums (United States). In addition, the film company often gets a piece of the record company's profits.

More commonly, these deals are made before the music is actually in existence. Depending on what everyone believes the music will be, and to a large degree depending on the reputation of the film director or producer (and the director/producer's prior history with soundtrack albums), the advances can still be high.

The record company will try to get some marketing requirements from the film company (for example, a contribution to videos, screen credit for the soundtrack album, use of the soundtrack music in ads for the film, and so forth).

COST COVERING

The most common deals these days are for the film company to pay all or part of the music costs of the film (recording costs, synchronization licenses, master licenses, songwriter fees, artist's fees and advances, composer's fees, and so forth) and get back what they can from the record company. Of course, whatever the record company pays is recoupable from the royalties.

OTHER ISSUES

The other major issues in soundtrack album deals are:

Release Timing

The record has to be released in coordination with the film. The film company wants maximum promotion for its film, and the record company wants maximum promotion for its record, all from the cross-advertising and cross-marketing of the film and album, radio play of the record, etc. Thus, both sides are extraordinarily touchy about delivery and release dates.

If there is an original single, or what's called a **tie-in** (meaning a track from an artist's upcoming album that's used in the film), the film and record companies want a single promoted about six weeks ahead of the film, and they want the album released right around the same time as, or a little before, the release of the film. This allows the single to gather steam by the time the film hits the theaters. A major reason for screwing up this ideal timing is the film company's changing its release date, based on a variety of film-related issues (for example, they have other films that are scheduled for release around the same time, the director isn't finished, etc.).

Film Release

The record company wants a guaranteed release of the film. They argue (quite rightly) that their album isn't worth much without a film to go with it. Film companies are very reluctant to do this, since they never give it to any of the actors, producers, directors, etc. For some film companies, it's an absolute no-no. For others, they'll work out some compromise.

The record companies also want to know how big a release it's going to be. Will it be a small release, in 200 to 400 theaters to see how it goes? Or a major release (called a **wide release**), on 2,000 to 4,000 screens? The film companies almost never guarantee a number of theaters, but they'll give an indication of what's happening "off the record."

Who Owns the Masters?

There are obviously two choices: the film company or the record company. The film company argues that it paid for the little darlings and thus should own them. The record company argues that the advance it pays under the soundtrack album deal pays for the masters, and thus the record company should own them. The record companies are particularly touchy when the master is recorded by one of their exclusive artists; they can't stand the idea of someone else owning that recording. So the record companies insist on owning the masters and licensing them back to the filmmaker, while film companies insist on owning them and licensing them to the record company.

Compromises run all over the map, but most often the record company owns the masters and licenses them to the film company. Occasionally, they split the ownership—the film company owns the recordings for the film and other non-record rights, while the record company owns them for phonograph records.

To me, the real issue isn't so much ownership as who controls the masters outside of the film, the soundtrack album, and singles. This means things like synchronization rights (for other films, television programs, commercials, etc.), and usages on records other than the soundtrack album and singles, like compilation packages, the artist's albums, etc. Both sides have legitimate arguments, and the answer depends solely on bargaining power. However, regardless of who ends up with the ownership and control, most film companies will insist (and most record companies will agree) that the film company has some level of control over licensing the masters for usage in other films, television programs, advertising, etc. The record companies are sensitive to the fact that these usages could dilute the film company's right to have the song identified exclusively with their movie.

Related to the issue of control is the question of who gets the money from usages outside the film and records. If the record company ends up with the rights, then the monies are split between it and the film company (or credited to the film company's account if unrecouped). If the film company keeps the rights, then it usually keeps the money (but not always). Results here also vary in proportion to bargaining power.

Bonus Tracks

These days, some record companies want **bonus tracks** on the album, meaning tracks that don't appear in the picture. The theory is that these extra tracks help drive sales of the album, though that's less of a plus in this day of single-song downloads. Often, the bonus tracks come from artists who are signed to the record company's label. Big surprise.

Videos

Who makes the videos and how are the costs recouped? The film company almost always supplies film footage without additional charge. The real question is whether the film company pays for part of the videos.

Credit

What type of credit will the record company have in the film? Will it be in film ads as well as onscreen? What credit will the film company get on the records and in record company ads?

Advertising

Will either company guarantee advertising of the album and/or the film?

Marketing

Will the film company pay any money for marketing, promotion, etc.? Will the record company? This is heavily negotiated, to make sure each side gets the most bang out of the other.

Conclusion

This concludes the informational portion of our program.

Congratulations! Whichever track you took through the book, you now have a better overview of the music business than 98% of your colleagues (or at least 97.63%). Despite my informal style of writing, I've given you a lot of info. So you've learned much more than you may think. In fact, you now have everything you need to go as far as your music and drive will take you, without being pillaged and plundered along the way (or at least you can only get zapped with your eyes open).

To get the most from this book, keep it handy as a reference. It was important for you to read it through as a solid framework on which to build, but it will be even more valuable as you apply it to specific situations in your life. When you get involved in a particular deal, look up that section and read it again. Seeing it for the second time, you'll pick up things you might have missed before. And it'll be far more meaningful in practice than it was in theory. Sort of like reading a book on flying when you're home in bed, then reading it again just before you pilot an airplane.

Now you're ready for takeoff, so . . .

Go get 'em!

Index

Page numbers in *italics* refer to illustrations

About the Author

Donald S. Passman is the author of *All You Need To Know About The Music Business* and a graduate of the University of Texas and Harvard Law School. He practices law with the Los Angeles firm of Gang, Tyre, Ramer & Brown, and has specialized in the music business for over thirty years.

He has lectured extensively on the music industry, including at Harvard Law School, Yale Law School, USC Gould School of Law, UCLA School of Law, the Los Angeles Copyright Society, and the Beverly Hills Bar Association. Don is also the author of three novels, *The Amazing Harvey*, *The Visionary*, and *Mirage*.

Don has been listed in the Best Lawyers in America for more than twenty years, as well as the Top 100 Lawyers in California, the Top 500 Attorneys in America, *Hollywood Reporter*'s Top 100 Entertainment Attorneys, *Billboard*'s Music's Most Powerful Attorneys, and Southern California's Super Lawyers.

Check out Don's website at www.donpassman.com.